THE ARDEN SHAKESPEARE FOURTH SERIES

General Editors: Peter Holland, Zachary Lesser and Tiffany Stern

TITUS ANDRONICUS

AF147820

THE ARDEN SHAKESPEARE FOURTH SERIES

TITUS ANDRONICUS

Edited by

CURTIS PERRY AND AYANNA THOMPSON

THE ARDEN SHAKESPEARE
LONDON · NEW YORK · OXFORD · NEW DELHI · SYDNEY

THE ARDEN SHAKESPEARE
Bloomsbury Publishing Plc, 50 Bedford Square, London, WC1B 3DP, UK
Bloomsbury Publishing Inc, 1359 Broadway, New York, NY 10018, USA
Bloomsbury Publishing Ireland, 29 Earlsfort Terrace, Dublin 2, D02 AY28, Ireland

BLOOMSBURY, THE ARDEN SHAKESPEARE and the Arden Shakespeare logo are trademarks of
Bloomsbury Publishing Plc

First published in Great Britain 2026

General Editors of the Arden Shakespeare Series

First Series (1899–1944): W.J. Craig and R.H. Case
Second Series (1946–82): Una Ellis-Fermor, Harold F. Brooks, Harold Jenkins and Brian Morris
Third Series (1995–2020): Richard Proudfoot, Ann Thompson, David Scott Kastan and H.R.
Woudhuysen
Fourth Series (current): Peter Holland, Zachary Lesser and Tiffany Stern

The Arden Shakespeare Fourth Series Fellows
Wendy Lennon, Vanessa Lim, Varsha Panjwani, Jennifer Park, Anita Raychawdhuri,
Kathryn Vomero Santos, Laura Seymour, Robert Stagg

Cover design by Eleanor Rose
Cover illustration by Emma Clinton / www.emmaclinton.com

Bloomsbury Publishing Plc does not have any control over, or responsibility for, any third-party
websites referred to or in this book. All internet addresses given in this book were correct at the
time of going to press. The author and publisher regret any inconvenience caused if addresses have
changed or sites have ceased to exist, but can accept no responsibility for any such changes.

A catalogue record for this book is available from the British Library.

A catalog record for this book is available from the Library of Congress.

ISBN: HB: 978-1-3500-7841-3
PB: 978-1-3500-7840-6
ePDF: 978-1-3500-7843-7
eBook: 978-1-3500-7842-0

Series: The Arden Shakespeare Fourth Series

Typeset by Newgen KnowledgeWorks Pvt. Ltd, Chennai, India
Printed and bound in Great Britain

For product safety related questions contact productsafety@bloomsbury.com.

To find out more about our authors and books visit www.bloomsbury.com
and sign up for our newsletters.

The Editors

Curtis Perry is Clayton and Thelma Kirkpatrick Professor of English and Professor of Classics at the University of Illinois Urbana-Champaign, USA.

Ayanna Thompson is Regents Professor of English and Executive Director of the Arizona Center for Medieval & Renaissance Studies (ACMRS) at Arizona State University, USA.

CONTENTS

LIST OF ILLUSTRATIONS

GENERAL EDITORS' PREFACE

The Arden Shakespeare has published world-class, authoritative and innovative critical editions for over 125 years, ever since Edward Dowden's edition of *Hamlet* in 1899. Just like its predecessors, the Arden Shakespeare Fourth Series is a series of single volumes, edited to meticulous standards, with detailed commentary and notes on the same page as the text. Each volume includes a full introduction that provides readers with crucial background and context for the work. These introductions will cover topics such as Shakespeare's composition of the work, its sources and influences, its early theatre productions and printed editions and its ongoing life in performance and criticism. The Fourth Series aims to be a twenty-first-century one, with all editions published in dynamic digital editions as well as in print. The in-depth commentary notes for which Arden has become known continue to appear in both print and digital editions, but the digital editions also offer shorter notes for those who want a more streamlined experience of the text. Greater attention has been paid to performances, adaptations, translations and appropriations of Shakespeare's plays and poems outside the UK and US, as well as to their life on film and in digital media.

We have asked Arden Shakespeare Fourth Series editors to begin by deciding on the particular performance or textual moment in the early history of Shakespeare's works that they will reconstruct through editing, and then, in the introduction, to give a rationale as to why: Shakespeare's original idea for the play? Its first performance? His revised ideas after initial performance? The collaborative approach of the playing company that first produced it? The play as it was put on at court? The play as it was adapted for later performance? Unlike some recent editions, therefore, the Arden Shakespeare Fourth Series does not present multiple texts of the same play when it exists in more than one version; we return to a single text for each play, as in the Second Series, but we open up the possibilities for what that text might represent. All the editions continue to offer the authoritative, reliable and expertly edited texts for which the Arden Shakespeare is recognized and valued.

This editorial policy recognizes that virtually all of Shakespeare's plays and poems have come down to us in ways mediated by printing and publishing. With the possible exception of two sheets of *Sir Thomas More*, which scholars have argued are in Shakespeare's hand, none of his manuscripts survive. We have the texts of his other plays – and all of his poems – only in printed editions, which have very different manuscripts behind them. Quartos and octavos, the single-volume texts often published in Shakespeare's lifetime, each have their own story of transmission: some are close to the author, some to the company (they may be versions of the prompter's book) and some have seemed so garbled that some scholars have theorized they were reconstructed from notes and memories. Even the thirty-six plays published together in Shakespeare's First Folio of 1623 have different sources: some may have come from pre-performance texts, some from prompters' books, some from transcripts for readers, some from court versions. Some may preserve something like Shakespeare's initial composition; others have been revised later, even after Shakespeare's death. Individually, each of these printed texts can represent only a snapshot in the history of a particular work, which will itself have been modified by the labour of many people in the printing house – compositors, press workers, scribes, proofreaders – as well as collaborating and revising authors and actors. Since the printed editions of Shakespeare's plays and poems are physical objects created by fallible human beings, they can never perfectly embody the author's intentions, nor the playing company's performance script, nor any other version of the work. Editing Shakespeare has therefore always been a form of reconstruction. The Arden Shakespeare Fourth Series celebrates that fact and foregrounds the editor's own activity in the chain of Shakespeare's textual transmission that is now more than 400 years old.

The Arden Shakespeare has long remained the premier scholarly edition of the plays and poems. Because it has always been a series of individually edited volumes, each edition offers the insights of its particular editor or pair of editors. This variety is a strength of the series, giving readers a range of approaches to Shakespeare's works and the benefits of the passionate and lengthy engagement of a single scholar with a single work. In putting editorial choice front and centre, our series continues and expands this Arden tradition. The result foregrounds the complexity of the printed text, and the work that editors do when recovering and reconstructing texts. It shows that editing itself involves judgements and choices and is as precarious, exciting and teachable as are the interpretations made by directors, actors, literary critics and readers.

Peter Holland (University of Notre Dame, USA)
Zachary Lesser (University of Pennsylvania, USA)
Tiffany Stern (Shakespeare Institute, University of Birmingham, UK)

HOW TO USE THIS EDITION

Like all editions of Shakespeare, the Arden relies on a set of conventions that aid in presenting the text in a clear, accessible form. In this section, we explain these conventions so that you can easily use and interpret them when reading the text. With this knowledge, you will be able to see clearly how Arden editors turn Shakespeare's early texts into modern editions for today's students and performers, understand the questions raised by the history of Shakespeare's texts and explore the interpretive and theatrical possibilities they offer.

TEXT

During Shakespeare's lifetime, many of his plays and poems were printed individually in quarto and octavo; seven years after his death, in 1623, thirty-six of his plays were collected in the larger folio format, including some that had not previously appeared individually. Some of Shakespeare's plays, therefore, exist in multiple versions, first as printed individually in quarto and then in the collected First Folio, and these versions do not correspond in every word, much less in spelling or punctuation. When faced with a variation between these early printings, therefore, an editor must decide which version to choose and why. And even those plays printed initially in the First Folio contain numerous typographical errors, apparent misreadings of handwriting and other obscurities. Here too editors are faced with many decisions about which word is 'correct', and here too that judgement will depend on the particular moment in the life of the play or poem that they wish to reconstruct. The Arden Shakespeare Fourth Series presents these texts as they have been curated by the expert scholarship of our volume editors, both to ensure the correct readings and to make the text clear and accessible to modern readers and performers.

Each page of the Arden Shakespeare presents the text of the play or poem, alongside commentary and textual notes. In plays, act and scene divisions (which usually do not appear in the early editions) are retained but are given less prominence on the page. Acts, scenes and line numbers used to be given in a strange mixture of Roman and Arabic numerals, such as III. ii.70–4. Nowadays they are marked in Arabic numerals, although they may have been indicated in the early texts with Latin words, such as *Actus Primus*; in these cases, the Latin form will be given in the textual notes. It also used to be traditional to add a location to the beginning of each scene but, since in virtually every case these have been invented by eighteenth-century editors, they have been removed from the text and placed in the commentary or omitted altogether.

The text of the work is in modernized British English spelling. Modernizing is a difficult process and a complex art. Its parameters can often seem a little unclear. But there is a significant and clear distinction for an editor between, say, altering the spelling of the First Folio (*F*) from 'who did bid thee ioyne with vs' in *Macbeth* to 'who did bid thee join with us' and altering Banquo's allusion to a bird called a 'Barlet' to 'martlet'. Since *i* was largely interchangeable with *j* (as a consonant) and with *y* (as a vowel) in early modern orthography, as were *u* and *v*, the first case simply brings the spellings of *ioyne* and *vs* in line with modern forms. The second, by contrast, changes a word, in this case because of a possible misreading of handwriting somewhere in the process of moving from Shakespeare's act of writing to the printing of *F*, as there is no known bird called a *barlet*. This latter example is not modernization but, rather, what editors call 'emendation': an alteration of the text based on the editor's educated guess as to the word that actually stood in the manuscript from which the early edition was printed.

Most straightforward modernization in the Arden Shakespeare is made without any comment. 'Heere' becomes 'here', 'go too't' becomes 'go to't', 'resolu'd' becomes 'resolved'. If the final syllable of 'resolved' ought to be sounded for metrical reasons, then a commentary note will make that clear:

92 **resolved** resolvèd

Punctuation, too, is silently modernized in accordance with modern practice. At the start of *The Tempest*, for instance, *F* prints 'or we run our selues a ground, bestirre, bestirre', where modern conventions require a semicolon or a full stop after 'aground'. No note is given, except where the alteration of punctuation raises questions about meaning (see pp. XX).

Split lines – verse lines that are divided between speakers – are marked in 'step' form, an editorial habit dating to the eighteenth century, showing when one speaker completes another's iambic line:

SOOTHSAYER
    Beware the Ides of March.

CAESAR   What man is that?

Whenever an editor has made changes or additions to stage directions, this text is put [in square brackets]. Some of these editorial additions are completely non-controversial: for example, indicating that a character exits at the end of a scene, a direction occasionally forgotten in the early printings. Others may be more interpretive, such as indicating precisely when a character speaks 'aside': Hamlet's first line ('A little more than kin and less than kind') is often considered an aside by editors and performers, but there is no indication in any of the early texts. Editors of the Arden Shakespeare Fourth Series have tried to add stage directions that are necessary to an understanding of the play, but without being too prescriptive or intrusive. Readers, actors and directors will find their own possible stagings – but only if they are alert to the fact that the information in those square-bracketed stage directions has been added to the early texts.

By contrast with stage directions, editorial emendations of the spoken text are not indicated by square brackets, otherwise the text would become difficult to read. To understand what has been altered, therefore, you need to look at the textual notes to see where and how the original text has been changed in the edition you are reading. The commentary notes may also elaborate on why such decisions have been taken, give some solutions tried by other editors and, in general, set out to clarify how the early text or texts become the text of the edition.

TEXTUAL NOTES

Textual notes appear at the bottom of the printed page, beneath the commentary notes. These notes tell readers when the edition makes changes to the early text(s) of the work, except for modernization of spelling and punctuation. Over the centuries, editors have developed an elaborate code for these notes, mainly in an attempt to save space on the page. Once this code is understood, the notes are easy enough to comprehend, and they allow you to follow the process we used to create our editions. The textual notes often reveal important variations within the Shakespearean text: does Hamlet wish that 'this too too sallied flesh would melt' as he does in the second quarto, or 'solid flesh' as he does in F, or 'sullied flesh' as the editor Dover Wilson first suggested? In cases like this one and many others, the textual note shows which words the editor has accepted or rejected from the early printed text(s), revealing possibilities for alternative meanings. A textual note for this moment in *Hamlet* might read:

129 sullied] *Wilson (conj. Tennyson)*; sallied Q2; solid F

Textual notes begin with the line number (129), followed by the reading as it appears in the Arden edition ('sullied'), and then a closing square bracket. Then follows an abbreviated citation of the source of this reading, whether an early printing or a later edition (*Wilson*); if someone had previously conjectured that this might be the right word, that person is credited in round brackets (*conj. Tennyson*). The Abbreviations and References section explains all such abbreviations. Following this, the note gives the reading as it stands in the early texts ('sallied' in Q2 and 'solid' in F) and any other particularly noteworthy guesses, each with an abbreviated reference to its source.

For those plays that exist in an early quarto text as well as in the First Folio, the textual notes record all significant variations between them, as in this example from *King Lear* when Lear says to the Duke of Burgundy that Cordelia will be 'Dowered with our curse':

196 Dowered] F; Couered Q

While the word 'Dowered', taken from *F*, represents the editor's informed judgement about what Shakespeare wrote, you might want to decide for yourself. The textual note allows you to do so.

Where the earliest instance of an emendation occurs in an adaptation of the play, that will be recorded in the textual notes, which will also give the first edition of the Shakespearean text to include this emendation:

352 SP PROSPERO] *Dryden, Theobald*[1]; *Mira.* F

In textual notes, the slash indicates a verse line ending:

179] *Pope; F lines* thoughts, / so. /

In this case, the editor has followed Alexander Pope in relineating the First Folio, but the note records the line endings in *F* so that you can reconstruct how the verse was originally printed.

Italic round brackets enclose distinctive spellings in the early texts, noted only when they might have an effect on meaning, for instance where the decision of how to modernize a word might be less obvious:

99 poured] F (powr'd)

Stage directions (SDs) take the number of the line within or immediately after which they are placed, except for entry SDs and for SDs longer than one line, which use a decimal format with the number after the decimal indicating the line within the SD. For example, 50.3 refers to the third line of the SD following line 50. SDs that begin a scene are numbered 0.1, 0.2, and so forth. Where only a line number, or a line number with SD, precedes the square bracket, as in 179] or 83 SD], the note relates to the entire line or the entire SD.

Speech prefixes (SPs) follow similar conventions. The form 123 SP] refers to the speaker's name for line 123. When a '+' is used following the line number, it indicates that the variation described pertains to all subsequent speech prefixes for that character in the scene:

1+ SP 1 WITCH] 1 F

This note tells the reader that throughout this scene in *Macbeth*, the character called '1 WITCH' in speech prefixes is simply called '1' in the First Folio.

The Arden Shakespeare does not attempt to record every proposed emendation or variation. It records all major variations from the early authoritative texts and any other emendations proposed in the history of Shakespeare editing that seem particularly significant to the Arden editor. Any rejected emendations that are listed will typically be discussed in a commentary note as well.

COMMENTARY

Commentary notes offer glosses of difficult or obsolete words and usages, highlight illuminating parallels in the play or in other works by Shakespeare or his contemporaries, discuss performance choices in the early theatre or in later productions, locate the passage in its critical or editorial history and explore textual variations and other points of interpretive interest. Commentary notes preceded by * indicate that the word or passage discussed is an editorial emendation, not found in the early authoritative editions. For the history of word usage, in addition to the *Oxford English Dictionary*, reference will often be made to EEBO-TCP (Early English Books Online-Text Creation Partnership), a searchable database of more than 30,000 texts from Early Modern England, and to *EarlyPrint*, an open-access database of early texts that enables complex linguistic queries. A headnote to an entire scene may discuss the imagined location of the action, its treatment of source materials, or questions of staging that affect the entire scene. Notes on the List of Roles (which rarely appeared in the early editions) may address variations in the naming of characters in the early texts, disguises adopted by characters, the comparative lengths of roles and their possible doubling in the early theatre, the pronunciation of names and historical information about characters.

ACKNOWLEDGEMENTS

One of the reasons we first proposed this volume is that we thought it might be fun to work together on a play we both love, and it has been! The General Editor assigned to this volume – Tiffany Stern – has been extraordinarily detail oriented, helpful and patient with us through numerous stages of this edition's development, and we are grateful too to people at Bloomsbury connected to the Arden Shakespeare who have been so helpful along the way, including Jade Grogan and Margaret Bartley (our shepherds!), Oliver Roxon (who helped with the technological aspects) and Ella Wilson (who helped with images and permissions). The Arden 4 team has gone out of its way to provide support and to facilitate a collaborative ethos, and we are also grateful to all the other editors who have been at meetings with us, and to Zack Lesser and Peter Holland and the Arden Fellows who have commented on drafts of every aspect of this text. Ayanna would also like to thank all the theatre practitioners who graciously shared their journeys with *Titus* and her students who opened new avenues into the play each semester. Curtis would also like to thank his early-modernist colleagues at the University of Illinois, and Jaya, who remains puzzled and tolerant with regard to his fondness for old revenge plays.

INTRODUCTION

THE PLAY

Titus Andronicus is a disturbing play, not only because it is extremely violent, though of course it is that, but also because of the way it alternates between horror and humour and generally refuses to allow its audience to inhabit a single attitude towards – or point of view about – the awful things that occur. The rape and mutilation of Lavinia in Act 2 are meant to be shocking and upsetting, but Marcus' response to them produces what Steven Mullaney has described as 'affective irony', in that the emotion Marcus expresses is meant to be consumed ironically even by an audience that is also meant to be sympathetic (Mullaney, 68–76). Likewise, subsequent acts of horrifying violence are made to feel like pranks or like absurdism (as with Aaron's trick to get Titus to cut off his own hand in Act 3), and the final spasm of violence, in which Titus, Tamora and Saturninus are all stabbed in rapid succession, has the dramatic rhythm of farce (5.3.58–64). Teachers often issue trigger warnings before asking students to read the play because of the graphic nature of the killings and dismemberments and the challenging nature of the sexual violence depicted in *Titus*. The tonal shifts between horror and humour can render the play's treatment of sexual violence insensitive, at best, or callously misogynistic, at worst. Moreover, the play has also tended to elicit treatments that simplify its moral position by reducing it to something wholly comic, as in the 2001 episode of *South Park* 'Scott Tenorman Must Die', in which a revenge plot ends with a character eating his parents in a chilli cook-off, or the 2020 pastiche *My Little Titus Andronicus*, where a cast of characters based on the cutesy 'My Little Pony' media franchise puts on *Titus* as if it were a cheerful children's show about friendship (Zolidis).

One way to describe what *Titus* is doing, in terms that would have been familiar to Shakespeare, Peele and their contemporaries, would be to say

Figure 1 In the 2001 episode of *South Park* 'Scott Tenorman Must Die', Cartman exacts revenge on the teenager Scott by tricking him into eating his parents in a bowl of chilli.

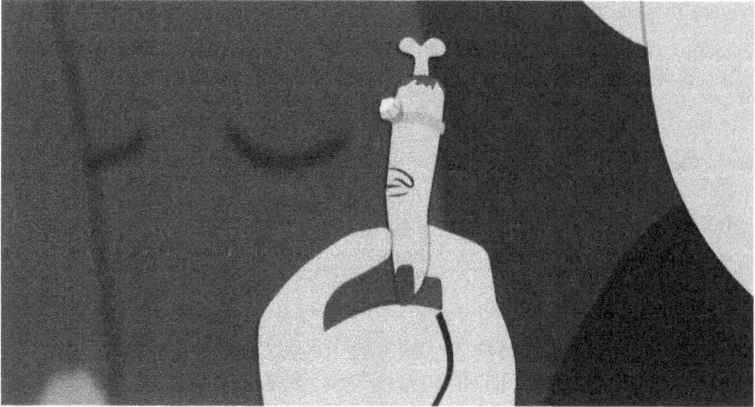

Figure 2 In the 2001 episode of *South Park* 'Scott Tenorman Must Die', Scott discovers his mother's finger in a bowl of chilli he has been eating.

that it is a play preoccupied with the production of indecorum. This is true in a literal, technical sense as well as in a colloquial one. In his well-known and highly influential verse-treatise *Ars Poetica* (written around 19 BCE) the Roman poet Horace lays out the principles of literary decorum; he opines that the characteristic styles and themes of comedy and tragedy should never be blended: 'a theme for Comedy refuses to be set forth in verses of Tragedy', he writes, and 'likewise the feast of Thyestes scorns to be told in strains of daily life that well nigh befit the comic sock' (lines 89–91, in Horace). The phrase 'comic sock' in Horace's Latin ('*socco*') names the sock or slipper worn traditionally by Greek comic actors, so mentioning it is a way of indicating comedy as a dramatic genre. And the point here is that cannibal banquets like the one in the story of Thyestes should not occur in comic drama. It would be hard to imagine how a play could flout Horace's rule more explicitly and programmatically than does *Titus Andronicus*. In 5.3, when the play stages its own version of the cannibal banquet of Thyestes (who was fed his own children in the Senecan play that bears his name), it has Titus dressed 'like a cook' (5.3.25 SD) as if he were a character in a comic play about daily life instead of the lead in a high-toned tragedy. Moreover, as the feast concludes, the play slips from blank verse into precisely the kind of shared rhyme scheme that one might more typically find in a late-Elizabethan comedy (5.3.51–65).

As Shakespeare and Peele would certainly have understood, the idea of decorum in classical literature involved the ability to fit literary language appropriately to the characters and situations depicted. In *Ars Poetica*, the dramatic writer is instructed to depict his characters according to a wise

Figure 3 In Julie Taymor's 1999 film *Titus*, Antony Hopkins, who plays Titus, ends the film dressed as a 'cook'.

understanding of real social customs, such that a play is both a fitting depiction of different kinds of people and inherently instructive of social and moral order:

> he who has learned what he owes his country and his friends, what love is due a parent, a brother, and a guest, what is imposed on a senator and a judge, what is the function of a general sent to war, he surely knows how to give each character his fitting part.
>
> (*Ars Poetica*, 309–16, in Horace)

If a decorous play, in Horace's sense, is one whose depiction of social life is reflective of a healthy social order, the wild indecorum spread throughout *Titus Andronicus* seems to be designed to reflect the loss of any correlative social order in the Rome it depicts. The wilful violation of literary decorum in 5.3 is in this sense the stylistic correlative to the play's sense of Rome as a place too amoral and too capriciously violent to sustain the type of moral and social wisdom that, for Horace, proper decorum reflects. This is one of the reasons that the play's last episode, in which Marcus and Lucius attempt to recuperate Roman identity (to 'knit again / This scattered corn into one mutual sheaf' [5.3.68–9]) rings false. For while they need the help of the Goths to 'knit' Rome together again, they also attempt to blame all of Rome's ills on Aaron the Moor and Tamora, the queen of the Goths. The Rome of the play – the Rome of Titus' sacrificial violence and of Saturninus' impulsive and petulant will – cannot be truly absolved or salvaged since its global reach and principle of incorporation are built into the very model of its empire.

For early modern English writers and audience members alike, thinking about politics inevitably entailed thinking about Rome.[1] This is true both because of the long-standing pervasiveness of the Latin language and a canon of Roman writers within European intellectual culture, and because of engrained habits of mind whereby Roman political history served as a primary reservoir of both positive exemplars and cautionary tales that were used for illustrative comparison with the early modern present. But

---

1 This is still true to some degree, at least if social media memes depicting American men's obsession with the corollaries between contemporary US politics and the fall of the Roman empire are to be believed (Clines).

the Rome on display in *Titus Andronicus* is populated by characters who seem to base their own sense of Rome on a rather indiscriminate anthology of historical and literary sources culled from different historical eras. In an oft-cited essay from the 1950s, T. J. B. Spencer wrote that *Titus Andronicus* 'includes all the political institutions that Rome ever had', and that it seems to be seeking 'not to get it all right but to get it all in' (Spencer, 32). For Spencer, this is evidence of Shakespeare's immaturity; he sees *Titus* as lacking 'the care and authenticity' evidenced in the later, Plutarchan tragedies. But we see it as having to do with the play's desire to depict a belated Roman milieu in which the characters themselves seek to relate their own stories to a hodgepodge of inherited Roman literary and political traditions.

Unlike Shakespeare's later Roman plays, which take up well-known incidents from actual Roman history and use the scaffolding provided by Plutarch's *Lives* to help render characters and places semi-realistic, *Titus Andronicus* tells a story that appears to be entirely made up. Scholars have sometimes argued that the play is meant to be set in some particular moment in Roman history (see Leibler, for instance, or Hunter, both of whom identify the playworld as Herodian's Rome), but we think it is more accurate to the play's overall aura of allusive belatedness to think of it as exploring ideas about the decadence of later imperial Rome without being more specific than that. After all, it would have been easy enough to locate the play's story in a specific historical moment via allusions to people and events if the authors had wished to accomplish that. The following quotation, from a remark by the poet Barnabe Googe, sums up an Elizabethan idea about late Rome that seems fitting for the play's setting:

> Rome, while she maintained her soldiers, was mistress and commandress of the whole world: but when she fell to her own delicacies, and neglecting of them, she became not only a triumph and contempt to the rude Vandal and barbarous Goth, but as yet she remains a spectacle of miserable ruin to the universal world.
>
> (Rich, sigs *4ᵛ–**1ʳ, here modernized)

This capsule summary of the idea of imperial Roman decline could almost be read as a gloss of the play's opening act, where Saturninus' neglect of Rome's greatest soldier is one of the things that sets the play in motion.

The idea of Roman decadence, as explored in *Titus Andronicus*, is bound up with the problematics of global empire. If, as in Googe's summary, 'delicacies' led to Rome's decline, then the global imperial reach made possible by military might was its precondition. Titus describes Saturninus as 'the wide world's emperor' (1.1.249), and all the foreign characters who come into the play's Rome from elsewhere are shown to be conversant in Roman literature, which is thus given as the playworld's de facto global culture. As for the play's repeated demolition of literary decorum, part of the underlying point is that a Rome that incorporates the whole wide world as well as all different eras of Roman history can no longer be said to have the kind of distinctive social and moral order that (for Horace) should provide the grounding of decorum. As Noémie Ndiaye has suggested, the interest of the play's initial audiences in the depiction of a decadent Rome likely had a great deal to do with the increasingly cosmopolitan nature of Elizabethan London itself, and with the mixture of desire and worry that the experience of such a global city might entail:

> early globalization did not only mean that England came to the world, but also that the world itself was coming to England, and in the process, turned London into a cosmopolitan world city replete with foreigners, Jews, and Afro-diasporic people, among others. *Titus Andronicus*, by means of a Roman anamorphosis, dreams of London as a cosmopolitan capital with imperial aspirations within a proto-colonial world economy.
>
> (Ndiaye, 'Race', 162–3)

Googe's remark about Roman decadence, quoted above, comes from a dedicatory epistle to a 1578 volume by Barnabe Rich that accuses England too of losing its martial spirit and caring too much about imported luxury goods ('vain trifles ... such things as do procure delights, wantonness and delicacy: the very vanities and vices of every Nation') instead of about the maintenance of domestic martial valour (Rich, sig. C4^r). *Titus Andronicus* depicts a global Rome that has lost itself, and does so partly as a cautionary exploration of what global empire could come to mean for early modern London.

The imperial action that sets the play in motion is the conclusion of a ten-year war with the Goths, in which the Roman general Titus loses twenty-one of his children in battle. While Titus enters the play with the Goths enslaved as his prisoners of war, the first act ends with the Goths freed and Tamora made 'incorporate in Rome' through her marriage to Saturninus (1.1.464). Like people stuffing themselves at a gluttonous feast, the late Roman empire of *Titus Andronicus* seems indiscriminate in its incorporation of foreign matter. And while the religions, cultures and even the races of the Romans and the Goths are initially described as being in opposition, the actions of the Romans continually work to undermine putatively essential differences. One key early example of this is Saturninus' attraction to Tamora's foreignness, as suggested by his declaration that Tamora's 'hue' pleases him more than Lavinia's (1.1.262). There is some evidence that the boy actors playing the parts of women in early modern plays regularly wore white make-up to signify female beauty: 'onstage, whiteface was probably the primary way of signifying femininity. It was an impersonation, just like blackface' (Callaghan, 84; see also Drew-Bear; Karim-Cooper, *Cosmetics*). Though it is not entirely clear how or if the different hues of Tamora and Lavinia would have been represented on stage, it is implied that Saturninus is attracted to Tamora because her skin colour is different than that of Roman women.[1] In *Titus*, the blending effects of imperial miscegenation coincide with the conventions of revenge narratives where (as many have noted) the moral and psychological distance and differences between the perpetrator and the revenger are shown to collapse: the revenger ends up resembling the perpetrator in terms of ethics, morality and character because of their unreasoning pursuit of revenge. It is not surprising, then, that *Titus Andronicus* puts pressure on what exactly differentiates the Romans from the Goths. By end of the bloody, cannibalistic banquet, the audience can be sure that the Goths do not have the market cornered in barbarism, despite the fact that both Aaron and Tamora are denigrated as being 'ravenous' tigers (5.3.5 and 5.3.193). What makes the play unique in the early modern revenge tragedy canon, however, is its employment of racial differences to emphasize the boundaries that are being indecorously crossed.

---

1   On the range of prosthetics used to depict skin-colour difference in early modern England, see also Smith, 'White Skin'.

Figure 4 Henry Peacham's illustration of lines from *Titus Andronicus*, 1595, offers one of the earliest pictorial examples of early modern stagecraft as racecraft.

It is important to ask why Aaron the Moor exists in *Titus Andronicus* in the first place. The only surviving picture of a Shakespeare play in production from his lifetime – the so-called Peacham drawing – includes characters from *Titus Andronicus*, and it is clear that Aaron the Moor was portrayed as racially distinct from the rest of the characters.[1] He is clearly rendered as a black man with closely cropped, curly black hair (perhaps a wig affixed with a headband) and with a black face, hands and legs. Aaron, then, is racially and culturally neither Roman nor Gothic; his backstory, or how he came to be associated with the Goths, is never revealed; and, though he wreaks havoc, he is not figured as a character seeking to exact revenge for specific wrongs suffered as the action unfolds. Yet he functions as the engine that drives and propels much of the action of the play: he encourages Chiron and Demetrius to share Lavinia 'by force' (2.1.118); he sets up Titus' sons, Quintus and Martius, to be accused of Bassianus' murder; he tricks Titus into cutting off his own hand; and he cuckolds Saturninus by having an affair

---

1   The image does not correspond exactly to any moment in the play and may be the product of a somewhat generalized memory of its action. The text under the image in the manuscript is headed by a stage direction that does not correspond to anything in the extant texts of the play ('Enter Tamora pleadinge for her sonnes going to execution'), and the page then features, as if a transcription of dramatic dialogue, Tamora's plea for Alarbus' life (1.1.104–20), a brief speech in response from Titus that cobbles together two half-lines from the play (1.1.121, 125) and conjoins them with two fabricated lines castigating Aaron, and then Aaron's lines from 5.1.125–44. The page ends with 'Alarbus' as a speech prefix, as if the dialogue might continue with him speaking, even though he has no lines in *Titus Andronicus*. For a transcription of the page's dialogue see Chambers, 'First'. On what the image might represent see Levin; Crosbie.

with and impregnating Tamora. At the end of the play, Marcus calls Aaron the 'Chief architect and plotter of these woes' (5.3.120). In a revenge tragedy in which multiple characters desire to exact revenge precisely because they feel disempowered, Aaron has a surprising amount of agency even though he does not function as a typical revenger or in a manner analogous to a typical revenger's nemesis.

While Aaron the Moor inspires a host of black characters in Renaissance dramas that were written after *Titus Andronicus*, including Shakespeare's *Othello*, he seems to come out of the medieval tradition of religious plays, George Peele's own earlier play about Spanish imperialism, and other early modern plays that explore the nexus and tension points of race, religion and empire. Scholars such as Anthony Gerard Barthelemy have noted that 'the association of blackness with evil has a long history on the English stage … In many medieval miracle plays, the souls of the damned were represented by actors painted black or in black costumes' (Barthelemy, 3–4). Similarly, Robert Hornback has argued that *Titus Andronicus* reflected the 'skewed religio-racial distinctions being constructed via European identity and fairness/whiteness as signs of Christianity against supposed physical and spiritual differences assigned to non-Christians'. He continues: 'Here we may recall the resort to a proto-racist definition embedded in Renaissance English representations of "Moors," a term which implicitly interpreted blackness as an external sign of religious and moral difference in the manner of moral allegory' (Hornback, 245).

Like the devils and Vice figures in medieval morality plays, Aaron is a 'sadistic trickster' who is frequently referred to as a 'devil' by other characters in *Titus Andronicus* (Hornback, 245). In this Aaron resembles George Peele's earlier evil Moor, Muly Mahamet in *The Battle of Alcazar*, whose black skin colour is understood to represent his evil, non-Christian soul. Muly Mahamet is described as being a 'negro', 'barbarous' and 'Black in his look and bloody in his deeds' (Peele, *Alcazar*, 1. Prologue, 7, 6 and 16). He is also 'accompanied … With devils coated in the shapes of men' (1. Prologue, 19–20). And like another theatrical non-Christian Vice figure – Barabas in Marlowe's *The Jew of Malta* – Aaron celebrates his villainy even up to the moment of his death. In *The Jew of Malta*, Barabas gloats, 'As for myself, I walk abroad o'nights, / And kill sick people groaning under walls. / Sometimes I go about and poison wells' (Marlowe, *JoM*, 2.3.176–8). Echoing the unmotivated wickedness of his Jewish/Vice forefather, Aaron lists crimes that outstrip any specific revenge agenda he could have:

> Oft have I digged up dead men from their graves
> And set them upright at their dear friend's door,
> Even when their sorrows almost was forgot,
> And on their skins, as on the bark of trees,
> Have with my knife carved in Roman letters,
> 'Let not your sorrow die though I am dead'.

(5.1.135–40)

Aaron, then, would have been a familiar type for the early modern audience: heretical and black on the inside and outside.

Yet what sets Aaron apart from his dramatic antecedents is his acute awareness of the racist associations between a black skin and a black soul. It is almost as if the character Aaron has seen *The Battle of Alcazar* and *The Jew of Malta* and taken notes about how blackness and racial difference are vilified and stereotyped as sadistic and devilish. When asked if he can enumerate his evil deeds and 'never blush' (5.1.121), Aaron retorts, 'Ay, like a black dog, as the saying is' (5.1.122). Black dogs are often associated with

Figure 5 In Julie Taymor's 1999 film *Titus*, Harry Lennix's Aaron is smart, stylish and clever.

the devil, the infernal and witchcraft in Elizabethan texts, and blackened men were often associated with the devil in medieval drama; Aaron, as always, reveals that he is well versed in racializing myths: 'If there be devils, would I were a devil, / To live and burn in everlasting fire, / So that I might have your company in hell / But to torment you with my bitter tongue' (5.1.147–50). At the same time, though, Aaron exhibits an unapologetic black pride that must have been startling to early modern English audiences. Reversing the logic of the superiority of whiteness, Aaron celebrates the power of black endurance. Although it is framed in terms of an essential proof of paternity, Aaron's black power speech makes it clear that black resilience will ultimately allow black people to outlive whites:

> What, what, ye sanguine, shallow-hearted boys,
> Ye white-limed walls, ye alehouse painted signs?
> Coal-black is better than another hue,
> In that it scorns to bear another hue:
> For all the water in the ocean
> Can never turn the swan's black legs to white,
> Although she lave them hourly in the flood.
>
> (4.2.98–104)

Appropriating the adage that it is impossible to 'wash the Ethiop white', Aaron embraces the tenacity and perseverance of blackness. *Titus Andronicus*, we might say, begins with the very Roman desire to memorialize the dead: Titus' first thought upon his return to Rome is about the need to guarantee an 'eternal sleep' (1.1.155) in the re-edified family monument for his deceased sons, a death that is imagined as a kind of eternal life in fame. Aaron – who knows he will have no such monument to rest in – asserts his own alternative, oceanic figuration of perpetual endurance. In doing so, he uncannily anticipates more recent scholarly accounts of black durability in the wake of attempted erasure: 'The amount of time it takes for a substance to enter the ocean and then leave the ocean is called residence time ... We, Black people, exist in the residence time of the wake, a time in which "everything is now. It is all now"' (Sharpe, 41). Death does not equal erasure for Aaron – even without a memorial monument – because of the innate endurance, resilience and survival of black life.

Aaron, this self-aware Vice figure, also functions as a father figure to Chiron and Demetrius (whose biological father is never mentioned in the course of the play), often translating and explaining Roman citations to them. His position as a stand-in father figure can be especially emphasized if the actors playing Chiron and Demetrius are made to look young. For instance, in Michael Fentiman's 2013 RSC production, the actors Jonny Weldon and Perry Millward were styled to look like teenagers. Their need for Aaron's guidance was pronounced precisely because they were so young and ignorant, and Aaron always seems to be as knowledgeable about Rome's literature and culture as the Romans themselves. In many ways, Aaron represents the perfect model of the imperial subject – the foreign subject who adopts the dominant culture as his own – for both good and ill. In fact, late Rome's destruction begins to resemble Aaron's ethos – a love of excess and chaos. The somewhat campy horror of the play's Roman denouement has some of

Figure 6 Photo from Michael Fentiman's 2013 RSC production of Jonny Weldon and Perry Millward as Chiron and Demetrius, who were styled to look like teenagers.

the prankish, humour-tinged quality that Aaron earlier in the play inspires and enacts. *Titus* asks us to ponder whether the imperial subject begins to absorb and take after the empire, or whether the empire, incorporating so many foreign subjects, begins to resemble its indecorous subjects.

Within this conundrum, Aaron's role as a father becomes even more central and weighty. There is an over-abundance of fathers in *Titus Andronicus*, and a scarcity of mothers: there is Titus with two dozen or so children, there is Marcus with his son Publius, there is Lucius with his son Young Lucius and there is Aaron with his biracial baby. The Romans exhibit several violent ways of treating their offspring. Titus willingly kills one of his sons at the beginning of the play as a show of loyalty to the new emperor Saturninus, literally putting the ties of empire above those of blood. Marcus and Lucius employ their sons as extensions of themselves, almost treating them like extra appendages for revenge. Marcus allows Publius to become one of Titus' assistants for enacting revenge at the end of the play, when Publius helps to bind and gag Chiron and Demetrius for their extrajudicial execution. And Young Lucius is made to articulate that if he 'were a man', even Tamora's 'bedchamber should not be safe' (4.1.106–7). Roman fathers, then, do not treat their children as individuals who are in need of care and nurturing; instead, they are treated as extensions of their fathers' public roles.

Aaron, too, describes his unnamed biracial baby as an extension, as 'this myself': 'The vigour and the picture of my youth' (4.2.108–9). Yet, for Aaron the baby's blackness, the very thing that reveals that the baby cannot be Saturninus', provides proof of his own paternity that necessitates not only celebration, but also preservation. While Aaron views his son as an extension of himself, that fact requires his protection: 'This before all the world do I prefer; / This maugre all the world will I keep safe' (4.2.110–11). Even when he knows that he will be executed, Aaron continues to plead for his son's life: 'Touch not the boy' (5.1.49); 'Lucius, save the child' (5.1.53); 'swear to me my child shall live' (5.1.68); 'vow ... To save my boy, to nourish and bring him up, / Or else I will discover nought to thee' (5.1.81–5). Unlike the Roman fathers who seem incapable of, or uninterested in, valuing their children for their own sake, Aaron repeatedly fights to save his child even in the face of his own imminent demise. Like Aaron's rhetoric of black durability, his ethic of paternal care is given as specifically anti-Roman; if

Figure 7 In Jane Howell's 1985 BBC film, it is clear that Aaron's baby has not survived through the use of a tiny black coffin that haunts Young Lucius (played by Paul Davies Prowles).

Figure 8 Julie Taymor's 1999 film version ends on an optimistic note with the next generation, Young Lucius (played by Osheen Jones), walking out of Rome with the biracial baby in his arms.

we are made to question whether the imperial subject begins to resemble the empire, or whether the empire begins to resemble its subjects, then Aaron's parenting points to a radically different alternative for imperial Rome. Directors have grappled with whether the lesson has been absorbed by the imperial centre. Some, like Jane Howell's 1985 BBC film version, make it clear that the baby has not survived: she ends her film with an image of tiny black coffin that contains Aaron's baby while Young Lucius looks on with horror. Others, such as Julie Taymor's 1999 film version, make it clear that the lesson has been learned, with Young Lucius walking out of Rome with the biracial baby in his arms. Either way, though the surviving Romans make every effort to recuperate *Romanitas* – their nostalgic idea of Roman-ness – and to blame outsiders for the play's horrors, the meaning of racial difference within a reasserted imperial hegemony remains an open question at the end of the play.

Likewise, *Titus Andronicus* forces its audience to ponder how gender roles function within imperial frameworks. It is important to acknowledge that Tamora and Aaron's baby is the only character in the play that has both parents present. No other character in *Titus Andronicus* has two parents. Despite the fact that Titus has dozens of children, their mother, his wife, is never alluded to in the course of the play – not even by her surviving children. While there are around thirty references to mothers within the play, the only ones mentioned are Tamora, Marcus and Titus' mother (when Marcus pleads to allow him to cut off his hand to ransom Titus' sons), and Young Lucius' mother/Lucius' wife. The late Roman Empire in *Titus Andronicus*, then, is a world of families and multiple generations, but without many mothers present. Practically speaking, this likely has something to do with the shortage of boy actors available when Shakespeare and Peele conceived of the play, but even so the authors make the most of this practical-theatrical situation by emphasizing Tamora's motherhood. The vast majority of references to mothers, mothering and motherhood in *Titus Andronicus* are all about Tamora. She is a mother to Chiron and Demetrius; she offers to be a 'loving nurse' and 'a mother to [Saturninus'] youth' (1.1.334); and she gives birth to Aaron's baby in the middle of the play. Tamora is fecund, and *Titus Andronicus* asks how maternal fecundity is employed in this late Roman empire. Tamora's

Figure 9 Indira Varma as Tamora in Lucy Bailey's 2006 production at Shakespeare's Globe in London.

fecundity is explicitly rendered monstrous and foreign by the Romans. Hers is the body that must not be incorporated into the Rome at the end of the play even when Lucius' return to Rome is predicated on his alliance with the Goths. Instead, her corpse is to be violently expelled from Rome: 'throw her forth to beasts and birds of prey. / Her life was beast-like and devoid of pity, / And, being dead, let birds on her take pity' (5.3.196–8).

While Tamora begins the play pleading for her son's life, kneeling before Titus to beg him not to sacrifice Alarbus, she is later more than willing to have her newborn child executed. As she is incorporated into Rome, and as her goals and desires come to be structured by the revenge plots she inhabits, Tamora ends up resembling and mirroring her nemesis, Titus, who begins the play by executing his own son and ends the play by killing his daughter. In the end, the audience is invited to ponder the value of fecundity in this late Roman empire. After all, fecundity is explicitly mocked by Titus' rape-like cannibalistic feast, in which he puts two children back into Tamora. Are we supposed to cheer, or endorse, this non-consensual act? To think it somehow just?

If Tamora is the play's 'ravenous' (5.3.193) and monstrously fertile mother, Lavinia is the model of restraint. Yet like almost all things in *Titus Andronicus* even this portrait and emblem of decorous womanhood is

Figure 10 Kate Mulgrew (as Tamora) and Keith David (as Aaron) in Michael Maggio's 1989 stage production of *Titus Andronicus* at the Delacorte Theater.

undermined. Since the play continually refuses to allow its audience to inhabit a single attitude towards the actions, it also refuses to allow the audience to inhabit a single point of view about the characters. Lavinia is named after the princess of Latium who is courted and married by Aeneas in Virgil's *Aeneid*. She represents an idealized version of Roman womanhood: she is obedient, chaste, mild-mannered and quiet. She does not speak up or protest when Titus agrees to have her marry Saturninus, even though we learn that she is already engaged to Bassianus. Lavinia's docility – a trait apparently lauded in a Roman woman – is quickly shown to come at a real price. All the men who purportedly love and admire Lavinia objectify her at one point or another: Titus believes Lavinia is his to give away to whom he chooses, and Bassianus believes that Lavinia is his property ('"Rape" call you it, my lord, to seize my own' [1.1.407]). When Marcus comes upon Lavinia after she has been raped and mutilated, he cannot think of her pain without referring to his own: 'O, that I knew thy heart, and knew the beast, / That I might rail at him to ease my mind' (2.4.34–5). Chiron and Demetrius' assault upon Lavinia is

Figure 11 Photo from Peter Brook's 1955 production with Vivien Leigh as Lavinia and Maxine Audley as Tamora. Lavinia was the portrait of restraint even when pleading to be killed by Tamora.

disgusting. Yet we are invited to compare their violent, non-consensual acts with Lavinia with the way she is positioned and treated by her loved ones. The tongueless Lavinia resembles the Lavinia of Act 1 who is the emblem of perfect womanhood in that both are silent. Lavinia's uncle and father in fact seem to experience some joy speaking for her as the play progresses. 'Shall I speak for thee?' Marcus asks, shortly after discovering the wounded Lavinia (2.4.33), and Titus proudly proclaims that he understands 'her signs' (3.1.144). Ultimately, Titus makes Lavinia his handmaiden for revenge when he instructs her to 'Bear thou my hand, sweet wench, between thy teeth' (3.1.283), and later in the play he has her hold the bowl to capture Chiron's and Demetrius' blood ''tween her stumps' (5.2.181). The play forces the audience to query whether silence is truly a virtue *and* whether silence can ever be interpreted as consent. When Titus kills Lavinia before revealing the ingredients of the cannibalistic banquet, she does not, cannot, protest vocally. On the page, this allows for a certain amount of ambiguity, but in performance actors and directors must decide if Lavinia willingly participates in her death (for more on this see the 'Reception and Performance History' section). Either way, the play has fully evacuated the notion that the silent woman is an uncomplicated ideal.

Just as the play turns stereotypes about blackness and femininity on their heads, so too does the play turn stereotypes about disability upside down. Anticipating the philosophy, language and rhetoric of crip theory, *Titus Andronicus* enables the audience to interrogate whether the able body is the most ideal form. While disability studies analyses how 'a culture of normalization reduces disability to lack or loss and positions disability as always in need of cure', crip theory is 'a particular mode of doing disability studies, deeply in conversation with queer theory' that

> affirms lived, embodied experiences of disability and the knowledges (or cripistemologies) that emerge from such experiences; at the same time, it is critical of the ways in which certain identities materialize and become representative to the exclusion of others that may not fit neatly within dominant vocabularies of disability.
>
> (McRuer and Cassabaum)

Figure 12 In Deborah Warner's 1987 RSC production of *Titus Andronicus*, Brian Cox played Titus as a man with multiple disabilities. Royal Shakespeare Company, at the Pit, Barbican, London, UK, 1988.

As Nicola Imbracsio has argued, 'the proliferation of social and symbolic dismemberment of the body in the English Renaissance, by punitive dismemberment on the scaffold, pictorial isolation in anatomy texts, or poetic blazoning in sonnets, attests to the cultural power of the fragment' (Imbracsio, 292). Yet most early modern representations of the disabled body were ones of dis-ability – that is, of bodies that lack ability. *Titus Andronicus*, however, depicts a revenge that is plotted and enacted by two disabled characters, Titus and Lavinia. Far from showing the dismembered body as weak or disempowered, the play hinges upon the ingenuity, adaptability and improvisation that many with disabilities are forced to develop. This is not to downplay the horror of the violence of the dismemberments enacted, but to emphasize that the play refuses to land on a lack of agency for the disabled. And, as we note below in our discussion of the play's reception and performance history, *Titus Andronicus* has become a play that contemporary actors and directors regularly turn to in order think through issues of disability and early modern theatre (on which, see p. 96).

AUTHORSHIP

In the epistle to the reader that prefaced his 1687 adaptation of *Titus Andronicus*, Edward Ravenscroft defended himself against the crime of stealing from Shakespeare by suggesting that the play had never really been Shakespeare's to begin with:

> I have been told by some anciently conversant with the Stage, that it was not Originally his, but brought by a private Author to be Acted, and he only gave some Master-touches to one or two of the Principal Parts or Characters; this I am apt to believe, because 'tis the most incorrect and indigested piece in all his Works; It seems rather a heap of Rubbish then a Structure.
>
> (Ravenscroft, sig. A2ʳ)

Ravenscroft's remarks are the first instance of the suggestion that Shakespeare collaborated with another writer on *Titus*. They also anticipate the manner in which later evaluations of the play's authorship have tended to become entangled with subjective aesthetic criteria; if the play is deemed to be crude and bad, and if Shakespeare is understood as the gold standard for literary excellence, then it must follow that the play was not *really* Shakespeare's.

In the long history of scholarly debate about *Titus Andronicus*, many critics and editors have argued against Shakespeare's authorship of the bulk of the play, and the play has been attributed, in whole or in part, to a rogue's gallery of Elizabethan playwrights on what have often been impressionistic and speculative grounds.

T. M. Parrott (who wanted to prove, in the early twentieth century, that *Titus* represented Shakespeare's revision of an older play) is sometimes credited with being the first scholar to attempt to set the question of the play's authorship on objective grounds, basing some of his arguments on reproducible quantitative tests linking attribution claims to specific semantic or prosodic features. But the ideological baggage that had been prominent in earlier arguments about the attribution of *Titus* persisted: his tests confirmed for him the presence of 'Shakespeare's hand at work in this ... distasteful play' (Parrott, 36). Fortunately, the increased scholarly attention the play has attracted in the last thirty years or so has made it possible to understand *Titus Andronicus* as more than just a 'heap of rubbish' while also putting questions of collaborative co-authorship on a firmer footing.

Early efforts at scientific authorship attribution tended to focus on countable attributes of diction and prosody felt to reveal a given author's habitual or automatic tendencies: things like the percentage of feminine endings in poetry (i.e., metrical lines with an unstressed syllable at the end), the use of interchangeable versions of the same word (such as has/hath) or the frequency of certain contractions. This approach involves identifying semantic tics and traits that are minor enough to occur prior to conscious stylistic choice and then using them as potential indicators of an authentic authorial fingerprint (see, e.g., Jackson, *Attribution*). With the growth of computer-assisted analysis, the science of attribution has become more sophisticated, and it is now possible to do things like search for recurrences of a given text's collocations (words occurring together) in a sizeable corpus of texts. Results yielded by this approach are sometimes controversial, and the majority of scholars in Shakespeare studies are not technically equipped to reproduce the experiments, but there is some reason to believe that this approach can provide good data on authorship even for a comparatively small segment of a play (see, e.g., Jackson, 'Determining'). In the case of *Titus Andronicus*, at least, older and newer objective methods of testing

Figure 13 Portrait of a young aristocrat assumed to be George Peele.

attribution have largely pointed in the same direction, and as a result there is now a widespread consensus that the play as we have it represents a collaboration of some kind between William Shakespeare and George Peele (1556–96).

Peele's hand had been suspected, especially in *Titus*'s long opening act, long before the intuition could be confirmed by modern, computer-assisted attribution studies. For instance, John Dover Wilson's landmark 1948 edition of the play discussed the many overt stylistic parallels between *Titus* and other works known to be by either Shakespeare or Peele and then offered the definitive early judgement that 'only two dramatists were concerned in the making of *Titus* as a whole, Peele and Shakespeare' (Cam², xxxiv). The history of speculative attributions for *Titus* is recounted and discussed in Vickers (148–243), as are early efforts to replace subjective speculation with more objective and reproducible methods of testing authorship attribution. Vickers' book, which pulls together prior authorship studies and details some additional tests of its own, can be credited with consolidating the groundwork for the current consensus that Peele was Shakespeare's co-author in *Titus Andronicus*: many of its central claims about the play have come to be widely accepted. This new consensus in attribution scholarship occurred alongside the growing acknowledgement that co-authorship was common enough within the culture of Elizabethan London's commercial theatres to be understood as the rule rather than the exception, and the recognition that playwrights were in fact often recruited to contribute scenes or episodes to fill in a plot scenario mapped out by another writer or by a third party (Stern, *Documents*, 8–35).

Still, Ravenscroft's informant, if in fact there was one, seems either to have invented or exaggerated his claims. Shakespeare wrote the lion's share of *Titus Andronicus*. There is now a strong scholarly consensus that Peele was the primary author of the play's opening scenes (1.1 and 2.1 in this edition), and that Shakespeare wrote most of the rest of the play. There is still some dispute as to whether Peele's hand can be detected after the initial scenes, however. Vickers assigned 4.1 to Peele, but some more recent studies, attempting to reassess attribution in light of the most up-to-date collocation-based attribution techniques, have argued that this scene too was written by Shakespeare (Weber, Pruitt). We find Mark C. Hulse's analysis persuasive, however: Hulse discovers experimental flaws in the tests that have led scholars to assign 4.1 to Shakespeare and demonstrates that both quantitative and qualitative data point towards Peele as the main author of 4.1. Hulse also points out that this reattribution has implications for the way we imagine Peele and Shakespeare as co-authors: if Peele only wrote the opening of our play, then it might be easier to imagine that Shakespeare took an old play by Peele in hand, or the opening of one, and composed *Titus* as we have it using Peele's opening movement as a starting point. If Peele wrote 4.1, however, it perhaps becomes easier to imagine the play's initial composition as more simultaneous in nature, with two writers contributing scenes to a single plotted-out story. Hulse's reattribution of 4.1, together with evidence that Shakespeare's own portions of *Titus* date from the very beginning of his theatrical career (Bruster and Smith), make it seem likely to us that Shakespeare and Peele both contributed to an early version of *Titus Andronicus* that was then revised for performance in some manner prior to its print publication in 1594 (see the section on 'Early Theatre History and Dating').

If Shakespeare and Peele were both assigned parts of *Titus* to write, Peele would have been the better known and more experienced of the play's co-authors. At the time of *Titus*'s likely composition, Shakespeare was a relatively unknown newcomer to the London theatrical milieu, and Peele had a reputation as a well-connected and comparatively high-status writer. Peele's father, James Peele, had been a learned and literate man who wrote London civic pageants and who published, among other things, the earliest surviving English book on double-entry book-keeping. His son George received his grammar school education at Christ's Hospital (a grammar school in London that was part of a charitable institution where his father was clerk), and matriculated at Christ Church, Oxford at the age of fourteen in 1571. He earned a BA in 1577 and an MA degree in 1579 (Barbour; Whitworth). Older editions of *Titus*, assembled before the general acceptance of Peele's co-authorship, have sometimes wondered how to square Shakespeare's respectable but not extraordinary level of classical erudition with some aspects of parts of the play we now attribute to Peele, such as the apparent allusion to Euripides' *Hecuba* at 1.1.136–8. Peele, having spent the better part of a decade as a student at Oxford, was as learned as any early modern British playwright could possibly be, and we even know – from a Latin commendatory poem by his Oxford contemporary Willian Gager – that Peele had himself translated one of Euripides' *Iphigenia* plays into English during his time in university (most likely *Iphigenia at Aulis*, which was quite well known in early modern European intellectual circles thanks to Latin translations by Erasmus and others [see Miola, 'Iphigenia']). The editor of any scene presumed to have been written by Peele can begin with the assumption that an unusual level of classical erudition lies behind the text. For modern readers, of course, Shakespeare is a towering figure and Peele is not. But Peele was a well-known writer in his day. Francis Meres, whose praise for Shakespeare in *Palladis Tamia* (1598) is often quoted to demonstrate Elizabethan appreciation for the Bard, also lists Peele as one of England's notable poets and as one of 'our best for Tragedie' (Meres, sigs Oo3^v–4^r).

Beginning in the early 1580s, Peele established himself as a writer in London, and he used his civic and university connections to help foster a reputation as a literary contributor to public affairs. His surviving *oeuvre* includes a number of narrative and occasional poems, high-profile commissioned pageantry (including two mayoral pageants) and a number of plays for the commercial theatre. Peele died in 1596, just two years after the initial print publication of *Titus Andronicus*, but his name remained familiar enough to have become attached to a posthumous jestbook – *The Merrie Conceited Jests of George Peele Gentleman* – that was first printed in 1607. There is no reason to think that the lively stories of pranks and cozenings detailed in this volume have any real biographical relation to Peele, or that anything in particular that he did during his lifetime led to this odd, posthumous reinvention, but the volume's existence does attest to the survival of Peele's modest literary celebrity, and to his remembered association with both gentlemanly elites and a predatory urban world associated with urban commercial theatres. The title page of the jestbook describes Peele as 'a man very well known in the City of London and elsewhere' (*Jests*).

Peele is perhaps best remembered today for a handful of successful plays, including *The Arraignment of Paris*, a full-length theatrical entertainment which was performed before Queen Elizabeth I by the Children of the Chapel a few years before its initial print publication in 1584; the comic romance *The Old Wives Tale* (sometimes dated to around 1591–2); and *The Battle of Alcazar* (which was likely first performed in 1588–9), a play based upon recent geopolitical events that anticipates some aspects of *Titus Andronicus*. *The Battle of Alcazar* features overtly Senecan revenge motifs, including a cannibal banquet performed in a dumb show, and a hammy, villainous dark-skinned Moor named Muly Mahamet. In fact, Muly has been described as the 'the first moor of any dramatic significance on the English stage' (Barthelemy, 76). Peele is now generally also thought to have been the author of the anonymous chronicle play *The Troublesome Reign of John, King of England* (1591), whose plot and structure Shakespeare imitated in *King John* (see the discussion in Peele, *Troublesome*).

Peele's verse may seem a bit stiff and archaic to modern ears: it makes heavy use of stylized formal techniques such as repetition and alliteration and has about it a sometimes inflexible metrical regularity. These traits, though, might also have made his verse seem particularly suitable for representing ceremonial stateliness on stage. For this reason, and because he had already been involved with the composition of mayoral pageantry in London as early as 1585, it would appear that Peele, in composing the highly public, political opening act of *Titus*, was playing to his strengths. In fact, the juxtaposition of the extended scene of public ritual and political conflict in Act 1 with Aaron's extended soliloquy at the opening of 2.1 is reminiscent of the juxtapositions of ceremonial public self-performance and villainous soliloquy in Peele's earlier *Battle of Alcazar* (Perry, *Senecan*, 214–21). Since Elizabethan plays were often assembled out of scenes and episodes farmed out to different writers, it is certainly possible to imagine that Peele, for instance, might have been asked to provide a suitably grand Roman opening scene for a play which Shakespeare would mostly be writing.

As a co-authored text, *Titus Andronicus* features a high level of internal thematic coherence. Ironies about Rome hinted at in Act 1 are paid off in spades in the remainder of the play, and thematic through-lines created by allusion to classical texts are not necessarily limited to only one author's sections of the play. To give just the most obvious of examples, the insistent parallel that characters within the play draw between Lavinia's rape and the Ovidian tale of Philomela is formally introduced, by Aaron, in a part of the play attributed to Shakespeare (2.3.43). But we believe that Peele wrote 4.1, where a copy of Ovid's *Metamorphoses* is brought on stage and Lavinia uses it to communicate with her family members about what has happened to her. This type of coherence may stem from the fact that the play draws on very well-known Roman texts in order to examine a set of widely held cultural preoccupations rather than from an especially active collaborative process. Perhaps writing a play like *Titus Andronicus* – one set in the late Roman empire that explores the inherent violence of Rome's cultural legacy – evoked a shared set of intertexts and approaches for both writers. It is also worth remembering, however, that even the earliest text we have of

Titus – that of Q1 – may represent the end-point of a protracted, iterative process of theatrical retransmission and revision involving an initial act of composition, informal revision by actors, revision in response to audiences, some process of being transmitted from acting company to acting company and relearned and at least one formal rewriting prior to print publication (see pp. 53–5). Early modern playtexts that we know were transmitted from company to company show tangible signs of having been altered by the repeated process of memorization and retransmission (Petersen), so it is possible, by the same logic, that some of the internal thematic coherence we detect in *Titus Andronicus* might be the product of a gradual, collaborative reshaping of the play during its labyrinthine preprint theatrical history. It is easy to imagine, certainly, that revisions to a well-known and successful play might serve to strengthen its internal thematic coherence by attempting to enhance what the original had been perceived as being about.

The other authorship-related question, about which there may not currently be consensus, concerns 3.2: the fly-killing scene. This scene is present only in the Folio text of the play, and there is good reason to think that it was written quite a bit later than the rest of the play, most likely in the context of a Jacobean theatrical revival. In the quarto versions of the play, the character of Lucius' son is first introduced in the subsequent scene (here 4.1), and because he is a new character there, being introduced to the audience for the first time, the text goes out of its way to specify Young Lucius' kinship relationships to the other characters in the scene (4.1.1–7). The mode of presentation used at the opening of 4.1 therefore seems to presume that the boy being chased by Lavinia would not already have been familiar to the audience. This in turn suggests that the play was originally staged without 3.2, where in the Folio version of the play the boy first appears (Kramer).

It is also anomalous that the characters who are on stage in 3.2 (Titus, Lavinia, Marcus and Young Lucius) should exit and re-enter as they do at the start of the next scene. The Elizabethan theatre did not use elaborate stage design or lighting effects to differentiate one time and place from another, and so clarity of theatrical narrative generally required that a group of characters not exit and immediately re-enter as if in a different time and place. Violations of this practical rule – which is sometimes referred to as the law of re-entry – rarely occur in early modern drama without the pause and separation of an act division to help clarify the spatio-temporal relationship between episodes (Taylor, 'Structure', 21–2): thus, it would seem, the re-entry of the Andronici at 4.1 can occur without causing confusion only because of the clarifying interruption represented by the interval between Acts 3 and 4. But it has also been argued that Shakespeare's theatrical company did not begin to build act divisions into their performances until after they began playing at the indoor theatre in Blackfriars in 1608 (Taylor, 'Structure'). Act divisions were required in an indoor theatre to attend to the candles used to light the stage, and they later came to be a structuring device that was imitated even in plays written for commercial theatres lit by natural light. If inserting the fly-killing scene into *Titus Andronicus* requires an act division, and if act divisions were not part of the performance of King's Men plays until after 1608, then that tells us something about when this scene may have been added to the play.

The insertion of act divisions into *Titus* as performed may also have required adding another scene in Act 3, for balance: without 3.2 the play's third act would be oddly brief and therefore potentially awkward as part of a theatrical experience. To be sure, there are Shakespearean plays whose acts are of significantly different lengths (as noted in the revised edition of Ard[3], 146), so it is certainly possible that the play could have been performed at some point after 1608 with a break between acts but no fly-killing scene. But in such a configuration the play might well have felt misshapen, with intervals after Act 2 and Act 3 coming too close together. It is therefore reasonable to hypothesize (with Taylor and Duhaime) that the fly-killing scene was added to the play at more or less the same time as act divisions were added to its performance: neither works well without the other. That means that the fly-killing scene was most likely added in the context of a Jacobean restaging of the play at some point between 1608 and the printing of the Folio text. An edition of the play that aims to recapture something like its original Elizabethan performance text should therefore omit or otherwise bracket off 3.2 (as Bate does in Ard[3]) and likewise either omit act divisions or treat them as a non-theatrical imposition upon the text. Since we are editing the play from the perspective of the Jacobean play it evolved into (see pp. 31–4), we include both 3.2 and the act intervals as they appear in F.

Taylor and Duhaime also present results of a series of computer-assisted, collocation-based tests which seem to show that the fly-killing scene was most likely written by Thomas Middleton rather than Shakespeare. And they argue that if the scene was not written by Shakespeare the additions must have taken place after he had retired from the theatre. Perhaps, though, it is also possible to imagine Shakespeare as not being especially proprietary, towards the end of his career, about a play that had been written and revised collaboratively and transmitted from company to company decades earlier. We see no reason to presume that Shakespeare would necessarily have been called upon to update or add to his own old play even if he was still active when the addition of 3.2 was made. The tests described in Taylor and Duhaime do seem to point away from Shakespeare, however, and towards either John Fletcher or (even more so) Thomas Middleton, and both authors are known to have been among Shakespeare's late collaborators (see, respectively, Munro; Smith, 'Collaborator'). For all the internal and contextual reasons suggested by Taylor and Duhaime, Middleton does at present seem to us to be the most likely candidate to have composed 3.2. He was a prolific professional freelancer who sometimes wrote for the King's Men and who some scholars have identified as a late reviser of the folio texts of other Shakespearean plays, such as *Measure for Measure* and *Macbeth* (Smith, 'Collaborator'). Still, it must be said that the question of who wrote the fly-killing scene has not yet been widely discussed in scholarship, and that the findings of Taylor and Duhaime on the matter have not yet received enough scholarly scrutiny and confirmation to be considered settled.

EARLY TEXTS

In the framing 'induction' to his Jacobean-era comedy *Bartholomew Fair*, the playwright Ben Jonson has a Scrivener write up a contract for his audience enjoining them to judge his play appropriately. Within this frame, Jonson makes fun of some audience members who still, in 1614, 'swear Jeronimo or Andronicus are the best plays yet'. Such audience members, Jonson's Scrivener declares, may be ignorant, but at least they are not fickle, for their judgement 'hath stood still these five and twenty or thirty years' (Jonson, *Bart. Fair*, 'Induction', 11). The implication is that *Titus Andronicus* (like Thomas Kyd's blockbuster *Spanish Tragedy* [1587], whose lead character is named Hieronimo) remained such a fan favourite, even towards the tail-end of Shakespeare's life, as to be annoying to writers like Jonson who wanted their audiences to appreciate their own more up-to-date offerings instead. The enduring popularity of *Titus Andronicus* seems to have made it one of early modern English drama's most restaged and retransmitted plays: there is some evidence that it had already been revised prior to its original printing in 1594, and (as we have seen) the Folio text contains an added scene and features a few other changes indicative of a later Jacobean staging.

Editors of Shakespeare have often quested after the pristine original text, the version of their play closest to the pure wellspring of authorial composition. We have not done that with this edition of *Titus*. For one thing, it seems quixotic to try to recover the pristine original of a play that shows signs of having been staged, transmitted between companies, restaged and revised even before its initial printing. For another, we believe that the play as a performance text may actually have been licked into shape by its early history of collaborative composition, staging, restaging, revision and addition. As much as is possible, we have therefore opted to present the play as the Jacobean audience might have seen it in revival, and as a play shaped by the collective agency of numerous hands, including those of its original authors.

We do not believe that this editorial goal is best accomplished by just printing the text as it appears in the Folio of 1623 (F), even though we do include the fly scene (3.2 – which is added for the first time in F), most of F's stage directions and numerous smaller changes to the text that first appear in F. The process of textual transmission linking the earliest printed text of *Titus Andronicus* (Q1) to the text in F seems mostly to have been independent of the play's onstage life, and the majority of the small variations between the earliest Quarto of the play (Q1) and the F text were actually introduced by the compositors (that is, typesetters) of the intermediary quarto texts, who made emendations and added errors of their own but who do not seem necessarily to have consulted anything but the previous quarto text in doing so. Even if one believes – as we do – that some of the changes to *Titus Andronicus* introduced in F bear witness to a Jacobean revival of the play, the F text contains many more variants that originate with the compositors of Q2 and Q3 than that can plausibly be seen as evidence of the play's evolving performance history. It is tempting, certainly, to see the Jacobean Folio text as the best approximation of what was staged in the play's Jacobean revival, but a more granular engagement with the play's history of textual transmission suggests that outside of 3.2 and the updated SDs this may not be the case.

The story of the textual transmission of *Titus Andronicus* from one early edition to another is relatively clear and has remained largely non-controversial since the rediscovery of Q1 and its integration into the play's editorial tradition in the early twentieth century (on which see, e.g., Bolton, 'Authentic'): the play's second quarto, dated 1600, was set from a copy of Q1 (1594) and Q3 (1611) is a reprinting of Q2 that even uses the same pagination. In each case some of the typographical errors in the previous base text were fixed by compositors, and in each case new errors were also added. The dialogue in the Folio text of the play is based primarily on Q3, though that text does include one new line in Act 1 that is not found in any quarto (1.1.400, on which see also pp. 40–2); more substantially, as mentioned in the previous section, the Folio text also introduces a scene that exists in no other early edition of the play (the fly-killing scene, which we include as 3.2). F also introduces act divisions for the first time, and differs most substantially from the quarto texts in terms of stage directions: Bolton counts seventeen Q3 stage directions that were emended in F, and nineteen new additions ('Authentic', 771). The Folio text of the play may therefore have been set from a copy of Q3 that had been marked-up in consultation with some sort of theatrical playbook, though there is little evidence that the compositors of the F text used anything other than just Q3 for most of the play's dialogue.

As the editors of the *New Oxford Shakespeare* (Oxf³) observe, Q2 was set from a copy of Q1 other than the sole copy that survives, and so it might possibly preserve otherwise lost textual variants within the play's initial printing. But we do not know that it does, and they also recognize that most of its new readings are 'obvious errors or sophistications, with no authority' (Oxf³, 133). Q3 adds its own fresh set of occasional emendations and errors. There is no real reason to think that any of the numerous small changes added to the Q1 text by the compositors of Q2 and Q3 have any demonstrable or recoverable relation to any other textual source or to the way the play may simultaneously have evolved as a living piece of theatre. F, as suggested above, bears a more complicated relation to the play's theatrical life, because its compilers do introduce new material and because of the text's apparent care with updated stage directions. At the same time, the compilers of F seem largely unconcerned to emend dialogue from Q3 and do not seem to have undertaken any kind of thorough revision of the Q3 text. The F text's compositors also add a significant number of obvious errors: approximately half of the minor variants that appear for the first time in F are the kind of self-evidently sloppy compositorial errors which would require editorial emendation in any edition. Our edition seeks to represent what the play became in performance as much as is possible, and we see no reason to assume that changes added in Q2 or Q3 and then carried over into F *must* reflect what was spoken on stage.

We do generally accept readings that originate with F when they are not self-evidently erroneous, though it must also be said that with small variants it is often impossible to tell the difference between something a compositor happened to change on his own and something that may have been altered in the marked-up copy he was consulting. Some unknowable percentage of the F readings we adopt here will have been the result of compositor choice rather than theatrical evolution. Q1 is clearly the best approximation we have of how the play was initially staged, and in the overwhelming majority of instances where F differs from Q1 the differences are either obvious errors or changes introduced by intermediary compositors. Attempting to edit a Jacobean-revival text of *Titus* will result in an approximation at best, and one question we have considered is this: what is more likely to reflect what was spoken on stage in the play's revival – a line from Q1 which presumably reflects early performance practice at least, or a variant introduced by a compositor who is unlikely to have given any consideration to performance at all? One can imagine speculative scenarios that would yield different answers to this question, but we have tended to assume that the former is more likely to be closer to what was eventually performed. As editors, therefore, we have chosen to work from Q1 as a base text and also generally to adopt alternative readings that originate with F. This approach makes it possible to distinguish more readily between changes added in different editions and to consider the variants enshrined in F differently depending upon when in the play's early textual transmission they first became part of the printed text.

On 6 February 1594, the stationer John Danter paid 6 pence to register his right to publish *Titus Andronicus*, and in a separate but adjacent entry he also registered his right to 'the ballad thereof' (SRO 3571).[1] Danter seems to have first registered the play, but then to have transferred his publishing rights to the two other stationers mentioned on the Q1 title page: Edward White and Thomas Millington; most likely they financed the book, and he simply printed it. Danter, a printer who specialized in ballads, may have bought and then transferred the publishing rights in order to drum up printing business for his press without having to bear the risk of financing and marketing an edition of a play. He had recently done something similar with Robert Greene's play *Orlando Furioso*: in late 1593 he registered that playbook, and then in May 1594 he formally transferred his rights to the stationer Cuthbert Burby, with the stipulation that he himself would 'have th[e] impryntinge thereof' for however many editions the play went through (SRO 3616). As per its title page, *Orlando Furioso* was then printed in 1594 by Danter for Burby and sold in the latter's shop (see Erne, 139–40; Murphy, 21–8). The title page of the *Titus* Q1 indicates that the book was to be sold at a bookseller's shop at 'the signe of the Gunne', which was Edward White's shop (Blayney, *Bookshops*, 87; Bishai). The Q2 title page indicates that it was printed 'by I.R. [James Roberts] for Edward White' and that it was to be sold at the same shop. And the Q3 title page likewise indicates that it was printed for White – in this case by Edward Allde – to be sold at his shop 'nere the little North dore of Pauls, at the sign of the Gun'.[2]

Shakespeare's modern editors have often proposed arguments about the degree to which various quarto texts seem to reflect playhouse practice, and *Titus Andronicus*'s previous editors have mostly agreed that Q1 was 'printed from an imperfectly corrected manuscript rather than a playhouse copy'

---

1   Since the eighteenth-century chapbook *The History of Titus Andronicus* (discussed in the section on 'Sources and Intertexts') was printed with the same ballad, some scholars have wondered if Danter might not have intended to print a now-lost earlier version of the chapbook history and ballad (Adams, 11). But since Danter's name was listed on the title page of Q1 of *Titus Andronicus* as the book's printer, this must be the book that he registered.

2   Although the Q3 title page does not name its printer, it features an ornament that was used by Allde from 1608 on (#18 in McKerrow, 'Typical'.)

(Cam³, 160). The evidence adduced for such an argument has had to do with those features of the Q1 text that might have been confusing for a working theatre company, such as sloppy entry and exit directions, inconsistent speech prefixes, internal evidence of revision and moments where speech prefixes fail to distinguish between different speakers, as when the different Goths speaking in 5.1 are identified only as 'Goth'. Paul Werstine, however, has now shown that each of these traits can also be found in manuscripts that we actually know were used by theatrical companies. We are, therefore, no longer as confident as some previous editors have been about the non-playhouse, authorial nature of the manuscript behind Q1.

Q1 does seem to contain internal evidence of revision, though we cannot say with certainty at which stage of the play's pre-print history revisions might have taken place. There are in Q1 at least two 'false starts' (as they are called in Ard³): moments where two versions of a scene, one superseding the other, seem both to be present next to one another in the text, as if a new section had been added without deleting an earlier idea. The clearest example occurs at 1.1.34–5, where Marcus' account of how his brother has come from battle 'bearing his valiant sons / In coffins from the field' also maintains that Titus has already 'at this day' (that is, today) 'To the Monument of that *Andronicy* / Done sacrifice of expiation, / And slaine the Noblest prisoner of the *Gothes*' (that is, sacrificed a Goth to expiate his sons' deaths). We omit these lines, which pre-empt the sacrifice of Alarbus, and the compositor of Q2 also omitted them, presumably for the same reasons (this means that they do not appear in Q3 or F either). They likely represent textual traces of an earlier conception of the opening of the play. For one thing, the episode involving the sacrifice of Alarbus does not occur in any of the other versions of the Titus story that might possibly reflect an early version of the play (on which see pp. 55–60). For another, Alarbus is missing from the subsequent stage direction indicating Titus' grand entry with his prisoners after 1.1.69. If the sacrifice of Alarbus was added to the play's story at some point after its initial conception, then it would seem that Marcus' remarks indicating that Titus has already performed an expiatory sacrifice of the 'the Noblest prisoner of the Gothes' is a holdover preserved from an earlier version of the action. Some scholars and editors have proposed emendations designed to preserve Marcus' lines, but we find them largely unsatisfactory. Bolton, for instance, suggested emending Q1's 'at this day' to 'at this door', to indicate that Titus had made a similar sacrifice on previous occasions at the door of his family monument ('Authentic', 780–82). Bate, who includes the lines in wavy brackets to indicate that they are suspect, nevertheless suggests that their sense could be preserved by taking the phrase 'at this day' to mean 'on the day corresponding to this' (Ard³, 99–100). However, since the lines in question were cut from Q2, it would seem that such readings were never idiomatic or self-evident, and also that the lines seemed extraneous even to the play's compositor in 1600.

The other passage in Q1 that seems to represent a false start occurs in 4.3.92–109, where an unnamed clown character interacts with Titus and Marcus before being sent unwittingly to his death at the hands of a violent and capricious emperor. As this exchange plays out, Titus awkwardly repeats virtually the same question verbatim ('Tell mee, can you deliver an Oration to the Emperour with a grace ... Sirra, can you with a grace deliver up a Supplication?'). John Dover Wilson, who proposed that this repetition could be internal evidence of revision, argued that the passage we print as 4.3.92–7 was a false start intended to be superseded (Cam², 143).[1] We find Waith's analysis (Oxf², 211–12) more persuasive – he sees two competing conceptions of the scene: one in which the letter that the Andronici give the Clown is referred to as an 'oration' (as at 95 and 105), and another in which it is referred to as a 'supplication'. The former, as Waith argues, is better integrated with the rest of the action: in the 'supplication' passage Titus indicates that he will be on hand when the Clown delivers his message to the emperor, but at line 108 (in our edition) Titus implies that he will be at home instead at that time, which is accurate to the events as they subsequently unfold in the play we have.

Since Q1 does seem to contain a few such false starts, it is reasonable for scholars to wonder if other lines or passages in the text might also be included erroneously or if Q1 otherwise contains evidence of revision. Dover

---

1   Unlike the presumed false start in Act 1, there is no compositorial intervention in this case: the two versions of the exchange occur in Q1 and are reprinted in the same fashion in Q2–3 and F. We see no reason, however, to assume that the lack of compositorial intervention means that the scene as printed, with both versions of the exchange, reflects what was performed at any given time.

Wilson, whose 1948 edition of the play did so much to open productive lines of inquiry about co-authorship and revision within the text, pointed out two additional places in Q1 that might be taken as internal evidence of revision. One concerns the obviously unmetrical line at 3.1.36:

> If they did hear,
> They would not mark me; if they did mark,
> They would not pity me: yet plead I must,
> And bootless unto them.
> Therefore, I tell my sorrows to the stones,
> Who though they cannot answer my distress,
> Yet in some sort they are better than the tribunes
> For that they will not intercept my tale.
>
> (3.1.33–40)

Here, as Dover Wilson suggested, the metre would be improved if the short line were cut and the other parts spliced together. Doing so would still yield a coherent text: 'yet plead I must; / Therefore, I tell my sorrows to the stones'. This passage has become a crux, in large part because of incoherent changes introduced by the compositor of Q3 (see 3.1.34–7n.), but we do not think that the short line in Q1 is necessarily evidence of error or revision in that text per se: there are other highly unmetrical lines in the text (like Aaron's very brief, unmetrical line at 2.1.9: 'So Tamora'), and myriad other ways that a line might be altered during its long journey from authorial copy to printed playbook.

The other argument that Dover Wilson broached concerning internal evidence of revision has to do with the killing and burial of Mutius in 1.1. There, he observed that the extended, ritualized burial of Mutius (1.1.343–92) is both preceded by Titus' speech about not being invited to the marriage of Saturninus and Tamora (1.1.340–2) and followed by Marcus and Titus speaking of Tamora's ascendancy. Thus, he wondered if the entire burial episode had been inserted in the middle of an episode that had originally focused on the emperor's marriage. The staging of Mutius' death also creates a series of awkward exits and entrances earlier in the scene (290–301), as if it too were a late addition poorly integrated into the scene's unfolding action (Cam², xxxvi–vii). Dover Wilson's account is suggestive enough to have been taken up by scholars like Wells (*Re-editing*), Boyd and Loughnane, who all treat the killing and burial of Mutius as a late addition to the opening scene. It may well be that the killing of Mutius was added to the first act at some point after the play's initial composition. This does not necessarily render it corrupt or unauthorial, however, especially since (as discussed below; see pp. 51–5) we think *Titus Andronicus* does seem to have been revised at least once and restaged as a marketably new play prior to its initial printing. Nor does it necessarily require editorial intervention: one of the advantages of editing the play as an evolving piece of theatre is that it frees us from the presumption that the task of an editor is to recapture a pristine original text. Our presumption is that the killing and burial of Mutius came to be part of *Titus Andronicus* as staged even if it was added to the long and complex opening act at some point in between the play's initial conception and the printing of Q1 in 1594.

The sole surviving copy of Q1 was rediscovered in Sweden in 1904, and its textual authority was established during the early part of the twentieth century. This means that the foundational editorial work establishing the texts of Shakespeare's plays was undertaken prior to the recovery of the first quarto of *Titus*, and also that the early editorial tradition surrounding the play relied primarily upon Q2 and the text of the play presented in the 1623 Folio. Early textual scholarship focusing on the relationship between Q1 and Q2 discovered that the text of Q2 was set from a copy of Q1 that had sustained damage at the bottom of its last sheet of paper: Q2 features fanciful additions apparently designed to fill in gaps at the bottom of each of the last two pages of its copy of Q1 (see Bolton, 'Authentic'; McKerrow, 'Note'; and the notes to 5.3.163–9 and 5.3.197–8). Though more errors were added than corrected in Q2, modern editors have typically praised the Q2 compositors for being unusually alert and willing to emend the text (Bolton, 'Authentic', 766; see also Cantrell and Williams, who attempt to distinguish between the work of two compositors in Q2). In addition to filling in gaps where their copy of Q1 was apparently damaged, they improved the punctuation of the text, made several acute emendations and (as we have seen) cut the lines from Q1 that awkwardly pre-empt the sacrifice of Alarbus. There are a few instances where Q2 clarifies or corrects classical references that are garbled in Q1, such as 1.1.227, where Q1 has 'Tytus' and Q2 corrects that to 'Tytans' (i.e., Titan's), or 4.2.96, where Q1's 'Alciades' (a rare but not unique spelling of an alternative name for Hercules) is corrected to the more usual 'Alcides'. Just as often, though, errors in Q1's classical names go uncorrected in Q2 despite its compositors' apparent eagerness to fill in or emend the text (see, for instance, 1.1.243, 1.1.318, 1.1.335, 2.3.236, 4.3.43 and 5.2.56). One place where we go against editorial tradition is 2.3.231–2, which we print, following Q1, as 'So pale did shine the moon on Priamus, / When he by night lay bathed in maiden blood' (see the note there). Previous modern editors, perhaps influenced by the long editorial tradition that established a text of *Titus* prior to the recovery of Q1, have accepted Q2's 'Piramus', which is then typically modernized into the name of the Ovidian figure Pyramus, who is best known now from the mechanicals' play in *MND*.[1] But 'Priamus' was an extremely common Latinate alternative for the name Priam, and the matter of Troy is of course very much on the minds of the characters in this play. Moreover, the Virgilian story of Priam's slaughter emphasizes the pathos of his death, in an outdoor courtyard at night, bathed in the blood of his young son Polites (as an adjective, 'maiden' could be used of innocent young men). Since the compositors of Q2, for all their care, do not seem to be especially expert in classical allusion, we believe that the change in Q2 is much more likely to have been the result of a simple transposition of letters than an informed, purposeful emendation.

As mentioned above, John Danter seems to have transferred his rights to publish *Titus Andronicus* to Edward White and Thomas Millington in 1594. This is likely even though (unlike the case of Greene's *Orlando Furioso*) there is no corresponding entry to that effect in the Stationers' Register. White sold all three quartos of *Titus Andronicus* in his bookshop and probably financed the editions. But Millington seems to have held a claim on the play too, since an entry in the Stationers' Register from April 1602 records the transfer from Millington to Thomas Pavier of rights to four books including 'Titus and Andronicus' (SRO 4536: and see footnote on p. 45). Pavier – who is best-remembered today for his involvement in the production of

---

1   As is typical, Q3 reproduces Q2's reading, and F reproduces Q3's ('*Piramus*').

Sammelbands containing Shakespearean and other quarto playbooks in 1619 (on which see Lesser) – does not seem for whatever reason to have invested in publishing an edition of *Titus*. But after Pavier's death, in 1625, his widow transferred publishing rights for a large number of books, including *Titus Andronicus*, to the stationers Edward Brewster and Robert Bird (SRO 8250). If indeed publication rights for the play flowed from Danter to White and Millington and then from Millington to Pavier, it is also possible that Pavier helped facilitate the play's inclusion in the 1623 Folio. Pavier, who owned rights to several Shakespeare plays, was a close, long-term associate of William Jaggard, a leading member of the consortium of stationers and actors behind the printing of the Folio.

Though invaluable for its added scene, its one restored line and its stage directions, the Folio text of the play is comparatively sloppy and introduces numerous small typographical errors into the text. Thanks to the work of Hinman, Bowers and Howard-Hill, it is generally believed that a good deal of the play's Folio text was set by a young and inexperienced apprentice compositor named John Leason – otherwise known as 'compositor E' – who was taken on as an apprentice by William Jaggard in November 1622 (Bowers, 181; Blayney, *Folio*, xxxvii; but see also Jansen, 15–21). He tended to be entrusted primarily with parts of those plays, like *Titus*, that were set from printed books instead of manuscripts, though he does seem to have undertaken the setting from manuscript of at least part of the fly-killing scene (Howard-Hill, 173). In one striking instance, the compositor of the Folio text emends a passage garbled in Q3 in a manner that may reflect the influence of the Q2 text. The Q1 version of the passage in question (3.1.33–6) is printed above as an example of a potential false start. Q2's version is quite close to Q1's, but with an added 'or' in line 34 that was probably meant to help regularize the metre. Here is the Q2 version of the lines in question, modernized:

> if they did hear,
> They would not mark me, or if they did mark,
> They would not pity me, yet plead I must,
> And bootless unto them.

The compositor of Q3 accidentally skips line 35, and – in a futile effort to salvage the sense of the passage – then changes 'and' to 'all'. Here are the Q3 lines, modernized:

> if they did hear,
> They would not mark me, or if they did mark,
> All bootless unto them.

The Folio text does not fully restore the original, but it salvages the sense of Titus' remark by reintroducing half of the Q2 line that the compositor of Q3 accidentally dropped. Here is the Folio version, modernized:

> if they did hear,
> They would not mark me; oh, if they did hear
> They would not pity me.

Since the compositor of the Folio text does not revert to the Q2 version of these lines, it seems unlikely that he had full and ready access to that text. There is another line in the play that the compositor of Q3 accidentally drops (4.4.102) and it is missing in the Folio text too. Perhaps the F compositor here was working from a marked-up copy of Q3 that had been annotated imperfectly? Dover Wilson's hypothesis – that the Folio text was set from a copy of Q3 that had been marked-up by somebody with access to an updated playbook of some kind – is compatible with the way the passage quoted above is only partially fixed in the Folio text. If Dover Wilson is correct, this annotator's hand would presumably have been the source for the Folio's added line at 1.1.400 too, which in turn might mean that the line was part of the play as it had come to be performed. Since the F text features carefully updated stage directions, Dover Wilson also suggested that whoever annotated Q3 for inclusion in the Folio might have been especially focused on updating the SDs for print, and that in marking up Q3 he might have skipped from stage direction to stage direction instead of reading systematically through and marking up the whole text. This might explain why just the one line was added to the Folio text in Act 1: it occurs right before a substantial stage direction, at a moment where a missing line might be noticed by somebody familiar with the updated play but who was mostly only paying attention to stage directions in the text (Cam², 96–7).

The fly-killing scene (3.2), which is unique to the Folio text of the play, was probably written later than the rest of the play and by another hand (see the section on 'Authorship' above). There are several anomalous features to the way it is presented in F. For instance, Titus is referred to as 'Andronicus' in his entry SD, and his speech prefix in this scene is 'An.' (instead of 'Titus.', 'Tit.' or 'Ti.', as in the rest of the play). And the name Tamora is rendered as 'Tamira' in the Folio text at 3.2.74. As Greg argued, these differences suggest 'a different scribal origin' than the original base text of Q1 (Folio, 204) – which is unsurprising if, as seems likely, this scene was a Jacobean addition inserted to refresh the play for a theatrical revival. It is possible that the people assembling the Folio had access to a copy of this scene as it was inserted into their marked-up copy of Q3, and it is also possible that they sought it out and included it because, by 1622–3, they considered it to have become part of the play. Though we have edited out anomalies like the name 'Tamira', we include 3.2 in our text of the play for the same reason: because we are using both Q1 and F to arrive at something that best approximates a Jacobean revival text of the play.

EARLY THEATRE HISTORY AND DATING

The title page of the 1594 quarto (Q1) of Titus Andronicus features what is possibly the most reliable piece of information we have about the play's early performance history: namely, that it had been performed by 'the right Honourable the Earle of Darbie, Earle of Pembrooke, and Earle of Sussex their servants'. That is, the Q1 title page says that Titus Andronicus had been associated with three different theatrical companies prior to its print publication: the company performing under the patronage of Ferdinando Stanley, Lord Strange, who had become the fifth Earl of Derby in 1593; the company performing under the patronage of Henry Herbert, second Earl of Pembroke; and the company performing under the patronage of Henry Radclyffe and/or his son Robert, who succeeded him as Earl of Sussex in the winter of 1593. This information has been the occasion of

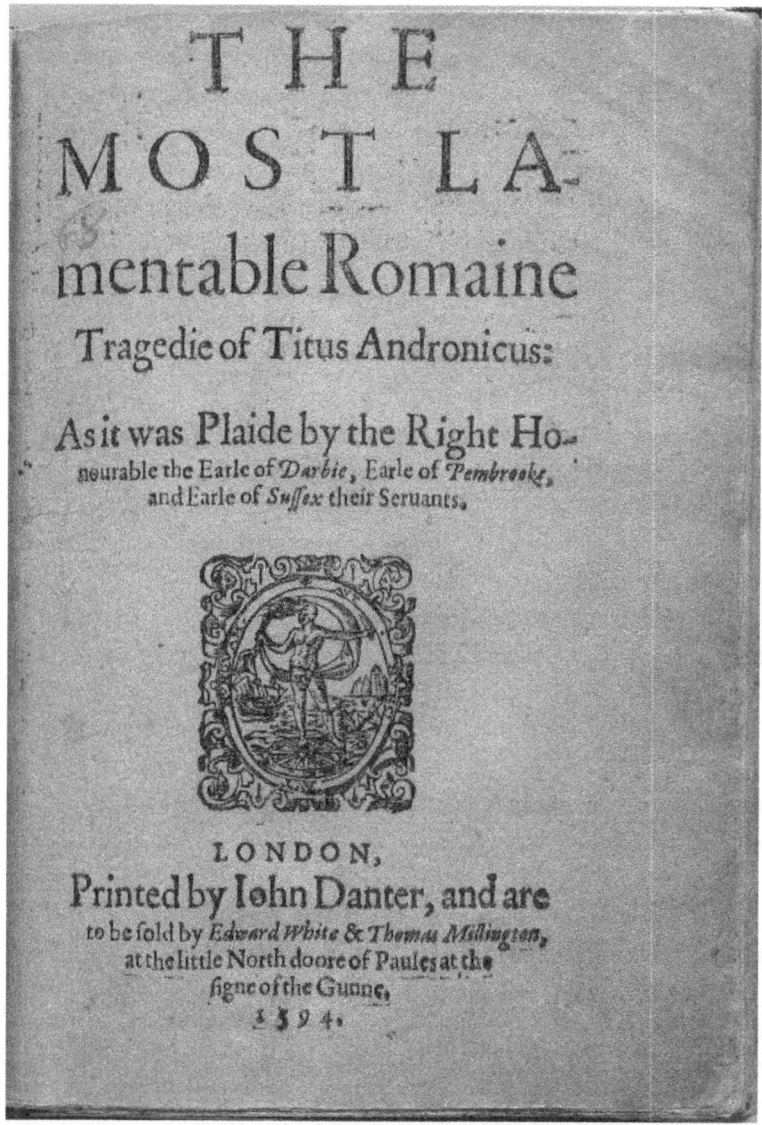

Figure 14 The title page of the 1594 quarto (Q1) of *Titus Andronicus* lists that it has been performed by 'the right Honourable the Earle of Darbie, Earle of Pembrooke, and Earle of Sussex their servants'.

considerable speculation and debate: does the order in which these names are listed matter? Should the attribution be understood as meaning that the play was performed by three discrete companies one after the other, or does it simply associate the play with different configurations of shifting personnel as actors moved from one company to another? Might it even refer to some kind of temporary merger or collaboration? Attributions to various theatrical companies are a common feature of the title pages of early English playbooks, and these ascriptions seem to be reliable as evidence, at least when a given play is printed within recent memory of its initial performance run (Syme, 'Alternative'). Thus, we can at least be fairly certain that *Titus Andronicus* had been performed by actors associated with Strange's Men, Pembroke's Men and Sussex's Men prior to its first printing. Beyond that, the early history of *Titus Andronicus* offers very little in the way of certainty.

   A great deal of the information we have about the day-to-day finances and operation of London's commercial theatre in the 1590s comes from a document known as Henslowe's Diary: an account book used for several years, starting in 1592, by Philip Henslowe, the entrepreneur who owned and managed the Rose Theatre in Bankside, south of the Thames. Among other things, Henslowe's records contain information about which plays were put on by what companies, and about how much money he received as a theatrical landlord. His ledgers include periods when the Rose was occupied by two of the three companies named on the Q1 title page of *Titus Andronicus*: Lord Strange's Men played at the Rose – off and on because of plague-related closures – from February 1592 until February 1593, and Sussex's Men played at the Rose from December 1593 until February 1594, and then again in some kind of collaborative arrangement with members of another company (The Queen's Men) from March to May of that same year. The first appearance of what is likely *Titus Andronicus* in Henslowe's diary occurs on 23 January 1594, and reads like this: 'ne – Rd at titus & ondronicus the 23 of Janeway........iij^{li} viij s' (Henslowe, 21). Despite Henslowe's apparently dittographical (with the 'and' sound repeated) rendering of the name, the identification of this entry with *Titus Andronicus* has only rarely been questioned, and the entry indicates that Henslowe received the comparatively robust sum of 3 pounds and 8 shillings as the gate receipts for that show.[1]

Henslowe's tantalizing annotation 'ne', which is used throughout the Diary, seems to be written by plays that are 'new or marketably new' (Knutson, 467). But Henslowe's 'ne' cannot simply mean new, since, for example, the now-lost play *Alexander and Lodowick* is listed as being performed 'ne' at the Rose by the Lord Admiral's Men on 14 January 1597, and as 'ne' again the next time it appears, on 11 February of the same year. One possibility is that 'ne' indicates the first performance of a newly licensed play, even if it was only a substantially revised version of an earlier play (Henslowe, xxxiv–xxxv; compare Syme, *History*, 19–24). Tiffany Stern has argued that audiences for a play's first public performance were invited to pass judgement and offer feedback, and she has suggested that Henslowe's 'ne' indicates a first performance of a new or newly revised play for which an audience therefore paid higher than normal admissions fees (Stern, *Rehearsal*, 115). Some of the plays that Henslowe marks as 'ne' do seem likely to represent newly revised and possibly relicensed versions of older plays, like *The Spanish Tragedy*, performed as 'ne' by the Admiral's Men in January 1597 (Henslowe, 55). In the case of *Alexander and Lodowick*, much more time elapses between two lucrative performances than is

---

1   In a provocative unpublished conference paper, Misha Teramura notes that a play referred to as 'Titus and Andronicus' is also mentioned in several other early modern documents, including: a stationer's register entry that transfers rights in a 'booke called Titus and Andronicus' from Thomas Millington to Thomas Pavier in 1602 (SRO 4536); another entry after Pavier's death that transfers his right to print 'Tytus and Andronicus' to two other stationers even though it also *separately* transfers to them 'Master Paviers right in shakespeare[']s plaies or any of them' (SRO 8250); a sloppy printed catalogue of plays from 1656 (appended to Goffe); and a less sloppy play list from the seventeenth century compiled by the collector Henry Oxinden (on which, see Dawson). If 'titus & ondronicus' is Henslowe's error, it is not clear how that error would find its way into these other documents, and so Teramura suggests that the name may refer instead to a lost play of that name (Teramura, 'Titus &'). If this were true, it would mean that *Titus Andronicus* left no trace in Henslowe's records as a property of either Strange's Men or Sussex's men, and yet we know from the Q1 title page that both of these companies played it. This might seem odd, since the play seems to have been popular with audiences, and since – if Henslowe's 'William the Conkerer' is the same as *Fair Em* – all of the other extant Elizabethan plays with title-page attributions to Strange's Men or Sussex's Men do show up in the Diary. It would also be an odd coincidence if printing rights to a lost play called 'Titus and Andronicus' happened to coincide with stationers (Millington and Pavier) who are otherwise linked to the provenance of *Titus Andronicus*. Teramura's line of inquiry certainly calls into question the meaning of Henslowe's entry, but further scholarly inquiry is required before we are ready to scrap Henslowe's entry as an anchor point. We are very grateful to Teramura for allowing us to consult the paper and we look forward to reading future scholarship debating the matter.

typical – twenty-three other performances are given in the interim – so it is possible to imagine that something happened after the initial performance that required extensive rewriting and/or relicensing. In any event, it seems likely that *Titus* was performed at the Rose in January 1594 as either a new play or one that had been revised and so was marketably new. Two more performances of 'titus & ondronicus' by Sussex's Men are recorded in late January and early February 1594 (Henslowe, 21).

In March and April 1594, Henslowe records a short season of eight performances at the Rose put on by Sussex's Men and the Queen's Men together; *Titus*'s absence from this set of records is perhaps notable since 'titus & ondronicus' had been one of the more popular plays put on by Sussex's Men earlier that same year. Perhaps the company had splintered and those performing at the Rose no longer owned the playbook (McMillin)? In June 1594 a play called 'andronicus' appears again in Henslowe's ledgers, but this time it is listed among a series of plays put on by the Lord Admiral's Men and the Lord Chamberlain's Men at a theatre to the south of London, in Newington Butts (Henslowe, 22). It is not clear why Henslowe had any interest at all in plays at Newington Butts, though the recorded receipts from this run of plays is low enough in comparison to the money taken in at the Rose to suggest that he may have been sharing the income with some other partner or perhaps managing performances in a venue owned by somebody else while the Rose was in hiatus (Rutter, 82).

Still, it remains difficult to square the information in Henslowe's Diary with the company attributions on the page of the earliest quarto edition of *Titus Andronicus*, since nothing resembling *Titus Andronicus* appears in any of Henslowe's records for Lord Strange's Men and since the Q1 title page says nothing about Lord Chamberlain's Men or the Admiral's Men. The difficulty is compounded by the porousness and fluidity of the companies themselves, especially in the early years of the 1590s. Narrative accounts of the movement of *Titus Andronicus* from one company's repertory to another are speculative and tend to hinge on hypotheses about key personnel moving from company to company and taking licensed playbooks with them. It has been postulated, for instance, that the Q1 title page lists the companies that owned the play in the correct chronological order, and that the playbook 'was carried along by one group of actors as they performed under a succession of patrons' – that is, that several members of Lord Strange's Men become key members of Pembroke's Men and then moved on to become Sussex's Men within a few years (McMillin, 217). It has also been tempting to imagine that Shakespeare himself may have brought the playbook with him from one company to another. Shakespeare had become a shareholding partner in the Lord Chamberlain's Men by the spring of 1595, and the play had certainly become part of the repertory of that company by the time the play's second quarto was printed in 1600. The Q2 title page advertises that the play 'hath sundry times beene played by the Right Honourable the Earle of Pembrooke, the Earle of Darbie, the Earle of Sussex, and the Lorde Chamberlaine theyr servants'.

The most convincing and satisfying speculative account that has so far been offered to reconcile Henslowe's Diary with the information contained on *Titus*'s Q1 title page is that of Holger Schott Syme, who reminds us that there is no reason to assume that Shakespeare himself owned the playbooks that he contributed to prior to joining the Lord Chamberlain's Men. In fact, Syme ('Alternative') is able to demonstrate convincingly that *Titus Andronicus* was not yet part of the repertory of the Lord Chamberlin's Men even shortly after Shakespeare joined that company. We know from a letter preserved in the papers of Sir Antony Bacon, and written by his Gascon secretary Jacques Petit, that '*la tragedie de Titus Andronicus*' was performed by a company of actors from London at the estate of Sir John Harington in Burley-on-the-Hill in Rutland on 1 January 1596 (Ungerer). Syme makes a strong case that the Lord Chamberlain's Men, who we know performed at court on 28 December 1595 and 6 January 1596, could not have been the troupe mentioned by Petit as performing at Rutland in the interim, and that instead the most likely company to have done so was Pembroke's Men, who may have been active at the Curtain Theatre in Shoreditch until 1597. If Pembroke's Men had *Titus Andronicus* in their repertory on 1 January 1596, then they were probably the last of the three companies listed on the Q1 title page to own the licensed playbook, and that would presumably mean that they started performing *Titus* at some point after the performances at Newington Butts recorded by Henslowe in early June 1594 and before the play's title page was designed in the same year.

Since title-page company attributions are part of a playbook's marketing, and since the Lord Chamberlain's Men were, in 1594, new and relatively unknown, Syme also speculates that the Q1 printer may have opted to go with a more established company name, which would be recognized by the play's potential readership, in the title-page list of theatre companies. Lord Strange's Men disbanded after their patron's untimely death in April 1594, and members of the company moved on to the Lord Admiral's Men and the Lord Chamberlain's Men (Manley and MacLean, 323–5). Henslowe indicates that these two companies performed together at Newington Butts in June of that same year. It is possible, therefore, that the amalgamated companies at Newington Butts might have seemed to a printer and to readers in 1594 to be identifiable as Strange's Men continuing in a different configuration. If so, the Q1 title-page attributions might reflect,

> in alphabetical rather than chronological order, the staging of the play from its first appearance in the 'Diary' in January (Sussex's Men) through its second appearance in June (at the hands of two companies that between them shared the major figures associated with Strange's, or, by 1594, Derby's Men) to what was by the time the book was published later in the year its final owners, the servants of the earl of Pembroke.
>
> (Syme, 'Alternative', 282)

Syme also offers an attractive account of how the licensed playbook of *Titus Andronicus* may have made its way from Pembroke's Men to the Lord Chamberlain's Men. We know that some sharers in Pembroke's Men were arrested in the controversy over the play *The Isle of Dogs* in 1597, and that some of the company's personnel at that point went over the Lord Admiral's Men taking some of the company's repertory with them (e.g., Chambers, *Stage*, 2: 132). Perhaps some also went to the Lord Chamberlain's Men at that point and brought the licensed copy of *Titus Andronicus* along with them (Syme, 'Alternative', 285).

Even if all this is accepted, questions remain about whether the play was in fact new (as opposed to newly revised or relicensed) when it was performed as 'ne' in 1594. The preponderance of evidence would seem to suggest that it was not. The impressionistic argument for this is simply that *Titus Andronicus* seems to be cut from the same cloth as plays like Thomas Kyd's *The Spanish Tragedy* (1587), Christopher Marlowe's *The Jew of Malta* (1589) and Peele's own *Battle of Alcazar* (1588–9). We discuss these plays as intertexts in the section on 'Sources and Intertexts'. As we have seen, Ben Jonson, writing from the vantage point of 1614, saw *Titus* and *The Spanish Tragedy* as two comparable old blockbusters of the same general vintage. The text of our play does seem to contain some traces of revision (see the section on 'Early Texts'), but this does not really prove much one way or another since traces of rewriting could easily be preserved in a manuscript playbook as the result of ordinary rewriting either prior to or just after a play's initial public performance.

More concretely, the 1594 quarto of the play *A Knack to Know a Knave*, which was performed as 'ne' at the Rose by Lord Strange's Men in June 1592, seems to contain an allusion to our play that might be evidence of its existence in repertory prior to 1594. There, a character named Osric welcomes his king with the following lines:

> My gratious Lord, as welcome shall you be
> To me, my Daughter, and my sonne in Law,
> As Titus was unto the Roman Senators,
> When he had made a conquest of the Goths:
> That in requitall of his service done
> Did offer him the imperiall Diadem:
> As they in Titus, we in your Grace still find
> The perfect figure of Princelie mind.

> (*Knack*, sig. F2ᵛ)

This is not exactly what happens in Act 1 of our play – Marcus in his role as Tribune offers Titus the crown on behalf of the people – but it is close enough to read like a reference to *Titus Andronicus*, especially since the Tribunes and Senators enter together at the start of *Titus* and since the political demarcation of these roles is not especially sharp in the play's imaginary Rome. Even if the quarto of *A Knack to Know a Knave* was patched together from memory by actors just before it was entered in the stationer's register on 7 January 1594 (as suggested in Bennett), it still predates the first performance of 'titus & ondronicus' recorded by Henslowe (see Wiggins, where *Tit* is #928).

It is possible, of course, that the allusion in A *Knack* refers to some now-lost precursor to our play, and there has certainly been a fair amount of scholarly speculation concerning the possibility of a lost ur-*Titus* (see, for instance, *Tito*, 42–6). One possibility that has been suggested (most recently by McCarthy and Schlueter) is that the version of the *Titus* story referred to in *A Knack to Know a Knave* is identical with another lost play, called 'Titus & Vespasia' by Henslowe, which we know was performed by Lord Strange's Men at the Rose contemporaneously with *A Knack*.[1] There is some reason to take this possibility seriously, though on the whole we still find it unlikely. The strongest piece of circumstantial evidence comes from the text of a German-language version of the *Titus Andronicus* story that was printed in Leipzig in 1620, and that was likely derived from a touring version of a *Titus Andronicus* play put on earlier by an English troupe (see *Tito*, 36–40). In that play – where many of the names differ from those of corresponding characters in *Titus Andronicus* – Titus' eldest son is named Vespasianus instead of Lucius. So perhaps the German play was based on an English original with these names as well, and maybe this is what appears in Henslowe as 'Titus & Vespasia'.

The problem with this hypothesis is simply that there is another very well-known story of Titus and Vespasian that seems much more likely to have been the subject of any new play with that name staged in 1592: the story the Roman emperor Vespasian, his son Titus and the siege of Jerusalem in 70 CE (see T&V; Wiggins, #923). There were numerous retellings of the siege of Jerusalem in circulation in Elizabethan England, and the story had even been recently dramatized, both in a (now-lost) pageant play put on in Coventry in 1584 (on which, see Groves) and as a three-part tragedy called *Solymitana Clades* by Thomas Legge (whose Latin university play about

---

1   In addition to seven entries in the Diary indicating performance by Strange's Men of a play called 'Titus & Vespasia' between April 1592 and January 1593, there are also three entries in Henslowe's Diary indicating performance of a play called just 'Titus' in January 1593 (Henslowe, 17–20). Since 'Titus & Vespasia' still seems to be in the repertory as of January 1593, and since there is no indication as yet that any new Titus-related play has entered the repertory of Lord Strange's Men, these seem to be the same play and the difference in titles would seem to just reflect Henslowe's evolving style of annotation.

Richard III demonstrably influenced subsequent commercial dramatizations of that story). It seems most likely that any play called 'Titus & Vespasia' in 1592 would have been based upon this story, and it is correspondingly easy to imagine that the author of the German *Tito Andronico* chose the name Vespasianus for Titus' son because of the recalled resonance of this other Roman story. If so, he may have associated the two Titus tales because they share some thematic details: the history of the siege of Jerusalem features a shocking cannibal banquet which the last part of Legge's *Solymitana Clades* recasts in imitation of Senecan-style tragedy, so a reader of one Titus story might well have been reminded of the other. Late Elizabethan writers and readers do seem sometimes to have cross-referenced these two Titus stories in their minds, even if they are quite far removed from each other in terms of narrative setting (on which, see also Moschovakis, 'Irreligious'). Thomas Nashe's pamphlet *Christ's Tears Over Jerusalem* (1593), which has been linked to *Titus Andronicus* via some suggestive verbal parallels with the play, includes a substantial account of the story of the siege of Jerusalem (see Streete). And even though the passage quoted above from *A Knack to Know a Knave* resembles the opening of *Titus Andronicus*, the Roman emperor Vespasian is prominently name-checked in the play as well (sigs A2ʳ and B3ᵛ).

One reason we think it likely that the *Titus* performed in 1594 was a newly revised version of a somewhat older play is that the text of Q1 itself shows signs of having undergone revision (as discussed in the section on 'Early Texts', pp. 35–8). Though we can only speculate about what an earlier, pre-revision version of the play might have looked like, it is notable that some of the places where the Q1 text shows internal signs of revision – especially around the sacrifice of Alarbus and the death and burial of Mutius in Act 1 – are also aspects of the play that are missing in other early retellings of the story. First, there is a ballad version, which survives in early seventeenth-century texts and which is likely the same one entered by Danter in the Stationers Register to accompany the 1594 printing of the play: in it, neither the sacrifice of Alarbus nor the death of Mutius is mentioned (the ballad is reprinted in Bullough, 6: 44–8 and in Oxf² as Appendix B). Then there is a German play, *Tito Andronico*, which was written by Friedrich Menius and printed in 1620 (*Tito*, 64–79) and which likely was derived in some way from an earlier English version of the story. It also tells the tale without the vivid sacrifice of Alarbus or the killing of Mutius. We will discuss these other versions of the story in the 'Sources and Intertexts' section, but it seems quite possible that both the ballad and the German play were influenced by an earlier version of our play to which these striking episodes had not yet been added.

It is therefore interesting to consider the possibility that Shakespeare and Peele may themselves have written an earlier version of our play. Douglas Bruster and Geneviève Smith, working with computer-aided analysis of evolving pause-patterns within Shakespeare's iambic pentameter line, have argued that Shakespeare's portions of *Titus Andronicus* represent the earliest extant writing in the canon, dating perhaps from 1590 or thereabouts (see Bruster and Smith). And Gary Taylor and Rory Loughnane adduce other arguments for an early dating of *Titus Andronicus*, such as the fact that only Shakespeare's pre-Chamberlain's Men plays require casts of the size that it would take to stage *Titus Andronicus* (Taylor and Loughnane, 450–1); they suggest that the size of *Titus's* cast is comparable with that of other plays that Shakespeare wrote prior to the plague-related closures of London's theatres in 1592, which may have thinned the ranks of available actors (493).[1] Does this mean that Shakespeare contributed to a version of the play and then partially rewrote it before it was played as 'ne' in 1594? If so, that would skew the data that Bruster and Smith draw upon since the text as we have it would then represent a mixture of later with earlier poetic lines. Peele had his heyday as a London dramatist circa 1588–92, so if in fact the play was first written as early as Bruster's and Smith's tests suggest, then Peele's hand in the play most likely originated then as well.

Wiggins, whose best guess as to the date of *Titus's* original composition is 1592, offers any time between 1584–94 as a possible writing date. It is difficult for us to imagine that *Titus* was written prior to the so-called 'lost years' of Shakespeare's early career, and so prior even to his likely arrival in

---

1 Bate estimated that the play would require 'an absolute minimum company size of between twenty-five and twenty-seven' (Ard³, 94), though this is based on an estimate of how many extras are required as followers of Saturninus and Bassianus and as Tribunes and Senators at the play's opening conflict. Since the play was put on in several different theatres (including a banqueting hall at Burley-on-the-Hill), there may have been circumstances where economizing was necessary, and it would be possible to get away with as few as twenty-two actors if there are only twelve on stage in the opening moment of conflict (three followers each for the brothers, three additional people supporting Marcus as Senators and Tribunes aloft).

London. Such speculation originates with the idea that *Titus Andronicus* is crude and amateurish juvenilia, which we do not think squares with the play's allusive sophistication. Peele was active as a writer from the early 1580s, but he does not seem to have been active as writer of commercial playbooks for the London theatres until somewhat later than that. We would suggest, therefore, that the window of possibility be narrowed to 1587–94. Our own best guess at a date of composition for the original state of the play is 1589–92, which is roughly in keeping with Cam³ and Ard², as well as with Bruster and Smith and with Taylor and Loughnane.

Nicholas Moschovakis has argued that the episode in 4.3 and 4.4, where the Clown first interacts with the Andronici and then is hanged for his trouble by Saturninus, is based on historical events that took place in London in the summer of 1591. If true, this would of course further narrow the date for *Titus*'s composition, but we do not feel that the argument is strong enough to be decisive. In July 1591, two sectarian puritans caused a disturbance by proclaiming, in the city streets, that one William Hacket was the Messiah and that Queen Elizabeth was not the true monarch. There are to be sure some suggestive parallels between this episode and *Titus* (as discussed in Moschovakis, 'Topicality'), but the most explicit link between the play and the historical episode is that Richard Cosin, in an account published in 1592, describes how Hacket's disciples had proclaimed that they brought 'newes from heaven' (Cosin, 55). This is the same phrase Titus uses when the clown appears on stage: 'News! News from heaven' (4.3.75). With the help of proximity searches in EEBO, however, it is possible to see that variations on the phrase 'news out of heaven' or 'news from out of heaven' are not at all uncommon in Elizabethan texts; it is quite possible that both Cosin and Shakespeare simply drew upon the same idiomatic and slightly comical phrase.

All accounts of the progress of *Titus Andronicus* through the guts of late Elizabethan London theatre are derived from highly speculative reconstructions of very fragmentary evidence. Here is a version of events that seems plausible to us given what we now know. If *Titus Andronicus* was first written circa 1589–92, it might well have been a collaborative effort, with various scenes farmed out to Shakespeare and Peele on the basis of some overarching plot design. Neither Shakespeare nor Peele would have had an exclusive relationship with any company at this time, and there is little basis for certainty about which company it might have been written for, especially given the easy way personnel and playbooks seem to have moved between different companies. Wiggins speculates that the play may have originally been written for Pembroke's Men, who are connected by title-page attributions to a number of early Shakespeare plays, but it is not clear that this company even existed in 1589–90 and its formation may have involved actors who had moved on from Lord Strange's Men (Chambers, *Stage*, 2: 128–31; Manley, 'From Strange's'). Robert Browne, the player who 'did most to acclimatize the English actors in Germany', between 1590 and 1620 was associated with personnel of the Lord Admiral's Men in 1589, and given the apparent popularity of the Titus Andronicus story in early modern German theatres this may provide a clue as the play's early provenance (Chambers, *Stage*, 2: 273).[1] Manley and MacLean make the case that the play originated with Lord Strange's Men, in the years before their performances at the Rose were recorded in Henslowe's Diary (109–10), though the absence of the play from Henslowe's records in 1592–3 might then be surprising. But plays and personnel moved relatively frequently between these companies in 1589–94. Peele's own roughly contemporary *Battle of Alcazar*, which is attributed to the Lord Admiral's Men on its Elizabethan title page, is likely the same play referred to as 'Mulo Mulloco' in the Strange's Men repertory from 1592–3 (Manley and MacLean, 75–81). Marlowe's play *The Jew of Malta* appears in Henslowe's records as part of the repertory of Lord Strange's Men in 1592–3, then again as part of the repertory of Sussex's Men in 1594, and thereafter as part of the repertory of the Lord Admiral's Men (McMillin). So, it is not difficult to imagine that an early version of *Titus Andronicus* was written for the Lord Admiral's Men or Strange's Men, then rewritten for Sussex's Men during their short-lived stay at the Rose in 1594, and then performed (as discussed above) in quick succession by actors formerly associated with Strange's Men at Newington Butts and by Pembroke's Men at the Curtain Playhouse. By the time a second quarto was printed, in 1600, it was part of the repertory of the Lord Chamberlain's Men, and (as discussed in the sections on 'Authorship' and

---

1   See *Tito*, 46–52 for a discussion of Titus plays performed in Germany in the seventeenth century.

'Early Texts') it seems to have been refreshed again by additions made in the Jacobean era and reflected in the text printed in the Folio of 1623.

SOURCES AND INTERTEXTS

There is no extant narrative source for *Titus Andronicus* from which the play's basic plot outline was clearly derived. This is unusual for an Elizabethan tragedy, but not unheard of. In fact, the two contemporary plays that are arguably closest to *Titus* in terms of theme and tone – Thomas Kyd's *Spanish Tragedy* and Christopher Marlowe's *The Jew of Malta* – both feature freshly invented plots – or, at least, plots for which we have not found sources. Still, since some aspects of later versions of the tale do not seem to have been derived from the play we have, there has been room for speculation about the possibility of some now-lost ur-*Titus*. Since we also think that the version of *Titus Andronicus* we have is likely a revision of an earlier version of the play by Shakespeare and Peele, speculation about a lost source becomes entangled with speculation about an earlier version of the play itself. If we find, in later texts, evidence suggestive of an ur-*Titus*, do we think we are seeing evidence of a lost source or of an earlier, pre-revision version of our play? In this section we will review the evidence and address this question before discussing the other kinds of sources and intertexts that the authors of *Titus Andronicus* were drawing upon.

When scholars speculate about versions of the Titus story that may have preceded the play, they typically base their arguments on variations among three later versions of the tale: the ballad (sometimes called 'Titus Andronicus's Complaint') that has survived in print from 1620, as well as in one manuscript that likely dates from earlier in the seventeenth century (Jackson, 'Editions', 249); a short prose narrative entitled *The History of Titus Andronicus, the Renowned Roman General, Newly Translated from the Italian Copy Printed at Rome* that was first printed (along with a version of the ballad) in the mid-eighteenth century; and a German play, called *Eine sehr klägliche Tragoedia von Tito Andronico vnd der hoffertigen Käyserin (A Very Lamentable Tragedy of Tito Andronico and the Haughty Empress)*, which was written by Friedrich Menius and printed in Leipzig in 1620. The first two of these are reprinted in Bullough (6:34–48) as well as in Oxf[2], and there has been a great deal of debate about their relationship to *Titus Andronicus* and to each other. The last of these, *Tito Andronico*, has until recently been harder to access and so less frequently discussed. We now finally have a strong, scholarly edition of this play, with a reliable English translation and a lengthy introduction that discusses the play's relation to *Titus Andronicus* and other versions of the story in detail (*Tito*, 1–45).

For much of the twentieth century, debates about the existence of a lost ur-*Titus* were centred around the chapbook *History of Titus Andronicus*. Joseph Quincey Adams – who discovered the volume in the Folger library – presented it to the scholarly community as a late printing of a lost source for the play (Adams, 7–9), and the chapbook was also reprinted as a 'probable' source for *Titus Andronicus* in Bullough (see also summary arguments in Metz and Oxf²). Both the chapbook and the ballad omit the sacrifice of Alarbus and the killing of Mutius, and so it has also seemed possible to some scholars that the ballad was based on the original story as enshrined in the chapbook rather than on the play. It seems much more likely to us, however, that the prose history was written after the ballad, and likely too that it was written with the ballad's version of the tale specifically in mind. In the *History of Titus Andronicus*, Lavinia reveals the names of her attackers by writing out a rhyming couplet with a 'wand between her stumps': 'The lustful sons of the proud Empress / Are doers of this hateful wickedness' (Oxf², 202). The same couplet appears in the ballad:

> For with a staff, without the help of hand
> She writ these words upon that plot of sand:
> 'The lustful sons of the proud Empress
> Are doers of this hateful wickedness'.
>
> (Oxf², 206)

This seems a strong indicator that the author of the history drew upon the ballad since, as Jackson argues, 'it is much more likely that the [chapbook author] has borrowed a key couplet from the ballad than that on the one occasion on which he attempted rhyme he fortuitously produced verse that perfectly fits the ballad's pentameter stanza' ('Editions', 249). The most likely argument, we feel, is that the ballad was based on the play and that the prose *History* was made (at least in part) from the ballad (and see also Ard[3] and Jackson, 'Play').

Those aspects of the prose history that seem to diverge most strikingly from the story in the play can often be understood as by-products of an effort to flesh out plot details from the much shorter ballad. To give one key example: in the chapbook *History* we are told that Lavinia had been engaged to the Saturninus character's 'only son by a former wife', but this odd detail is likely based on a misunderstanding of the ballad, where she is said to be betrothed to 'Caesar's son' (Oxf², 200 and 205, respectively). Bassianus introduces himself as 'Caesar's son' when he first introduces himself in *Titus Andronicus* (1.1.10), so it seems likely that the ballad's turn of phrase was based on the play and that the author of the chapbook in turn was trying to build out narrative detail based upon his misunderstanding of the phrase in the ballad (Jackson, 'Play'). Imagining that Lavinia's fiancé is the current emperor's son necessitates other aspects of the chapbook's version of the story as well: for instance, this means that the emperor is actively supportive of Lavinia's marriage and so her fiancé has to be kidnapped by the Tamora figure and her Moor lover and hidden in the woods for a while before being killed. This in turn means that his murder and the assault on Lavinia become more temporally distinct events in the chapbook version of the story.

The most likely scenario, therefore, is that the ballad (which is probably the same ballad entered into the Stationer's Register by John Danter when he registered the play) was written on the basis of an early version of the play, and that the author of the prose history used the ballad to produce his tale. As Adams first ascertained, the chapbook *History of Titus Andronicus* was printed between 1736 and 1764 by Cluer Dicey, who was a prolific publisher of ballads, chapbooks and other print ephemera. Dicey was a wholesale dealer in cheap print, and his stock of histories and ballads indicates that he trafficked in popular antiquarianism. But he was also in the business of selling short histories and novellas that were meant to be easily accessible to ordinary readers of his day, and meeting consumer demand for such material likely was more important to him than being scrupulous about textual provenance: the Dicey catalogue of chapbooks includes, for example, a short, contemporary sounding jestbook that was called *Canterbury Tales* and that was attributed on the title page to a Chaucer Junior (*Catalogue;*

on the Dicey chapbooks, see Neuburg; Stoker). The title page of Dicey's *History of Titus Andronicus* indicates that it was 'newly translated from the *Italian* Copy printed at *Rome*', but that seems likely to be fictional – part of the marketing of the book, rather than a credible account of how it came into Dicey's possession (Oxf², 195; compare Mincoff). One would not necessarily expect to find a carefully preserved Elizabethan novella in the Dicey catalogue, in short, and it would not be at all surprising to find there a recasting of an older story written in accessible prose. Since Dicey was himself a dealer in ballads, one can easily imagine him commissioning the chapbook history of Titus as a retelling of the ballad.

The German play *Tito Andronico* was self-evidently written after *Titus Andronicus*, of course; its relevance to the topic of an ur-*Titus* has to do with the fact that it was likely derived from an early touring version of some English Titus Andronicus play. Though there are many elements in this play that do seem to derive from something like our *Titus* – so much so that we have often used the play's SDs to illustrate possible early staging choices throughout this edition – there are also aspects of it that differ from our play in ways that cannot be explained as simplification or bowdlerization. For instance, the German play's Aaron figure, who is named Morian (after the German word for Moor), offers a surprisingly detailed account of his prehistory with the Tamora figure (who in the German play is made into the Queen of Ethiopia):

> Everyone thought I was merely the Queen's servant – but no, I was her secret lover and slept more often with her than the King of Ethiopia, her husband, so that at last he noticed the mischief between me and the Queen, and had me closely watched so that I could not go near her. The Queen became very impatient with her husband, for I could not come near her for fourteen days, being guarded so closely, and the King could not pluck her strings half as vigorously as I. Therefore, she took poison and gave it to the King in a goblet of wine so that again I had free access to her.
>
> (*Tito*, 1.1.89–100)

Later in the same speech he gives a detailed account of his own military prowess and his defeat at the hands of the Romans in the play's immediate prehistory:

In battles and perilous wars I fought like a formidable lion – not like a man but like a very devil. Thus, eventually, I became known throughout the whole world for my great, superhuman, manly exploits and was given the title of 'Thunder and Lightning of Ethiopia'. My fame finally reached the Romans, who armed themselves mightily and came for us in Ethiopia, devastating and destroying the land with unheard-of cruelty. I went out against them with my army and thought they would cause me little trouble and be driven back so that none would return to Rome alive. But when the fight began, I saw how dreadfully old Tito Andronico hit back; he surpassed me and was ten times more fierce. In all my life I had not seen an army more warlike and battle-hardened than these Romans. This frightened me, and I saw my ranks dissolve, beaten like dogs. Before long, old Tito rushed at me and – something that no man had ever done before – struck me off my horse with his lance so fiercely that I didn't know whether I were dead or alive. They cut everyone down, so that no-one escaped. They took many spoils, among them me, the Queen, and her sons, and brought us to Rome.

(*Tito*, 1.1.107–30)

The vivid particulars provided here – about the poisoning of the queen's old husband, about warlike exploits and about Morian's actual physical conflict with Tito – are full of arresting narrative specificity and are of course wholly absent from the *Titus Andronicus* play we have.

Morian's expository prehistory is presented as part of an extended soliloquy at the end of *Tito*'s first act, a soliloquy that is loosely analogous in the play's structure to Aaron's first speech in *Titus Andronicus* (2.1.1–25). As pointed out by the editors of the recent edition of *Tito Andronico*, there is even some evidence of a genealogical link between Morian's soliloquy and Aaron's. Morian, for example, 'pulls off the old cloak' he has been wearing near the beginning of his soliloquy (*Tito*, SD after 1.1.83), while Aaron (who may or may not physically remove a garment on stage) declares: 'Away with slavish weeds and servile thoughts' (2.1.18). Where the German Morian tells us that he had been known as the 'Thunder and Lightning of Ethiopia', the Aaron in our play reflects, in the equivalent speech, that Tamora 'sits aloft, / Secure of thunder's crack or lightning flash' (2.1.2–3).[1] It is possible

---

1 As is noted in the gloss on this speech in *Tito*. Such echoes are discussed in *Tito*, 7–19, and in the glosses provided throughout that text.

to imagine the kinds of similarities and differences between the two plays as the end product of a German reinvention of our play, but it is also possible that they have to do with shared reliance upon some now-lost earlier version. This is the scenario that the recent editors of *Tito Andronico* find most plausible: that '*Tito* does not derive from *Titus* but is based on an earlier version, a lost *Ur-Titus*, which revision turned into Shakespeare and Peele's *Titus Andronicus*' (*Tito*, 46).

The editors of *Tito Andronico* also identify parallels between the ways that the prose history and *Tito Andronico* each differ from *Titus Andronicus* (as discussed in *Tito*, 40–6), on the theory that the chapbook *History* may reflect some version of the tale other than the ballad or the play. The key argument here is that in both the *History* and in *Tito* Titus sacrifices his hand to save his imprisoned sons before encountering his mutilated daughter. In the ballad, the order of these events more closely resembles *Titus Andronicus*, as is consistent with the idea that the ballad was based on an early version of the play. If the prose history and *Tito* each differ from both the ballad and the play in ways that parallel one another, then (the argument goes) there may be some reason to hypothesize the existence of some other earlier version of the story, in which the cutting off of Titus' hand precedes his discovery of Lavinia's rape. While it remains possible that the German play may contain traces of some lost ur-*Titus* (if not just of an earlier version of *Titus Andronicus*), we do not find the argument about the similarities between *Tito* and the chapbook to be especially persuasive, and (as discussed above) we feel that the reordering of events in the chapbook can be explained as a result of its author's misunderstanding of the ballad narrative.

Setting aside the tantalizing question of an ur-*Titus*, we can also see that *Titus Andronicus* makes sophisticated use of a wide range of classical and contemporary intertexts, which give shape to aspects of the play's story and which are designed to help orient readers and observers towards the play's thematic concerns. Because the play is set in the later Roman empire, its characters are repeatedly shown turning to canonical Roman literature in order to make sense of the playworld they inhabit. Titus compares himself to King Priam, the legendary king of Troy, in his very first speech (1.1.79–80), thereby indicating his membership in a style of imperial

Roman self-understanding evocative of Virgil's *Aeneid*. He sees himself, accordingly, as representing a timeless imperial ethos in which military virtue and dutiful civic piety take precedence over anything personal. His daughter, Lavinia, is named after the daughter of King Latinus whose marriage to Aeneas, in Virgil's epic, paves the way for the founding of Rome. Aaron, as he leads Chiron and Demetrius towards the rape of Lavinia, first evokes the Livian/Ovidian story of the rape of Lucrece (2.1.108) and then the Ovidian story of the rape of Philomela (2.3.43). Each of these stories becomes a recurring comparative framework for understanding the action in the play (e.g., 2.4.38–43; 4.1.62–3; 4.1.88–93; 5.2.193–4), and, of course, Ovid's *Metamorphoses* is eventually brought on stage and used by Lavinia to explain what has happened to her (4.1.30–57). Demetrius, meanwhile, as he accedes to Aaron's rape plot, misquotes Seneca's *Phaedra* (2.1.135), thereby aligning himself with Senecan themes of uncontrolled passion and the relinquishment of moral rectitude. One striking feature of the play's insistent allusiveness is that all the characters, even those first brought into Rome as prisoners of war in 1.1, make easy, constant use of Roman literature to explain or examine their circumstances. The play imagines Rome as a global empire whose culture has perforce become universal among the play's characters, even though several of them hail from the empire's periphery.

Because the play's late-Roman characters look back to canonical Latin literature from a temporal distance, their relation to the texts they cite and allude to often resembles that of Peele, Shakespeare and their contemporaries, who also looked to Roman texts as the shared stuff of culture, and who also sometimes thought of themselves as Rome's belated heirs. This parallelism is part of the play's design, and it even provides explicit material for an anachronistic joke in 4.2, when Young Lucius delivers a scroll with two lines from one of Horace's Odes to Chiron, Demetrius and Aaron. Chiron, proud of himself, declares 'O 'tis a verse in Horace, I know it well. / I read it in the grammar long ago' (22–3): the joke is that the grammar in question is an Elizabethan grammar-school textbook which Shakespeare himself likely used (Lily's *A Shorte Introduction of Grammar*: see the note at 4.2.23). Because the play's authors and consumers share an immersion in Roman culture with its characters, allusions like the ones mentioned in the previous paragraph convey thematic information or expectations about plot.

The story of Procne, Philomela and Tereus plays an especially important role as an insistent, recurring model for the play's action. The best-known version for Shakespeare, Peele and their contemporaries was from Ovid's *Metamorphoses* (6.401–674), where the tale begins with the marriage of Tereus, a powerful Thracian king, to the Athenian princess Procne. After living in her husband's kingdom for several years, Procne asks Tereus to bring her sister Philomela to Thrace for a visit. Tereus sets sail for Athens to fulfil the request, but he is waylaid by his own tyrannical desires. He rapes Philomela on the journey from Athens to Thrace and attempts to hide his crime by locking her away and cutting out her tongue to prevent speech. Philomela, though, weaves the story of her rape into a tapestry and has it delivered to her sister by a trusted servant. To get revenge, Procne murders the son she has had with Tereus, and the two sisters prepare the son's body as a cannibal feast for his unwitting father. This narrative pattern, in which the crime of violent rape is avenged via cannibal banquet, gives shape to the early modern Titus Andronicus story, and characters within the playworld often seem to understand that they are living out a twisted re-enactment of the Ovidian tale. When Marcus discovers Lavinia with her tongue and hands cut off, his initial reaction is that she must have fallen victim to a 'craftier Tereus' who, knowing the Ovidian original, has tried to forestall discovery by cutting off those hands 'that could have better sewed than Philomel' (2.4.41–3). By the end of the play, when Titus uses the device of the cannibal banquet to get his revenge, there is a sense that the characters all know they are one-upping an Ovidian original: 'For worse than Philomel you used my daughter, / And worse than Procne I will be revenged' (5.2.193–4). Both the play's authors and the characters treat the Ovidian story as a narrative source to draw on, in other words, which gives the play's exceptionally violent denouement a weirdly knowing and recursive quality, as if the characters on stage were battling over who had interpretive control over the re-enactment.

The other legendary Roman story that acts as a narrative source for both the play's characters and its authors is the story of the rape of Lucrece and its aftermath. Shakespeare, of course, wrote a long narrative poem on the subject that was also first printed in 1594. In *Titus*, the story is first evoked by Aaron (who compares Lavinia's chastity to that of Lucrece at 2.1.108) and is thereafter called upon as an exemplary narrative of tyrannical crime and politically efficacious vengeance. As recounted both in Ovid's *Fasti* (2.6685–852) and at the end of the first book of Livy's *History of Rome* (1.57–60), the chaste Lucrece is raped by the son of a tyrannical Roman king named Lucius Tarquinius Superbus who had earlier usurped power from his own father-in-law by force and whose ascendancy is described by Livy as marking the end of lawful kingship in Rome (1.43.8–9). Lucrece summons her father, her husband and their close associates, tells them what has occurred and commits suicide, whereupon her male relatives, together with Lucius Junius Brutus, lead an uprising that culminates with the banishment of the Tarquins and the establishment of the Roman republic. The story of the rape of Lucrece is thus also the story of the purging of tyrannical government and the founding of a new, reformed Rome.

This is how the Andronici understand the meaning of the rape of Lucrece, and they wish to cast their own vengeance for Lavinia's rape as analogous to this story. Marcus asks his kinsmen to

> ... swear with me – as, with the woeful fere
> And father of that chaste dishonoured dame,
> Lord Junius Brutus sware for Lucrece' rape –
> That we will prosecute, by good advice,
> Mortal revenge upon these traitorous Goths,
> And see their blood or die with this reproach.
>
> (4.1.88–93)

Lucius, similarly, imagines himself as another Lucius Junius Brutus when he vows to make Saturninus and Tamora 'beg at the gates like Tarquin and his queen' (3.1.299). The point is that the Andronici see themselves not just as revengers acting out of a sense of deep personal grievance (like Procne, say), but rather as political reformers purging Rome of tyranny. The play itself may be cynical about the restoration offered by Lucius and Marcus at the end, which is effected by making Aaron and Tamora into scapegoats for faults that also belong to Titus and Saturninus and thus to Rome, but both the Andronici and the play itself draw upon the story of the rape of Lucrece as an exemplum in which the sometimes unruly impulse to vengeance is made to serve the public good.

Scholarly discussions of the pervasive allusiveness of *Titus Andronicus* have sometimes treated it as a symptom of Shakespeare's artistic immaturity. Acknowledging the older Peele as co-author challenges this assumption, in that while there has sometimes been a reluctance to credit Shakespeare's erudition, nobody doubts Peele's. In any event, we do not treat the play as juvenilia, and we think it is more appropriate to see *Titus* as instantiating an earlier, less character-based form of theatrical and literary sophistication than some of Shakespeare's later tragedies. Instead of featuring central protagonists who articulate core thematic content in meditative soliloquies, early Elizabethan blockbusters by writers like Marlowe and Kyd often use tonal instability and unexpected juxtapositions of events to provoke and elicit audience response. Kyd's *The Spanish Tragedy* is arguably as searching and interrogatory as *Hamlet* about the ethics and psychology of revenge, but it lacks a Hamlet-like character to articulate its core questions explicitly. *Titus Andronicus* explores the legacy of its Roman setting by juxtaposing classical allusions in such a way as to create richly suggestive metadramatic dissonance: the move into the Ovidian woods prompts re-evaluation by disrupting the stately Virgilian thematics of the opening act (James), for instance, and the metatheatrical sense of one-upmanship in relation to Ovid's story of Procne and Philomela may itself be derived from the Senecan tragedy *Thyestes* (Schiesaro, 70–3), which also provides an influential dramatic precursor for the play's cannibal feast. Titus' antic comportment during the cannibal banquet scene may also represent a specifically satiric rejoinder to a Roman idea of artistic decorum articulated influentially in Horace's *Ars Poetica* (Perry, 'Satire'). It has also been suggested that the characterization of Aaron as the play's instigator of cruelly comic pranks and New-Comedy style subplots owes something to the understanding that the comic playwright Terence was himself an African in Rome (Teramura, 'Black'). In general, incisive and sometimes ironic evocations of well-known Roman literary texts and authors are one of the main ways that both the play's authors and its characters contextualize and provide commentary on the action as it unfolds.

Titus Andronicus is also a product of the theatrical culture of its own moment, of course, and as such it often seems to be in dialogue with the thematic concerns of other roughly contemporary plays. The most important dramatic intertext is probably Thomas Kyd's *The Spanish Tragedy*, an influential play whose popularity and brilliance set a template for a good deal of subsequent revenge drama. It is not a coincidence that Titus' character arc – from a fully integrated member of his milieu into a cynical outsider teetering on the edge of madness and wreaking vengeance on the powers that be – mirrors that of Hieronimo, the central figure in Kyd's play. There are several moments in *Titus Andronicus* where Titus' reactions seem to have been written with imitation of Hieronimo in mind, and some moments that are so self-conscious in their imitation of *The Spanish Tragedy* as to suggest that eliciting comparison with the earlier play was part of *Titus*'s design.

In 3.1, when Aaron leaves with Titus' severed hand and the remaining Andronici are given a moment to reflect on the devastation they have experienced, the neo-Senecan poetic extremity of Titus' reaction owes something to Hieronimo's grief at the murder of his son (see the note at 3.1.222–30, as well as Ard³, 285–6). Then Aaron's messenger re-delivers Titus' severed hand, along with the heads of the sons he had hoped to save by allowing it to be removed, and even Marcus acknowledges that he can no longer ask Titus to contain his grief (3.1.260–4). Titus' reaction is laughter ('Ha, ha, ha' [3.1.265]) – a jarring indication that the character has responded to trauma by vacating the canons of seemliness and decorum constitutive of Roman elite public identity earlier in the play. This idea of the revenger's devolving mindset is also based upon Kyd's play, where Hieronimo in his extreme grief begins to make jokes and to laugh on stage. In *The Spanish Tragedy*'s third act, two Portuguese functionaries approach Hieronimo to ask where they can find Lorenzo, one of the play's main villains. In an exchange that is itself a model for Titus' own antic fantasies about seeking justice out in Pluto's court (4.3.6–16, and see 4.3.4n.), Hieronimo gives them directions to the underworld (*Spanish Tragedy*, 3.11.10–29). And then, in his suffering, Hieronimo laughs at his own futile conceit: 'Ha, ha, ha! / Why ha, ha, ha! Farewell, good, ha, ha, ha!' (3.11.30–1).

Kyd's revenger seeks redress from his king, but the villainous Lorenzo prevents him from presenting his case properly. This prompts the formerly public-minded Hieronimo to give up on civic justice and instead to adopt the persona of a Senecan avenger. He announces this change intertextually:

> *Vindicta mihi!*
> Ay, heaven will be revenged of every ill,
> Nor will they suffer murder unrepaid:
> Then stay, Hieronimo, attend their will,
> For mortal men may not appoint their time.
> *'Per scelus semper tutum est sceleribus iter.'*
> Strike, and strike home, where wrong is offered thee;
> For evils until ills conductors be,
> And death's the worst of resolution.
>
> (3.13.1–9)

As Hieronimo's gloss implies, the first of this passage's Latin quotations (which translates to 'vengeance is mine') comes from a well-known scriptural passage that enjoins followers to leave the execution of vengeance to God (Romans 12.17–13.2). The second Latin tag ('for crime the prudent path is always through crimes') is an adaptation of a widely circulated adage from Seneca's *Agamemnon* (l. 115). Hieronimo quotes Senecan tragedy here as a rebuttal of a Christian trust in God's inscrutable justice, and this in turn marks his full commitment to the pursuit of his own extralegal vigilante justice.

Something similar occurs, albeit in a more compressed manner, at the moment in *Titus Andronicus* where Titus fully commits to a project of revenge. This occurs in 4.1, after Lavinia is finally able to communicate the names of her rapists by writing them in the sand. Titus' reaction, like Hieronimo's, is Senecan: '*Magni dominator poli, / Tam lentus audis scelera, tam lentus vides?* (80–1; 'Ruler of the great heavens, do you listen to crimes so sluggishly, see them so sluggishly?'). The Latin exclamation is loosely adapted from Seneca's *Phaedra*, where Hippolytus learns that his stepmother Phaedra is in love with him and reacts with shocked horror ('*Magne regnator deum, / tam lentus audis scelera? Tam lentus vides?*' [671–2]). But, suggestively, Titus' version actually seems like a wilful conflation of two very different Senecan sources. The phrase in line 80 – '*magni dominator poli'* – is most likely derived from the first line of a poem or prayer quoted in Seneca's *Moral Epistle* 107: a call for obedience to god and nature that begins '*Duc, o parens celsique dominator poli'* ('lead me, o my father, master of the lofty heavens' [107.11]). This short stoic prayer, like the epistle it is drawn from, was well-known in early modern Europe, in part because St Augustine (attributing it to Seneca) used it to exemplify the nature of stoic appeals to fate (Augustine 5.8). The epistle where Seneca quotes it was chosen for a Christianizing translation by Queen Elizabeth herself in about 1567 (Mueller and Scodel, 409–21). Since Titus' exclamation begins with what sounds like an allusion to this poem before veering off into *Phaedra*, it is as if Titus, like Hieronimo, first cites a text advocating an ethic of passive, obedient acceptance to God's justice and then transforms into a Senecan cry for revenge. One way to understand Titus' confusingly intertextual exclamation is as a highly compressed homage to Hieronimo's own moment of transformation, which likewise indicates a decisive movement away from self-subordinating rectitude and into the territory of vengeful Senecan criminality.

The other roughly contemporary play whose influence upon *Titus* has been widely recognized is Christopher Marlowe's *Jew of Malta* (ca. 1589), which was even part of the same Sussex's Men repertory as *Titus* in early 1594. The main point of comparison is between the semi-comic creative energy of Marlowe's villain Barabas and Aaron, whose scene-stealing and improvisatory wickedness sometimes seems to overflow the strict demands of the play's revenge plot. Aaron's enumeration to Lucius of a whole list of past crimes unconnected to the plot of the play (5.1.124–44) gestures towards a career of ludic destructiveness, and it is reminiscent of a similar list of unmotivated crimes shared between Barabas and his newly purchased slave Ithamore in Marlowe's play (2.3.176–213). *The Jew of Malta* is, among other things, a study of disaffiliation: it gives us an anti-hero whose playful amorality stems from having no real connections with any family or community (political or religious), and so the play can be said to explore the anarchic freedom of complete individualism. Aaron differs conspicuously from Marlowe's Barabas in the seriousness of his concern for his own child, but he is an outsider among both the Romans and the Goths, and his actions are often either unmotivated pranks (as with the severing of Titus' hand) or instigations of others' desires (as with his encouragement of Chiron and Demetrius in 2.1). *The Jew of Malta* is not really a revenge tragedy, in the sense that it does not follow a central character, like Titus or Kyd's Hieronimo, who seeks justice and gradually loses faith in the norms, decorums and practices of civic life, but its examination of radical disaffiliation connects with revenge tragedy's deep thematic interest in what it means to find oneself alienated from the society within which one lives.

Other commonalities between *Titus Andronicus* and roughly contemporary extant plays stem from mutual participation in a commercial London theatre culture that was often collaborative, imitative and ready to adopt borrowed motifs and conventions as representational shorthand. The theatre historian Louise George Clubb coined the term 'theatergrams' to name the kinds of recurring, 'reshuffleable' theatrical units (such as character types, episodic actions, speech genres, motifs and images, and so on) that provide evidence of routine borrowing in a vibrant theatre culture (Clubb, 4). *Titus* can certainly be said to share theatergrams with several roughly contemporary plays. The character-type of the scheming and wicked dark-skinned Moor, for instance, owes something to the character of Muly Mahamet in Peele's own earlier *Battle of Alcazar* (1588–9), as we have noted. And Saturninus' sudden attraction to the 'hue' (1.1.262) of the conquered, white-skinned Tamora can likewise be understood as a theatergram representing autocratic will that was shared with other contemporary plays: in Marlowe's *Tamburlaine* (1587) the title character falls in love with his fair-skinned captive Zenocrate, and in *The Tragedy of Locrine* (which was probably written by Robert Greene ca. 1591) the title character falls suddenly and disastrously in love with his hyper-white captive Estrild. In each case, emphasizing the hyper-white fairness of the love object is a way of signalling her elite status and desirability, and the ruler's sudden and total attraction signals his characterological absolutism: his willingness to be led by his own impulses, and his rejection of expected norms associated with the acceptance of ordinary social contingency.

As noted above, students coming to *Titus Andronicus* in the context of a university-level Shakespeare class are likely to find the play's extreme violence upsetting, and to be disoriented by the way the play teeters uneasily between being horrifying and farcical. These effects too might be considered the product of theatergrams derived from the long tradition of Senecan-influenced tragedy and then refined and shared in the London drama of the 1580s and 1590s. There are onstage dismemberments in other, roughly contemporary plays, such as Robert Greene's *Selimus* (1591) where a character's hands are also cut off on stage, and *Titus*'s tonal oscillation between horror and humour is likewise anticipated in plays like Kyd's *Spanish Tragedy* and Marlowe's *Jew of Malta*, which we have discussed above. Given the level of uncertainty surrounding the dates of composition and initial performance for many of these plays – including *Titus* itself – it is often impossible to speak concretely about which play might have been a source for another's actions but noticing that *Titus Andronicus* shares theatergrams with other contemporary plays can enrich our understanding of how the play might have been understood in its original performance context.

RECEPTION AND PERFORMANCE HISTORY

In an essay published in 2015, Laura Estill, Dominic Klyve and Kate Bridal sought to trace changing attitudes towards plays in the Shakespeare canon over time by using the resources of the World Shakespeare Bibliography database to compare scholarly and theatrical practice in two five-year periods: 1960–4 and 2000–4. What they found was that the overall volume of publications about Shakespeare grew significantly from one sample to the other, and that *Hamlet* was consistently the most written about and performed play in both samples. They also found that *Titus Andronicus* went from being only the twenty-eighth most written about play in the Shakespeare canon in the early 1960s to being close to the middle of the pack in terms of scholarly activity at the start of the twenty-first century, and that no Shakespeare play other than *The Tempest* enjoyed a greater increase in popularity from one sample to the next (Estill et al.). This study confirms the most striking thing about the reception history of *Titus Andronicus* – namely, that the play was not at all held in high esteem prior to the 1990s, and that it has experienced a marked increase in scholarly, theatrical and classroom interest since then.

As mentioned previously, Edward Ravenscroft, *Titus*'s Restoration-era revisor, described the play he took up in 1687 as 'a heap of Rubbish' (Ravenscroft, sig. A2ʳ). T. S. Eliot, writing two-and-a-half centuries later, described *Titus Andronicus* as 'one of the stupidest and most uninspired plays ever written, a play in which it is incredible that Shakespeare had any hand at all, a play in which the best passages would be too highly honoured by the signature of Peele' (Eliot, 67). One way to characterize this long history of critical disfavour would be to say that it lionizes putatively Shakespearean virtues that the play lacks, such as a realistic representation of a tragic milieu, a heroic central character who articulates his suffering in richly written and inward-searching soliloquies, or the kind of cathartic machinery which enables an audience to feel ennobled by its encounter with tragic violence. Those scholars who contributed most significantly to the play's critical recuperation are therefore those who, instead of continuing to focus on what our play does not do, found productive ways of understanding what it actually does. Heather James' widely cited 1991 article on the play was in this regard a watershed in the play's critical history, since it demonstrated a new way to think of the play's intrusive allusiveness as staging a meta-conversation about the meaning of Rome, in which Ovidian associations with the woods in Act 2 undermine or contaminate the strong Virgilian register of Act 1 (James). This argument, whose implications are still being expanded and worked out by other scholars, made it possible to see classical allusion as something deployed with intelligence – and even brilliance – in the play, instead of as evidence of the regrettable clumsiness of Shakespearean juvenilia.

Jonathan Bate's Arden 3 edition of the play, which was published in 1995, cemented and expanded James' insight about the brilliance of the allusive meta-discourse in the play, and has probably done more than any other single intervention to make the play interesting and fresh to subsequent generations of scholars and theatre practitioners. As Bate later noted in the remarks he added to the revised and updated version of his edition,

> Editing *Titus* in the early 1990s was still a defensive operation. As one of the volumes marking the launch of the third series of the Arden Shakespeare, the edition had to undo the dismissive work of J. C. Maxwell's second series Arden and to demonstrate that the play was worthy of its place in the front rank of the new series ...
>
> (Ard³, 123)

By starting with the premise that the play was worthy of critical interest and respect and editing it accordingly, Bate was able to make the play's design legible to subsequent scholars not as a pile of overly allusive rubbish, but as 'a complex and self-conscious improvisation upon classical sources' (Ard³, 3). Bate's edition also helped pave the way for Julie Taymor's landmark 1999 film *Titus*, which captured the brilliance of the play's tonal complexity and made it viscerally accessible to a wide audience. In an introduction he penned to an illustrated screenplay for Taymor's film, Bate argued that 'Shakespeare's innovative discovery in *Titus Andronicus* is that extreme trauma reveals the strange proximity of horror to comedy' (Taymor, *Screenplay*, 9). His edition and Taymor's film both put this insight at the centre of our understanding of the play.

One other key early essay that helped rekindle interest in *Titus* was Francesca T. Royster's now-classic 2000 essay on *Titus*'s examination of the 'unstable continuum of racial identities' (Royster, 432). By looking at racial constructions in the play as something more complex than a black/white binary, and by noting that Tamora is depicted as whiter than the Romans (and was performed in whiteface) just as Aaron is depicted as blacker than the Romans and the Goths (and was performed in blackface), Royster is among the earliest scholars to recognize that we should look to early modern texts for their own distinctive ideas about race and race-making. In effect, Royster's essay made it clear that we should be using *Titus* to think about the constructed nature of all races in the early modern period, and she showed that the play allows readers and students a fresh purchase on urgent contemporary concerns having to do with race-making and racism. It may have taken some time for this lesson to take hold, but the study of race-making is, as we write this, one of the liveliest areas of current scholarly interest in *Titus*.

The fortunes of *Titus Andronicus* as a play in theatrical performance mirror its critical history: it was put on relatively rarely prior to its critical rejuvenation in the 1990s and has been performed much more frequently in this millennium. While some of Shakespeare's plays are consistently popular in performance, such as *Hamlet*, *Romeo and Juliet*, *Macbeth* and *King Lear*, some are consistently unpopular, such as *Two Noble Kinsmen* and *Henry VIII*. *Titus* is unique in that among the plays that are performed roughly as often (*Pericles*, *Cymbeline* and *Antony and Cleopatra*), it has had a much higher percentage of performances after 2000. Looking at performance data in the World Shakespeare Bibliography (WSB), we see that while other plays with roughly the same total number of recorded performances since 1960 have had on average about 50 per cent of their productions staged after 2000, *Titus* comes in at well over 60 per cent.[1] The other anomalous aspect of *Titus*'s performance history is that it has been entrusted to women directors 25 per cent of the time since 2000 – a much higher percentage than for other Shakespearean tragedies, which are directed by women less than 20 per cent of the time. This likely has to do both with the way Bate foregrounded gendered violence in his Arden 3 edition of the play and with the high-profile example of heralded stage and film productions by Julie Taymor. *Titus Andronicus* provides an excellent case study for the ways that textual editing and performance can be mutually influencing.

As noted in other sections of this Introduction, there is good reason to think that *Titus Andronicus* was a very popular play in late Elizabethan and early Jacobean England. Jonathan Bate and Eric Rasmussen argue that *Titus Andronicus* may also have been the catalyst for Shakespeare's turn away from the 'highly formalized physical gestures that characterized' the acting by the 'top box office star of … the early 1590s, Edward Alleyn' (*RSC*, 1598). If, as they speculate, the actor Richard Burbage came to play Titus, then it may be (as Bate and Rasmussen argue) that Shakespeare enabled him to develop a 'subtler [acting] style' that explored the 'inner life' of the character differently (*RSC*, 1598). As Shakespeare's first revenge tragedy, *Titus Andronicus* sets the stage for *Hamlet*, in which the eponymous revenger explicitly disparages the older acting model perfected by Alleyn. Anticipating Hamlet's admonishment to the players to rely less on highly formalized gestures ('do not saw the air too much with your hand' [3.2.4–5]), Shakespeare's Titus grows to realize that the stylized forms of grief that Marcus suggests are useless ('Rend off thy silver hair, thy other hand / Gnawing with thy teeth' [3.1.261–2]).

It is striking, therefore, that by the time of the Restoration the play's first major adaptor felt the need specifically to strengthen the play's depiction

---

1   Using the World Shakespeare Bibliography's data on performances – a data set that seeks to be a comprehensive source for professional or semi-professional theatrical productions of Shakespeare since 1960 – we find that *Cymbeline* has had 220 productions since 1962 (110 since 2000), *Pericles* has had 250 productions since 1964 (135 since 2000), *Antony and Cleopatra* has had 275 productions since 1960 (130 since 2000) and *Titus Andronicus* has had 257 since 1967 (162 since 2000).

of character. While many scholars have focused on Edward Ravenscroft's structural changes to *Titus*, he also claimed that he 'heighten'd' 'most of the principal characters' (Ravenscroft, sig. A2'). This seems to have entailed moral simplification: where Shakespeare's characters in *Titus Andronicus* are morally enigmatic because so many are involved in entangled revenge plots, Ravenscroft's characters have clear motives that delineate and differentiate the heroes from the villains. As Joyce Green MacDonald writes, Ravenscroft's alterations, 'while ignoring the original's imperial concerns, more clearly forced spectator and reader identification with dominant perspectives on cultural value: male instead of female, white instead of black' (MacDonald, 187).

Published in 1687 but probably first acted in 1678, Ravenscroft's adaptation changed both structure and character. As Michael Friedman summarizes, 'Gone completely from the 1687 *Titus* are: (1) 2.2 (the preparation for the hunt); (2) 3.2 (the fly-killing scene); (3) most of 4.3 (the onstage arrow-shooting); and (4) the clown of 4.3 and 4.4' (Friedman, 10). Unlike Shakespeare's play, Ravenscroft's *Titus Andronicus* moves most of the violence offstage, so the audience only sees the aftermath, such as Titus splattered with blood 'like an Executioner' after the killing of Chiron and Demetrius (Ravenscroft, 51). Ravenscroft also made numerous plot alterations, including hinting at a new backstory when Titus and Lucius defend their right to sacrifice Tamora's son Alarbus by referring to an episode in which Tamora herself had been 'deaf like the Gods when Thunder fills the Air' when she had killed a captive son of Titus' earlier in the war (Ravenscroft, 4).

But the largest set of changes involves Aaron the Moor. As Joyce Green MacDonald argues, 'Ravenscroft set about correcting Shakespeare's play by strengthening its characters' revenge motives and adding prominence to the role of Aaron the Moor' (MacDonald, 187). In his first soliloquy, Ravenscroft's Aaron makes clear that he too views himself as a revenger, and that his motive for revenge is anti-black racism:

> Hence abject thoughts that I am black and foul,
> And all the Taunts of Whites that call me Fiend,
> I still am Lovely in the Empress Eyes,

Lifted on high in Power, I'le hang above
Like a black threatning Cloud o're all their heads
That dare look up to me with Envious Eyes

(Ravenscroft, 15)

While Ravenscroft's Tamora becomes less sympathetic and explicitly more villainous (for example, she kills her biracial baby herself), his Aaron is granted a much clearer motive than Shakespeare's.

James Quin, a famous Restoration actor whose portrait by Thomas Gainsborough still resides in Buckingham Palace, used the role of Raven-scroft's Aaron to launch his career as an actor who excelled in exotic, blackface performance. Quin also played Bajazet in Nicholas Rowe's *Tamerlane*, Zanga in Edward Young's *The Revenge* and Othello in remountings of Shakespeare's play. Michael Friedman argues that Quin was 'the first of many actors ... who found grand opportunities in the role of Aaron' (Friedman, 9). Part of the appeal of the role stemmed from Ravenscroft's dramatically revised ending, which opens with 'The Moor discover'd on a Rack' and Titus, as the torturer, barking orders to 'Stretch him' and 'Disjoynt his Limbs' (Ravenscroft, 53). Unphased by his torture, Aaron remains silent until Marcus threatens to kill his baby. Only in an attempt to save the child's life does Aaron reveal who killed Bassianus, raped and mutilated Lavinia and framed Titus' sons for Bassianus' murder. In the end, Lucius announces, 'It was decreed he [Aaron] should expire in flames, / Around him kindle straight his Funeral Fire' (Ravenscroft, 56). Ravenscroft's stage direction then reads 'The Fire flames about the Moor', as Lucius continues 'He shall at once be burn'd and Rack'd to death' (Ravenscroft, 56). As Eugene Waith argues, this revised ending provided 'a final virtuoso turn for the interpreter of Aaron's part' (Oxf², 46). Michael Friedman adds that the prospect of playing Ravenscroft's Aaron 'had obvious appeal for a James Quin or any other bravura actor' (Friedman, 13).

Eighteenth-century productions of *Titus Andronicus* were all based on Ravenscroft's adaptation instead of Shakespeare's. In fact, Shakespeare's version of the play was not remounted until the early twentieth century. In his note to the printed edition of the play, Ravenscroft claims that his adaptation had become 'a stock-play' (sig. A2ᵛ), meaning that it was performed regularly. Once James Quin started performing as Aaron, it became a regular part of his performance repertory too. He performed in a dozen productions between 1717 and 1724, including two benefit performances for himself. In other words, Ravenscroft's *Titus* was a hit in performance in the eighteenth century.

Unsurprisingly, there were very few nineteenth-century productions of *Titus Andronicus*. Victorian era sensibilities did not align with the violence and moral ambiguity of Shakespeare's play. The two notable exceptions to the nineteenth-century performance lacuna were American-led adaptations. In 1839, at the Walnut Street Theatre in Philadelphia, the oldest theatre in the independent United States, N. H. Bannister played Titus opposite his wife's Lavinia. There are two extant playbills for performances in January, and while one claims that the production retains the language of 'the immortal Bard', the other announces that 'every expression calculated to offend the ear has been studiously avoided' (quoted in Oxf², 47). It appears that Bannister adapted the text to preserve the poetical language while excluding the horrors of the violence. As Waith writes, 'It is unfortunate that we do not know exactly what horrors were excluded nor which offensive expressions were avoided' (Oxf², 47).

The other American-led adaptation of *Titus Andronicus* was devised by the African American actor Ira Aldridge. A free-born New Yorker who obtained a classical education in the African Free School, Aldridge began his acting career at the African Theatre, a theatre designed by and for free blacks that regularly staged Shakespearean productions. In his memoir, Aldridge claimed to have performed as Romeo at the African Theatre, but, as George Thompson argues, 'it seems unlikely that Aldridge could have been a prominent member of the African company so early in its history' since he would have only been in his early teens (Thompson, *Documentary*, 46). But Aldridge may have performed leading Shakespearean roles after James Hewlett, the African Theatre's star, left the company in March 1822 (Aldridge would then have been fourteen or fifteen years old). James McCune Smith, a classmate of Aldridge's at the African Free School, later claimed that when Aldridge's religious father found out he was acting, he made him leave the company (Smith, 'Aldridge', 32). Regardless of that claim's veracity, we know that Aldridge sailed to England in 1824, and by

Figure 15 'Mr. Ira Aldridge as Aaron'. The London Printing and Publishing Company, 1852.

October 1825 (when he was still only seventeen or eighteen years old) he was performing in leading roles in smaller London venues.

Aldridge, who adopted the moniker 'the African Roscius', made his reputation playing black tragic roles. Not unlike James Quin's blackface performance repertoire, Aldridge regularly performed as Oroonoko in Southerne's adaptation of Aphra Behn's novella of the same name, Zanga in Edward Young's *The Revenge* and Othello in Shakespeare's play (Marshall and Stock, 70). It was only later in his career that he added Aaron the Moor, and in doing so Aldridge sought to change Aaron's character into a fully sympathetic one. Working with the playwright C. A. Somerset, Aldridge dramatically altered *Titus Andronicus*. Touring with *Titus* as part of his repertoire, Aldridge performed his adaptation in England, Scotland and Ireland between 1849 and 1860. As the reviewer of the 1857 production at the Britannia Theatre in Hoxton explains, 'The *Titus Andronicus* produced under Mr. Aldridge's direction is a wholly different affair; the deflowerment of Lavinia ... and gross language which occur in the original are totally omitted.' The reviewer continues, explaining that 'Aaron is elevated into a noble and lofty character. Tamora, the Queen of Scythia, is a chaste though decidedly strong-minded female, and her connection to the Moor appears to be of a legitimate description' (Aldridge review, 10). The villain in this version of the play is Saturninus, and

> Thus altered, Mr. Aldridge's conception of the part of Aaron is excellent – gentle and impassioned by turns; now burning with jealousy as he suspects the honour of the Queen; anon, fierce with rage, as he reflects upon the wrongs which have been done him – the murder of Alarbus and the abduction of his son; and then all tenderness and emotion in the gentle passages with his infant.
>
> (Aldridge review, 10)

Aldridge played opposite an English cast, including Miss Adelaide Cooke as Tamora, Mr J. Reynolds as Titus, Mr F. Wilton as Marcus and Mrs K. Yarnold as Lavinia.

Aldridge frequently concluded his performances with the two-act comic operetta *The Padlock* (music by Charles Dibdin, lyrics by Isaac Bickerstaffe). Although originally written to be a blackface performance that ridiculed an enslaved West Indian, Aldridge altered that role as well. Nonetheless, the 1857 reviewer lauded the performance: 'After the tragedy Mr. Aldridge, whose genius is of a versatile character, appeared as Mungo in the eccentric burletta of *The Padlock*, and here his humour created as much merriment as his pathos had before excited sympathy' (Aldridge review, 10). Attentive to demonstrating his acting range, Aldridge found that by pairing his tragic Aaron the Moor with his humorous Mungo he could demonstrate his diverse acting skills.

Aldridge's attention to the ways his acting techniques could be rendered visible through the pairing of Aaron with comic black(face) roles was noted even seventy years later. Henry Chance Newton, writing under the pen name 'Carados', remarked that Aldridge's pairing was 'a wonderful tour de force for any actor, black or white!' ('Carados', n.p.). What emerges from the first 300 years of *Titus* in performance, then, is an appreciation for the play (including its adaptations) as an acting text. Although there are consistent remarks about the grotesque nature of the play, there are also consistent remarks about the characters providing star turns for the actors playing them, especially for the actors playing Aaron. These sentiments are voiced directly in the next recorded performance of *Titus*: a production at the Old Vic in 1923. Summing up his opinion in *The Referee*, Newton wrote that 'notwithstanding all its accumulated horrors upon horror's head, *Titus Andronicus* proved a powerful acting play' ('Carados', n.p.). Under the management of Lilian Baylis at the Old Vic, Robert Atkins directed the first professional production in the twentieth century, starring Wilfrid Walter as Titus, Ian Swindley as Saturninus, Florence Saunders as Tamora, George Hayes as Aaron (in blackface) and Jane Bacon as Lavinia.

The following year, at Yale University in New Haven, Connecticut, the first twentieth-century performance of *Titus Andronicus* was produced in the United States. Directed by Edgar Montillion 'Monty' Woolley, who went on to be a stage and film star, and John Milton Berdan, a professor in Yale's English Department, the 1924 production was staged 'in the upper room of Alpha Delta Phi' fraternity for two nights in April. A review in *The Yale Daily News* by Professor Alexander Maclaren Witherspoon, who edited the 1926 Yale Shakespeare edition of *Titus*, remarked that 'Many a play which, like *Titus*, is consumedly dull in the pages of a book takes on life and colour to a surprising degree when transferred to the boards' (Witherspoon, 386). The production starred Arthur Milliken as Titus, G. L. King as Lucius, J. C. Orr as Marcus and J. L. McKeon as Aaron (in blackface), whose performance inspired 'interesting questions as to the inception of both Othello and Iago' (Witherspoon, 386). Witherspoon concludes his review with remarks that will become standard in reviews of *Titus* in the twentieth century:

> All in all, it must be conceded that *Titus Andronicus* is far too bloody and unpleasant a play to become popular, even if it had all the virtues of a great tragedy. But despite the fact that it is a sort of geometrical progression of horrors, the members of the cast made the roles convincing, and commanded the interest of the audience throughout.
>
> (Witherspoon, 386)

For much of the twentieth century, then, performance reviews contain similar caveats: despite the fact that a production is well received, and despite the fact that critics praise the play as a great acting vehicle, and despite the fact that the play's unique performance history is part of a production's promotional materials, *Titus Andronicus* was pigeonholed as a second-rate play. It was therefore staged only irregularly in the early twentieth century.

Most performance critics grant a great deal of space to Peter Brook's 1955 production at Shakespeare's Memorial Theatre (which would later become the home of the Royal Shakespeare Company). While it is indeed a key production, it is important to situate it within the changing modes of the performance of blackness in the mid-twentieth century. For while Brook's production was revolutionary in the way it presented *Titus* as a serious tragedy, it was also conservative in the way it presented the performance of blackness: as the domain of white Shakespearean actors. After all, Anthony Quayle, who played Aaron in Brook's production, did so in full blackface make-up, as he did when he played Othello one year earlier in 1954 in a production that he himself directed. And like the critical responses to the actors who had played Aaron before him, Quayle's blackface performance was lauded for revealing his 'energy and versatility ... he showed what an eminently actable role it is' (Oxf², 55).

Figure 16 Anthony Quayle as Aaron the Moor in blackface in Peter Brook's 1955 production at the Shakespeare Memorial Theatre (later the RSC).

Yet the 1950s also saw a shift in performance modes with many black actors, inspired in part by Paul Robeson's performances of Othello in 1930 at The Savoy Theatre in London, in 1943 in the Theatre Guild's Broadway run in New York, and in 1959 at the Shakespeare Memorial Theatre in

Stratford-upon-Avon, beginning to seek out opportunities to perform in Shakespearean productions. Thus, in the 1956 New York Shakespeare Festival production of *Titus*, Roscoe Lee Browne became the first black American actor since Ira Aldridge to play Aaron, almost exactly 100 years later. Joseph Papp, who founded the New York Shakespeare Festival in 1954, did so for the explicit purpose of creating Shakespearean productions that were accessible to the entire New York population, including blacks and Hispanics. He is thought to have been the first professional director to employ inclusive casting practices. This is all to say that it seems clear in hindsight that Peter Brook's *Titus Andronicus* was staged amidst radically changing performance modes with regard to race. Brook's was by no means the last production to employ a white actor as Aaron, after all – subsequent productions cast the likes of Derek Jacobi (1963 at the Birmingham Rep), Peter Postlethwaite (1978 at the New Vic Bristol) and Alan Scarfe (1978 at the Stratford, Ontario Festival) – but looking at his production now reveals the tensions of the changing times.

Brook's production was revolutionary in the way it depicted the horror of the violence in a stylized way. With Vivien Leigh as Lavinia, playing opposite her husband Laurence Olivier as her father Titus, Brook staged her rape and dismemberment not in a realistic manner but with ribbons that represented the blood streaming from her mouth and hands. Michael Friedman argues that Brook's production ushered in one of the four performance lines of descent for *Titus Andronicus* – a physically stylized mode that often invites the cutting of the text so that the representation of violence speaks for itself without what Jonathan Bate called the play's 'verbal stylization' (Friedman, 28; Ard³, 59). As Eugene Waith noted, 'there was no diminution of the impression of horror. The entrance of the raped and mutilated Lavinia was a moment of extraordinary power, mentioned by most of the reviewers at the time' (Oxf², 55). The famous 2006 Japanese production of *Titus Andronicus*, directed by Yukio Ninagawa, clearly borrowed Brook's stylized technique, even having his Lavinia, played by Hitomi Manaka, with red silk streamers billowing from her hands and mouth (more on this production , p. 90).

Brook's production was conceived and conveyed in 'the totality – the sound, the visual representation, everything interlocking' (Beauman, 224). And the production was wildly successful across Europe: 'When we toured

Figure 17 Yukio Ninagawa's 2006 Japanese production of *Titus Andronicus* borrowed from Peter Brook's stylized technique, even having his Lavinia, played by Hitomi Manaka, with red silk streamers billowing from her hands and mouth.

Europe with *Titus Andronicus*, it was not only the academic audiences that besieged the theatres. It was everyone, every class, every level whether in bourgeois Vienna or socialist Warsaw' (Brook, 16). Brook claimed the success of the production was in part due to its embrace of a stylized approach, and he argued that the audience grappled with the realities of 'violence, hatred, cruelty, pain' because the unrealistic nature of the storytelling 'transcended the anecdote and became for each audience *quite abstract and thus totally real*' (Brook, 17; emphasis in original). In this vein, Marcus' long speech when he encounters the raped and mutilated Lavinia in the woods was completely removed. The RSC's prompt book – the annotated copy of the play that includes all the specific performance cues for that particular production – shows that the scene moves directly from the exit of Chiron and Demetrius in 2.4 to Titus' entrance when he is pleading with the Roman senators and tribunes in 3.1 (the prompt book labels these scenes as 1.3 and 1.4 respectively). Likewise, much of Act 5 was shortened, allowing for a more visual and presentational style of storytelling, with the bodies piled up on the banquet table becoming a visual emblem of the cannibalistic nature of violent revenge. Interestingly, Gerald Freedman's 1967 New York Shakespeare Festival production employed a very similar stylized approach, eschewing realism at almost every turn in the production. Nonetheless, Freedman cast realistically in terms of race, with the black actor Moses Gunn as Aaron, who won an Obie Award for his performance.

The success of these stylized productions, however, did not prevent realistic approaches from gaining traction as well. Trevor Nunn's 1972 RSC production – part of the RSC's 'The Romans' season – aimed for hyper-realism. Influenced in part by the violence of the war in Vietnam, Nunn wanted to show the built-in destructive elements of all empires – that the Hobbesian, combative nature of man inevitably leads to self-destructive social orders. Colin Blakely, who played Titus, remarked that the stylized nature of the Brook production would not work in 1972 'when people can see what violence is really like when they watch the news on television' (quoted in Cook, 88). Thus, the decapitated heads of Titus' sons were realistic renderings of the actors. Lavinia (played by Janet Suzman) could barely walk after her rape and mutilation and stumbled around in a realistic representation of trauma in contradistinction to Vivien Leigh's ribboned/ballet-like entrance. The Bahamian actor Calvin Lockhart played Aaron on the RST, but when the play transferred to the Aldwych Theatre in London, Patrick Stewart took on the role of Aaron and performed in blackface. It appears that realism had its limits when it came to portraying blackness in that moment in *Titus*'s performance history in the UK.

In 1981, a relatively new theatre in Wisconsin, the American Players Theatre, marked an important milestone in the history of *Titus* in performance: the first professional production directed by a woman. Anne Occhiogrosso, who served as one of the artistic directors of the outdoor theatre, was the first in what would become an unusually long line of women to direct the tragedy. Shortly thereafter Jane Howell, the only female director included in the BBC Television Shakespeare series, directed *Titus Andronicus* in 1985 (see Howell, BBC). In 1987, Deborah Warner directed *Titus* at the RSC. Before Julie Taymor's ground-breaking 1999 film, there were at least nine other productions directed by women (Jeanette Lambermont in 1989, Donna Northcott in 1990, Erica Prahl in 1991, Carole Tweedy in 1993, Sarah Wilson in 1993, Dorothee Steinbauer in 1994, Julie Taymor in 1994, Eva Maria Niedermeiser in 1998 and Annecy Lax in 1999). And since Taymor's 1999 film, the number of women directing *Titus* has surpassed those for any other tragedy. In many ways, *Titus* has become the tragedy most often entrusted to female directors – perhaps because of its horrific depiction of violence against women, or perhaps because it is not considered one of Shakespeare's major tragedies, or both.

Deborah Warner's 1987 RSC production, for example, became well known and well received because it was one of the first to treat the full text as important and stageable. Unlike Brook's highly edited production, Warner started without a concept and worked with the actors to create the playworld or *mise en scène*. Opting for minimalist staging in the RSC's Swan Theatre, Warner's production made the most of a stage ladder and a few other set pieces. In addition, the costuming was vaguely ancient, but the actors wore contemporary hairstyles and footwear. Alan Dessen praised the show for being 'one of the best Shakespeare shows I have seen in recent years (a verdict shared by many theatrical professionals who saw it)' (Dessen, 223). He went on to explain that the word most often used to describe Warner's process was 'trust': 'trust in the script, in the audience, in the Swan (a major component in the success of this show), in each other. What happens when you do trust Shakespeare' (Dessen, 223). Brian Cox, who played Titus, for instance, insisted that they not cut lines from 3.1 because 'to cut a line is to short-circuit the process' and psychology of his character (Dessen, 224). Furthermore, Cox portrayed Titus as a 'muscular, gritty, battered warrior, out of touch with politics and people (including Lavinia and Mutius, who were mere objects to him), already a little touched in the head' at the play's opening (Dessen, 224). Sonia Ritter's Lavinia, Estelle Kohler's Tamora and Donald Sumpter's Marcus were all singled out in reviews for providing surprising and effective performances that challenged older assumptions about *Titus's* unstageability. Yet, as Kevin Crawford notes, none of the laudatory reviews mentioned that a white actor, Peter Polycarpou, played Aaron: 'Dessen's 1988 account of the performance for *Shakespeare Quarterly* ... doesn't mention Aaron once' (Crawford, 114). A Cypriot actor who applied prosthetics to darken his skin for the 1987

Figure 18 Deborah Warner's 1987 RSC production, starring Brian Cox as Titus and Sonia Ritter as Lavinia.

RSC production, Polycarpou was out of place in this production. Michael Billington assessed Polycarpou's Aaron as having a 'deficiency of evil' (Billington, 'Horror'), and Warner 'agreed afterwards that Aaron should have been "a black, black, black man"' (Goy-Blanquet, 43). While it is not clear why Warner felt the need to repeat how black Aaron should have been, it is clear that Polycarpou's Aaron did not land memorably.

The exact opposite can be said of Harry Lennix's performance as Aaron in Julie Taymor's 1994 Theatre for a New Audience production and in her 1999 film version. A classically trained black American actor from Chicago, Lennix brought a strength and wit to Aaron that was celebrated in many reviews. Taymor understood Aaron as being central to the structure of *Titus*, arguing that 'Titus and Aaron are mirrors, absolute mirrors of each other. As you watch Titus become a monster, you watch Aaron become a father' (quoted in Johnson-Haddad, 36). Explaining her approach to Aaron, Taymor contrasted his characterization with the stereotypical black saviour figure in many contemporary films in the 1990s:

Aaron is not PC, but compare him to the big black guy in *The Green Mile* – you want to die at *The Green Mile*, to die of shame and embarrassment. The NAACP should have gotten up there and objected – to have a black man at this point [in history] who's playing a dumb Jesus Christ and saying those lines made me ill. Shakespeare's written someone who is nihilistic, very modern, and yet he's not Iago, not white. You understand, perhaps, how this man got to that place, when you see how much hatred is directed towards him, and when his own lover delivers their child and orders him to kill it.

(quoted in Johnson-Haddad, 36)

As David McCandless argues, Harry Lennix's portrayal of Aaron

attracts the superimposition of contemporary stereotypes in the white cultural imaginary ... he presents the image of the seemingly assimilable (if marginalized), highly intelligent black man whose secret ambition is to sleep with white women and destroy white men.

(McCandless, 494)

Like many black actors, Lennix found playing Aaron to be revelatory. In conversation with Lennix, Laurence Fishburne said,

that whole diatribe, that whole fucking tirade that Aaron has, the one that you did so beautifully with the child in your arms? That whole fucking thing? I mean, come on. That's the righteous fucking indignation ... That's brilliant shit.

(Lennix and Fishburne, 408)

If Taymor's direction of Lennix seemed to crack Aaron open for a new era of empowered performances by black actors, her direction of Miriam Healy-Louie as Lavinia seemed to challenge many male directors' previous approaches to the character. While preceding productions varied in style (realistic versus stylized) and historical setting (any time from ancient Rome to the contemporary moment), most assumed that Lavinia's death was her father's doing. That is, most directors before Taymor made Titus the agent of action, while Lavinia was passive and acted upon (even if tacitly agreeing to her own death). Taymor's change was to make Lavinia an active agent. As David McCandless summarizes, Taymor's 'stage Lavinia essentially kills herself, impaling herself on one of her own prosthetic talons that, at her bequest, Titus had removed and extended toward her' (McCandless, 506). Feminist scholarship had long challenged the assumption that Lavinia's enforced silence aligned neatly or clearly with passivity, and Taymor's 1994 stage production seems to be the first to put that challenge into action. By having Lavinia take control of her own death, Taymor gave Lavinia an agency that most male directors had previously denied her.

Taymor revealed that Jonathan Bate's Arden 3 edition of *Titus Andronicus* 'inspired me', and that his close attention to the interlocking and repeated symbolic imagery of the play informed 'every image' she created on stage (quoted in Johnson-Haddad, 35). Yet it is also clear that Taymor was inspired by Jane Howell's 1985 BBC Television Shakespeare series version of *Titus*. This comes through most clearly through Taymor's use of Young Lucius as a framing device. Howell's film begins with a tight shot of a bespectacled Young Lucius (played by Paul Davies Prowles), and the film ends with Young Lucius mourning over a small black coffin that contains Aaron and Tamora's biracial baby. For Howell, then, the full impact of the tragedy rested on the damage inflicted on the next generation. Describing Taymor's 1994 TFANA production, David McCandless writes:

> onstage Aaron's baby does not survive but is represented in the final scene by a tiny black coffin, on which Young Lucius obsessively fixes his gaze in the play's final moments. He rests his hand on the coffin as the lights begin to dim and the sound of wailing babies and screeching birds of prey fill the space.
> (McCandless, 509)

Taymor's 1999 film version also begins with Young Lucius (played by Osheen Jones) who, though not bespectacled, is wearing a brown paper bag mask which similarly frames his eyes, emphasizing that his is the gaze through which the audience should look. Taymor's film ends differently than her stage production, though, with Young Lucius walking out of Rome with the living biracial baby in his arms. Explaining the film's new ending, Taymor wrote: '*Titus* will premiere as the millennium comes to an end. May the child finally exit the Colosseum as the new millennium rolls in' (Taymor, *Playing*, 233).

If Julie Taymor's first stab at *Titus* nodded subtly to Jane Howell's 1985 film, the legacy of Taymor's film has haunted twenty-first century

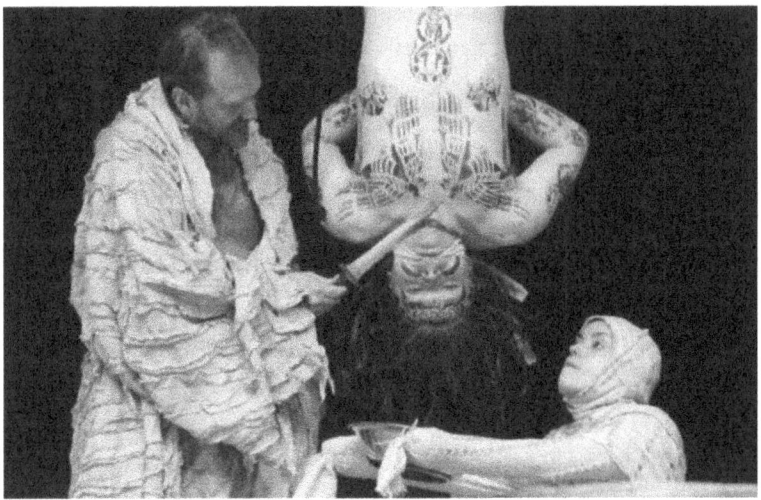

Figure 19 Julie Taymor's 1999 film *Titus* cast a long shadow on productions, including Lucy Bailey's 2006 production at Shakespeare's Globe with Douglas Hodge (Titus Andronicus), Richard Riddell (Chiron) and Laura Rees (Lavinia).

productions not so subtly. It is almost as if the directors who have staged *Titus* after Taymor cannot unsee her film. For instance, to mark the Goths as foreigners in Rome visually, Taymor created tribal tattoos that covered large portions of their upper bodies. Lucy Bailey's 2006 and 2014 Shakespeare's Globe productions and Michael Fentiman's 2013 RSC production used the same visual rhetoric. Taymor had Titus (played by Antony Hopkins) hang Chiron and Demetrius from their feet so that he could slit their throats and bleed them out like pigs, and so did Lucy Bailey in her Globe productions and Blanche McIntyre in her 2017 RSC production. Taymor's Lavinia (played by Laura Fraser) is figured with an animal head when she remembers the horrors of her rape and mutilation, and Michael Sexton's 2011 Public Lab production employed a bird's head for his Lavinia (played by Jennifer Ikeda). And Taymor's coolly styled Aaron (played by Harry Lennix) saw him outfitted in beautifully tailored suits, as did Michael Sexton's Aaron (played by Ron Cephus Jones) in his 2011 production. When one considers the first quarter of the twenty-first century's productions of *Titus*, one can see the long shadow that Julie

Taymor's film has cast, especially with regard to her very particular visual rhetoric and styling.

Non-anglophone productions of *Titus*, though, tend to live under a different set of long shadows. Much less popular than other Shakespeare plays in translation, *Titus* still occupies a niche spot. Interestingly, there are more productions in Germany than in any other non-anglophone country. This may stem from the early-seventeenth-century translation of *Titus* in German creating a longer performance tradition, or it may stem from the way the play inspires experimental productions. Either way, in any given year there is at least one professional production in Berlin, Bern, Dresden, Magdeburg, Munich or Stuttgart. Many of the German productions of *Titus* lean into a stylized, minimalistic staging. For instance, in the 2012 Staatsschauspiel Dresden production directed by the Polish director Jan Klata, German actors played the Romans and Polish actors from the Teatr Polski Wrocław played the Goths (the German translation was by Wolf von Baudissin, and the Polish surtitles were by Maciej Słomczyński). Klata's spare staging for the provocative content made the production shocking and shockingly dark in tone, including his use of a fully blackfaced performance of Aaron by the white Polish actor Wojciech Ziemiański. Leaning into the stereotype of the black devil, Ziemiański was blacked up with large-scale devil horns on his head and a giant, two-foot-long prosthetic penis hanging out of the fly of his trousers. Likewise, the rape of Lavinia (Paulina Chapko) was staged in very realistic terms, with Lavinia stumbling around the stage in torn undergarments with blood dripping down her legs. Because the minimalist set design by Justyna Łagowska-Klata only featured about a dozen black trunk cases (the kind used for moving music equipment) and a large screen for the Polish subtitles that were at times superimposed onto the actors' bodies, all the attention was focused on the actors and the horrific actions of the revenge tragedy. The theatre advertised the production as 'erbarmungslos pessimistische Stück – Hasstirade und Schlachtruf gegen Kultur und Natur des Menschen' (a mercilessly pessimistic piece – a tirade of hatred and a battle cry against human culture and nature), and this is the tone that many German productions put forward (see Staatsschauspiel).

There have also been many productions of *Titus* in Japan, although at about half the rate of those in Germany. Unlike the very long performance history of the play in Germany, most of the Japanese productions have been inspired by the hugely popular and oft-cited 2006 production directed by Yukio Ninagawa. A highly stylized production, the white stage featured a large white statue of the she-wolf that suckled Romulus and Remus, the founders of Rome, and most of the costumes were all-white, allowing the red silk ribbons of blood to stand out visually. As Michael Billington wrote in his 2006 review of the production at the RSC,

> Ninagawa, echoing the fact that Remus was the victim of fraternal slaughter, emphasizes the fatal consequences of Rome's animalistic origins ... But, for all the murderous mayhem, there is not a trace of stage blood in Ninagawa's production ... At times I felt that Ninagawa, through stylized images and Handelian music, unduly aestheticized violence. But, more positively, he turns the play into a prolonged lament for the suffering imposed by an imperialist society.
>
> (Billington, Review)

Ninagawa's production was unique in the way it invited the audience to contemplate what protracted stress and distress does to both individuals and to societies. Labelling the style 'victim art', Howard Y. F. Choy writes that Ninagawa's production

> reminds its non-Japanese Asian audience of World War II: Do the acts of redemption in [*Titus*] imply that the Japanese were mere victims of atomic bombings by understating their nation's responsibility for starting the war in the Pacific theatre and massacring their Asian neighbors?
>
> (Choy, 49)

The implicit political valences of the production seemed to open the door for many other Japanese adaptations. Since Ninagawa's production there have been five other distinct productions in Tokyo alone, directed by Takayuki Ayanogki (2007), Yasuhiro Yosuda (2010), Eiji Nishizawa (2010), Hideki Yashiro (2011) and Mitsuka Kusunoki (2011).

Titus Andronicus is much less popular in China. Nonetheless, there was a remarkable 2009 production in Hong Kong directed by Tang Shu-wing, which blended Shakespeare's first tragedy with Chinese storytelling. Employing seven actors, *Titus Andronicus 2.0* 'is rewritten into a story, that is, a narrative in which the plotline and each character's lines are assigned to various actors of a common chorus. By so doing, the characters are detached from any particular actor' (Choy, 53). Adele Lee writes:

> the production seemed to promote both Eastern collectivism and Western individualism, while the acting style oscillated (rather incongruously, at times) between Eastern stylization and Western realism. Thus, in terms of style and content, the production revealed the hybrid identity of the former colony and this theatre troupe which had been appropriately called 'No Man's Land' when it was first formed.
>
> (Lee, 111)

Employing a bare set with only chairs facing the audience, Tang collaborated with his cast to create symbolic, non-mimetic movements that encapsulated the play's moods and themes. For example, between Acts 4 and 5 there was a 'tableaux of handstand on chair ... to demonstrate a world that is upside down' (Choy, 56). In the concluding cannibalistic feast, Tang inserted long moments of pause (up to six minutes in length), humming and spinning that encouraged the audience to contemplate cycles of violence in a meditative framework. Likewise, he had Lucius, instead of Young Lucius, assume responsibility for Aaron and Tamora's biracial child. As Howard Choy notes, 'Tang leaves the question for us to answer by closing *Titus 2.0* in a turning meditation performed by the actors' (Choy, 58).

Since 2000, there have been two or more productions of *Titus Andronicus* in France, Spain, South Korea, China, Poland and Hungary, and one-off productions in Italy, Turkey, the Czech Republic, Romania and Sweden. We would like to highlight one production from 2019 in Iran. Directed by Masoud Tayebi at the IranShahr Theater in Tehran, this translation/adaptation of *Titus* by Shahram Ahmadzadeh was titled *There Will Be Blood*. Described by the theatre as a production that challenges the 'social, cultural, and political circumstances' and notions of power in which people 'destroy each other for the sake of each other's power', *There Will Be Blood* was 'an experimental work in a very modern and contemporary style' (Theater Iran). As a professional theatre, IranShahr often stages translations and adaptations of Western canonical texts, including Sophocles' *Antigone* (2018), Chekhov's *Ivanov* (2016) and in 2022 an adaptation of *Hamlet* called *Ophelia* (written and directed by Tayebi and influenced by his readings of Jan Kott and Emma Jung). The most detailed account we have been able to find of *There Will Be Blood* is from a scholarly article showing how staging plays set in Rome makes it possible for Iranian directors 'to address the current state of affairs in Iran' and also to 'get past the surveillance bodies by ensuring them that "This is not a true story"' (Javanian, 133). Because we have not been able to find theatrical reviews of *There Will Be Blood*, we wonder how the play's depiction of a dying empire set within a 'modern and contemporary style' was received by the audiences. This could have been a production that critiqued Western empires and/or one that subtly critiqued Iran's attempts to revive a Persian one.

As many will know, India has a rich filmic tradition of adapting Shakespeare's plays, and the 2017 film *The Hungry*, written and directed by Bornila Chatterjee, appropriates *Titus* to contemporary New Delhi. Set against the backdrop of a large Indian wedding, *The Hungry* uses *Titus*'s double revenge plot to interrogate corruption in contemporary India's business and politics. More pointedly, the film's graphic depiction of the rape of the Lavinia character, Loveleen (played by Sayani Gupta), implicitly referenced the infamous 2012 Nirbhaya case in New Delhi in which a 22-year-old woman was beaten, raped and tortured by a group of five men and a boy on a private bus. When the woman died from her injuries, India erupted in protests, as women blamed the government for the lack of measures to protect them. Chatterjee's adaptation of *Titus*, then, seems to ask what it takes for a society to protect women even as it relishes in a true villainess in the Tamora figure, Tulsi (played by Tisca Chopra). Thea Buckley notes,

> Throughout the film, Chatterjee focuses on the double standards applied to women, and their continual escapism. Tulsi is a name that evokes Hindu wifely chastity, the herb worshipped for a husband's wellbeing, yet ironically she is having an affair ... Loveleen is expected to remain pure, yet grinds onstage at the wedding party in a nautch-style dance number, and chugs whiskey.
>
> (Buckley, 290–1)

The film ends with a herd of goats eating the remains of the feast, 'leaving the viewer with an uneasy sense of closure sans redemption' (Buckley, 292).

It becomes clear, then, that the directors of the productions we have discussed in Japan, Hong Kong, Iran and India see something in *Titus* that allows them to explore the specific contemporary political and cultural issues they are facing. We will end with one last production that exemplifies the appeal of turning to *Titus* as a vehicle for a cultural-political critique. Although it was performed in English, the 1995 production of *Titus Andronicus* at the Market Theatre in Johannesburg, South Africa (directed by Gregory Doran) used the play to explore what empire, power, race and gender look like in a post-apartheid world. The Romans were staged as the divided Afrikaners in South Africa, and the Goths were invading guerrilla forces. Antony Sher, as a General Patton-like Titus, entered the first act in a war-ravished Jeep that had to be pulled by the captured Goths. As Michael Billington writes, however, the production 'sometimes veers awkwardly between realism and stylisation. The appalling violence towards Lavinia, for instance, is minimised by being perpetrated on a shop-window dummy' (Billington, 'Brutal'). And yet the production 'puts the play into a specifically South African context and, even though the historical fit is not perfect, it confirms *Titus*'s status as Shakespeare's first masterwork' (Billington, 'Brutal').

As we think about what the future holds for *Titus Andronicus* in performance there are a few clues that point in different directions. There are beginning to be more feminist-informed productions, such as Lise Bruneau's 2013 Riot Grrrls production with an all-female cast. By depicting Chiron and Demetrius as young teenage boys (played by Amanda Forstom and Teresa Spencer), Bruneau forced the audience to interrogate the 'boys will be boys' excuse frequently used to justify violence against girls and women. An egregious example of this type of excuse occurred in 2016 when the father of a convicted teenage rapist argued for leniency on the grounds that a prison sentence would be too 'steep a price to pay for 20 minutes of action out of his 20 plus years of life' (quoted in Samuels). With an all-female cast, Bruneau's production was unrelenting in its condemnation of toxic masculinity and societies that foster, enable and promote such behaviour. A similar tack was taken by Michael Fentiman in his 2013 RSC production.

Figure 20 Lise Bruneau's 2013 Riot Grrrls production with an all-female cast forced the audience to interrogate the 'boys will be boys' justification for violence against girls and women. Amanda Forstom and Teresa Spencer as Chiron and Demetrius.

Although the actors playing Chiron and Demetrius (Jonny Weldon and Perry Millward) were both twenty years old at the time of the production, Fentiman styled them to look closer to fourteen or fifteen years of age. By having so many boys on stage (Young Lucius, Chiron, Demetrius and the biracial baby), Fentiman invited the audience to probe how violent men are actually made.

Likewise, Fentiman's production incited the audience to ask how ethical Titus' interpretations of Lavinia's desires really are. While the bloody banquet scene is often staged with Lavinia willingly submitting to her death (as a type of suicide by father), in the 2013 RSC production Titus (played by Stephen Boxer) had to grapple with and subdue Lavinia (played by Rose Reynolds), who seemed unaware of his plan and unwilling to submit to it. How much agency Lavinia has in a world in which her lovers, brothers, uncle and father frequently objectify her and speak for her is a question that feminist approaches to *Titus* reveal, expose and explore.

Figure 21 In Matthew R. Wilson's 2014 Faction of Fools production Miranda Medunga's Lavinia made it clear that her male relatives did not speak for her. L–R: Nello DeBlasio (Titus), Matthew Pauli (Lucius), Miranda Medunga (Lavinia) and Toby Mulford (Marcus).

In Matthew R. Wilson's 2014 Faction of Fools production, for instance, Lavinia (played by the deaf actress Miranda Medungo) signed all of her lines until she was raped and mutilated by Chiron and Demetrius (played by Tyler Herman and Charlie Ainsworth). With her hands cut off, Lavinia no longer had any means to communicate. Nonetheless, she was demonstrably annoyed that her father (played by the hearing actor Nello DeBlasio) was attempting to interpret her non-signed ideas and emotions. She made it visibly clear to the audience that he did not understand her thoughts or desires, and this came to a head when she physically resisted participating in the killing of Chiron and Demetrius. Wilson's production was staged at Gallaudet University, an American university that teaches deaf and hard of hearing students in a bilingual learning environment, featuring American Sign Language (ASL) and English, and the cast featured two deaf performers (Charlie Ainsworth as Demetrius and Miranda Medugno as Lavinia) who signed all of their lines. Lavinia's disdain for being both ignored and spoken for – a frequent complaint of deaf individuals – gave Wilson's production a decidedly feminist and disability-justice slant, and made Shakespeare's lines seem new and fresh.

Furthermore, Wilson's production points to another rising trend in *Titus* performances: disability-informed, and in particular deaf, interpretations. Although it is difficult to pinpoint the first professional production of *Titus* that incorporated deaf actors, Carole Tweedy's 1993 Octagon Theatre (Bolton, England) production looks to have been one of the first. The production received an Arts Council 'Be Bold' award to create a bilingual production in English and British Sign Language (BSL) with a cast that included deaf performers, including Paula Garfield as Lavinia. Some of the sign language was created specifically for the production, including one for 'Andronicus', which consisted of placing an open palm on the top of the signer's head to represent a plumed Roman helmet. There are several other forthcoming professional productions that will incorporate ASL and BSL, including one in development by Gregg Mozgala, Kim Weild and Katherine Williams (through Apothetae and The Public Theater), and another by Howie Seago, Lezlie Cross and Christine Albright-Tufts (supported by Play On). These productions are labour intensive because they require Shakespeare to be translated twice, as the deaf actor Andrew Morrill explains: 'ASL is a different playground from English and Shakespearean English. ... Technically, Shakespearean English is my third language, therefore, I will need to go through the process from Shakespearean English to English to ASL' (quoted in Ebanks). Nonetheless, the time and energy that many deaf actors are putting into *Titus Andronicus* feels like a significant shift in contemporary understandings of the play. They are shining a light on the disability built into the play itself and staking a claim for the rights of disabled actors to inhabit significant roles in this disability rich text. Regardless of the historical realities of disabled people in early modern England, contemporary disabled artists want to establish *Titus Andronicus* as a vehicle for exploring and discussing disability. While it is too soon to make major predictions, this performance shift feels akin to the one that occurred around the portrayal of Aaron's blackness.

The future of the afterlife of *Titus Andronicus* is particularly interesting as we enter the second quarter of the twenty-first century. As the shadow of

Julie Taymor's influence shortens, there will not only be innovative 'straight' productions, but also imaginative retellings. One retelling of particular note had its initial realization in a seemingly unlikely venue: the 2021 reboot of the teen soap opera *Gossip Girl*. In the third episode, some of the main characters attend an experimental performance. Here's how *The New York Times* described the scene:

> We hear him before we see him come across the screen: Aaron howls and barks then gallops, on all fours, onto a white, wooden thrust stage, ringed on three sides by the audience. This enraged man – the son of Aaron the Moor from 'Titus Andronicus' – is stark naked and covered in blood. 'What? What? Have I not arrived as you assumed I would?' he demands, panting and sniffing, shouting into the faces of the seated theatregoers. 'Like the black dog, as the saying is.'
>
> (Zornosa)

This scene within a scene of *Gossip Girl* was written by the Tony-nominated playwright Jeremy O. Harris, and he has been commissioned by The Public Theater in New York to write *The Bloody and Lamentable Tale of Aaron*. This play will take up where *Titus Andronicus* left off, with young Aaron 'named after his father, in his 20s. He has been raised by Lucius Andronicus, now in his 60s. And he's thirsty for revenge' (Zornosa). Harris explained his approach, indicating that Aaron's son's thinking is not 'I'm evil because I'm Black' but 'I'm evil because you guys have socialized me. You have socialized rules around what Black means and what maleness means' (quoted in Zornosa). Once this appropriation comes fully to life, the afterlife of *Titus Andronicus* promises to move in directions that cannot be fully anticipated now. This indecorous play that weds horror and humour, a play written well over four centuries ago, continues to inspire artists globally to explore their own environments' political and cultural excesses. *Titus* is proving to be one of Shakespeare's most adaptable plays in the twenty-first century precisely because the world is grappling with the ramifications of the corrupting nature of excess. Teachers and artists continue to be drawn to *Titus* to ask: Who will Young Lucius and Young Aaron grow up to be? What world will they build in the wake of their parents' world's collapse into brutal indecorum?

Figure 22 Jeremy O. Harris wrote the scenes featuring *The Bloody and Lamentable Tale of Aaron: The Moor's Nigga Prince* for *Gossip Girl*'s 2021 reboot, and The Public Theater then commissioned him to write a sequel to *Titus Andronicus*.

TITUS ANDRONICUS

LIST OF ROLES

ROMANS

SATURNINUS	*eldest son of the late Emperor,*	
	subsequently Emperor	
BASSIANUS	*younger brother of Saturninus*	
TITUS Andronicus	*patrician Roman general in wars*	
	against the Goths	5
MARCUS Andronicus	*brother of Titus; a Tribune of Rome*	
LAVINIA	*daughter of Titus; betrothed to*	
	Bassianus	
LUCIUS		
QUINTUS	*Titus' surviving sons*	10
MARTIUS		
MUTIUS		
YOUNG LUCIUS	*son of Lucius, grandson of Titus*	
PUBLIUS	*nephew of Titus, son of Marcus*	
Sempronius		15
Caius	*kinsmen of the Andronici*	
Valentine		
EMILLIUS	*a high-ranking Roman*	
CAPTAIN		
MESSENGER		20
NURSE		
CLOWN		
ROMAN LORD		
ROMANS	*Tribunes, Senators, Attendants,*	
	Soldiers	25

GOTHS AND ASSOCIATES

TAMORA	*Queen of the Goths, and later Empress of Rome after*	
	marrying Saturninus	
AARON	*a Moor brought to Rome as Titus' prisoner of war;*	
	Tamora's lover	30
Alarbus		
CHIRON	*sons of Tamora*	
DEMETRIUS		
GOTHS	*an army*	

101

1   **SATURNINUS** A name associated with the Roman god Saturn, and so appropriate for a member of the ruling family of Rome. Also perhaps meant to evoke the idea of having a saturnine (influenced by the planet Saturn) temperament, which exhibited traits such as sullenness or a readiness to anger (*OED* 1.a; see also the note at 2.3.30–1). Hunter first noted that the names Saturninus and Bassianus appear in proximity to one another (naming figures who seem wholly unrelated to the characters in this play) in the work of the historian Herodian, whose Greek-language *History* covers 180–238 CE. But the name is not that uncommon (EEBO-TCP turns up instances in more than forty English books before 1590) and could have been encountered as a characteristic Roman name by Shakespeare and/or Peele in more widely known volumes by writers like Sallust and Plutarch, too. Sometimes referred to as 'Emperour' in SPs in the early texts, and occasionally as 'King' (see the note at 1.1.114).

3   **BASSIANUS** A name associated with two different Roman tyrants who feature in Herodian's *History* (as well as in numerous other English books touching on Roman history): the cruel Caracalla, whose birth name was Lucius Septimius Bassianus (Herodian, 3.10–4.13), and the louche Elagabalus, whose birthname was Sextus Varius Avitus Bassianus (Herodian, 5.3–5.8). Both figures could be seen as relevant to the idea of Rome underpinning this play, though neither seems to have anything in common with this character in particular. Caracalla was known for fierce rivalry with his brother Geta, whom he had killed. Elagabalus is a figure associated with imperial excess and decadence. It is not clear that Herodian is a direct source for the name, which may have been selected for its association with imperial-era Roman power.

4   **TITUS ANDRONICUS** Titus is introduced as having the surname 'Pious' (1.1.23, and see note), but this is never mentioned again.

7   **LAVINIA** Named after the daughter of the king of Latinum, whose marriage to Aeneas is both the precondition for the founding of Rome and the cause of the rivalry between Aeneas and Turnus that is the central subject of the second half of Virgil's *Aen*. She would have been played by a boy actor, likely using white facial make-up to represent feminine beauty.

9   **LUCIUS** A very common Latin name, strongly associated with Lucius Junius Brutus, who led the uprising that expelled the Tarquin family and established the Roman republic. See 4.1.88–90.

13   **YOUNG LUCIUS** Referred to as 'Lucius sonne' and 'young Lucius' in entry SDs in Q1, but SPs in Q1 call him 'Puer' [Latin for 'boy'] and those in F refer to him as 'Boy'. In Q1, which lacks 3.2, he is added to the play at the start of Act 4.

14   **PUBLIUS** One of the kinsmen assisting Titus with his schemes in 4.3 and 5.2. Titus is referred to as his uncle at 4.3.25 and since there is no mention in the play of Titus having another brother it is implied that he is the son of Marcus.

15–17 **SEMPRONIUS, CAIUS AND VALENTINE** Non-speaking roles; kinsmen who continue to support Titus, Marcus and Lucius even after they have lost all support in Saturninus' Rome. Publius, Sempronius and Caius are the kinsmen named in 4.3 who play along with Titus and shoot arrows to the gods; Publius, Caius and Valentine are the names given for the Andronici who come in to bind and gag Chiron and Demetrius in 5.2. It is possible that the name Sempronius is replaced with Valentine through error: it seems unnecessary to have different actors play these roles.

18   **EMILLIUS** Described as a 'nuntius' [Latin, 'messenger'] in the SD at 4.4.59.1, but apparently a much more high-ranking figure than the unnamed messenger who delivers Aaron's message to the Andronici after 3.1.234.

22   **CLOWN** In the sense of a low, rustic person, but also a role likely played by an actor who specialized in comic parts. See the note on the SD at 4.3.74.1.

23   **ROMAN LORD** An aged figure of generic respectability who speaks on behalf of Rome as the surviving Andronici try to reconstitute the broken polity at the end of the play. See note to the SP at 5.3.71.

26   **TAMORA** In the fly-killing scene (3.2), which was added for the first time in F, she is referred to by the name 'Tamira'. Like Lavinia, she would have been played by a boy actor in whiteface: her fair hue is specifically what catches Saturninus' eye.

29   **AARON** 'Aron' or 'Moor' in SDs and SPs in Qq; sometimes Aaron in F. The name is an odd choice, since it would have been strongly associated with the Old Testament priest Aaron, the brother of Moses. Ken Jackson, who reads the play as a meditation on the sacrificial energies associated with the Old Testament story of Abraham, sees Titus' willingness to sacrifice his sons for Rome as

proto-Christian and so reads Aaron's unwillingness to do the same as un-Christian, and believes the Old Testament name invokes this notion (Jackson, *Abraham*, 83–95). The role would have been played by an actor in blackface.

31–2   **CHIRON, DEMETRIUS** Unlike Alarbus (whose sacrifice may have been a late addition to the play), the two sons of Tamora who speak in the play have names taken from Greek mythology, which may mark them as extrinsic to Rome but as part of the larger world subsumed by Rome.

THE MOST LAMENTABLE ROMAN TRAGEDY OF TITUS ANDRONICUS

[1.1]   *Flourish. Enter the Tribunes [including* MARCUS] *and Senators*
aloft. And then enter SATURNINUS *and his followers at one door,*
and BASSIANUS *and his followers at the other,*
with drum and colours.

SATURNINUS

Noble patricians, patrons of my right,
Defend the justice of my cause with arms.

0.1–4   ***Flourish ... and colours*** The SD in F calls for an introductory flourish, typically an offstage trumpet
fanfare announcing an important arrival. The SD in Qq is less precise: '*Enter the Tribunes and Senatours
aloft: and then enter Saturninus and his followers at one dore, and Bassianus and his followers, with
Drums and Trumpets*'. The sonic and spectacular quality of this opening is clarified by the SD in F, which
also indicates that each of the opposing factions enters with a drummer and a standard-bearer carrying
the group's emblematic banner ('colours').

***including* MARCUS** Since Marcus is a Tribune, his entrance is implied here. F has him entering with the
crown just before his first speech at 18.

aloft The opening act in particular makes elaborate use of a balcony space to represent the elevated
authority of Roman officials. This tells us something about how the early texts imagine the stage
configuration. However, since *Tit* was likely performed at several different Elizabethan theatres, as well
as at the estate of Sir John Harington (see p. 47), staging should be understood as fluid and adaptable.

at one door ... at the other The two factions enter through two different doors, which again tells us
something about the stage configuration presumed by the early texts.

1   **patricians** the Roman aristocracy, who are socially more elevated than the common plebeians

---

TITLE] Q1; The Lamentable Tragedy of *Titus Andronicus* F   1.1] *Actus Primus. Scaena Prima* F; not in Qq
0.1 *Flourish*] F, not in Qq   *including* MARCUS] *Riv subst.*   0.3 *at the other*] F, not in Qq   0.4 *drum*] Q3, F;
drums Q1–2   *colours*] F; *trumpets* Qq

And countrymen, my loving followers,
Plead my successive title with your swords.
I am his first-born son, that was the last   5
That wore the imperial diadem of Rome.
Then let my father's honours live in me,
Nor wrong mine age with this indignity.

BASSIANUS

Romans, friends, followers, favourers of my right,
If ever Bassianus, Caesar's son,   10
Were gracious in the eyes of royal Rome,
Keep then this passage to the Capitol,
And suffer not dishonour to approach
The imperial seat, to virtue consecrate,
To justice, continence, and nobility,   15

---

4   **successive title** 'successive' ('coming one after another in an uninterrupted sequence' [*OED adj.*])
     because Saturninus' claim is based on primogeniture and his status as the eldest son of the recently
     deceased emperor

5   **I am ... last** F's version of this line ('I was the first born son, that was the last') is comprehensible,
     but makes Saturninus' relation to the previous emperor much more difficult to understand at the
     very moment where it is being introduced as a key point; it could also partly be the product of a
     compositorial eye-skip, a duplication of the 'was' from the second half of the line in the first half of
     the line.

6   **diadem** a crown, wreath, or band emblematic of its wearer's authority

8   **this indignity** i.e., the indignity of having his legitimacy as ruler questioned

9   **friends** Bassianus, whose claim is based on merit and election rather than primogeniture, speaks to his
     followers in the language of egalitarian republican comradery. The conflict between the two brothers
     thus introduces an implied conflict about the nature of Roman civic government.

10   **Caesar's son** Caesar is here used as a title rather than as a proper name: Bassianus, like his brother
     Saturninus, is son to the last Roman ruler.

12   **this passage ... Capitol** Technically, the Capitol refers to the temple of Jupiter on the Capitoline Hill
     in Rome, but it is here treated as the location of the Senate house and seat of Roman civic politics.
     Compare *JC* 1.2.186–7, where Brutus says that Cicero looks 'As we have seen him in the Capitol / Being
     crossed in conference by some senators'. In terms of staging, 'Bassianus establishes one [stage] door as
     the entrance to the Capitol; he and his followers hold it, while Saturninus tries to enter' (Cam[3]). He is
     both concerned that his path to power not be blocked figuratively and also that his literal access to the
     Capitol through one stage door be protected.

14   **consecrate** consecrated; dedicated with sacred purpose

15   **continence** self-restraint; the ability to rein in passions and desires

---

5 I am his] *Qq*; I was the *F*   6 wore] *F*; ware *Qq*   9] *Q1*; *F lines* Followers, / Right: /

But let desert in pure election shine,
And, Romans, fight for freedom in your choice.
MARCUS (*Aloft, [steps forward] with the crown.*)
Princes, that strive by factions and by friends
Ambitiously for rule and empery,
Know that the people of Rome, for whom we stand   20
A special party, have by common voice
In election for the Roman empery
Chosen Andronicus, surnamed Pious
For many good and great deserts to Rome.
A nobler man, a braver warrior,   25
Lives not this day within the city walls.
He by the senate is accited home

---

18 SD   **Aloft ... crown** In Qq, Marcus' speech is introduced by the phrase 'Marcus Andronicus with the
         Crowne', which is centred. F interprets this by indicating an entrance. However, since Marcus is also a
         Tribune, we follow Ard³ in thinking that he must already have entered aloft with the other Tribunes
         at the start of the play. We preserve the spirit of F's SD by having Marcus step forward from the other
         governmental figures aloft to deliver his speech.
19   **empery** the office or role of emperor
20–1   **for whom ... party** Marcus is a tribune, which is an office in Rome that was meant to represent the
         interests of the plebeians; here they are said to be representatives ('special party') acting on behalf
         of the people. Shakespeare dramatizes the origin of the office in Cor. Over time, the representative
         function of the office was weakened, and Marcus is neither a plebeian himself nor especially aligned in
         the rest of the play with the interests of the plebeians as a group.
22   **election** choice; in a political context, the word 'election' would have indicated the formal choosing of
         a person for an office, dignity, or position (OED 1), but at this point the succession remains undecided,
         so it would seem that Titus has been identified by the people of Rome as a favourable candidate to
         become the next emperor. This is further clarified at 179–86 below.
23   **surnamed** surnamèd
         Pious as an epithet or adjective, Pious (or 'Pius', as it is spelled in Qq) is strongly associated with
         Aeneas, the legendary founder of Rome in Virgil's Aen; there, it names both reverence to the gods
         and a commitment to public duty characteristic of Aeneas; here, the surname and its Virgilian echoes
         associate Titus with a nostalgic brand of Roman moral orthodoxy and civic-mindedness.
27   **accited** summoned

---

18 SP] Rowe; not in Qq, F   18 SD Aloft ... forward] this edn; Marcus Andronicus with the Crowne Qq; Enter
Marcus Andronicus aloft with the Crowne F   23 Pious] Qq (Pius); Pious F

From weary wars against the barbarous Goths,
That, with his sons, a terror to our foes,
Hath yoked a nation strong, trained up in arms.   30
Ten years are spent since first he undertook
This cause of Rome, and chastised with arms
Our enemy's pride. Five times he hath returned
Bleeding to Rome, bearing his valiant sons
In coffins from the field.   35
And now, at last, laden with honour's spoils,
Returns the good Andronicus to Rome;
Renowned Titus, flourishing in arms.
Let us entreat, by honour of his name
Whom worthily you would have now succeed,   40
And in the Capitol and senate's right,
Whom you pretend to honour and adore,

28   **barbarous Goths** This initial reference to the Goths as Rome's enemy would likely have indicated to
      the play's early audiences that the story was set in the decadent late empire. See pp. 4–7.
30   **yoked** subjugated
32   **chastised** chastisèd
35–6 **field ... now** Q1 here prints several lines not present in any of the later quartos nor in F: 'In Coffins
      from the field, and at this day, / To the Monument of that *Andronici* / Done sacrifice of expiation, /
      And slaine the Noblest prisoner of the *Gothes*' ... Since these lines pre-empt the sacrifice of Alarbus
      later in the scene, it is usually assumed that they are an unexpunged trace of an earlier draft of the
      scene, though some scholars have proposed emendations to make their inclusion make sense. See
      pp. 35–6. We prefer the irregular, shortened line at 35 to the narrative inconsistency created by the
      inclusion of these remarks.
38   **Renowned** renownèd
      flourishing in arms displaying his arms in a triumphal manner
39–40 **by honour ... succeed** The meaning of Marcus' injunction has been variously interpreted, and it
      is grammatically unclear whose name the brothers are being enjoined to honour ('his'). Capell's
      emendation – 'Whom worthily you would have now succeeded' – has Marcus asking the brothers to
      be peaceful out of respect for their late father. Ravenscroft omits 40 altogether, so that the brothers
      are enjoined to stand down in honour of Titus. The remark as it stands, though, would appear to
      mean something like 'in honour of his name, whomever ... you would have succeed'. Since each
      brother hopes to rule, each has some vested interest in preserving political order, and Marcus asks
      each of them to follow the political process out of respect for their own best interest as a potential
      successor.
42   **pretend** claim; the word does not imply that the claim is false (*OED v.* 4).

35–6 field ... And] Q2–3, F; field, and at this day, / To the Monument of that *Andronici* / Done sacrifice of
expiation, / And slaine the Noblest prisoner of the *Gothes*, / And Q1   40 Whom ... succeed] Qq, F; Whom ...
succeeded *Capell*

That you withdraw you, and abate your strength,
Dismiss your followers and, as suitors should,
Plead your deserts in peace and humbleness.   45

SATURNINUS
How fair the tribune speaks to calm my thoughts.

BASSIANUS
Marcus Andronicus, so I do affy
In thy uprightness and integrity,
And so I love and honour thee and thine –
Thy noble brother Titus and his sons,   50
And her to whom my thoughts are humbled all,
Gracious Lavinia, Rome's rich ornament –
That I will here dismiss my loving friends,
And to my fortunes and the people's favour,   54
Commit my cause in balance to be weighed.   [*Exit Soldiers.*]

SATURNINUS
Friends that have been thus forward in my right,
I thank you all, and here dismiss you all,
And to the love and favour of my country
Commit my self, my person, and the cause.   [*Exit Soldiers.*]

43   **abate** diminish
44   **suitors** petitioners
45   **Plead your deserts** argue for what you deserve
47   **affy** trust
51–2 **her … ornament** the first indication of Bassianus' relation to Lavinia; it later becomes clear that they
      are engaged to be married, but it is not clear that Titus – who has been away fighting – knows this. See
      also the note at 277.
55   **in balance … weighed** determined impartially, in a scale, as opposed to by arms
56   **forward** ready to promote

46] *Q1; F lines* speakes, / thoughts. / 55 SD] *Capell subst.*   56] *Q1; F lines* beene / Right, /   59 SD] *Capell subst.*

109

Rome, be as just and gracious unto me   60
As I am confident and kind to thee.
Open the gates and let me in.
BASSIANUS
Tribunes, and me, a poor competitor.

Flourish. They go up into the senate house.

Enter a CAPTAIN.

CAPTAIN
Romans, make way. The good Andronicus,
Patron of virtue, Rome's best champion,   65
Successful in the battles that he fights,
With honour and with fortune is returned
From whence he circumscribed with his sword
And brought to yoke the enemies of Rome.

61   **confident and kind** Saturninus is confident of Rome's election because he is well disposed towards
      Rome (*OED* kind *adj. and adv.* 10), but also perhaps in that he has a birthright claim to his father's title
      (*OED adj. and adv.* 3) and in that he is native and to the manner born (*OED adj. and adv.* 4).
62   **Open ... in** The tetrameter line may be intended to make Saturninus sound impatient or peremptory.
63   **competitor** a rival candidate for office, as the Latin word '*conpetitor*'
63 SD **They ... senate house** Bassianus and Saturninus go aloft, clearing the main stage for Titus' entrance. The
      SD refers to a 'senate house' that is not itself a staged location in the play. The sense may be that they
      go off to attend to political business, and that may mean that they mingle with the other senators and
      tribunes who are also aloft. Some editions have them re-enter prior to Saturninus' next spoken line (at
      202), but we follow Ard³ in having them remain aloft in the interim. It is unlikely that they would exit
      altogether and miss an important public event of some significance to their own affairs.
65   **Patron** protector, supporter
68   **circumscribed** circumscribèd; imposed restraints upon

63.1 SD *Flourish*] *F; not in Qq*   64 SP] *F; not in Qq*   68 whence] *F; where Qq*

Sound drums and trumpets, and then enter two of Titus' Sons [including LUCIUS*].*
After them, men bearing coffin[s] covered with black, then two other Sons.
After them, TITUS *Andronicus, and then, [as prisoners,]* TAMORA *the Queen of Goths,*
and her [three] sons, [Alarbus], CHIRON *and* DEMETRIUS*, with* AARON *the Moor, and*
others, as many as can be. They set down the coffin[s], and TITUS *speaks.*

69.1–5   F and Qq have substantially the same stage direction here with very minor verbal differences, and ours is based on F. Titus' entrance is evidently meant to be as grand as possible ('*as many as can be*'), so it is likely that this entrance redeploys the actors who had earlier made up the retinues of Saturninus and Bassianus, with the drummers but presumably without the 'colours' used to indicate factions in their initial entry (0.4). Trevor Nunn's 1972 RSC production took a maximalist approach with a cast of thirty-seven, and Yukio Ninagawa's influential Japanese production, which was also staged as part of a Royal Shakespeare Company festival in 2006, had a cast of thirty. In both productions many were employed in this opening pageant. The spectacle of the black Aaron and the northern Goths paraded as captives in a Roman triumph visually signals the all-encompassing global power of the play's Rome. Oxf² has Titus entering in a chariot, based on Titus' remark at 250; we omit this since it is not specified in the SDs and not explicitly indicated in the text. It is not clear that the earliest Elizabethan stagings of the play would even have had access to such a prop (Tavares). It is possible of course that a Jacobean revival might have used one to make the scene grander, but a revival informed by memories of earlier productions would not have assumed that such a device was called for. While Deborah Warner's 1987 metatheatrical RSC production used a wheeled stage ladder as Titus' chariot without disguising its stage-tech function, Gregory Doran's 1995 Market Theatre production (South Africa) used a war-battered Jeep that had to be towed in by the Goths.

69.2   *men bearing coffin[s]* The SD in Qq and F specifies that there are 'two men bearing a coffin'. We follow Oxf¹, since Titus in this scene inters more than one son, and since, in the SD at 149, Qq's 'coffin' is changed in F to 'coffins'. The word 'coffin' could also refer more generally to a bier (*OED n.* 3b) so it would also be possible to imagine that two bodies are being conveyed together upon a carried platform of some kind. The prompt book for Deborah Warner's 1987 RSC production had two coffins, while Peter Brook's 1955 RSC production had three coffins on stage.

69.4   *Alarbus* Alarbus' role is a non-speaking one, but his presence on stage is required. It may be that his omission from his stage direction in all the early texts reflects an earlier version of the scene in which his death was only reported. See 35–6n. above, and also pp. 51–2.

69.4–5   *and other … be* The practicality and informality of this SD has been seen as representative of the insider/authorial nature of the Q1 SDs (Greg, *Folio*, 137). Since it is now believed that Peele wrote this scene, it is noteworthy that there is a similarly open-ended SD in Peele's roughly contemporary play *King Edward the First* (printed in 1593), where an entry SD for a public state event likewise requires '*others as many as may be*' (Peele, *Edw. 1*, sig. A2'). On SDs as evidence for Peele's authorship of Act 1 of *Tit*, see Jackson, 'Stage Directions'. See also Dessen and Thomson on 'permissive stage directions' (161–2).

69.1] *including* LUCIUS] *this edn*   69.1–2 *After them … After them* F; *and then … then* Qq   69.2–5 *men bearing coffins … coffins*] Oxf¹; *two men bearing a coffin … coffin* Qq, F   69.3 *as prisoners*] Ard³   69.3–4 *three sons … Alarbus*] Rowe *subst.*; *two sonnes* Qq, F   69.5 *be. They*] F; *be, then* Q1

TITUS

Hail, Rome, victorious in thy mourning weeds.   70
Lo, as the bark that hath discharged his freight
Returns with precious lading to the bay
From whence at first she weighed her anchorage,
Commeth Andronicus, bound with laurel boughs,
To resalute his country with his tears –   75
Tears of true joy for his return to Rome.
Thou great defender of this Capitol,
Stand gracious to the rites that we intend.
Romans, of five-and-twenty valiant sons,
Half of the number that King Priam had,   80
Behold the poor remains, alive and dead:
These that survive, let Rome reward with love;
These that I bring unto their latest home,

---

70   **mourning weeds** funereal clothing
71   **Lo** a now-archaic interjection used to create emphasis or to call attention to something that is about to be said
        bark ship
        freight The early texts all have 'fraught' (a burden or load); though the *OED* has an entry for 'fraught', it is given as an obsolete word, with 'freight' as a modernized alternative.
72   **lading** cargo
73   **weighed her anchorage** raised its anchors
74   **bound … boughs** having laurel branches encircling his head; laurel was worn by Roman commanders in the triumphal celebrations of their victories. In the so-called Peacham drawing, which seems to depict this episode in *Tit*, the Titus figure is shown to be literally wearing a laurel wreath (see p. 8).
75   **resalute** greet in return
77   **Thou … Capitol** an address to Jupiter, whose temple was located on the Capitoline Hill in Rome. See 12n.
78   **Stand** be
80   **King Priam** the legendary last king of Troy, said to have had 50 sons, many of whom were killed during the Trojan War; Titus, whose surname 'Pious' also evokes Aeneas and the Trojan origins of Rome, compares himself to the great Trojan king and so positions himself as a representative of the heroic, Virgilian version of Rome's origin myth.
83   **latest** final

70] Q1; F *lines* Rome: / Weedes: /   71 freight] *Rowe;* fraught *Qq, F*

With burial amongst their ancestors.

Here Goths have given me leave to sheathe my sword.   85

Titus, unkind and careless of thine own,

Why sufferst thou thy sons, unburied yet,

To hover on the dreadful shore of Styx?

Make way to lay them by their brethren.   *They open the tomb.*

There greet in silence, as the dead are wont,   90

And sleep in peace, slain in your country's wars.

O sacred receptacle of my joys,

Sweet cell of virtue and nobility,

How many sons hast thou of mine in store

That thou wilt never render to me more.   95

LUCIUS

Give us the proudest prisoner of the Goths,

That we may hew his limbs and on a pile

---

85   **Goths ... sword** a roundabout way of describing victory over the Goths without seeming to brag or take too much personal credit

86   **unkind** unnatural, un-familial

87–8   **unburied ... Styx?** The mythical river Styx encircles the classical underworld. In *Aen.*, 6.317–32, Aeneas discovers that the infernal ferryman Charon will only transport the spirits of those who have received proper burial across the river Acheron to their final resting place. Titus apparently has something similar in mind, though he names a different infernal river.

89   **brethren** a variant form of the word brothers, here pronounced with three syllables (and spelled accordingly in Q3 and F: 'bretheren')

89 SD   Opening the tomb here likely entailed opening the stage's trap door, at least in commercial London theatre performances, but a discovery space or even just a door could also have been used, especially at touring performances such as the one at Sir John Harington's estate in 1596. Contemporary stagings tend to be split between using a trap door (like Blanche McIntyre's 2017 RSC production) and using the discovery space (like Peter Brook's 1955 RSC production). Productions that use a trap door for the tomb tend also to use it for the pit in 2.3.

92   **receptacle** vessel or repository (as in *OED* II.4.a) but also with the connotation of a shelter or safe haven (II.5.a); here and at 2.3.235 the natural stress in the iambic line falls on the first and third syllable (rèceptàcle).

93   **cell** a small room

94   **in store** implying preservation rather than loss

---

94 hast thou of mine] Q1–2; of mine hast thou Q3, F

Ad manes fratrum sacrifice his flesh
Before this earthly prison of their bones,
That so the shadows be not unappeased,   100
Nor we disturbed with prodigies on earth.

TITUS

I give him you, the noblest that survives,
The eldest son of this distressed queen.

TAMORA [*Kneels with her sons.*]

Stay, Roman brethren, gracious conqueror,
Victorious Titus, rue the tears I shed,   105
A mother's tears, in passion for her son;
And if thy sons were ever dear to thee,

---

98   *Ad manes fratrum* (Latin) 'to the spirits of our brothers'; though this Latin is not quoted directly from
      any known source, it serves to make the sacrifice seem like a traditional and required part of Roman
      funeral rites. Hunter has suggested that the phrase may have been derived from Livy (1.25.12) where, in
      a duel between two sets of triplets to determine sovereignty, the sole surviving Roman brother exults
      that he has given two of his opponents to the shades of his bothers ('*Duos ... fratrum Manibus dedi*')
      as he prepares to kill the third. There is wide agreement in classical literature that human sacrifice
      was incompatible with civility, but (as Peele, who likely wrote this scene, would have known) Aeneas
      sacrifices prisoners in retribution for the death of Pallas in *Aen.* 11.81–4. Peele was probably also
      familiar with Plutarch's discussion of Roman attitudes towards human sacrifice in 'Roman Questions'
      83. There, Plutarch discusses the hypocrisy of Roman objections to human sacrifices conducted by
      'barbarous' peoples: 'this seemeth to be verie absurd, that they themselves should do those things,
      which they reprooved in others as damnable' (Plutarch, *Morals*, 878). A similar irony underpins this
      episode in the play.
99   **earthly** F's 'earthly' seems to have been interchangeable with Qq's 'earthy' in early modern discourse.
100   **shadows** the shades or spirits of the dead brothers: the '*manes fratrum*' referenced at 98
101   **prodigies** unnatural, portentous events; the implication is that failure to appease the spirits of the
      deceased Andronici may result in hauntings or other disturbances of the natural order.
103   **distressed** distressèd
104 SD *Tamora later promises to avenge herself on the Andronici and to 'make them know what 'tis to let a
      queen / Kneel ... and beg for grace in vain' (1.1.456–7). The Peacham drawing, which seems loosely to
      be based on this scene, also shows Tamora and two of her sons kneeling (see p. 8).
104   **brethren** brothers; Tamora proposes an idea of universal brotherhood in order to counteract the logic
      of the Roman sacrifice, whereby a Goth must be killed by the Andronici to appease the spirits of their
      Roman brothers.
105   **rue** regard with sorrow

---

98 *manes*] F3; *manus Qq, F*   99 earthly] F; earthy *Qq*   104 SD] *Oxf² subst.*

O, think my sons to be as dear to me.
Sufficeth not that we are brought to Rome
To beautify thy triumphs, and return   110
Captive to thee, and to thy Roman yoke,
But must my sons be slaughtered in the streets
For valiant doings in their country's cause?
O, if to fight for king and commonweal
Were piety in thine, it is in these.   115
Andronicus, stain not thy tomb with blood.
Wilt thou draw near the nature of the gods?
Draw near them then in being merciful.
Sweet mercy is nobility's true badge;
Thrice-noble Titus, spare my first-born son.   120

109   **Sufficeth not that** is it not enough that
110   **To beautify** to decorate or ornament
       triumphs A triumph was the formal celebration of a Roman general's military victory.
       return Tamora is not from Rome, but here presents herself as participating in Titus' return.
113   **doings** deeds
114   **king** It would be natural enough for Peele and Shakespeare to have thought of the head of state as a
       king, and in fact Saturninus is sometimes referred to as either 'King' or 'Emperour' in SPs in all the early
       texts. Tamora presumably refers to the Roman emperor as king in this generic sense – as ruler of a state.
       But emperors of post-republican Rome were typically careful to distinguish their office from that of the
       kings who were expelled and replaced after the rape of Lucrece. Titus also refers to Saturninus as a king
       at 1.1.248.
       commonweal an older form of the word commonwealth, which here means the polity or the state and
       also the shared well-being of its members
115   **thine ... these** i.e., 'your sons ... my sons'
117–18 **Wilt thou ... merciful** The proverbial nature of Tamora's phrase (Dent, M898: 'it is in their mercy that
       kings come closest to gods') is appropriate for her attempt at universal appeal, but the idea behind
       this expression dates back to the Roman philosopher Seneca's Neronian treatise *De Clementia*, where
       mercy is presented as the central, praiseworthy attribute of the Roman emperor's extraordinary power.
       Tamora's appeal is designed to garner broad audience sympathy while catering specifically to an idea of
       Roman imperial magnanimity.
119   **badge** sign, indicator

108 sons] *F*; sonne *Qq*

TITUS

Patient yourself, madam, and pardon me.
These are their brethren whom your Goths beheld
Alive and dead, and for their brethren slain
Religiously they ask a sacrifice.
To this your son is marked, and die he must,   125
T'appease their groaning shadows that are gone.

LUCIUS

Away with him, and make a fire straight,
And with our swords upon a pile of wood
Let's hew his limbs till they be clean consumed.

Exit Titus' [four] sons with Alarbus.

TAMORA [*Rises with her sons.*]

O cruel, irreligious piety.   130

CHIRON

Was never Scythia half so barbarous.

---

121   **Patient yourself** be patient
122   **their brethren whom** the brothers of those whom
122–3 **beheld … dead** saw alive and then dead; killed
123   **their** i.e., my sons'
124   **Religiously** ceremonially, in accordance with religion
125   **marked** designated, chosen
126   **groaning shadows** groaning ghosts; since 'groaning' implies the experience of suffering or grief (*OED* groan 1.a), Titus perhaps implies that the spirits of his dead sons are suffering and calling for expiatory sacrifice. Compare *JC* 3.2.275, where Antony imagines a world full of 'carrion men, groaning for burial'.
127   **straight** immediately
128–9 **And with … consumed** The Romans apparently plan to cut up ('hew') Alarbus' body as it burns.
129   **clean** completely
130   **irreligious piety** a pointed oxymoron that comments on the ironies of this gruesome episode
131   **Scythia** The Scythians were a nomadic people to the northeast of the Mediterranean world, often treated as uncivilized by classical Greek and Roman writers and their early modern English imitators. Compare *Lear* 1.1.117–21: 'The barbarous Scythian, / Or he that makes his generation messes / To gorge his appetite, shall to my bosom / Be as well neighboured, pitied and relieved, / As thou my sometime daughter'.

---

122 their] Qq; the F   your] Q1; you Q2–3, F   129 SD *four*] Rowe subst.; *Exit Titus Sonnes with Alarbus Qq; Exit Sonnes with Alarbus F*   130 SD] *Oxf*² subst.   131 never] Q1; euer Q2–3, F

DEMETRIUS

Oppose me Scythia to ambitious Rome.
Alarbus goes to rest, and we survive
To tremble under Titus' threatning looks;
Then, Madam, stand resolved, but hope withal   135
The self-same gods that armed the queen of Troy
With opportunity of sharp revenge
Upon the Thracian tyrant in his tent,
May favor Tamora, the queen of Goths
(When Goths were Goths, and Tamora was queen),   140
To quit the bloody wrongs upon her foes.

Enter the sons of Andronicus [MUTIUS, MARTIUS, QUINTUS, LUCIUS] *again.*

LUCIUS

See, lord and father, how we have performed
Our Roman rites: Alarbus' limbs are lopped,

132   **Oppose me** compare for me
       ambitious 'desiring success to an excessive or immoderate degree; arrogant, overbearing' (*OED* 1); the
       implication is that Rome, in its might and arrogance, does things that are worse than barbaric.
136–8 **the queen of Troy ... his tent** A reference to the story of the revenge of Hecuba, who had previously
       been queen of Troy, upon the Thracian king Polymestor. Polymestor killed Hecuba's son Polydorus
       in the aftermath of the Trojan War, and Hecuba in response kills Polymestor's sons and blinds him
       by stabbing him in the eyes. Peele – who we know translated a different play by Euripides while a
       student at Oxford – would have known this story both from Ovid, *Met.,* 13.533–75 and from Euripides'
       play *Hecuba*, which was among the best-known Greek plays in the Renaissance (see Pollard, 100–1).
       The location of the revenge in a tent is most likely a reference to Euripides' play, where Hecuba lures
       Polymestor into her tent and blinds him. Theobald emended the text to indicate that the revenge was
       carried out in 'her' tent, and that may be appropriate if there is a printing error here. It is also quite
       possible, of course, that Peele simply misremembered a somewhat minor detail in the story and wrote
       these lines as they appear. Given the recurring Roman allusions in this scene to Priam, Aeneas and
       Rome's Trojan origins, it is striking that the Goths, too, compare themselves to Hecuba and understand
       their experience with reference to the larger story of Troy's fall.
141   **quit** repay
143   **Roman rites** echoes Titus' language at 75, and clarifies that the sacrifice is understood by the Romans
       as part of a funereal ritual
       lopped trimmed, as with tree branches (*OED* 1.a)

132 me] F; not *Qq*   134 looks] F; looke *Qq*   138 his] *Qq*, F; her *Theobald*   141.1 MUTIUS ... LUCIUS] *Rowe subst.*

And entrails feed the sacrificing fire
Whose smoke, like incense, doth perfume the sky.   145
Remaineth nought but to inter our brethren
And with loud 'larums welcome them to Rome.

TITUS

Let it be so, and let Andronicus
Make this his latest farewell to their souls.

> *Flourish. Then sound trumpets, and lay the*
> *coffins in the tomb.*

In peace and honour rest you here my sons,   150
Rome's readiest champions, repose you here in rest,
Secure from worldly chances and mishaps.
Here lurks no treason, here no envy swells,
Here grow no damned drugs, here are no storms,
No noise, but silence and eternal sleep.   155
In peace and honour rest you here, my sons.

> *Enter* LAVINIA.

---

145   **perfume** pronounced with the stress on the second syllable; the connotations of the word may have
       been medicinal, associated with cleansing or disinfecting the air (*OED* v. 1.a).
147   **'larums** for 'alarums': loud noises, alarms, clamours (*OED* n. 2)
       welcome them to Rome Lucius imagines his bothers' being placed in the family monument as a
       successful return home. This is for the Andronici the culmination of a ritual predicated upon the idea
       that the dead were 'groaning' in pain (126) and unable to find rest (87–8) prior to the sacrifice of
       Alarbus.
149   **latest** final
149 SD F specifies that there is both an initial trumpet flourish and then more martial music played as the
       bodies are placed in the monument.
150–6 **In peace ... sons** In yet another of this scene's many allusive evocations of the matter of Troy, this
       speech is loosely modelled on part of a choral ode from Seneca's *Agamemnon*, where a chorus of
       bereaved Trojan women describe death as a haven from the hardships of life (*Aga.*, 589–610).
151   **readiest** most prompt to action
154   **damned** damnèd
       drugs poisonous plants or manufactured poisons
156 SD Lavinia enters and her first line echoes a line of Titus' that she has apparently not overheard. This could
       mean that her entry SD is misplaced in Qq and F and that she should enter a few lines earlier. However,
       since interring the deceased Andronici is depicted as a civic ritual, the repetition could also indicate
       that both Titus and Lavinia are speaking in a ritualistic or formulaic manner.

---

149 SD] *F; Sound Trumpets and lay the Coffin in the Tombe Qq coffins*] *F; coffin Qq*   154 drugs] *Q1–2;* gruddges
Q3; grudges *F*

LAVINIA

In peace and honour live Lord Titus long;

My noble lord and father, live in fame.

Lo, at this tomb my tributary tears

I render for my brethren's obsequies,   160

[*Kneels.*] And at thy feet I kneel, with tears of joy

Shed on this earth for thy return to Rome.

O, bless me here with thy victorious hand,

Whose fortune Rome's best citizens applaud.

TITUS

Kind Rome, that hast thus lovingly reserved   165

The cordial of mine age to glad my heart.

Lavinia, live; outlive thy father's days

And fame's eternal date, for virtue's praise.   [*Lavinia rises.*]

---

159   **tributary** offered in tribute
160   **obsequies** funeral rites; in the sole surviving copy of Q1, this word has been scored through and
        replaced, in what looks to be a typical Elizabethan-era secretary hand, with the synonym 'exequies'.
        The two words were sometimes treated as synonymous, but 'exequies' is the more correct Latin form
        (directly derived from the classical Latin word *exequia* – 'funeral rites' – where 'obsequies' is derived
        from spurious medieval Latin) and is also much less common in Elizabethan texts. See the notes in Ard³
        and Oxf³ for further discussion of the relationship between the two words.
166   **cordial** something medicinal to the heart; Titus thanks Rome for preserving Lavinia, who gladdens his
        heart with her presence.
167–8   **outlive ... praise** 'may you outlive your father, and may the praise of your virtue outlive even the
        eternal duration of fame'.

---

157 SP] Q3, F; *not in* Q1–2   161 SD] *Bevington subst.*   162 this] Q1; the Q2–3, F   164 fortune] F; fortunes Qq
165] Q1; F lines Rome, / reseru'd /   168 SD] *Bevington subst.*

MARCUS [*aloft*]

　Long live Lord Titus, my beloved brother,

　Gracious triumpher in the eyes of Rome.　　　　170

TITUS

　Thanks, gentle tribune, noble brother Marcus.

MARCUS [*aloft*]

　And welcome, nephews, from succesful wars,

　You that survive, and you that sleep in fame.

　Fair lords, your fortunes are alike in all,

　That in your country's service drew your swords,　　　　175

　But safer triumph is this funeral pomp,

　That hath aspired to Solon's happiness

　And triumphs over chance in honour's bed.

　[*Displays white robe.*] Titus Andronicus, the people of Rome,

　Whose friend in justice thou hast ever been,　　　　180

　Send thee by me, their tribune and their trust,

---

169 SD *aloft The F SD at 234 suggests that all the characters who have been aloft come down to the lower stage at that point. It may (as Bate suggests in Ard[3]) make good dramatic sense to have Marcus come down from the upper stage here and greet his brother face to face. Cam[1] has Marcus enter on the main stage here, with Saturninus and Bassianus re-entering aloft. But in the subsequent exchange Marcus is still speaking formally, as a Tribune, and this authority at the start of the play is associated with speaking from an elevated position.

173　**sleep in fame** Like Titus, Marcus imagines the dead in the family tomb as timelessly preserved and free from the tumults of life.

174　**Fair lords ... all** i.e., 'the living and the dead share the same honour' (RSC); in this line, F's new reading – 'are all alike in all' – seems to be an obvious compositor error.

176　**safer ... pomp** Titus' return to Rome is the occasion of two ceremonies: his triumphal entry as victor and the funeral pomp honouring his fallen sons. Marcus suggests that the funeral celebration is the more trustworthy or durable of the two: while the fortunes of the living may be altered, the fame of the dead is preserved forever.

177　**Solon's happiness** Solon was an early Athenian politician who famously advised the Lydian King Croesus that, given the fickleness of human fortune, no one should be accounted fully happy prior to their death.

---

169 SD] *Oxf*[1]　171] *Q1; F lines* Tribune, / Marcus. /　172 SD] *this edn; implied in Oxf*[1]　174] alike *Qq;* all alike F　179 SD] *this edn*

This palliament of white and spotless hue,
And name thee in election for the empire
With these our late-deceased emperor's sons.
Be *candidatus* then and put it on,   185
And help to set a head on headless Rome.

TITUS

A better head her glorious body fits
Than his that shakes for age and feebleness.
What should I don this robe and trouble you –
Be chosen with proclamations today,   190
Tomorrow yield up rule, resign my life,
And set abroad new business for you all?
Rome, I have been thy soldier forty years,
And led my country's strength successfully,
And buried one-and-twenty valiant sons,   195
Knighted in field, slain manfully in arms,

182   **palliament** a candidate's robe; this is a rare word that first appeared in print in Peele's 1593 *The Honour of the Garter*, a poem which compares a king's garments to 'a Romaine palliament' (Peele, *Honour*, sig. B2ᵛ). Peele, who wrote this scene too, likely derived the term from the Latin word *pallium* ('cloak') and cognates. Our SD at 179 indicates that Marcus may hold up a white robe or a folded garment. SDs for the presentation of the robe have varied in recent editions: Folg has Marcus entering on the main stage at 168 and 'carrying a white robe'. Bevington, who has Marcus aloft here, indicates that a robe is brought by someone to Titus.

183   **name thee in election** nominate you as a candidate for election; Marcus feels authorized to offer Titus the 'empery' at 201, and has indicated earlier that Titus has popular support (see the note at 22), but since Titus has never formally become a candidate there does not seem to have been anything like a formal vote. 'Election' here names the mechanism by which a new emperor will be appointed, but that mechanism seems to be an informal one.

184   **late-deceased** late-deceasèd

185   *candidatus* (Latin) candidate, but also, literally, somebody who is dressed in the white (Latin: *candida*) robe indicative of candidacy for an office

186-7 **a head … fits** Marcus imagines Rome as body parts and then Titus imagines 'her' as a woman. These conventional, corporeal metaphors for the body politic help to establish thematic resonance for all the literal dismemberments to come in the play.

189   **What should** why should; a fairly common idiomatic usage in Early Modern English

192   **set abroad** create, initiate

196   **Knighted in field** The chivalric terminology, referring to the practice of awarding knighthoods to soldiers to reward military valour, is anachronistic to the Roman setting. Such anachronisms are common enough in early modern drama (and see 3.1.170n.), but Peele – who is generally thought to have written this scene – tends in particular to give the action in his plays and poems 'a generalized chivalric-ethical colouring' regardless of its suitability to the historical setting (Vickers, 177).

In right and service of their noble country.
Give me a staff of honour for mine age,
But not a sceptre to control the world.
Upright he held it, lords, that held it last.   200

MARCUS [aloft]

Titus, thou shalt obtain and ask the empery.

SATURNINUS [aloft]

Proud and ambitious tribune, canst thou tell?

TITUS

Patience, prince Saturninus.

SATURNINUS [aloft]

Romans, do me right!
Patricians, draw your swords and sheath them not   205
Till Saturninus be Rome's emperor.
Andronicus, would thou were shipped to hell
Rather than rob me of the people's hearts.

LUCIUS

Proud Saturnine, interrupter of the good
That noble-minded Titus means to thee.   210

---

197   **right** duty
198–9 **staff of honour … sceptre** Titus indicates that it would be more appropriate for him to be given a staff
       (in the sense of 'a rod, baton, or wand carried by the holder of a particular post or position as an official
       symbol of authority or badge of office' [OED 1.5.c]) as a sign of earned civic authority, rather than a
       sceptre, which is an emblem of imperial rule. In the context of a speech where he calls attention to his
       old age, there may also be a suggestion that he could use a staff to lean on (OED 1.3) and is too old
       to rule.
200   **Upright** wordplay meaning both straight up and with integrity, but Titus is also playing on the idea
       that he – in contrast to the previous emperor – is old and bent and in need of a staff
201   **obtain … empery** obtain the position of emperor if you ask for it
207   **would thou were** Q3 changes 'were' to 'wert', which is a grammatical improvement (and compare
       3.1.294). But the phrase 'would thou were' could also be idiomatic and (per EEBO) appears in numerous
       early modern texts. Since we do not believe that Q3's edits reflect performance, we here opt for Q1's
       reading.
209–10 **Proud Saturnine … thee** Lucius probably does not know exactly what Titus plans to do here, but he
       seems to understand that his father's conservative brand of civic piety favours Saturninus' claim as
       eldest son of the emperor.

---

201 SD] this edn; implied in Oxf¹   202 SD] Ard³   204 SD] Ard³   207 were] Q1–2; wert Q3, F

TITUS

    Content thee, prince, I will restore to thee

    The people's hearts and wean them from themselves.

BASSIANUS [*aloft*]

    Andronicus, I do not flatter thee,

    But honour thee and will do till I die.

    My faction, if thou strengthen with thy friends,   215

    I will most thankful be; and thanks, to men

    Of noble minds, is honourable meed.

TITUS

    People of Rome, and people's tribunes here,

    I ask your voices and your suffrages.

    Will ye bestow them friendly on Andronicus?   220

TRIBUNES [*aloft*]

    To gratify the good Andronicus,

    And gratulate his safe return to Rome,

    The people will accept whom he admits.

---

212   **wean … themselves** to wean a child is to accustom it to managing without mother's milk; Titus
        uses the word figuratively, as meaning 'to reconcile by degrees to the privation of something' (*OED*
        v. 2): he promises to teach the people to accept that they cannot have the emperor of their choice.
        But the literal meaning of wean is also thematically relevant in that Titus implies the plebeians are
        moral toddlers who should be made to give up their childish judgement. It should be noted that the
        mother of Titus' children is never named or even mentioned, and that Saturninus marries the maternal
        Tamora. Titus' brand of Roman virtue is symbolically associated with the containment or rejection of
        the maternal, but by the end of this opening scene the maternal (in the person of Tamora) has been
        reincorporated into Rome.
217   **meed** reward
218   **People of Rome** Bassianus has just made a direct appeal for Titus' support. Titus does not acknowledge
        it and speaks instead to the whole assembly.
219   **your voices … suffrages** your votes; Titus asks the people for permission to choose their next emperor.
222   **gratulate** celebrate; express joy on a happy occasion (*OED* 3)
223   **The people will accept** The Tribunes speak for the people, but not necessarily in accordance with their
        wishes: we already know from 212 above that Titus considers his choice to be unpopular.

213 SD] *Ard³*   221 SD] *this edn; implied in Oxf¹*

TITUS

> Tribunes, I thank you, and this suit I make,
> That you create our emperor's eldest son,　　　　　　　225
> Lord Saturnine, whose virtues will, I hope,
> Reflect on Rome as Titan's rays on earth,
> And ripen justice in this commonweal.
> Then, if you will elect by my advice,
> Crown him and say 'Long live our emperor'.　　　　　　230

MARCUS [aloft]

> With voices and applause of every sort,
> Patricians and Plebeans, we create
> Lord Saturninus Rome's great emperor,
> And say, 'Long live our emperor Saturnine'.
>
> [Marcus crowns Saturninus.]
>
> A long flourish till they come down.

224　　**suit** petition; F has 'sure', but the change is likely derived from a compositorial misreading of Q3's 'sute'.

225　　**create** i.e., as emperor

227　　**Titan's** Titan is a common name of the Roman sun god, and thus for the sun itself.

228　　**ripen justice** The metaphor here is that justice will ripen in Rome under Saturninus' virtue as plants ripen in sunshine.

231　　**applause ... every sort** applause of every sort of people: that is, of both the Patricians and Plebeians

234 SD1　***Marcus crowns Saturninus** The SD at 18 indicated that Marcus was holding a crown, so presumably he here bestows it upon Saturninus. In the early-seventeenth-century German *Tito Andronico*, which may possibly reflect the staging of an earlier version of this play, it is instead the Titus character who crowns the new emperor (*Tito*, SD at 1.1.33). On the relationship between the German play and the play by Peele and Shakespeare, see pp. 58–60. Trevor Nunn's 1972 RSC production follows this older tradition by having Titus (played by Colin Blakely) crown Saturninus (played by John Wood).

234 SD2　**A ... down** This SD, which is only in F, makes good sense with the flow of the action, marking closure of one episode and clearing the upper stage for the next development as the business of electing a new emperor is completed. The upper stage has been occupied since the initial entry of senators and tribunes at the start of the play, and Saturninus and Bassianus have likewise been aloft since 63, so this offers a chance to stage another substantial processional.

---

224 suit] Qq; sure F　225 our] Q1; your Q2–3, F　227 Titan's] Q2–3, F (Tytans); Tytus Q1　231 SD] *this edn*; implied in Oxf¹　234 SD1] *this edn*　234 SD2 *A long flourish ... down*] F; *not in Qq*

SATURNINUS

Titus Andronicus, for thy favours done   235
To us in our election this day,
I give thee thanks in part of thy deserts,
And will with deeds requite thy gentleness.
And for an onset, Titus, to advance
Thy name and honourable family,   240
Lavinia will I make my empress,
Rome's royal mistress, mistress of my heart,
And in the sacred Pantheon her espouse.
Tell me, Andronicus, doth this motion please thee?

TITUS

It doth, my worthy lord, and in this match   245
I hold me highly honoured of your grace,
And here, in sight of Rome, to Saturnine,
King and commander of our commonweal,
The wide world's emperor, do I consecrate
My sword, my chariot, and my prisoners,   250

---

236   **election** pronounced with four syllables
237   **in part ... deserts** as partial compensation for what you have deserved
238   **requite thy gentleness** repay your courtesy
239   **for an onset** as a start
241   **empress** pronounced with three syllables
243   **Pantheon** a temple in Rome dedicated to all the gods
       espouse marry
244   **motion** proposal
246   **hold me** consider myself
248   **King** see the note to 114 above; it is perhaps more surprising that Titus refers to the emperor as a king than that an outsider like Tamora has done so.
249   **consecrate** dedicate solemnly, as to a sacred purpose (OED 1.a)
250   **My sword ... prisoners** Ravenscroft has a SD here indicating that Titus 'Presents his captives to the Emperor' (p. 8), but Titus' announcement is itself adequate to indicate that he is handing them over. Subsequent editors have sometimes also taken this line to imply other stage business, like having Titus enter in chariot earlier and here offer it up (on which, see 69.1–5n. above) or having him hand over his sword here (as in Ard³). But Titus still seems to be armed at 293, when he kills Mutius, so perhaps Titus is speaking figuratively here, pledging his ongoing military support to the new emperor. Regardless of the stage business, Titus is literally ceding possession of his prisoners to Saturninus.

243 Pantheon] F2; Pathan Qq, F

Presents well worthy Rome's imperious lord.
Receive them then, the tribute that I owe,
Mine honour's ensigns humbled at my feet.

SATURNINUS
Thanks, noble Titus, father of my life.
How proud I am of thee and of thy gifts   255
Rome shall record, and when I do forget
The least of these unspeakable deserts,
Romans forget your fealty to me.

TITUS [to Tamora]
Now, Madam, are you prisoner to an emperor:
To him that for your honour and your state   260
Will use you nobly and your followers.

SATURNINUS
A goodly lady, trust me, of the hue
That I would choose were I to choose anew.

---

253   **ensigns** representative symbols
254   **father of my life** important benefactor; Saturninus imagines Titus as a paternal supporter and mentor,
      a formulation which accords with Titus' own highly patriarchal idea of piety. Later in this scene,
      however, the emperor casts the paternal figure Titus aside in favour of the maternal figure Tamora.
257   **unspeakable** inexpressible, beyond words
258   **fealty** dutiful obligation
260   **for** because of
      state estate, status; Titus expects that Saturninus will treat her well, as befits an honourable and well-
      born prisoner.
262–3 **A goodly ... anew** This self-contained, rhyming couplet could well be construed as an aside, in which
      case it would mark the first moment in the play where a character articulates a feeling that they don't
      want to share publicly. But Saturninus is generally shameless about expressing even antagonistic
      thoughts aloud, and he seems to take pleasure in testing out his new-found power by provoking
      others, as if to see what he can get away with. Another example of this is when he asks Lavinia if she
      minds his address to Tamora at 271.
262   **hue** Though 'hue' could just mean appearance generally (*OED n.* 1), the word is self-evidently describing
      skin colour when used later in the play (2.3.73; 4.2.72, 100–1, 118; 5.1.28). Moreover, imperious rulers
      in several other roughly contemporary plays also fall in love with captives who are conspicuously fair-
      skinned (and at 264 Saturninus also refers to Tamora as 'fair'). Saturninus is attracted to Tamora partly
      because, as a Goth, her skin is lighter than that of the Romans (see p. 68 on this as a 'theatergram').

251 imperious] Q1–2; imperiall Q3, F   253 my] F; thy Qq   259 SD] Johnson   259 you] Qq; your F   260 your
honour and your] Qq; you honour and your F

[*to Tamora*] Clear up, fair queen, that cloudy countenance;
Though chance of war hath wrought this change of cheer   265
Thou com'st not to be made a scorn in Rome;
Princely shall be thy usage every way.
Rest on my word, and let not discontent
Daunt all your hopes. Madam, he comforts you
Can make you greater than the queen of Goths.   270
Lavinia, you are not displeased with this?

LAVINIA

Not I, my lord, sith true nobility
Warrants these words in princely courtesy.

SATURNINUS

Thanks, sweet Lavinia. Romans, let us go.
Ransomless here we set our prisoners free.   275
Proclaim our honours, lords, with trump and drum.
> [*Sound drums and trumpets; Tamora, her sons, and
> Aaron are set free. Saturninus attends to Tamora.*]

---

264   **cloudy** gloomy, sullen
265   **chance of war** the fortunes of war; Saturninus switches to accessible, proverbial language (Dent,
       C223: 'the chance of war is uncertain') to address his new foreign captive.
       change of cheer change of mood
268   **Rest on** rest assured of
270   **greater ... Goths** To be favoured by the all-powerful Roman emperor, Saturninus implies, is better
       than just being queen of Goths.
272   **sith** since
273   **Warrants** authorizes
276 SD *The sounding of drums and trumpets and the release of the prisoners are not indicated in the early
       texts but are implied by Saturninus' speech. Editors since Rowe (who added 'The Emperor courts
       Tamora in dumb shew') have often supplied a stage direction here to indicate that Saturninus is
       distracted and paying attention to Tamora when Bassianus steps forward to lay claim to Lavinia.

---

264 SD] Rowe³   265] Q1; F lines warre / cheere, /   chance Q2–3, F; change Q1   270 you] Qq; your F
276.1–2 Sound ... free] Ard³ subst.   Saturninus ... Tamora] Rowe subst.

BASSIANUS

Lord Titus, by your leave, this maid is mine.

TITUS

How, sir? Are you in earnest then, my lord?

BASSIANUS

Aye, noble Titus, and resolved withal

To do myself this reason and this right.   280

MARCUS

Suum cuique is our Roman justice;

This prince in justice seizeth but his own.

LUCIUS

And that he will, and shall, if Lucius live.

TITUS

Traitors, avaunt! Where is the Emperor's guard?

Treason, my lord! Lavinia is surprised.   285

SATURNINUS

Surprised? By whom?

BASSIANUS   By him that justly may

Bear his betrothed from all the world away.

---

277   **this maid is mine** It is implied that Lavinia and Bassianus have previously been engaged to be married,
and Marcus' reply suggests that he knew of this already too. This may even be why Saturninus seeks
Lavinia as his bride – because he covets whatever his brother has. It is possible that Titus, who has
been away from Rome fighting the Goths, may have been unaware of any engagement. Bassianus, here
and in the exchange that follows, primarily defends his claim to marry Lavinia on the basis of his own
property rights. Lavinia, silenced later, is also effectively spoken for throughout Act 1.

280   **do ... reason** to do justice for myself (*OED reason, n.*[1] II.7.a)

281   **suum cuique** (Latin) 'to each his own'; the phrase is common enough in well-known Latin texts to
render exact identification impossible, but Peele, writing this scene, may possibly have had Cicero in
mind here: in *DND* (3.38) Cicero describes *iustitia* ('justice') as '*quae suum cuique distribuit*' ('that which
gives to each its own'). On the phrase's legal resonance, see Hadfield.

285   **surprised** seized

286   **By whom?** Saturninus' surprise likely indicates that he has been distracted by Tamora and thus
inattentive during the previous exchange.

---

281 *cuique*] F2; *cuiqum* Q2; *cuiquam* Q3, F

MUTIUS

Brothers, help to convey her hence away,

And with my sword I'll keep this door safe.

> [*Exit Bassianus at one door, bearing off Lavinia,*
> *guarded by Marcus, Lucius, Quintus, and Martius,*
> *with Mutius following.*]

TITUS [*to Saturninus*]

Follow, my lord, and I'll soon bring her back.   290

> [*Saturninus exits at the other door with Tamora,*
> *Chiron, Demetrius, and Aaron.*]

MUTIUS

My lord, you pass not here.

TITUS

What, villain boy? Barr'st me my way in Rome?

MUTIUS

Help, Lucius, help!   [*Titus*] *kills him.*

> [*Re-enter* LUCIUS.]

---

289 SD   *The early texts do not provide adequate guidance for the hectic onstage action of this episode, but since Marcus and the other Andronici have entrance SDs later it makes sense to assume that they all exit here with Bassianus and Lavinia. Our SD follows Capell and implies that Mutius is in effect defending the rear of the exiting party. On editorial speculation that the killing of Mutius may have been a late addition to the script, and the attendant difficulties of recreating its staging, see Loughnane and also pp. 37–8.

290 SD 2   *The timing of Saturninus' exit is not specified in the early texts, and has been variously assigned by editors as occurring either at 276, before Bassianus steps forward to claim Lavinia, or (following Cam¹) during Titus' quarrel with his sons. We follow Ard³, where Saturninus refuses Titus' instruction that he follow Lavinia and instead exits with his retinue out of the other stage door. This staging underscores Saturninus' refusal to be instructed by Titus, which hardens into outright hostility after his re-entry aloft. In Ravenscroft, the stage is cleared here for the end of the first act (p. 9).

292   **Barr'st ... way** do you block my way

289.1–3 SD] *Capell subst.*   290 SD *to Saturninus*] *this edn* 290.1–2 *Saturninus exits ... Aaron*] Ard³
subst.   293 SD] Q3, F (*He kills him*); *not in* Q1–2 293.1 *Re-enter Lucius*] Capell

LUCIUS

My lord, you are unjust, and more than so;
In wrongful quarrel you have slain your son.   295

Enter aloft the Emperor [SATURNINUS] *with* TAMORA *and her two sons* [CHIRON *and* DEMETRIUS] *and* AARON *the Moor.*

TITUS

Nor thou, nor he, are any sons of mine:
My sons would never so dishonour me.
Traitor, restore Lavinia to the Emperor.

LUCIUS

Dead, if you will, but not to be his wife   299
That is another's lawful promised love.   [*Exit.*]

295.1–2 *This SD is placed after 300 in Qq, F, as if prompted by Saturninus' speech aloft at 301ff. Entry SDs in early modern playbooks are often tied to speeches and sometimes even replace SPs. Since Saturninus' speech at 301 is his refusal of Lavinia, it is generally assumed that Saturninus is awkwardly resuming the conversation he was having with Titus before his earlier exit (see, for instance, the note in Ard³). But if Saturninus enters here and listens from above for a moment as Titus and Lucius argue about Lavinia then his sudden refusal of her at 301 makes a great deal more organic sense.

299–300 **Dead ... love** Lucius' willingness to consider killing Lavinia is grounded in his assumption that she represents the family honour in her role as the chaste property of her prospective husband. This is here seen as a normative Roman attitude towards women's honour, but it is exposed as grotesque later in the play: compare, for instance, 5.3.36–44 and notes.

300 SD *Exit Editors differ as to whether or not Lucius carries Mutius' body off stage when he exits. We follow Capell in having Lucius exit here, leaving the body of Mutius on stage: having the body remain visible is more in keeping with the grotesque quality of violence in a play where audiences are frequently forced to gaze upon corpses and mutilated body parts. In Deborah Warner's 1987 RSC production, Mutius' corpse remains slumped on the stage ladder that had been used as Titus' chariot. The SD provided in Oxf¹ specifies that Lucius carries Mutius' body off. Ravenscroft, whose re-envisioning of the scene may or may not be based on recollections of an earlier staging, specifies that Mutius' body is carried back on stage when the sons re-enter (p. 11).

295.1–2 *Enter aloft ... Moor*] after line 300 in Qq, F   295.1 SATURNINUS] *Cam¹ subst.*   295.2 CHIRON and DEMETRIUS] *Cam¹ subst.*   300 SD] *Capell; not in Qq, F*

SATURNINUS

No, Titus, no, the Emperor needs her not;
Nor her, nor thee, nor any of thy stock.
I'll trust by leisure him that mocks me once,
Thee never, nor thy traitorous haughty sons,
Confederates all thus to dishonour me. 305
Was none in Rome to make a stale
But Saturnine? Full well, Andronicus,
Agree these deeds with that proud brag of thine
That said'st I begged the empire at thy hands.

TITUS

O monstrous! What reproachful words are these? 310

SATURNINUS

But go thy ways. Go give that changing piece
To him that flourished for her with his sword.
A valiant son-in-law thou shalt enjoy,
One fit to bandy with thy lawless sons,
To ruffle in the commonwealth of Rome. 315

302 **stock** bloodline, kin
303 **by leisure** at my leisure i.e., slowly, reluctantly
306 **Was ...** a F2 awkwardly emends this tetrameter line ('Was there none els in Rome to make a stale of').
stale a lover whose devotion is turned into ridicule for the amusement of a rival or rivals (OED n.³ 6)
307–9 **Full well ... hands** This is the pure product of Saturninus' imagination, generated out of thin air to save face. As such, it may also reflect Saturninus' larger desire to avoid any sense of indebtedness to Titus. One advantage of choosing Tamora is that, as an outsider to Rome, she is free from all constraining prior ties to Roman society.
311 **changing** fickle; Saturninus accuses Lavinia of changing her mind even though to this point she has done nothing other than acquiesce to both Saturninus and Titus.
piece a derogatory, objectifying way to refer to a woman as a sex object (OED II.9.b)
312 **flourished** waved his weapon in a theatrically showy manner (OED v. 9.b)
314 **bandy** brawl
315 **ruffle** stir up trouble

306 Was ... stale] Qq, F; Was there none els in Rome to make a stale of F2

TITUS

These words are razors to my wounded heart.

SATURNINUS

And therefore, lovely Tamora, queen of Goths,
That like the stately Phoebe 'mongst her nymphs
Dost overshine the gallant'st dames of Rome,
If thou be pleased with this my sudden choice,   320
Behold I choose thee, Tamora, for my bride,
And will create thee empress of Rome.
Speak, queen of Goths, dost thou applaud my choice?
And here I swear by all the Roman gods,
Sith priest and holy water are so near,   325
And tapers burn so bright, and everything
In readiness for Hymenaeus stand,

316   **These words … heart** A vivid bodily image for heartache that ironically anticipates the violent horrors
       still to come in this play. It is striking too that Saturninus so completely ignores Titus' agonized reaction
       to him.
318   **Phoebe** another name for the Roman goddess Diana, a figure associated with the white luminosity of
       the moon and with chaste virtue
318–19 **That like … Rome** Saturninus' praise of Tamora recalls a description of Dido's loveliness from Thomas
       Phaer's translation of *Aen.* 1.496–504 (a comparison originally credited to the antiquary Joseph Ritson
       in Steevens² [13: 268]). In Phaer, Dido is said to be 'faier of hewe' and 'like unto *Diana* bright whan
       she to hunt goth out', such that 'thousands of the ladie *Nymphes* awaite to do her will' but she 'al
       them overshynes' (Phaer, sig. Bii'). Saturninus may thus be reiterating his attraction to Tamora's fairness
       while also associating himself with Aeneas by casting his own foreign love as another Dido (who is the
       abandoned love of Virgil's hero). Tamora too compares herself to Dido at 2.3.20–4.
319   **gallant'st** most gorgeous (*OED* gallant *adj.* 1.a)
322   **empress** pronounced with three syllables; unlike the similar instance at 241, the pronunciation here is
       implied by the spelling in Q1 ('emperesse').
325   **priest and holy water** Christian-sounding ceremonial appurtenances anachronistically imagined
       as Roman
326   **tapers** candles, especially those used in religious ceremonies
327   **Hymenaeus** Roman god of marriage
       stand Idiomatic modern English would indicate that everything stands in readiness; the verb is plural
       because all the items Saturninus has listed (priest, holy water, tapers) stand ready.

318 Phoebe] *F2; Thebe Qq, F*

I will not resalute the streets of Rome,
Or climb my palace, till from forth this place
I lead espoused my bride along with me.   330

TAMORA

And here, in sight of heaven, to Rome I swear,
If Saturnine advance the queen of Goths,
She will a handmaid be to his desires,
A loving nurse, a mother to his youth.

SATURNINUS

Ascend, fair queen, Pantheon. Lords, accompany   335
Your noble emperor, and his lovely bride,
Sent by the heavens for prince Saturnine,
Whose wisdom hath her fortune conquered.
There shall we consummate our spousal rites.

Exeunt omnes [except Titus].

---

329   **climb** Saturninus is already aloft, and this makes it sound like he is at ground level. Bate, in Ard³, suggests that this may be a continuity error stemming from the addition of the killing of Mutius to this scene after the play's earliest performance but before its first printing. See also the note at 335 below.

333–4 **handmaid ... youth** Tamora indicates that she will be a servant who will fulfil Saturninus' desires, and a nurse and mother who will love and nurture him (which might be taken to infantilize the emperor and reverse the inherent power dynamic of the situation). Tamora gives birth at 4.2.50, and it does not seem that months have elapsed, so it is possible to imagine that the young Saturninus is here attracted to her pregnant, maternal body. But Saturninus later presumes the child is his, which would suggest that he does not register here that she is pregnant. We are not aware of any contemporary production of the play that stages Tamora as visibly pregnant in Acts 1–2. See also 4.2.50n.

335   ***Ascend ... Pantheon** see the note at 243 above; the word 'Pantheon' gave the compositors of Q1 and the other early texts trouble, both here and at l. 243 (where it is rendered as 'Pathan'). Here, following Q1, the early texts have 'Panthean', which is apparently mistaken for an adjectival form modifying Lords. Pope's sensible emendation has been widely accepted. As with 'climb' at 329, Saturninus' 'ascend' may be an error, since he is already aloft, or perhaps it indicates to the audience that his offstage movement should simply be imagined as a further ascent.

338   **Whose wisdom ... conquered** whose wisdom (in accepting his offer of marriage) has overcome the prior setback to her fortunes
       conquered conquerèd

339   **There** i.e., at the Pantheon

339 SD *Exeunt omnes* (Latin) 'they all exit'

335] Q1; F lines Qeene, / accompany /   Ascend ... Lords] Pope subst.; Ascend faire Queene: Panthean Lords Q1; Ascend Faire Qeene, Panthean Lords F   339 SD except Titus] Theobald subst.

TITUS

    I am not bid to wait upon this bride.   340

    Titus, when wert thou wont to walk alone,

    Dishonoured thus and challenged of wrongs?

       Enter MARCUS *and Titus' sons* [LUCIUS, QUINTUS, *and* MARTIUS].

MARCUS

    O Titus, see! O, see what thou hast done:

    In a bad quarrel slain a virtuous son.

TITUS

    No, foolish tribune, no. No son of mine,   345

    Nor thou, nor these, confederates in the deed

    That hath dishonoured all our family,

    Unworthy brother, and unworthy sons.

LUCIUS

    But let us give him burial, as becomes:

    Give Mutius burial with our brethren.   350

TITUS

    Traitors, away. He rests not in this tomb.

    This monument five hundred years hath stood,

    Which I have sumptuously re-edified.

    Here none but soldiers and Rome's servitors

    Repose in fame. None basely slain in brawls.   355

    Bury him where you can, he comes not here.

---

340   **wait upon** attend to; Titus notes that he is not invited to participate in the Emperor's wedding.
342   **challenged** challengèd; accused
346   **Nor thou, nor these** Titus disavows kinship with Marcus and his remaining sons.
349   **as becomes** as is proper or becoming
350   **brethren** pronounced with three syllables
353   **re-edified** rebuilt, restored
354   **servitors** servants

342.1 LUCIUS, QUINTUS, and MARTIUS] *Rowe subst.*

MARCUS

My lord, this is impiety in you.

My nephew Mutius' deeds do plead for him:

He must be buried with his brethren.

QUINTUS *and* MARTIUS

And shall, or him we will accompany. 360

TITUS

And shall? What villain was it spake that word?

QUINTUS

He that would vouch it in any place but here.

TITUS

What, would you bury him in my despite?

357 **impiety** absence of reverence or filial duty (*OED* 1, 2); this rebuts the initial idea of Titus as one 'surnamed Pious' (23) and echoes the Goths' description of Titus' sacrifice of Alarbus at 130.

359 **brethren** pronounced with three syllables (as at 350)

360 SP *Quintus and Martius are named only in the SPs for 2.2, and they are never spoken of by name by other characters in the play. In the SPs and SDs of 1.1 they are simply referred to as the second and third son. Ard³ leaves them unnamed in 1.1 since they 'serve their dramatic purpose better as an anonymous pair' (93). This is a fair assessment of the degree to which these sons are not individuated as characters, and arguments about who should get which speech here are based on slender evidence. Bolton ('Notes') assigns the second son's lines to Martius, on the grounds that he seems more spirited in 2.2. Bate (Ard³, 95) suggests that Quintus may be the second son here, both because he initiates the dialogue in 2.2 and because his name suggests that he is the fifth of Titus' 25 sons and thus among the oldest of them. Since lines given to these characters do need to be spoken by individual actors, we here give the second son's lines to Quintus and the third son's lines to Martius.

361 **What ... word** Titus, who objects to the assertiveness implied by his sons' peremptory 'shall', wants to pin the blame on one of them.

362 SP *If the two sons together speak 360, then Titus' demand in 361 amounts to a request to know which of them to single out as leader. The early texts do not specify which of the two sons answers (the early texts only indicate that 'Titus sonne speakes') but it would make sense if the elder of the two came forward. In the subsequent exchange (370–1, where lines are given to the third and second son respectively in the early texts), the third son is more cautious and the second more assertive.

362 **vouch** defend

363 **in my despite** in contemptuous defiance of me (*OED* despite *n.* 5.a)

360 SP] Capell subst.; 2 & 3 sons Ard³; not in Qq, F, but implied by SD Titus two sonnes speakes   362 SP] Rowe subst.; Qq, F have centred SD Titus sonne speakes   vouch] Qq; vouch'd F

MARCUS

No, noble Titus, but entreat of thee
To pardon Mutius and to bury him.   365

TITUS

Marcus, even thou hast struck upon my crest
And with these boys mine honour thou hast wounded.
My foes I do repute you, every one,
So trouble me no more, but get you gone.

MARTIUS

He is not with himself; let us withdraw.   370

QUINTUS

Not I, till Mutius' bones be buried.
                The brother and the sons kneel.

MARCUS

Brother, for in that name doth nature plead –

QUINTUS

Father, and in that name doth nature speak –

TITUS

Speak thou no more, if all the rest will speed.

MARCUS

Renowned Titus, more than half my soul –   375

---

366   **crest** an emblematic figure worn on a soldier's helmet; since Titus associates his crest, figuratively, with
      family honour, the term as he uses it has heraldic connotations that are anachronistic to the play's
      Rome (on which see also 196n. above).
370 SP *F assigns this line to '1. Sonne', and some editors have followed suit by giving the line to Lucius. Since
      Lucius is named in SPs in this exchange, the Qq reading ('3. Sonne.') seems preferable. We here continue
      to assign the third son's lines to Martius (see 360n).
      not with himself not in full possession of his faculties; not himself
371   **buried** burièd
374   **speed** succeed or prosper
375   **Renowned** renownèd

---

366 struck] *Qq, F (stroke)* 370 SP] *Malone subst.; 3. Sonne. Qq; 1. Sonne. F; Luc. / Rowe*   371 SP] *Rowe subst.;
2. Sonne. Qq, F*   373 SP] *Rowe subst.; 2. Sonne. Qq, F*

LUCIUS

    Dear father, soul and substance of us all—

MARCUS

    Suffer thy brother Marcus to inter

    His noble nephew here in virtue's nest,

    That died in honour and Lavinia's cause.

    Thou art a Roman, be not barbarous.   380

    The Greeks upon advice did bury Ajax

    That slew himself, and wise Laertes' son

    Did graciously plead for his funerals;

    Let not young Mutius then, that was thy joy,

    Be barred his entrance here.   385

TITUS   Rise, Marcus, rise, [*They rise.*]

    The dismal'st day is this that e'er I saw;

    To be dishonoured by my sons in Rome.

    Well, bury him, and bury me the next.   *They put him in the tomb.*

LUCIUS

    There lie thy bones, sweet Mutius, with thy friends,

    Till we with trophies do adorn thy tomb.   390

381–3 **The Greeks ... funerals** In the aftermath of the Trojan War, the hero Ajax, who was infuriated not to have been given the armour of Achilles, vowed revenge against the leaders of the Greek army. Athena filled him with delusional madness, such that he instead wreaked his revenge upon the cattle and herdsman serving the Greek army. Ashamed, Ajax killed himself, and Odysseus ('Laertes' son') persuaded the Greek generals to bury him instead of leaving his body to be eaten by wild animals. The tale is told in Sophocles' *Ajax*. Marcus, in effect, asks Titus to treat Mutius' actions as a form of temporary madness equivalent to Ajax's and thus to allow him burial accordingly. Editors since Steevens have wondered how Shakespeare knew this story (see the discussion in Ritson, 157–8), but Peele, who is now thought to have written this scene, was definitely familiar with some Greek tragedy.

389   **friends** kinsmen (*OED* 3)

390   **trophies** items commemorating military victories; in spite of Titus' objections, Lucius treats Mutius as an honourable military hero.

382 wise] *Qq; not in F*   385 SD] *Bevington*

ALL [*kneeling*]

No man shed tears for noble Mutius,
He lives in fame that died in virtue's cause.

Exit all but Marcus and Titus.

MARCUS

My lord, to step out of these sudden dumps,
How comes it that the subtle queen of Goths
Is of a sudden thus advanced in Rome?   395

TITUS

I know not, Marcus, but I know it is –
Whether by device or no, the heavens can tell.
Is she not then beholden to the man
That brought her for this high good turn so far?   399
Yes, and will nobly him remunerate.   *Flourish.*

---

391   The early texts and most editors have all of the Andronici kneeling and participating here.
[SP and SD] Bate, in Ard³, points out that it is odd to have Titus participating in this after so strenuously
            opposing Mutius' burial, and so excludes him. These lines read like a purely ritualistic
            utterance, however, so when Titus agrees to Mutius' burial he may also be agreeing to speak
            these words, however reluctantly, over his body.
393   **step out of** change the subject from
            dumps fits of melancholy
394   **subtle** cunning, wily, or devious (*OED adj.* 2.a)
397   **by device** i.e., by Tamora's contrivance
398   **the man** i.e., Titus, without whom Tamora would not have been brought to Rome in the
            first place
400   **Yes … remunerate** This line, which is not present in Qq, concludes Titus' speech in F. Dyce
            assigned the line to Marcus, and editors since then have been divided as to its assignment.
            Bate, in Ard³, finds its 'worldly-wise, ironic tone' characteristic of Marcus and so treats it as
            his reply to Titus. But (as Waith argues in Oxf²), the 'naïve confidence in Tamora's gratitude is
            more characteristic of Titus'.

---

391 SP and SD] Qq, F (*centred SD they all kneele and say*); MARCUS & TITUS' SONS [*kneeling*] Ard³   392 SD]
Qq; Exit F   393 sudden] F; dreary Qq   398 beholden] Qq, F (*beholding*)   400 Yes … remunerate] F; *not in*
Qq; Dyce (*conj. Malone*) *assigns to Marcus*   400 SD1 Flourish.] F, *not in Qq*

Enter the Emperor [SATURNINUS], TAMORA *and her two sons* [CHIRON
and DEMETRIUS], *with* [AARON] *the Moor at one door. Enter at the
other door* BASSIANUS *and* LAVINIA, *with* [LUCIUS, QUINTUS, *and* MARTIUS].

SATURNINUS

So, Bassianus, you have played your prize;
God give you joy, sir, of your gallant bride.

BASSIANUS

And you of yours, my lord, I say no more,
Nor wish no less, and so I take my leave.

SATURNINUS

Traitor, if Rome have law, or we have power,   405
Thou and thy faction shall repent this rape.

BASSIANUS

'Rape' call you it, my lord, to seize my own,
My true betrothed love, and now my wife?
But let the laws of Rome determine all;
Meanwhile am I possesed of that is mine.   410

SATURNINUS

'Tis good, sir. You are very short with us.
But if we live we'll be as sharp with you.

---

401   **you ... prize** entered into a sporting competition (*OED* prize *n.*³ 2); treating his brother's defence of a
       prior marriage agreement as a trivial contest is insultingly dismissive on Saturninus' part.
406   **rape** In idiomatic Early Modern English, as well as in both Roman and common law, the word 'rape'
       could be used to describe either the theft of a woman from another man (regardless of her consent)
       or a sexual assault (see, e.g., Helms, 557). Saturninus treats Bassianus' abduction of Lavinia as a type
       of theft. Bassianus' response is likewise about his property rights rather than about Lavinia's wishes or
       consent
408   **betrothed** betrothèd
411   **short** rudely abrupt, curt (*OED* II.10.a)

400.1 SATURNINUS *Rowe subst.*   400.1–2 CHIRON *and* DEMETRIUS] *Rowe subst.*   400.2 AARON] *Cam*¹   400.3 LUCIUS,
QUINTUS, *and* MARTIUS *Oxf*¹; *others Qq, F*   410 am I] *Q1*; I am *Q2–3, F*

BASSIANUS

   My lord, what I have done, as best I may,
   Answer I must, and shall do, with my life.
   Only thus much I give your grace to know: 415
   By all the duties that I owe to Rome,
   This noble gentleman, Lord Titus here,
   Is in opinion and in honour wronged,
   That in the rescue of Lavinia
   With his own hand did slay his youngest son   420
   In zeal to you, and highly moved to wrath
   To be controlled in that he frankly gave.
   Receive him then to favour, Saturnine,
   That hath expressed himself, in all his deeds,
   A father and a friend to thee and Rome.   425

TITUS

   Prince Bassianus, leave to plead my deeds:
   'Tis thou, and those, that have dishonoured me.
   [*Kneels.*] Rome and the righteous heavens be my judge
   How I have loved and honoured Saturnine.

TAMORA

   My worthy lord, if ever Tamora   430
   Were gracious in those princely eyes of thine,

---

418   **opinion** reputation
422   **To be** because he was
     controlled … gave i.e., Titus was angry about being restrained ('controlled') after he had freely ('frankly') given away Lavinia. The implication is that Titus had intended the bestowal of Lavinia to be a noble act of magnanimity.
426   **leave to plead** stop defending
427   **those** i.e., the other Andronici
428 SD   *As pointed out in Ard³, Titus is asked to rise at 461 so he must kneel: this seems like the most likely moment.

428 SD] *Bevington subst.*

Then hear me speak indifferently for all,
And at my suit, sweet, pardon what is past.

SATURNINUS
What, madam, be dishonoured openly,
And basely put it up without revenge?   435

TAMORA
Not so, my lord; the gods of Rome forfend
I should be author to dishonour you.
But on mine honour dare I undertake
For good Lord Titus' innocence in all,
Whose fury, not dissembled, speaks his griefs.   440
Then at my suit look graciously on him;
Lose not so noble a friend on vain suppose,
Nor with sour looks afflict his gentle heart.
[*aside, to Saturninus*]
My lord, be ruled by me, be won at last:
Dissemble all your griefs and discontents;   445
You are but newly planted in your throne.
Lest then the people, and patricians too,
Upon a just survey take Titus' part,

---

432   **indifferently** impartially
435   **put it up** set it aside; the phrase is an idiomatic metaphor derived from the fact that to put a sword
        or weapon up meant to sheathe it.
436   **forfend** forbid
437   **author** cause, source
438   **undertake** vouch
440   **fury** passionate disorder of mind (*OED* 1.a)
442   **vain suppose** unnecessary supposition
444 SD *Line 444 is indented in Qq, perhaps to indicate that this part of the speech is spoken as an aside to
        Saturninus. This extended aside marks a departure from the relentlessly public nature of discourse in
        the scene so far.
447   **people, and patricians** the plebeian commoners and the elite patrician class, from whom Saturninus
        had previously drawn support (as indicated at 1 above)
448   **survey** examination; the emphasis falls on the second syllable

---

436] Q1; F lines Lord, / for-fende, /   444] indented in Qq   444 SD] Rowe subst.; not in Qq, F

And so supplant you for ingratitude,
Which Rome reputes to be a heinous sin,　　　　450
Yield at entreats, and then let me alone.
I'll find a day to massacre them all,
And race their faction and their family –
The cruel father and his traitorous sons,
To whom I sued for my dear son's life –　　　　455
And make them know what 'tis to let a queen
Kneel in the streets and beg for grace in vain.
[to all] Come, come sweet emperor, come Andronicus.
Take up this good old man, and cheer the heart
That dies in tempest of thy angry frown.　　　　460

SATURNINUS
Rise, Titus, rise; my empress hath prevailed.

TITUS [Rises.]
I thank your majesty and her, my lord:
These words, these looks, infuse new life in me.

TAMORA
Titus, I am incorporate in Rome,
A Roman now, adopted happily,　　　　465
And must advise the Emperor for his good.
This day all quarrels die, Andronicus,

451　**at entreats** to entreaties
　　　let me alone leave it to me to take care of
453　**race** erase, eradicate; the word is often modernized to 'raze' which is nearly synonymous and
　　　etymologically similar, but see OED race v.² 2.b. and v.¹ 2.
457　**Kneel** The dramatic impact of Tamora's aside is amplified if Titus is also kneeling and awaiting
　　　Saturninus' forgiveness.
459　**Take up** both 'invite to stand up' and 'welcome back into your favour'
464　**incorporate** legally admitted to the body politic and figuratively absorbed into Rome
465　**adopted** taken voluntarily into any relationship legally or informally, as heir, father, friend, etc. (OED 2.a)

---

449 you] Q1–2; us Q3, F　　458 SD] Hanmer subst.　　461] Q1; F lines rise, / preuail'd.　　462 SD] Bevington
462-3] Q1; F lines Maiestie, / Lord. / looks, / me. /

And let it be mine honour, good my lord,
That I have reconciled your friends and you.
For you, Prince Bassianus, I have passed   470
My word and promise to the Emperor
That you will be more mild and tractable.
And fear not, lords, and you, Lavinia:
By my advice, all humbled on your knees,
You shall ask pardon of his majesty.   475
  [*Marcus, Lavinia, Lucius, Quintus, and Martius kneel.*]

LUCIUS

We do, and vow to heaven and to his highness
That what we did was mildly as we might,
Tendering our sister's honour and our own.

MARCUS

That, on mine honour, here do I protest.

SATURNINUS

Away, and talk not; trouble us no more.   [*He begins to leave.*]   480

---

476 SP   *The Q1 text has no SP here, and 476–8 are there set as a continuation of Tamora's speech, which is
          self-evidently erroneous. The compositor of Q3, noting the error, assigns the speech to 'All', which
          suits the overall tenor of the moment but disregards the fact that its mention of 'our sister's honour'
          implies a more specific relationship. F assigns the speech to an unspecified 'Son', which has the virtue
          of being responsive to the relationship claimed in the lines themselves. The assignment of the speech
          to Lucius, which makes dramatic sense given his authority as the eldest son, was first made by Rowe.
477   **mildly as we might** as calmly and moderately as we could
478   **Tendering** having regard for
479   **That** i.e., that he too was acting in defence of Lavinia's honour and that of her brothers (and not out
          of disrespect to the emperor)
480 SD   *At 483, Tamora asks Saturninus to 'look back'. This could be construed figuratively as a request to
          remember – as if Tamora calls on Saturninus to remember himself and reconsider his impulse to
          peevishness – but it makes more sense to read it (as in Bevington) as a response to onstage action
          indicating that Saturninus has begun to turn away and leave.

473] Q1; F lines Lords: / Lavinia, /   475 SD] Oxf²   476] Q1; F lines doe, / Highnes, /   SP] Rowe; no SP Q1–2;
indented Q2; All Q3; Son F   479 do I] Q1; I do Q2–3, F   480 SD] this edn; He turns away. Bevington

TAMORA

    Nay, nay, sweet emperor, we must all be friends.

    The tribune and his nephews kneel for grace.

    I will not be denied. Sweetheart, look back.

SATURNINUS

    Marcus, for thy sake, and thy brother's here,

    And at my lovely Tamora's entreats,   485

    I do remit these young men's heinous faults:

    Stand up.   [*Marcus and the others rise.*]

    Lavinia, though you left me like a churl,

    I found a friend, and sure as death I swore

    I would not part a bachelor from the priest.

    Come, if the Emperor's court can feast two brides,   490

    You are my guest, Lavinia, and your friends.

    This day shall be a love-day, Tamora.

---

486   **remit** pardon (*OED* I.3.a)

487   **Stand up** Qq and F all set the phrase 'stand up' as if it were the start of 488, which creates an uncharacteristically long and hypermetrical line. Pope, ever attentive to metre, omitted the phrase, and Capell (whom we follow here) preserved the metre of 488 by relineating 'stand up' as a curt and commanding stand-alone line. Dyce speculated that 'stand up' might actually be a mis-set stage direction, since the Andronici have all recently knelt to Saturninus. But Waith (in Oxf[2]) notes that most (if not all: see the SD at 2.3.116) of the stage directions in Q1 take the form of statements, and that one would therefore expect a misplaced SD to read 'they stand up'.

488   **churl** a person of low rank (*OED* 2.a); pejoratively, the opposite of a king, noble, or person of rank (*OED* 2.b)

481] Q1; F *lines* nay, / friends, /   484] Q1; F *lines Marcus,* / heere,   487 Stand up] Qq,F; *om. Pope; as SD Dyce*
487–88 Stand ... churl] *Capell subst.; one line in* Qq,F   487 SD] *Dyce*[2] *subst.*   489 swore] Qq; sware F

TITUS

Tomorrow, and it please your majesty
To hunt the panther and the hart with me   495
With horn and hound, we'll give your grace *bonjour.*

SATURNINUS

Be it so, Titus, and gramercy too.   *Exeunt.*

494   **and** if
495   **the panther and the hart** panthers and stags; the choice of panthers is striking. Staged hunts and
         gladiatorial events involving panthers in Rome required the animals to be imported, a practice which
         dates back to the defeat of Carthage in the Punic Wars. The use of panthers was therefore connected
         to imperial magnificence and exotic display. Peele might have been familiar with this practice from
         reading Cicero's *Epistulae ad Familiares*, which contains letters from Marcus Caelius Rufus to Cicero
         when he was governor in Cilicia (in what is now Turkey) asking for panthers to be sent to Rome for
         games (See Cicero, *Letters*, 1.78, 82, 88, 90).
496   ***bonjour*** (French) 'good morning'; Titus' use of French is anachronistic to the play's Rome, but (given
         early modern English stereotypes) likely signals an attempt on Titus' part to adopt a courtly tone as
         suitable for royal festivities.
497   **gramercy** thank you
497 SD Act divisions were first added in F, which also clears the stage here and has Aaron re-enter at the
         beginning of Act 2. In the quarto texts, which do not have act divisions, the SDs here specify that Aaron
         remains on stage. We follow F, using the logic that if the added act divisions reflect evolving theatrical
         practice (rather than just textual convention) then the way F handles Aaron's soliloquy may do so as
         well. See the Introduction, p. 29.

496] Q1; F lines Hound, / iour. /   497 SD] F; Exeunt. sound trumpets, manet Moore Qq

[2.1]   *Flourish. Enter* AARON *alone.*

AARON

Now climbeth Tamora Olympus' top,
Safe out of fortune's shot, and sits aloft,
Secure of thunder's crack or lightning flash,
Advanced above pale envy's threatening reach,
As when the golden sun salutes the morn,   5
And having gilt the ocean with his beams,
Gallops the zodiac in his glistering coach,

0.1   ***Flourish*** Since flourishes are most frequently used to announce the entrance of a politically important personage, as at the start of this play (see Dessen and Thomson), it is odd that F adds one here at the start of the second act for the entry of Aaron. In Qq, where there are no act divisions, a trumpet sounds to indicate the departure of the Emperor and his court, and Aaron remains on stage, so the Flourish here may be a holdover suggested by that older staging. At the same time, the flourish as it appears in F seems also to take Aaron at his own estimation, perhaps lending sonic contextualization to the boasts he makes in the soliloquy that follows, and it may also signal something metadramatic about how the importance of the character was expected to be understood in revival by those audience members who might have been at least broadly familiar with this long-popular play.

1   **Olympus' top** Mount Olympus was the home of the gods in Greco-Roman mythology. This reference is an indicator of Aaron's fluency with the cultural codes of his Roman captors, which is already on full display in this first soliloquy.

2   **out of ... shot** out of range of being hurt by anything Fortune shoots

3   **Secure of** safe from

4   **above** F's alternative reading – 'about' – is likely just a compositorial misreading of Q3's 'aboue'.
      pale envy's Envy is commonly imagined as pale in early modern texts, as near the end of *H5* where the chalky shores of England and France are said to be 'pale / With envy of each other's happiness' (5.2.244–5). Aaron is later shown to be especially attuned to discourses concerning skin colour and may use the phrase for this reason.

7   **Gallops ... coach** Tamora in her new pride of place is compared to the sun riding through the sky in a shining ('glistering') coach. The image of the sun's chariot galloping across the zodiac is a characteristically Peelean way of representing celestial movement. Compare this, from the opening speech of Peele's *Descensus Astraeae* (1591): 'Time hath turnd his restles wheele about / And made the silver moone: & heavens bright eie / Gallop the Zodiacke and end the yere' (Peele, *Descensus*, sig. A2^r).

2.1] *Actus Secunda F; not in Qq.*   0.1] F; *Sound trumpets, manet Moore Qq*   4 above] *Qq; about F*

And overlooks the highest-peering hills:

So Tamora.

Upon her wit doth earthly honour wait, 10

And virtue stoops and trembles at her frown.

Then, Aaron, arm thy heart and fit thy thoughts

To mount aloft with thy imperial mistress,

And mount her pitch, whom thou in triumph long

Hast prisoner held, fettered in amorous chains 15

And faster bound to Aaron's charming eyes

Than is Prometheus tied to Caucasus.

Away with slavish weeds and servile thoughts.

---

8   **overlooks** looks down upon, as from on high
      highest-peering Aaron's image is of the sun looking down upon hills, but the hills are here also imagined as 'peering'. Since Aaron is expressing delight about Tamora's new social elevation, there may be a punning reference to 'peers' as members of the highest ranks of the nobility: she now flies above the highest peers.

10   **wit** intelligence or cleverness

11   **virtue stoops** (1) virtuous people will be over-awed by Tamora; (2) she now has power to subvert virtue

14   **mount her pitch** a hawking term, meaning to rise to a height (*OED* pitch *n.*² V.21.c); but Aaron is also using suggestive language that has other connotations: he combines a sexually suggestive phrase, meaning to copulate (as associated with *OED* mount II.14.a.; see also Partridge), with a racially suggestive word 'pitch', which could also refer to a 'tenacious resinous substance, of a black or brown colour' and which comes to mean blackness in general and defilement in particular (*OED* pitch *n.*¹).

14–15   **in triumph ... chains** Aaron entered the play (at 1.1.70) as a prisoner on display in Titus' triumph, so he also imagines his own amorous power over Tamora as analogous to a Roman military conquest. Aaron is characteristically sensitive to Roman modes of expression, and characteristically creative in his appropriation and redeployment of them. The image may also serve to extend the hawking image implied by 'mount her pitch', envisioning Tamora as a hawk tethered to Aaron, her falconer, with chains.

16   **charming** magically enchanting

17   **Prometheus ... Caucasus** The titan Prometheus stole fire from the gods and gave it to humankind. For this, he was punished by being chained to a rock in the Caucasus mountains where every day an eagle would devour his eternally regenerating liver. Elsewhere, Peele similarly uses the story to figure the emotional extremity of love: 'Advise my love be rendered to my hand: / Tell them the Chaines that *Mulciber* erst made, / To tie Prometheus lims to Caucasus, / Nor furies phanges shal hold me long from her' (Peele, *Edw. 1*, sigs D1ᵛ–D2ᵛ).

18   **Away ... slavish weeds** Weeds are clothes. The phrase is not just a figure of speech, since Aaron was an enslaved prisoner of war in Titus' triumph. In the seventeenth-century German play based on the same story, the Aaron character (named Morian) throws off his ragged old cloak during his initial soliloquy in anticipation of his new alliance with the emperor (*Tito* 1.1.83 SD). Aaron might do the same here, or maybe Peele's speech merely contains a verbal recollection of a staging from an earlier

---

18 servile] *Q1–2*; idle *Q3, F*

I will be bright and shine in pearl and gold
To wait upon this new-made empress.   20
To wait, said I? To wanton with this queen,
This goddess, this Semiramis, this nymph,
This siren that will charm Rome's Saturnine,
And see his shipwreck and his commonweal's.
Hallo, what storm is this?   25

Enter CHIRON *and* DEMETRIUS *braving.*

DEMETRIUS

Chiron, thy years wants wit, thy wits wants edge
And manners, to intrude where I am graced,

---

19   *Titus* play from which the German play also derived. In Blanche McIntyre's 2017 RSC production, Aaron (played by Stefan Adegbola) took off his prisoner's clothing here, but Michael Sexton's 2011 Public Lab production had Aaron (played by Ron Cephus Jones) dressed in a tight-fitting business suit from the beginning.

19   **pearl and gold** precious goods symbolic of the wealth of empire; Aaron imagines himself both partaking in this opulence and as serving an ornamental function in Tamora's court.

20   **empress** pronounced as a three-syllable word (and Q1 has 'Emperesse')

21   **wanton** indulge in amorous or lascivious behaviour (*OED v.* 1.c)

22   **Semiramis** pronounced with the accent on the second syllable; a legendary Queen of Assyria; judging from a survey of allusions to her in other early modern texts, audiences likely associated the name with exoticism, beauty, queenly governance, impetuousness and/or lascivious desire.

23–4   **siren ... shipwreck** Sirens, in classical myth, are creatures who lure sailors to their death with enchanting song.

25   **Hallo** an exclamation of surprise

25.1   *braving* swaggering and challenging each other; Chiron and Demetrius here reprise the theme of sibling rivalry associated with Saturninus and Bassianus in Act 1.

26   **thy years ... edge** This is Q1's version of the line, and the use of 'wants' with a plural noun was grammatically acceptable in Elizabethan English (Hope 2.1.8a). The line was changed in Q2 to read 'thy wits want'. F2 first brought the line into alignment with idiomatic modern English ('thy years want wit, thy wits want edge').

         thy years Chiron is a 'year or two' (2.1.31) younger than Demetrius, but their ages are not otherwise specified. Most modern productions cast the brothers as being in their early twenties, but the age of the actors playing these characters can have a significant impact how they are perceived. In Lise Bruneau's 2013 Riot Grrrls (all-female) production, the actors playing Chiron and Demetrius (Amanda Forstom and Teresa Spencer) were dressed and staged as teenage boys. That same year, Michael Fentiman's RSC production also staged Tamora's sons as teenagers (Jonny Weldon and Perry Millward).

---

22 nymph] *Q1–2*; Queene *Q3, F*   26 years wants] *Qq, F*; years want *F2*   wits wants] *Q1*; wit wants *Q2–3, F*

And may, for ought thou knowest, affected be.

CHIRON

Demetrius, thou dost overween in all,
And so in this, to bear me down with braves.   30
'Tis not the difference of a year or two
Makes me less gracious, or thee more fortunate;
I am as able and as fit as thou
To serve, and to deserve my mistress' grace,
And that my sword upon thee shall approve,   35
And plead my passions for Lavinia's love.

AARON

Clubs, clubs! These lovers will not keep the peace.

DEMETRIUS

Why, boy, although our mother, unadvised,
Gave you a dancing-rapier by your side,
Are you so desperate grown to threat your friends?   40
Go to. Have your lath glued within your sheath,
Till you know better how to handle it.

CHIRON

Meanwhile, sir, with the little skill I have,
Full well shalt thou perceive how much I dare.

DEMETRIUS

Aye, boy, grow ye so brave?   *They draw.*

---

28   **affected** loved
29   **overween** presume superiority
30   **to bear ... braves** to oppose me strongly with swaggering challenges
35   **approve** prove
37   **Clubs, clubs** i.e., 'bring clubs': an idiomatic expression used to call for armed assistance, here used sarcastically as if calling for intercession to help stop a brawl in the streets; compare the character Simplicity in *The Three Lords and Three Ladies of London* (1590): 'Clubs, clubs, nay come neighbours come, for here ... I left them, arrant theeves, rogues, cosoners' (Wilson, *Three*, sig. F4ᵛ).
38   **unadvised** imprudently
39   **dancing-rapier** a sword worn only as an ornament at a dance; Demetrius implies that Chiron is too immature to carry a real sword. Since a sword is a commonplace symbol of phallic potency this is also a sexual slight.
40   **threat** threaten
41   **Go to** an expression of defiant indifference
      lath a strip of wood used to make a pretend weapon

AARON Why, how now, lords? 45
So near the Emperor's palace dare ye draw
And maintain such a quarrel openly?
Full well I wot the ground of all this grudge.
I would not for a million of gold
The cause were known to them it most concerns, 50
Nor would your noble mother for much more
Be so dishonoured in the court of Rome.
For shame put up.

DEMETRIUS Not I, till I have sheathed
My rapier in his bosom, and withal
Thrust those reprochful speeches down his throat 55
That he hath breathed in my dishonour here.

CHIRON
For that I am prepared and full resolved,
Foul-spoken coward, that thundrest with thy tongue,
And with thy weapon nothing dar'st perform.

AARON
Away, I say! 60
Now, by the gods that warlike Goths adore,
This pretty brabble will undo us all.

---

47   **maintain** The metrical stress falls on the first syllable.
48   **wot** know, understand
49   **million** pronounced with three syllables
51   **for much more** i.e., for much more than a million of gold
53   **put up** sheathe, put away (your sword)
54   **withal** in addition
55   **Thrust ... throat** as in the modern idiomatic phrase 'to make somebody eat their words'
61   **by ... adore** It is characteristic of Aaron to appeal to the gods whom others worship rather than invoking a belief system of his own.
62   **pretty** unwelcome (this ironic use is OED 3.c)
        brabble noisy dispute

---

46 ye] Q1; you Q2–3, F   55 those] Q1–2; these Q3, F   58] Q1; F lines Coward, / tongue, /   62 pretty] F; petty Qq

Why, lords, and think you not how dangerous
It is to set upon a prince's right?
What, is Lavinia then become so loose,   65
Or Bassianus so degenerate,
That for her love such quarrels may be broached
Without controlment, justice, or revenge?
Young lords, beware; and should the Empress know
This discord's ground, the music would not please.   70

CHIRON

I care not, I, knew she and all the world!
I love Lavinia more than all the world.

DEMETRIUS

Youngling, learn thou to make some meaner choice:
Lavinia is thine elder brother's hope.

AARON

Why, are ye mad? Or know ye not in Rome   75
How furious and impatient they be,
And cannot brook competitors in love?
I tell you, lords, you do but plot your deaths,
By this device.

64   **set upon** attack
67   **broached** publicly aired
68   **controlment** constraint
69–70   **should ... please** a metaphor that links social conflict to unpleasant music, including puns on the
        terms 'ground' (the melody on which a descant is raised [*OED* II.6.c.]) and 'discord' as implying the
        musical term chord
71   **knew she ... world** if Tamora and the whole world knew
73   **Youngling** youngster
        meaner more common, of lower status
76   **impatient** pronounced with four syllables
77   **brook** tolerate
79–81   **By ... strange** This exchange, as laid out here, draws on a tradition of editorial relineation that dates
        back to Hanmer and whose aim is to leave as few partial lines as possible. The premise behind such
        emendation is that the play is largely composed in blank verse, and so hanging half-lines that could
        easily be resolved into iambic lines that scan well without creating other problems probably reflect
        compositor's errors and should be emended. In Qq and F Chiron's iambic line is 'Aaron, a thousand
        deaths would I propose', which means that in all the early texts the preceding half-line ('By this
        device') is left as an unmetrical stub. We adopt a relineation first proposed in Bevington, where the
        exchange is resolved into a series of interlocking metrical lines.

64 set] *F; jet Qq*   70 discord's] *Qq; discord F*   73] *Q1; F lines* Youngling, / choise, /   79–81] *Bevington;
Qq, F lines* deuise. / propose / loue / how / strange? /; *Hanmer lines* device. / deaths / love. / how! / strange?/

CHIRON   Aaron, a thousand deaths
Would I propose to achieve her whom I love.   80
AARON
To achieve her how?
DEMETRIUS   Why mak'st thou it so strange?
She is a woman, therefore may be wooed;
She is a woman, therefore may be won;
She is Lavinia, therefore must be loved.
What, man? More water glideth by the mill   85
Than wots the miller of, and easy it is
Of a cut loaf to steal a shive, we know.
Though Bassianus be the Emperor's brother,
Better than he have worn Vulcan's badge.

80   **to achieve ... love** To achieve means 'to accomplish some objective', so this formulation treats Lavinia
        as a prize to be schemed for (as Aaron immediately recognizes). There is a striking parallel here with
        sonnet 15 of Barnabe Barnes' roughly contemporary Petrarchan sonnet sequence *Parthenophil and
        Parthenophe* (printed in 1593), where the lover complains that he is 'Barr'd from her loves which my
        desertes atchived' (15, l. 4, in Barnes). Barnes's sequence, notably, ends with a vivid and disturbing
        rape fantasy. It is unclear whether Barnes's sequence was written before or after this scene, or if Peele
        could have known it, but it seems clear that both pieces explore the violent potential implicit in the
        conventional language of love in similar ways.
        to achieve pronounced as two syllables ('t'achieve'), both here and in the next line
81   **Why ... strange** 'why do you make it out to be so surprising?'
82–3   **She ... won** proverbial (Dent, W681: 'All women may be won'); Demetrius has recourse to generalizing,
        proverbial language to rebut Aaron's claim that his behaviour is inappropriate in Rome in particular.
85–7   **More water ... know** Demetrius continues to defend himself by drawing upon proverbial language,
        here combining Dent, W99 ('Much water goes by the mill that the miller knows not of') and Dent,
        T34 ('It is safe taking a shive of a cut loaf'). The rusticity of these expressions is jarring after the more
        elevated (if still conventional) love talk earlier in the scene.
87   **shive** slice of bread; the sense of this crude remark is that once a woman has lost her virginity it is
        easier for another man to have illicit sex with her without arousing suspicion.
89   **Better ... Vulcan's badge** The god Vulcan was cuckolded when his wife Venus slept with Mars;
        'Vulcan's badge' is therefore the sign of the cuckold (i.e., horns). This is an unmetrical line unless an
        extra syllable is added to the pronunciation of either 'worn' or 'Vulcan's'. The latter is perhaps more
        likely, since Vulcan is often referred to by the Latinate name *Vulcanus* in early modern texts.

80 love] Q1–2; do loue Q3, F   81 mak'st] F; makes Qq

AARON [*aside*]

    Aye, and as good as Saturninus may.   90

DEMETRIUS

    Then why should he despair that knows to court it

    With words, fair looks, and liberality?

    What, hast not thou full often struck a doe

    And borne her cleanly by the keeper's nose?

AARON

    Why then, it seemes some certain snatch or so   95

    Would serve your turns.

CHIRON   Aye, so the turn were served.

DEMETRIUS

    Aaron, thou hast hit it.

AARON   Would you had hit it, too,

    Then should not we be tired with this ado.

    Why, hark ye, hark ye, and are you such fools

    To square for this? Would it offend you, then,   100

    That both should speed?

CHIRON

    Faith, not me.

---

91   **knows to court it** knows how to woo elegantly, like a courtier

93–4   **struck … nose** struck and killed a deer and then snuck the body out adroitly past the gamekeeper

95   **snatch** a trap or snare (*OED n.* 2), a quick grab at something (*OED n.* 3), and a crude, colloquial expression for female genitalia (*OED n.* 6b and 14)

96   **turns** carries a euphemistic sexual sense; Partridge's glossary notes several instances, including the exchange from *A&C* where Cleopatra asks what 'good turn' Antony has gone to Octavia for and is told that he has gone 'for the best turn i'th' bed' (2.5.58–9).

97   **hit … hit** Demetrius uses a hunting metaphor to indicate that Aaron is correct: he has hit the bullseye; Aaron adds a sexual meaning in his response. Partridge lists several instances in Shakespeare where the word 'hit' has a sexual connotation, as it does here. Aaron's sense is 'if you had already had sex with Lavinia, we would not now be dealing with this disturbance'.

100   **square for** quarrel over

101   **That … speed?** This half-line is missing in F, and the question mark is there moved up to the end of the previous line. The omission makes the sense of Aaron's question hard to follow and so seems like an error.

       speed succeed

90 SD] *Theobald*   93 struck] *Q1* (stroke); strucke *Q3, F*   101 That … speed?] *Qq; not in F*

DEMETRIUS   Nor me, so I were one.

AARON

For shame, be friends, and join for that you jar:
'Tis policy and stratagem must do
That you affect, and so must you resolve   105
That what you cannot as you would achieve,
You must perforce accomplish as you may.
Take this of me: Lucrece was not more chaste
Than this Lavinia, Bassianus' love.
A speedier course than lingering languishment   110
Must we pursue, and I have found the path:
My lords, a solemn hunting is in hand;
There will the lovely Roman ladies troop.
The forest walks are wide and spacious,
And many unfrequented plots there are,   115
Fitted by kind for rape and villainy.

102   **so** so long as
103   **join … jar** join forces to get what you have been fighting over
104   **policy** cleverness
104–5 **do … affect** accomplish what you want
106–7 **what … you may** 'What you cannot achieve in the manner you'd like, you accomplish in the manner
       you can'. Aaron, having heard Chiron and Demetrius speak in proverbial language, uses it too in order
       to persuade them. Compare Dent, M554: 'Men must do as they may, not as they would'.
108   **Take … me** take it from me
       Lucrece A virtuous Roman wife who killed herself after being raped by Tarquin, thus setting off the
       chain of events leading to the end of early Roman monarchy and the foundation of the republic.
       A well-known story with thematic implications for the play's depiction of Rome. See the discussion in
       the Introduction at pp. 62–4.
110   ***than** Qq and F all have 'this', but Rowe's emendation is generally accepted; it would be easy for a
       compositor to err while glancing at the words 'than this' in the previous line.
       lingering languishment protracted lovesickness; lingering is spelled 'lingring' in Qq, F, and that also
       reflects pronunciation.
112   **solemn** stately, ceremonial
114   **spacious** The metre suggests that this would have been pronounced with three syllables.
115   **plots** areas, places
116   **by kind** by their nature

110 than] *Rowe;* this *Qq, F*

Single you thither then this dainty doe,
And strike her home by force, if not by words:
This way, or not at all, stand you in hope.
Come, come, our empress, with her sacred wit   120
To villany and vengeance consecrate,
Will we acquaint withal what we intend,
And she shall file our engines with advice,
That will not suffer you to square yourselves,
But to your wishes' height advance you both.   125
The Emperor's court is like the house of Fame,
The palace full of tongues, of eyes and ears.
The woods are ruthless, dreadful, deaf, and dull:
There speak, and strike, brave boys, and take your turns;
There serve your lusts, shadowed from heaven's eye,   130
And revel in Lavinia's treasury.

CHIRON

Thy counsel, lad, smells of no cowardice.

117   **Single** separate it from the herd, a phrase drawn from hunting (*OED v.*¹ 2)
        dainty delicately pretty
118   **strike her home** make an effective stroke with a weapon (*OED* home *adv.* 4.a)
        force ... if not words i.e., by rape, rather than persuasion
120–1   **sacred wit ... consecrate** Aaron's religious language suggests both that Tamora's wit is specially
        devoted to villainy and vengeance, and also that it is to be revered for its abilities. Bate (drawing on
        OED adj. and n. 6) makes the interesting suggestion in Ard³ that the word 'sacred' may also have the
        sense of accursed or horrible, as in the Latin root-word *sacer*. If Peele wrote this scene, as we now
        believe, it increases the likelihood that this Latinate sense of the word was intended at least as part
        of the connotation. Tamora's wit is thus perhaps sacred in the sense of being terrifyingly hungry for
        vengeance and villainy.
122   **acquaint withal** familiarize with
123   **file our engines** smooth out and refine our schemes
124   **to square yourselves** to fight with each other
126–7   **emperor's court ... ears** In Ovid's *Met.*, Fame is said to live in a house that 'roreth every way /
        Reporting dowble every word it heareth people say' (Golding, 12:51–2).
131   **treasury** goods, a euphemism for Lavinia's sexual body that downplays the violence of rape by
        opening up a second, allegorical meaning in which the Goth interlopers are able to seize upon the
        wealth of Rome
132   **smells ... cowardice** has nothing about it of cowardice

122 what] *Q1; that Q2–3, F*   127 and] *Q1–2; of Q3, F*   130 lusts] *F; lust Qq*

DEMETRIUS

Sit fas aut nefas; till I find the streams

To cool this heat, a charm to calm these fits,   134

Per Stygia, per manes vehor.   *Exeunt.*

[2.2]   *Enter* TITUS Andronicus *and his three sons* [LUCIUS, QUINTUS, *and*

MARTIUS], *making a noise with hounds and horns, and* MARCUS.

TITUS

The hunt is up, the moon is bright and grey,

The fields are fragrant, and the woods are green.

Uncouple here, and let us make a bay,

And wake the Emperor and his lovely bride,

And rouse the prince, and ring a hunter's peal,   5

That all the court may echo with the noise.

133   **Sit fas aut nefas** (Latin) 'be it right or wrong'; this is not a direct quotation, and indeed 'the conjunction
      of "*fas*" and "*nefas*" is proverbial enough not to require any particular source' (Chaudhuri, 794). Bate, in
      Ard³, suggests two thematically apt and well-known Latin texts that Peele (who wrote this scene) may
      have had in mind. They are: Horace, *Odes* 1.18.10–11, where Thracians in the throes of sexual desire
      are unable to distinguish between right and wrong ('*fas atque nefas*'); and from *Met.*, where Ovid is
      describing Procne's conflation of right and wrong ('*fasque nefasque / confusura ruit*', 6.585–6).
135   **Per Stygia, per manes vehor** (Latin) 'I am carried through the Stygian realms, through the realm of shades'.
      This is an adaptation or misquotation of a line from Seneca's *Phaedra*, where the queen, having caused her
      stepson's death by falsely accusing him of rape, regrets it and vows to pursue him to the underworld: '*per
      Styga, per amnes igneos amens sequar*' ('I will madly follow you through Styx and rivers of fire' [*Phae.*, 1180]).
      It is ironic that Demetrius, as he plans a rape, should allude in this way to a moment where Phaedra repents
      accusing Hippolytus of rape. Perhaps Peele is using this irony to characterize Demetrius, suggesting that
      he does not possess the same mastery of apt Latin allusions that other characters have? Changing *sequor*
      to *vehor* turns Phaedra's purposeful expression of regret and frustration into 'an expression of personal
      abandonment to evil' (Miola, *Classical*, 14); transposing the letters of *amnes* into *manes* also recalls the
      sacrifice of Alarbus *ad manes fratrum* at 1.1.98, so that Demetrius here alludes 'not only intertextually to
      Senecan tragedy but also intratextually to the sacrifice of Alarbus' (Chaudhuri, 796).
1   **moon** Q3 clarified the temporal setting by substituting 'morne', but the original idea seems to have
      been that this scene is taking place in early morning light with the moon still visible in the sky.
3   **Uncouple** release the dogs, previously fastened ('coupled') together, for the chase
      bay prolonged barking of hunting dogs in pursuit of their prey
5   **hunter's peal** 'horn-blowing to set the dogs barking' (Oxf²)
6   **court** Perhaps this indicates that Titus imagines their location as an outdoor courtyard of some kind, or
      perhaps the presence of the emperor and his retinue makes the woods seem like a royal court to him.

133 Sit] *Qq; Sij F*   133 streams] *F; streame Qq*   134 these] *Q1–2; their Q3, F*   2.2] *Rowe subst.; not
in Qq, F*   0.1 LUCIUS, QUINTUS, and MARTIUS] *Capell subst.*   0.2 and MARCUS] *F; not in Qq*   1 moon] *Q1–2;
morne Q3, F*

Sons, let it be your charge, as it is ours,
To attend the Emperor's person carefully.
I have been troubled in my sleep this night,
But dawning day new comfort hath inspired. 10

Here a cry of hounds, and wind horns in a peal: then enter SATURNINUS,
TAMORA, BASSIANUS, LAVINIA, CHIRON, DEMETRIUS, *and their* Attendants.

Many good morrows to your majesty;
Madam, to you as many and as good.
I promised your grace a hunter's peal.

SATURNINUS
And you have rung it lustily, my lords,
Somewhat too early for new-married ladies. 15

BASSIANUS
Lavinia, how say you?

LAVINIA   I say no.
I have been awake two hours and more.

SATURNINUS
Come on, then, horse and chariots let us have,
And to our sport. [*to Tamora*] Madam, now shall ye see
Our Roman hunting.

MARCUS   I have dogs, my lord, 20

8   **To attend** The metre requires elided pronunciation: 't'attend'.
10.1–2   The SD as printed here is substantially the same in all the early texts, but in F it is prefaced by an
         additional note to 'Winde Hornes'. Though we generally use the SDs from F in this edition, the
         addition seems redundant.
10.1   *cry* barking
        wind blow
13   **promised** promisèd
17   **I say no** Lavinia denies Saturninus' racy implication that all the new-married ladies might be tired
        out from their wedding nights and wanting to sleep in. This might be taken as prim, on Lavinia's
        part, though it could also just be her way of refusing the familiar intimacy presumed by Saturninus'
        remark.

10.1 *Here a cry of hounds, and wind horns in a peal*] Qq; *Winde Hornes. / Heere a cry of houndes, and winde
hornes in a peale* F   11 Qq, F repeats SP   16–17 *I ... more*] *lineated as* F; *one line in* Qq   17 been awake] F;
been broad awake Qq   19 SD] *Johnson*

Will rouse the proudest panther in the chase
And climb the highest promontory top.

TITUS

And I have horse will follow where the game
Makes way and runs like swallows o'er the plain.

DEMETRIUS [aside]

Chiron, we hunt not, we, with horse nor hound,   25
But hope to pluck a dainty doe to ground.   Exeunt.

[2.3]   Enter AARON alone [with a bag of gold, which he hides].

AARON

He that had wit would think that I had none,
To bury so much gold under a tree

---

21   **chase** hunting ground
22   **promontory** mountain ridge; the meaning of the word is close to that of its Latin root-word
        (*promunturium*).
24   **runs** grammatically, in this image, it is the wild game, scattering over the plain, that is chased by the horse
26   **dainty doe** Demetrius returns to the hunting metaphor used in 2.1 for the violent, non-consensual
        sexual act he and his brother intend.
0.1   ***with … hides** The early texts provide no stage directions for the business Aaron does here with the
        gold. Capell first added stage directions with Aaron's entrance indicating that he hides the bag of gold.
        Editors since Malone have divided Capell's SD into two, to indicate that Aaron enters with a bag of
        gold and then hides it at some point during or after his soliloquy. Malone added the SD 'hides the gold'
        after 8 and most editors have tended to follow suit or to place a similar SD at the end of the speech.
        There is little basis for specifying when Aaron hides the gold, but the simplest solution is to have him
        come out, hide the gold and then speak about his actions.
1–9   **He that … chest** Where Aaron's first soliloquy, at the beginning of 2.1, can be read as meditative or
        self-expressive, this one is more expository and seems to be addressed directly to the audience. This
        kind of direct audience address, which may have been associated with playful mastery over the layers
        of dramatic illusion that the audience is experiencing, is associated with theatrically improvisational
        stage villains dating back to the Vice figures in late-Medieval morality plays.
2   **under a tree** The recovery of the bag, later in this same scene, 'Among the nettles at the elder tree /
        Which overshades the mouth of that same pit' (272–3) suggests that the bag is hidden in or near the
        trapdoor. Waith (in *Oxf³*) notes the presence of a tree and moss banks as props in Henslowe's *Diary*
        and suggests that such items might have been used to make hiding the bag seem realistic. The woods
        in this scene are not imagined in consistent or realistic terms, however (see 93–8n. below), and a pillar
        or the trapdoor space could also have been used to indicate dramatically that the bag is hidden.

---

24 runs] Qq, F; runne F2   like] Qq; likes F   25 SD] Capell   26 SD] Q1 (Exeuut); Exeunt Q2–3, F   2.3] Capell
subst.; not in Qq, F   0.1 with a bag of gold, which he hides] Capell; not in Qq, F

And never after to inherit it.

Let him that thinks of me so abjectly

Know that this gold must coin a stratagem,   5

Which, cunningly effected, will beget

A very excellent piece of villainy.

And so repose, sweet gold, for their unrest,

That have their alms out of the Empress' chest.

Enter TAMORA *to the Moor.*

TAMORA

My lovely Aaron, wherefore look'st thou sad,   10

When everything doth make a gleeful boast?

The birds chant melody on every bush,

The snakes lies rolled in the cheerful sun,

The green leaves quiver with the cooling wind

And make a checkered shadow on the ground.   15

---

4   **thinks ... abjectly** considers me to be so low and servile
5   **coin** produce (a figurative use that is also a pun under the circumstances)
8–9   **And so ... chest** Aaron is implying that those who receive this money from Tamora's treasury will be
         discomfited by it. Later in the scene, we learn that Aaron and Tamora have staged things to make it
         appear that the money was meant for Titus' sons as payment for killing Bassianus, so in this sense it
         does bring unrest. But Aaron's rhetoric is also characteristically playful and complex, first contrasting
         the gold's own 'repose' with the unrest it will cause, and then hinting that Tamora's charitable
         generosity in providing the money ('alms') will bring about uncharitable results ('unrest').
10   **sad** serious
11   **gleeful boast** happy display
12–15   **The birds ... ground** Tamora's sustained description of her surroundings here provides an imaginary
         supplement to what would have been, by our standards, a bare stage. The description – birdsong,
         sunshine, a cooling breeze, shade – recalls numerous set-piece descriptions in classical literature
         of similarly idyllic landscapes, which came to be recognized as a trope or commonplace: the '*locus
         amoenus*' or pleasant place. Shakespeare (who is believed to have written most of the play from 2.2
         on) likely had in mind the many *loca amoena* in Ovid's *Metamorphoses*, where 'there is a characteristic
         tension ... between the beautiful setting and the sufferings which befall most of the characters
         who inhabit or enter it'; the play exploits the way such descriptions in Ovid seem to 'provide a
         narratological "cue" for' subsequent episodes of sexual violence (Hinds, 130–1).
13   **snakes lies** The agreement of a plural noun with what looks to us like a singular, third-person, present-
         tense verb is grammatically acceptable in Elizabethan English (see also 2.1.26n.). Here, it also echoes
         'birds' in the previous line.
         rolled rollèd

9.1 *Enter* TAMORA.] F; *Enter Tamora alone Qq*   10] *Q1; F lines* Aaron, / sad, /   13 snakes lies] *Q1–2; snake
lies Q3, F*

Under their sweet shade, Aaron, let us sit,
And whilst the babbling echo mocks the hounds,
Replying shrilly to the well-tuned horns
As if a double hunt were heard at once,
Let us sit down and mark their yelping noise;   20
And after conflict, such as was supposed
The wandering prince and Dido once enjoyed –
When with a happy storm they were surprised
And curtained with a counsel-keeping cave –
We may, each wreathed in the other's arms,   25
Our pastimes done, possess a golden slumber,
Whiles hounds and horns and sweet melodious birds
Be unto us as is a nurse's song
Of lullaby, to bring her babe asleep.

AARON

Madam, though Venus govern your desires,   30

---

17   **babbling** the sound of dogs barking too loudly in a hunt (*OED* babble *v.*¹ 1.d)
20   **yelping** The quarto texts have 'yellowing', which could mean yelling or bellowing (*OED* yellow *v.*²). Q1
        may be the earliest use of 'yellowing' in this sense – it is the earliest use attested to in the *OED* – and it
        is quite a rare use of the word. F's emendation might be an attempt to clarify a word that was obscure
        even to early modern readers.
22–4   **wandering prince ... cave** The wandering prince is Aeneas, whose love for the Carthaginian queen
        Dido was consummated in a cave (*Aen.* 4.160–72). For Tamora to liken her tryst with Aaron to the
        epic Virgilian story of Dido and Aeneas is an act of characteristically audacious appropriation that
        amplifies the interracial dynamics of Aeneas' assignation with his African queen.
23   **happy** fortunate
24   **curtained with** concealed by
        counsel-keeping secret-keeping, private
25   **wreathed** wreathèd
30–1   **Venus ... Saturn** Aaron's literal meaning is that while Tamora is thinking of love (Venus is the
        Roman goddess of love), he is grimmer and more saturnine (a mental state supposedly associated
        with the influence of the planet Saturn). The same contrast of opposites underpins a witticism in
        2H4, when the prince teases Falstaff by asking if 'Saturn and Venus' are 'this year in conjunction'
        (2.4.266). Aaron may also enjoy appropriating the emperor's name for himself.

---

20 yelping] F; yellowing Qq   30] Q1; F lines Madame, / desires, /

Saturn is dominator over mine.
What signifies my deadly-standing eye,
My silence, and my cloudy melancholy,
My fleece of woolly hair that now uncurls
Even as an adder when she doth unroll   35
To do some fatal execution?
No, madam, these are no venereal signs:
Vengeance is in my heart, death in my hand,
Blood and revenge are hammering in my head.
Hark, Tamora, the empress of my soul,   40
Which never hopes more heaven than rests in thee,
This is the day of doom for Bassianus.
His Philomel must lose her tongue today.
Thy sons make pillage of her chastity,
And wash their hands in Bassianus' blood.   45
　　　[*He gives Tamora a letter.*]
See'st thou this letter? Take it up, I pray thee,
And give the king this fatal-plotted scroll.
Now question me no more; we are espied.
Here comes a parcel of our hopeful booty,

32–6　**signifies ... execution** A remarkable self-description that articulates Aaron's awareness of his racial
　　　distinction in Rome, with protruding eyes and tightly curled hair. This moment invites the audience
　　　to ponder the actor's 'originary whiteness [that] creates a metatheatrical awareness of blackness as a
　　　dramatic role' (Vaughan, 110). Aaron glosses his own looks as a series of 'signs' (l. 37) indexing a scary
　　　predatory animality, even to the point of reversing Tamora's notion that the snake is curled asleep in
　　　the sun in 13 above. Aaron's, in contrast, is unrolled and ready to attack.
32　　**standing** protruding (*OED* standing *adj.* II.8, which cites '*stantes oculi*' from Ovid, *Fasti* 6.133); in Ovid,
　　　the phrase describes the eyes of a kind of greedy, predatory bird descended from harpies.
36　　**execution** the metre suggests that this should be pronounced as a five-syllable word
37　　**venereal** having to do with Venus and love
41　　**hopes** hopes for
　　　heaven pronounced as one syllable, 'heav'n'
43　　**Philomel** The sister of Procne in classical myth, who was raped by her brother-in-law Tereus; he cut
　　　out her tongue to prevent her telling her story. This narrative, especially as recounted in Ovid's *Met.*, is
　　　a recurring model for the action of the play. See the Introduction, p. 62.
44　　**make pillage of** plunder
47　　**fatal-plotted** planned as part of a death-dealing scheme
49　　**parcel ... booty** a portion of the plunder we hope for

---

45 SD] *Bevington subst.*　　49 hopeful booty] *Q1* (hopeful lbootie); hopefull bootie *Q2–3, F*

Which dreads not yet their lives' destruction.   50

Enter BASSIANUS *and* LAVINIA.

TAMORA
Ah, my sweet Moor, sweeter to me than life.

AARON
No more, great empress, Bassianus comes.
Be cross with him, and I'll go fetch thy sons
To back thy quarrels whatsoe'er they be.   [*Exit.*]

BASSIANUS
Whom have we here? Rome's royal empress,   55
Unfurnished of her well-beseeming troop?
Or is it Dian, habited like her,
Who hath abandoned her holy groves
To see the general hunting in this forest?

TAMORA
Saucy controller of my private steps,   60
Had I the power that some say Dian had,
Thy temples should be planted presently
With horns as was Actaeon's, and the hounds
Should drive upon thy new transformed limbs,

---

50   **destruction** pronounced as a four-syllable word
56   **Unfurnished ... troop** without her appropriate retinue of attendants; Bassianus implies that it is
      unseemly for Tamora to be alone with Aaron.
57   **Dian** Diana, the classical goddess of the hunt, and also associated with chastity and the moon;
      Bassianus' comparison is meant sarcastically.
      habited like her dressed like her, because Tamora is in fact dressed for hunting
58   **abandoned** abandonèd
60   **Saucy** presumptuous
      controller This could just mean 'censorious critic' (*OED n.* 3), but the word's primary association is
      with an official who manages household finances (*OED n.* 1–2). As Bate notes (Ard³), Tamora is pulling
      rank by treating Bassianus like a nosy and officious underling.
61–4 **Dian ... transformed limbs** Tamora alludes to the well-known Ovidian story of Actaeon, a hunter
      who (as recounted in *Met.* 3.137–252) stumbled upon the goddess Diana while she was bathing.
      Enraged, Diana threw water in Actaeon's face and transformed him into a stag, whereupon he was
      chased down and torn apart by his own hounds.
64   **transformed** transformèd

51] *Q1; F lines* Moore: / life. /   54 quarrels] *Q1–2;* quarrel *Q3, F*   54 SD] *Rowe*   55] *Q1; F lines* heere? / Empresse, /
55 Whom] *F;* Who *Qq*   56 her] *Q1–2;* our *Q3, F*   60 my] *Q1–2;* our *Q3, F*   64 thy] *Q1–2;* his *Q3, F*

Unmannerly intruder as thou art.   65

LAVINIA

Under your patience, gentle empress,
'Tis thought you have a goodly gift in horning,
And to be doubted that your Moor and you
Are singled forth to try experiments.
Jove shield your husband from his hounds today: 70
'Tis pity they should take him for a stag.

BASSIANUS

Believe me, queen, your swarth Cimmerian
Doth make your honour of his body's hue:
Spotted, detested, and abominable.
Why are you sequestered from all your train,   75

---

66   **Under your patience** 'if I may be permitted': a faux-polite start to a cutting retort
67–71   **in horning ... stag** Lavinia proves to be both quick-witted and outspoken in private, which may
        come as a surprise given her formality and quiet obedience in Act 1. She reverses Tamora's allusion
        to Actaeon by suggesting that Tamora is giving horns (the traditional emblem of the cuckold; see
        2.1.89n.) to Saturninus by having an affair with Aaron.
68   **to be doubted** one suspects
69   **singled ... experiments** gone off alone to experiment (in cuckold-making)
70   **Jove** a common name for the highest of the Roman gods
72   **swarth** swarthy, dark-skinned; Qq have 'swartie', an alternative form of the word swarthy. F's
        emendation improves the metre.
        Cimmerian Cimmerians were a nomadic people originating just past the north-eastern edge of
        the Mediterranean world in antiquity, but the name is also associated with a legendary people
        (the *Kimmerioi*) at the world's end who were said in Homer's *Odyssey* (11.14) to live in mist and
        darkness beyond the reach of the sun. In early modern English texts, the name is often associated with
        infernal darkness, as when Theridamas, near the end of 2 *Tamburlaine*, says that 'Death with armies of
        Cymerian spirits / Gives battle gainst the heart of Tamburlaine' (Marlowe, *Tamb.* 2: 5.3.8–9), or with
        what John Marston called 'Cymerian darknes' (Marston, 39). Bassianus thus associates Aaron with
        darkness, because of his 'swarth' skin, but also perhaps because of his foreignness and devilishness.
        Ndiaye suggests that the word as printed in Q1 ('Cymerion') may also have evoked the Spanish word
        'cimarrón' – a word for runaway African enslaved persons 'that entered English literary culture under
        the influence of Sir Francis Drake, who first encountered black cimarrones in Panama in the 1570s'
        ('Aaron's Roots', 66). It is possible that audience members would have heard this regardless of what the
        writer intended.
74   **Spotted** stained, morally disfigured, but also (in the context of the remark about Aaron's 'body's hue'
        in the previous line) a metatheatrical reference to the black make-up that might be expected transfer
        from the actor playing Aaron in racial prosthetics to the actor playing Tamora
75   **sequestered** separated.

---

69 try] Q2–3, F; trie thy Q1   72 swarth] F; swartie Qq; swart Capell

Dismounted from your snow-white, goodly steed,
And wandered hither to an obscure plot,
Accompanied but with a barbarous Moor,
If foul desire had not conducted you?

LAVINIA

And being intercepted in your sport,   80
Great reason that my noble lord be rated
For sauciness. [to Bassianus] I pray you, let us hence,
And let her joy her raven-coloured love;
This valley fits the purpose passing well.

BASSIANUS

The king my brother shall have notice of this.   85

LAVINIA

Aye, for these slips have made him noted long;
Good king, to be so mightily abused!

TAMORA

Why, I have patience to endure all this.

76–8   **snow-white … Moor** Although Bassianus is literally talking about the whiteness of Tamora's horse,
racially coded opprobrium structures this entire exchange: having dismounted, 'the implication is
that she will be mounted by a black "barbarous Moor"' (Williams, *Glossary*, 211). It is not simply
that Tamora is alone with a man in the woods, but more specifically that she has left a 'goodly' white
horse to be with a black man – the height of moral depravity, according to Lavinia's and Bassianus'
rhetorical logic.

77   **obscure** the stress is on the first syllable

81   **rated** rebuked angrily

83   **joy her raven-coloured love** enjoy her lover, who is the black colour of a raven; again, Lavinia implies
that Aaron's blackness makes Tamora's assignation especially scandalous.

84   **passing** surpassingly, exceedingly

86   **slips** errors in conduct
        noted notorious
        long Since Saturninus has only been married to Tamora for one evening, the idea that her conduct
        has caused him scandal for a long time makes little sense. Ard[3], noting that Tamora's two subsequent
        speech prefixes in Q1 (both just as '*Queene*') differ from the norm, suggests that the error may be the
        result of textual corruption rather than of authorial sloppiness. But either explanation seems possible,
        since temporal sloppiness of this kind is not at all unusual in Shakespeare, or in early modern English
        plays generally (and compare 4.2.50n.).

---

78 but] Q1–2; *not in* Q3, F   82 SD] Oxf[2]

Enter CHIRON *and* DEMETRIUS.

DEMETRIUS

How now, dear sovereign and our gracious mother,

Why doth your highness look so pale and wan?   90

TAMORA

Have I not reason, think you, to look pale?

These two have 'ticed me hither to this place:

A barren, detested vale you see it is,

The trees, though summer, yet forlorn and lean,

O'ercome with moss and baleful mistletoe.   95

Here never shines the sun, here nothing breeds

Unless the nightly owl or fatal raven.

And when they showed me this abhorred pit,

They told me, here at dead time of the night,

A thousand fiends, a thousand hissing snakes,   100

Ten thousand swelling toads, as many urchins,

---

92   'ticed enticed
93–8   **barren, detested ... pit** Tamora, who described this same landscape as a *locus amoenus* near the
        beginning of this scene (see 12–15n. above), now offers a radically different description of her
        surroundings. This has sometimes been thought of as authorial sloppiness (see the note on 2.3.93 in
        Yale, for instance) but it shows how Tamora's improvisational creativity can reshape the scene. This
        rhetorical reinvention of the landscape is enabled by a relatively bare stage and calls explicit attention
        to the imaginative work audiences are asked to do to understand the setting of an early modern play.
95   **O'ercome** overgrown
        baleful mistletoe 'baleful' (deadly) perhaps because it was seen as parasitic, growing in trees and
        sapping their vitality, or perhaps because of the way it thickens tree cover and blocks out the light; in
        Richard Johnson's roughly contemporary *History of the Seven Champions of Christendom*, St Patrick
        is described entering 'a dismall shady thicket beset about with balefull misselto, a place of horror'
        (Johnson, *History*, 78).
97   **fatal** ominous
        raven Tamora may recall that Lavinia compared Aaron to a raven at 83 above.
98   **abhorred** abhorrèd
        pit The improvisational reimagining of what would have been a mostly blank stage calls attention to
        the trapdoor.
100   **hissing snakes** The fluidity of the way Tamora describes the landscape in this scene is emblematized
        by her descriptions of snakes: here, Tamora's account of the horror of hissing snakes stands in sharp
        contrast to the snakes she earlier described as 'rolled in the cheerful sun' (13); Tamora may also recall
        Aaron's description of his own hair unrolling like 'an adder' at 35.
101   **urchins** hedgehogs

89] Q1; *F lines* Souerainge / Mother, /

Would make such fearful and confused cries,
As any mortal body, hearing it,
Should straight fall mad, or else die suddenly.
No sooner had they told this hellish tale,   105
But straight they told me they would bind me here
Unto the body of a dismal yew
And leave me to this miserable death.
And then they called me 'foul adulteress',
'Lacivious Goth', and all the bitterest terms   110
That ever ear did hear to such effect.
And had you not by wondrous fortune come,
This vengeance on me had they executed.
Revenge it as you love your mother's life,
Or be ye not henceforth called my children.   115

DEMETRIUS

This is a witness that I am thy son.   *Stab him.*

CHIRON

And this for me, struck home to show my strength.
        [*Stabs Bassianus, who dies.*]

---

107   **dismal yew** The yew tree is poisonous and was known to be so (see Price); it is also a common feature
       of dismal or even infernal landscapes associated with death in Roman literature (for example: *Met.*
       4.432 or *Thy.* 654).
110   **'Lascivious Goth'** Tamora is inventing threats and insults putatively aimed at her by Lavinia and
       Bassianus; she ascribes to them a pun hinging on the similar pronunciation of Goth and goat, as in
       AYL 3.3.7–9 (a parallel first noted in Herford).
115   **Or ... my children** The phrase 'be ye not henceforth' has often been emended by editors to smooth
       out the metre: Capell makes the line into tetrameter ('Or be not henceforth call'd my children.');
       Pope gives it as 'Or be ye not from henceforth call'd my children'; and *Oxf* emends 'henceforth' to
       'henceforward'. We print the line as it appears in Qq and F and note that it can be metrical (with
       a feminine ending) if 'called' is pronounced with two syllables and that it can also be an effective,
       staccato line that doesn't sound unmetrical if the actor playing Tamora adds a slight pause for
       emphasis before the word 'henceforth'.
117   **struck home** struck effectively (compare 2.1.118)

---

110 Lacivious] Q3 F; Lauicious Q1–2   115 Or ... my children] Qq, F; Or be not henceforth call'd my children
Capell; Or be ye not from henceforth call'd my children *Pope*; Or be ye not henceforward called my children *Oxf*
117] Q1; F lines me, / strength. /   117 SD] *Capell subst.*

LAVINIA

Aye, come, Semiramis! Nay, barbarous Tamora,
For no name fits thy nature but thy own.

TAMORA

Give me the poniard. You shall know, my boys,   120
Your mother's hand shall right your mother's wrong.

DEMETRIUS

Stay, madam, here is more belongs to her:
First thrash the corn, then after burn the straw.
This minion stood upon her chastity,
Upon her nuptial vow, her loyalty,   125
And with that painted hope braves your mightiness:
And shall she carry this unto her grave?

CHIRON

And if she do, I would I were a eunuch.
Drag hence her husband to some secret hole,
And make his dead trunk pillow to our lust.   130

---

118   **Semiramis** see 2.1.22n.
120   **poniard** dagger; we know (from 2.1) that both brothers carry weapons, and they have both just used
       them to stab Bassianus, so Tamora could be addressing either son here.
122   **belongs to her** is due to her
123   **thrash the corn** to thresh or thrash literally means to separate grains from husks and straw by
       hitting or shaking them; the euphemistic sense – in which 'to thrash in a woman's barn' has a sexual
       meaning – is proverbial (Dent, B89.1).
124   **minion** a derogatory term that can describe either an overly fastidious underling (OED n.¹ 2) or a
       sexual plaything (OED n.¹ 1b); both connotations are in Demetrius' sneering remark.
126   **painted** false, deceptive; because this line is hypermetrical, it has proven tempting to emend the text
       by swapping in a one-syllable word for 'painted', and the most widely adopted alternative is Oxf¹'s
       'quaint'. Emendation, however, gets rid of the specifically misogynistic connotations that the word
       'painted' often had in idiomatic early modern discourse because of its association with women's use
       of putatively duplicitous make-up for cosmetic purposes (as in OED 1.c). The phrase 'painted hope'
       could mean something like 'false, put-on bravado' here.
129–30 **Drag hence ... lust** As first noted by Ebbs, these lines bear a striking resemblance to a description,
       from Thomas Nashe's The Unfortunate Traveller (1594), of a rape in which the dead body of the
       victim's husband is 'made a pillow to' the 'abhomination' (Nashe, sig. K4ᵛ). Because of the uncertainties
       surrounding the date of Tit's original composition, it remains difficult to ascertain which account
       might have been composed first.

---

118 Aye, come] Qq, F (I come)   120 the] Q1–2; thy Q3, F   126 painted] Qq, F; quainte Oxf¹   128] Q1; F
lines doe, / Eunuch, /

TAMORA

But when ye have the honey we desire,
Let not this wasp outlive, us both to sting.

CHIRON

I warrant you, madam, we will make that sure.
Come, mistress, now perforce we will enjoy
That nice-preserved honesty of yours.   135

LAVINIA

O Tamora, thou bearest a woman's face –

TAMORA

I will not hear her speak; away with her.

LAVINIA

Sweet lords, intreat her hear me but a word.

DEMETRIUS [*to Tamora*]

Listen, fair madam, let it be your glory
To see her tears, but be your heart to them   140
As unrelenting flint to drops of rain.

LAVINIA

When did the tiger's young ones teach the dam?
O, do not learn her wrath, she taught it thee.

---

131   **we desire** F2's emendation of 'we' to 'ye' is understandable, but Tamora is clearly herself invested in
       her sons' predatory aggression.
132   **wasp** Wasps were not clearly distinguished from bees in early modern texts, and were thought to
       have honey.
       outlive survive (*OED* 3.a); the comma, first introduced by Theobald, clarifies the intransitive usage
       of the verb. Ard² prints the line as we do but notes that the intransitive usage (which is the sole
       attestation in the *OED* entry) is unusual and suggests that it may be a compositor error for 'o'erlive'.
133   **warrant** pronounced as one syllable
135   **nice-preserved** nice-preservèd; fastidiously protected
136   **bearest** pronounced as one syllable
141   **flint ... rain** Demetrius combines two proverbial ideas: the notion of a heart as hard as flint (Dent,
       H311) and the idea that constant water drops will wear away stone (D618); however, since he is
       suggesting that stone is 'unrelenting' to water drops he is reversing the meaning of the latter.
142   **dam** mother
143   **learn her** instruct her in

---

131 we] *Qq, F;* ye *F2*   132 outlive, us] *Theobald;* out liue us *Q1;* out-liue us *Q2–3, F*   136 woman's] *Qq;*
woman *F*   139 SD] *Oxf²*

The milk thou suck'st from her did turn to marble:
Even at thy teat thou hadst thy tyranny.   145
Yet every mother breeds not sons alike;
Do thou entreat her show a woman's pity.

CHIRON

What, wouldst thou have me prove myself a bastard?

LAVINIA

'Tis true, the raven doth not hatch a lark;
Yet have I heard – O, could I find it now –   150
The lion, moved with pity, did endure
To have his princely paws pared all away.
Some say that ravens foster forlorn children
The whilst their own birds famish in their nests.
O, be to me, though thy hard heart say no,   155
Nothing so kind, but something pitful.

---

144   **The milk ... marble** The idea that a child's character might be influenced by its mother's milk was so
       widely accepted that the notion of 'sucking evil from the dug' was proverbial (Dent, E198): Tamora's
       milk has rendered her sons' dispositions hard and inflexible, like marble (*OED*, marble 1.c).
       suck'st The quarto texts have 'suckst', and as Bate points out in Ard³ Shakespeare also uses 'suckst' in
       place of a past tense verb at *1H6* 5.4.28. Ravenscroft (p. 22) and Rowe both corrected the word's tense
       by adding a d ('suck'dst'). That makes it something of a tongue-twister, and if the 'd' sound were to be
       swallowed the difference might not even be audible on stage. F's contraction 'suck'st', which we adopt,
       acknowledges both the tense of the verb and its likely pronunciation.
148   **bastard** to do so would be to call his legitimacy into question
149   **the raven ... lark** An alternative version of the proverbial wisdom that 'the eagle does not hatch a
       dove' (Dent, E2) that picks up the raven's association with blackness (83) and ominousness (97) earlier
       in the scene.
150   **find it** (1) find it to be true; (2) remember it
151-2 **The lion ... away** Lavinia's general point is a proverbial one, namely that even the ferocious lion shows
       mercy towards supplicants (Dent, L316). But her specific example of leonine gentleness is apparently
       drawn from a half-remembered Aesopian fable in which a lion who falls in love with a woman allows
       his claws to be pared and his teeth filed and is then killed by the woman's kin (*Fables*, 98). This fable
       and the example offered about ravens in the following lines are both stories in which pity proves
       self-destructive. Titus' Roman response to Tamora in Act 1 precluded pity, and Lavinia's unpersuasive
       examples perhaps suggest some residual Roman ambivalence about the value of acting on pity.
154   **birds** i.e., their own young offspring
156   **Nothing ... pitiful** if not as kind as the raven, then at least somewhat compassionate

---

144 suck'st] *F*; suckst *Qq*; suck'dst *Rowe³*   147 woman's] *Q1*; woman *Q2–3, F*   148] *Q1; F lines* What, /
bastard? /   153 Some] *Q1* (So me); Some *Q2–3, F*

TAMORA

    I know not what it means. Away with her.

LAVINIA

    O, let me teach thee, for my father's sake,

    That gave thee life when well he might have slain thee.

    Be not obdurate; open thy deaf ears.   160

TAMORA

    Hadst thou in person ne'er offended me,

    Even for his sake am I pitiless.

    Remember, boys, I poured forth tears in vain

    To save your brother from the sacrifice,

    But fierce Andronicus would not relent.   165

    Therefore, away with her, and use her as you will:

    The worse to her, the better loved of me.

LAVINIA   [Kneels and clings to Tamora.]

    O Tamora, be called a gentle queen,

    And with thine own hands kill me in this place.

    For 'tis not life that I have begged so long: 170

    Poor I was slain when Bassianus died.

TAMORA

    What begg'st thou then, fond woman? Let me go.

LAVINIA

    'Tis present death I beg, and one thing more

    That womanhood denies my tongue to tell:

    O keep me from their worse-than-killing lust,   175

---

157   **it** i.e., pity

160   **obdurate** hardened, stubborn; metrically, the stress falls on the second syllable.

168 SD   *A SD is required because Tamora demands that Lavinia let her go at 172.

172   **fond** foolish

173   **present** immediate

---

160 ears] Q3, F; yeares Q1–2   164 brother] Q1 (brothet); brother Q2–3, F   168] Q1; F lines Tamora, / Queene, / SD Kneels and ... Tamora] this edn; clinging to Tamora Ard³; embracing Tamora's knees Oxf²; she tugs at Tamora's garments Bevington (at 171)   175 their] Q1 (there); their Q2–3, F

And tumble me into some loathsome pit,
Where never man's eye may behold my body.
Do this and be a charitable murderer.

TAMORA

So should I rob my sweet sons of their fee;
No, let them satisfy their lust on thee.   180

DEMETRIUS

Away, for thou hast stayed us here too long.

LAVINIA

No grace, no womanhood! Ah, beastly creature,
The blot and enemy to our general name,
Confusion fall –

CHIRON   Nay then, I'll stop your mouth.   [*Kisses her forcibly.*]
[*to Demetrius*] Bring thou her husband.   185

---

176   **tumble** throw down (*OED* 4.a); the word also has sexual connotations which are ironic in context (see *OED* 9.a, which gives the following example from *Ham*: 'Quoth she, "before you tumbled me, / You promised me to wed"' [4.5.62–3])
177   **man's eye** Lavinia construes being made into a spectacle for men as itself a kind of violation.
181   **stayed** delayed
183   **our general name** i.e., the good name of all women
184–5 **Confusion ... husband** The lineation – with Chiron interrupting Lavinia and completing her iambic line – is adopted from Ard³. The early texts all have Chiron's reply ('Nay then ... husband') as one long, hypermetrical line. Relineation here makes sense dramatically as well as metrically.
184   **Confusion** destruction
184 SD *There are no SDs in the early texts and Chiron could simply be threatening Lavinia verbally. However, some method of silencing Lavinia is implied (Ard³ has '*Grabs her, covering her mouth*') and the brothers do intend to make a sexual assault. There is a parallel editorial question near the end of *Ado*, where most modern editions (though not the Ard³ edition), after Benedick tells Beatrice 'I will stop your mouth', add a SD indicating a kiss (see, for instance, in Bevington, at 5.4.96). In Gregory Doran's 1995 Market Theatre production (South Africa), a shop window dummy was substituted for Lavinia in this scene of violence.

---

180 satisfy] Q1 (satisfiee); satsifie Q2–3, F   181] Q1; F lines Away, / long. /   182–5 No grace ... husband] Ard³; Qq lines creature, / name, / fall / husband, /; F lines Garace, / creature, / name, / fall – / mouth / husband, /   184 fall—] Q3, F; fall Q1; fall. Q2   SD] *this edn; Grabs her, covering her mouth* Ard³   185 SD] Oxf²

This is the hole where Aaron bid us hide him.
> [*Demetrius throws the body of Bassianus into the pit;*
> *he and Chiron exit dragging Lavinia.*]

TAMORA

Farewell, my sons, see that you make her sure.
Ne'er let my heart know merry cheer indeed
Till all the Andronici be made away.
Now will I hence to seek my lovely Moor,   190
And let my spleenful sons this trull deflower.   *Exit.*

> *Enter* AARON *with two of Titus' sons* [QUINTUS *and* MARTIUS].

AARON

Come on, my lords the better foot before;
Straight will I bring you to the loathsome pit
Where I espied the panther fast asleep.

QUINTUS

My sight is very dull, whate'er it bodes.   195

186.1–2 *The pit here is represented by the stage trapdoor. When Quintus falls into the pit, he describes it as being covered with 'rude-growing briars' (199), so Waith's SD in Oxf² has Demetrius covering the trapdoor opening with branches. This is unnecessary, and it is also predicated on an idea of dramatic realism that the play's other staging choices in this scene do not support: compare 3n. and 93–8n. Quintus' language at 199 provides an imaginative cue for the audience regardless of the use of props.

187   **make her sure** make sure of killing her

189   **made away** done away with

191   **spleenful** impetuous, appetitive, mercurial; the spleen was thought to play a role in the production of humoral imbalance leading to emotional instability, and Shakespeare often uses the word 'spleen' as a metonym for erratic moodiness, as in *V&A*: 'A thousand spleens bear her a thousand ways' (l. 907).
        trull whore

192   **the better foot before** put your best foot forward; Aaron uses highly accessible, proverbial language (Dent, F570: 'to set the best foot forward') to encourage the sons and get them to where he needs them to be.

194   **Where ... panther** Panther-hunting is the ostensible backdrop for the events in Act 2, and Aaron is luring Titus' sons by using the hunt as a false pretext.

195   **dull** obscured, as by darkness; but also, as Martius' response suggests, implying sluggishness

---

186 SD] *Capell subst.*   191 SD] *F; not in Qq*   191.1 QUINTUS *and* MARTIUS] *Capell subst.*   192 SP] *F; not in Qq but implied by preceding entry SD*

MARTIUS
    And mine. I promise you, were it not for shame,
    Well could I leave our sport to sleep awhile.   [*Falls into the pit.*]
QUINTUS
    What, art thou fallen? What subtle hole is this,
    Whose mouth is covered with rude-growing briars
    Upon whose leaves are drops of new-shed blood   200
    As fresh as morning dew distilled on flowers?
    A very fatal place, it seems to me.
    Speak, brother, hast thou hurt thee with the fall?
MARTIUS
    O brother, with the dismal'st object hurt
    That ever eye with sight made heart lament.   205
AARON [*aside*]
    Now will I fetch the king to find them here,
    That he thereby may have a likely guess
    How these were they that made away his brother.   *Exit.*
MARTIUS
    Why dost not comfort me and help me out
    From this unhallowed and bloodstained hole?   210
QUINTUS
    I am surprised with an uncouth fear,

197   **to sleep awhile** Martius' bizarre, unexplained drowsiness inaugurates a dream-like tonal instability that pervades this episode and the environment of the 'subtle hole' (198), encompassing Quintus' uncanny, anticipatory fears at 211, the insistently overdetermined bodily language used to describe the pit, and the semi-farcical stage business of Quintus himself falling into the pit, which Cam³ describes as 'potentially ludicrous, like Gloucester's leap from a non-existent cliff' in *Lear*. In performance, this shift has been signaled by actors who portray Martius as extremely hung over, sleep deprived, or blinded by fog (as in both the 2006 Bailey and 2017 McIntyre productions).
198   **subtle** hidden
199   **mouth ... briars** see 186.1–2n. above
204   **object** spectacle
      hurt Martius uses the term figuratively and then elaborates in 205.
210   **bloodstained** bloodstainèd
211   **surprised** suprisèd
      uncouth unfamiliar

197 SD] *Rowe subst.*   198] *Q1; F lines* fallen? / this, /   201 morning] *Q1–2;* mornings *Q3, F*   204] *Q1; F lines* Brother, / obiect /   hurt] *Q1–2; not in Q3, F*   206 SD] *Johnson*   210 unhallowed] *F;* unhollow *Qq*

A chilling sweat o'erruns my trembling joints,
My heart suspects more than mine eye can see.

MARTIUS

   To prove thou hast a true-divining heart,
   Aaron and thou look down into this den,   215
   And see a fearful sight of blood and death.

QUINTUS

   Aaron is gone, and my compassionate heart
   Will not permit mine eyes once to behold
   The thing whereat it trembles by surmise.
   O, tell me who it is, for ne'er till now   220
   Was I a child to fear I know not what.

MARTIUS

   Lord Bassianus lies berayed in blood,
   All on a heap, like to the slaughtered lamb,
   In this detested, dark, blood-drinking pit.

QUINTUS

   If it be dark, how dost thou know 'tis he?   225

MARTIUS

   Upon his bloody finger he doth wear
   A precious ring that lightens all this hole,

---

215   **den** in the now-archaic sense of a hollow, cavern or pit
219   **The thing ... surmise** i.e., the thing it (my heart) anticipates and trembles at
220–1 **ne'er till ... what** i.e., never until now have I felt fear of the unknown, as does a child
222   *berayed dirtied, defiled; Dover Wilson's emendation of Q1's 'bereaud' in Cam² is commonly accepted, and his speculation that the Q1 compositor may have misread the handwritten word 'bereied' is plausible. A proximity search of EEBO-TCP makes it clear that berayed in (or with) blood was a familiar idiomatic formulation. The only known copy of Q1 has the phrase 'bereaud in blood' scratched out and replaced by the phrase 'heere reav'd of lyfe' written in a secretary hand. If nothing else, this suggests that a contemporary reader too saw the need for emendation. The same impulse probably explains the emendation in Q2–3 and F, where 'embrewed heere' replaces 'bereaud in blood'.
227   **A precious ring ... hole** The idea that gemstones could be luminescent predates the play. For example, Pliny the Elder describes a precious stone called 'Chrysolampis' that is found in Ethiopia: 'all the day long of a pale colour, but by night it glowes in manner of a cole of fire' (Pliny the Elder, 1.626).

---

220 who] *Q1–2*; how *Q3, F*   222 berayed in blood] *Cam²*; bereaud in blood *Q1*; embrewed heere *Q2–3, F*
223 the] *F*; a *Qq*   227 this] *Q1–2*; the *Q3, F*

Which, like a taper in some monument,
Doth shine upon the dead man's earthy cheeks
And shows the ragged entrails of the pit.   230
So pale did shine the moon on Priamus,
When he by night lay bathed in maiden blood.
O brother, help me with thy fainting hand –
If fear hath made thee faint, as me it hath –
Out of this fell devouring receptacle,   235

228   **monument** tomb, as in the monument of the Andronici in Act 1; by comparing the pit to a family tomb, Martius evokes Act 1 and – since the trapdoor used for the pit was also likely used for the monument – creates a moment of possible metadramatic recognition for the audience.

229   **earthy** earth-like; 'used figuratively of a human body, esp. a dead body' (*OED* I.1.c)

230   **entrails** interior; the word's bodily meaning was as predominant in Shakespeare's day as in ours, and the comparison of the pit to a body is picked up in the rest of this scene.

231–2 **So pale ... blood** Priamus was the last king of Troy, killed by Pyrrhus when the Greek army sacked Troy at the end of the Trojan War. In Virgil, the killing of Priamus takes place in an open-air courtyard, amidst general carnage, at night, and the narrative emphasizes how the old king is soaked in the blood of his own son, Polites. In Q2, the name was changed to Piramus, and since the modernized text of *Tit* predates the early-twentieth-century rediscovery of Q1 there has been a long-standing editorial tradition of seeing this name as an allusion to the figure Pyramus, an Ovidian character that Shakespeare also uses in the last act of *MND*. The compositor of Q2 is often quite sloppy with classically derived words and names, however, so transposition of letters seems as likely an explanation to us as does purposeful emendation. And the exceptionally well-known story of Priam's death from Book 2 of *Aen.* (512–58) arguably better corresponds to the political and moral stakes of what Martius feels he has discovered here in the pit. The Latinate version of the Trojan king's name – 'Priamus' – was used in literally hundreds of early modern English-language books, and in poems and plays it was often used interchangeably with the now more familiar name Priam for metrical reasons: see, for instance, *T&C* 2.2.207 ('You valiant offspring of great Priamus') and 5.3.54 ('Not Priamus and Hecuba on knees'). On the decision to opt for the Q1 reading over the more familiar reading used in Q2–3 and F, see also pp. 38–9.

232   **maiden blood** The word 'maiden' could be used for a sexually inexperienced man (*OED* 2.b) – and editors who have glossed this line as an allusion to Pyramus have sometimes thought that the maiden blood referred to might be his (see, for instance, Ard³). Accounts of the death of Priam tend to emphasize the pathos of the fact that Priam was soaked in the blood of his own son Polites, and several early modern accounts also emphasize Polites' youthfulness: in *Fenne's Fruits* (1590), Polites is described as a 'fearfull youth' (Fenne, sig. Ee3ᵛ), for example, and in Thomas Heywood's *Troia Britanica* (1609) Polites is referred to as 'the Youth' and 'the child' (Heywood, *Troia*, 414). In the play *The Faithfull Shepherdess* (1610) the phrase 'maiden blood' denotes the collective innocence of a group of young men and women (Fletcher, sig. B3'), so it is also possible that Martius likens the bloodstained body of Bassianus to an image of Priam wet with the blood of innocent young victims of war.

235   **receptacle** The tomb of the Andronici is likewise described as a 'sacred receptacle' at 1.1.92. The metrical emphasis here – as there – falls on the first and third syllable of the word ('rèceptàcle').

229 earthy] *Q1–2*; earthly *Q3, F*   230 the] *F*; this *Qq*   231 Priamus] *Q1*; *Piramus Q2–3, F; Pyramus / Rowe*

As hateful as Cocytus' misty mouth.

QUINTUS

Reach me thy hand that I may help thee out
Or, wanting strength to do thee so much good,
I may be plucked into the swallowing womb
Of this deep pit, poor Bassianus' grave. 240
I have no strength to pluck thee to the brink.

MARTIUS

Nor I no strength to climb without thy help.

QUINTUS

Thy hand, once more; I will not loose again
Till thou art here aloft or I below.
Thou canst not come to me; I come to thee. [*Falls in*] 245

Enter the Emperor [SATURNINUS, *with Attendants,*] *and* AARON *the Moor.*

SATURNINUS

Along with me! I'll see what hole is here
And what he is that now is leapt into it.
Say, who art thou that lately didst descend
Into this gaping hollow of the earth?

---

236 **Cocytus' misty mouth** Cocytus is a river in the classical underworld. Shakespeare was probably thinking of the description, in *Aen*. 7.560–71, of the Vale of Amsanctus: the cavern, replete with mist and roaring waters, through which the fury Allecto returns to Cocytus (Law, 149). If so, this allusion to the Virgilian story of a vengeful fury coming to wreak havoc in the world anticipates the more general invocations of the idea of Revenge coming from the underworld in Acts 4 and 5.

239 **swallowing womb** The idea of earth as a womb swallowing up its offspring is common in Shakespeare. Dover Wilson (in Cam²) compares *R&J* 2.3.5–6 ('The earth that's nature's mother is her tomb, / What is her burying grave, that is her womb') and *R2* 2.1.82–3 ('a grave, / Whose hollow womb inherits naught but bones'). The image here, however, is also literalized in the cannibalism of the play's denouement.

245.1 ***with Attendants*** Subsequent action in this scene – pulling the Andronici out of the pit and guarding them as prisoners – would seem to demand attendants, though none are indicated in the early texts. Some editors, following Theobald, have attendants enter with Tamora at 258.1, but the emperor would likely be presumed to travel with a retinue, and his first words in what follows ('Along with me!') may be understood as urging them to keep up. Ravenscroft (p. 24) also has attendants enter with Saturninus here.

---

236 Cocytus'] *Qq, F (Ocitus); Cocitus F2* 245 SD] *Pope; Boths fall in F; not in Qq* 245.1 SATURNINUS, *with Attendants,*] *Oxf¹ subst. and*] *Q1–2; not in Q3, F*

MARTIUS

The unhappy sons of old Andronicus,   250
Brought hither in a most unlucky hour
To find thy brother Bassianus dead.

SATURNINUS

My brother dead? I know thou dost but jest.
He and his lady both are at the lodge
Upon the north side of this pleasant chase.   255
'Tis not an hour since I left them there.

MARTIUS

We know not where you left him all alive,
But – out, alas! – here have we found him dead.

Enter TAMORA, [TITUS] Andronicus *and* LUCIUS.

TAMORA

Where is my lord the king?

SATURNINUS

Here, Tamora, though griped with killing grief.   260

---

258   **out, alas!** an idiomatic exclamation of lament, as at *3H6* 1.4.18–19: 'With this we charged again, but, out, alas, / We budged again'

260   ***griped** seized (as in *OED* gripe *v.*[1] 3); the early texts all have versions of the implausibly awkward and redundant phrase 'grieved with killing grief', and various emendations have been suggested. Cam[2] first proposed 'griped' at the suggestion of J. C. Maxwell, whose own subsequent Ard[2] edition defends the plausibility of this unusual compositor error (of p for u/v) in some detail (see the note in that text). Ard[3] emends the word to 'gride', a very rare word meaning to wound or pierce. Oxf[3] argues that 'gride' would have been so rare as to have been unintelligible to the play's early audiences, and that (Maxwell notwithstanding) a compositor would have been unlikely to mistake p for a u/v, and so proposes 'percde' (pierced) on the theory that it would be easier for a compositor to mistake p for g in late Elizabethan handwriting. However, the fact that the word appears in such close proximity to the word 'grief', which was presumably written in the same hand in the manuscript, makes it seem less likely to us that a compositor would have misconstrued the 'gr' at the start of the word in question in whatever manuscript hand he was working with. Despite Oxf[3]'s reasonable objections, therefore, we here adopt the Cam[2] emendation and preserve the alliteration from the early texts. A search of EEBO-TCP reveals that variations on the phrase 'griped by/with grief' or 'griping grief' are relatively common in early modern texts (though this may also have to do with the contextual indistinguishability of the words 'griped' and 'gripped' in Elizabethan spelling). For a roughly contemporary example, see Gardiner: 'He was round about griped and galled with grief' (86).

---

250 sons] *Q1*; sonne *Q2–3, F*   256 them] *Q1–2*; him *Q3, F*   257 him] *F*; them *Qq*   258.1 TITUS] *Cam¹*
260 griped] *Cam² (conj. J. C. Maxwell)*; griude *Q1*; greeu'd *Q2*; grieud *Q3*; grieu'd *F*; gride *Ard³*; percde [pierced] *Oxf³*

TAMORA

　　Where is thy brother Bassianus?

SATURNINUS

　　Now to the bottom dost thou search my wound:

　　Poor Bassianus here lies murdered.

TAMORA

　　Then all too late I bring this fatal writ,

　　The complot of this timeless tragedy,   265

　　And wonder greatly that man's face can fold

　　In pleasing smiles such murderous tyranny.

　　　　She giveth Saturnine a letter.

SATURNINUS　(*Reads the letter.*)

　　And if we miss to meet him handsomely,

　　Sweet huntsman – Bassianus 'tis we mean –

　　Do thou so much as dig the grave for him.   270

　　Thou know'st our meaning. Look for thy reward

　　Among the nettles at the elder tree

　　Which overshades the mouth of that same pit

　　Where we decreed to bury Bassianus.

　　Do this and purchase us thy lasting friends.   275

262　**Now … wound** 'now you've touched on the truth of what is hurting me'

263　**murdered** murderèd

264　**writ** a written document, in this case the note

265　**complot** conspiracy; Tamora implies that the note she brings lays bare the alleged plot.

　　　timeless untimely

266–7　**man's face … tyranny** The folds of skin made by smiling are imagined as covering over or enfolding hidden treachery.

　　　tyranny any violent, lawless action

268　**miss** fail

　　　handsomely readily, conveniently

272　**elder tree** associated with duplicity and betrayal, as when the Elizabethan writer Lewis Evans compares Papist hypocrites to elder trees: 'We gather that they be lyke unto the elder tree, which havinge a faire & pleasaunt flowre, yet bearth a contageous, and a most noysome fruite' (Evans, sigs B4v–B5r); see also *LLL* 5.2.600: 'Judas was hanged on an elder'. On the staging of the bag as putatively hidden at the elder tree see 2.3.3n.

275　**purchase us thy** acquire us as your

---

268 SP and SD] Qq, F (*Saturninus reads the letter.*)

O Tamora, was ever heard the like?
This is the pit and this the elder tree.
Look, sirs, if you can find the huntsman out
That should have murdered Bassianus here.

AARON   [*Finds the bag of gold.*]

My gracious lord, here is the bag of gold.   280

SATURNINUS   [*to Titus*]

Two of thy whelps, fell curs of bloody kind,
Have here bereft my brother of his life.
Sirs, drag them from the pit unto the prison.
There let them bide until we have devised
Some never-heard-of torturing pain for them.   285

TAMORA

What? Are they in this pit? O wondrous thing!
How easily murder is discovered.

[*Attendants drag Quintus, Martius, and Bassianus' body from the pit.*]

TITUS   [*Kneels.*]

High emperor, upon my feeble knee
I beg this boon, with tears not lightly shed,
That this fell fault of my accursed sons –   290
Accursed, if the faults be proved in them –

SATURNINUS

If it be proved? You see it is apparent.

---

281   **whelps** offspring of dogs
        fell curs … kind cunning dogs, violent by nature; the word 'kind' could mean natural disposition,
        parentage, or kinship (*OED* III.10.a).
287   **easily** pronounced with two syllables
        discovered discoverèd
290, 291 **accursed** accursèd

276] *Qq, F repeat SP*   280 SD] *Bevington subst.*   281 SD] *Rowe*   286] *Q1; F lines* pit, / thing! /   287 SD]
*Oxf*¹   288 SD] *Bevington subst.*

179

Who found this letter? Tamora, was it you?

TAMORA

Andronicus himself did take it up.

TITUS

I did, my lord, yet let me be their bail,   295
For by my fathers' reverend tomb I vow
They shall be ready at your highness' will
To answer their suspicion with their lives.

SATURNINUS

Thou shalt not bail them. See thou follow me.
Some bring the murdered body, some the murderers.   300
Let them not speak a word; the guilt is plain.
For, by my soul, were there worse end than death,
That end upon them should be executed.

TAMORA

Andronicus, I will entreat the king.
Fear not thy sons, they shall do well enough.   305

TITUS

Come, Lucius, come; stay not to talk with them.

*Exeunt [with Attendants carrying Bassianus' body
and others leading the prisoners].*

293–5   **Who found … lord** Aaron gives the letter to Tamora at 2.3.46 and she produces it here, so it is
not clear why Titus is said to have found it or why he would agree to have done so. In 5.1, when
Aaron is proudly describing the crimes he has committed and has no further use for subterfuge,
he tells Lucius 'I wrote the letter that thy father found' (106). This seems to be a continuity error,
attributable either to authorial sloppiness or perhaps to the play's history of revision prior to its
first print edition.

296   **fathers'** There is no apostrophe in the early texts to specify whether the word is singular or plural, but
we know that the monument of the Andronici is a family tomb.

298   **their suspicion** the suspicion they are under

300   **murderers** pronounced with two syllables ('murd'rers')

305   **Fear not thy sons** i.e., fear not for them

295] Q1; F lines Lord, / baile, /   296 reverend] *Rowe;* reuerent *Qq, F*   306] Q1; F lines come, / them. /   SD
Exeunt] F; not in Qq   with … prisoners] *Bevington subst.*

[2.4]   *Enter the Empress' sons* [CHIRON *and* DEMETRIUS], *with* LAVINIA, *her hands cut off, and her tongue cut out and ravished.*

DEMETRIUS

    So now go tell, and if thy tongue can speak,
    Who 'twas that cut thy tongue and ravished thee.

CHIRON

    Write down thy mind, bewray thy meaning so,
    And if thy stumps will let thee play the scribe.

DEMETRIUS

    See how with signs and tokens she can scrawl.   5

CHIRON

    Go home, call for sweet water, wash thy hands.

DEMETRIUS

    She hath no tongue to call, nor hands to wash,
    And so let's leave her to her silent walks.

CHIRON

    And 'twere my cause, I should go hang myself.

0.2   ***ravished*** On the early modern stage, the boy actor playing Lavinia probably entered with his costume soaked in animal blood to signify that Lavinia had been raped and mutilated. In modern productions, directors tend to swing between hyper-realistic portrayals of the effects of violent rape (like in Bornila Chatterjee's 2017 Indian film *The Hungry*) or stylistic ones that eschew blood in favour of ribbons (like in Yukio Ninagawa's 2006 Japanese production) or nothing at all (like in Tang Shu-wing's 2009 No Man's Land production [Hong Kong]).

1   **and if** if

3   **bewray** reveal

5   **scrawl** gesticulate (*OED v.*¹ 1); *Tit* predates the *OED*'s earliest uses of 'scrawl' as a verb to refer to hasty or inelegant writing by a few decades, though EEBO-TCP reveals that this meaning of the word, while rare, was not unheard of in late Elizabethan England (see, e.g., the discussion of a cipher 'raggedly scrawled' in *Discursive*, 52). Demetrius may possibly be punning on this emergent meaning of the word in response to Chiron's remarks about how Lavinia cannot write. F's 'scowl' is likely a compositorial misreading of Q3's 'scrowle' and makes less sense in the context of the brother's banter about trying to write without hands.

6   **sweet water** fresh water (*OED* sweet 3.b)

9   **And if**
    cause case, situation

2.4] *Dyce subst.; not in Qq, F*   0.1 CHIRON *and* DEMETRIUS] *Rowe subst.*   5 scrawl] *Qq* (scrowle); scowl *F*   6] *Q1; F lines* home, / hands. /

DEMETRIUS

If thou hadst hands to help thee knit the cord.   10

Exeunt [Chiron and Demetrius].

Wind horns. Enter MARCUS *from hunting, to Lavinia [who begins to flee].*

MARCUS

Who is this? My niece, that flies away so fast?

Cousin, a word – where is your husband?

[*Lavinia turns towards him.*]

If I do dream, would all my wealth would wake me;

If I do wake, some planet strike me down

That I may slumber an eternal sleep.   15

Speak, gentle niece, what stern ungentle hands

Hath lopped and hewed and made thy body bare

Of her two branches, those sweet ornaments

10.2   ***from hunting*** The fact that this is part of the SD suggests that Marcus' clothing should indicate in a visible way that he has been hunting. Dessen and Thomson note that SDs indicating that characters in early modern plays enter in hunting costumes are typically generic and do not specify what this entails.

who begins to flee Bevington was the first modern editor to use the SD to make explicit what is implied by Marcus at 11. In the seventeenth-century German version of the play, the Lavinia character '*flees into the forest*' (*Tito*, SD after 4.2.9) when first discovered after the assault and then has to be brought back to the stage by her brother (at 4.2.12).

11   ***Who ... fast?*** Because Lavinia is trying to avoid Marcus, he does not immediately recognize the violence that has been done to her.

12   ***Cousin*** a kinship term used of any relative more distant than a brother or sister who is not in a direct line of descent

13   ***If ... wake me*** 'If this is a dream I would give all my wealth to wake from it'

14   ***If I*** There is a small printer's error here: line 14 is the first line on sig. E2ᵛ in Q1, and the catchword ('I') on sig. E2ʳ leads one to expect that the next word will be 'I'. The lines are obviously correct as printed, however.

    some planet ... down 'To be planet struck' (Dent, P389), as a proverbial or idiomatic expression, meant to be blasted by some planetary force, resulting in destruction or utter paralysis. Marcus imagines himself being rendered eternally insensible or killed.

17–18   ***lopped ... branches*** The word 'lopped' comes from forestry and is associated with tree-trimming, as in Marcus' extended metaphor. Compare 1.1.129 and 143.

18   ***ornaments*** adornments; here Lavinia's hands and, by extension, her arms

---

10 SD *Exeunt] Q1, F; not in Q2–3   Chiron and Demetrius] Theobald   10.2 Wind horns ... Lavinia] F; Enter* MARCUS *from hunting Qq   who begins to flee] Bevington subst.   11 SP] not in Qq, F, but implied by entry SD   12 SD] Ard³ subst.   14 If I] Qq, F; 'I' is catchword on previous page in Q1   15 an] Q1; in Q2–3, F*

Whose circling shadows kings have sought to sleep in
And might not gain so great a happiness 20
As half thy love? Why dost not speak to me?
Alas, a crimson river of warm blood,
Like to a bubbling fountain stirred with wind,
Doth rise and fall between thy rosed lips,
Coming and going with thy honey breath. 25
But sure some Tereus hath deflowered thee
And, lest thou shouldst detect him, cut thy tongue.
Ah, now thou turn'st away thy face for shame,
And notwithstanding all this loss of blood,
As from a conduit with three issuing spouts, 30
Yet do thy cheeks look red as Titan's face,
Blushing to be encountered with a cloud.

19 **Whose circling … in** 'in whose embrace kings have sought to sleep'; Marcus maintains the tree-related imagery from the previous lines, likening Lavinia's arms to encircling, shadow-casting branches. It is an awkward, strained metaphorical conceit: Marcus' language in this scene is full of elaborate metaphorical conceits that can seem grotesque given the nature of Lavinia's visible trauma.

21 **as half … love** Theobald's emendation of 'half' to 'have' has not generally been accepted in modern editions. Marcus' point is that those kings who had sought to sleep in Lavinia's embrace were unable to achieve even the happiness that winning half of her love would entail.

24 **rosed** rosèd; rosy

26 **some Tereus** see 2.3.43n.; Tereus raped his sister-in-law Philomela and cut out her tongue to prevent her from telling what had happened. The story was a model for Shakespeare and Peele, as well as for characters within the play seeking to understand or advance the play's action. Marcus returns to the Ovidian story at 38 below.

27 ***him** The early texts have 'them' here, and editors have generally followed Rowe in correcting the grammar of the sentence: as Bate notes in Ard[3], it was very easy for a compositor to mistake 'him' for 'them' in Elizabethan handwriting. Since Lavinia has been mutilated by two people, it may also possibly be an authorial slip to think of her attackers as plural rather than singular.

30 **conduit … issuing spouts** a fountain or pipe for distributing water, here figuring the three wounds from which Lavinia is bleeding; the early texts have 'their issuing spouts', which is grammatically awkward since conduit is singular. We adopt Hanmer's emendation, which is plausible since a compositor could easily mistake 'thre' in manuscript for 'ther' (as suggested in Ard[2]).

31 **Titan's** the sun's, as at 1.1.227

32 **encountered with** confronted with, obscured by

21 half] *Qq, F*; have *Theobald*   27 him] *Rowe*; them *Qq, F*   30 three] *Hanmer*; their *Qq, F*

Shall I speak for thee? Shall I say 'tis so?
O, that I knew thy heart, and knew the beast,
That I might rail at him to ease my mind.   35
Sorrow concealed, like an oven stopped,
Doth burn the heart to cinders where it is.
Fair Philomela, why she but lost her tongue,
And in a tedious sampler sewed her mind.
But, lovely niece, that mean is cut from thee: 40
A craftier Tereus, cousin, hast thou met,
And he hath cut those pretty fingers off
That could have better sewed than Philomel.
O, had the monster seen those lily hands
Tremble like aspen leaves upon a lute   45

33   **Shall I speak for thee** Lavinia, who was spoken for by her father in 1.1 and who is spoken for many
      times subsequently, may react demonstratively, but Marcus' speech gives no indication that he has
      understood her. While many productions choose to depict Lavinia as silenced and traumatized,
      others choose to depict her agency more directly. For instance, in Matthew R. Wilson's 2014 Faction
      of Fools production, the deaf actor playing Lavinia, Miranda Medugno, was visibly exasperated
      whenever anyone spoke for her.
34   **the beast** i.e., the rapist
36–7 **an oven ... cinders** The image is proverbial (Dent O89.1, 'an oven dammed up bakes soonest');
      compare *V&A* 331–4: 'An oven that is stopped, or river stayed, / Burneth more hotly, swelleth with
      more rage: / So of concealed sorrow may be said'.
38   **Fair ... tongue** We retain Q1's reading despite its hypermetrical quality. Some editors, since Cam[1],
      have shortened Philomela to Philomel, and Q3 and F regularize the line by dropping the word 'why'.
      Marcus' speech is conspicuously mannered and poetic, but he is also reacting to a horror and the
      rhetorical choppiness created by the extra syllable may reflect his disturbance.
39   **tedious** laborious
      sampler 'a piece of embroidery serving as a pattern to be copied' (*OED n*[1] 3.a); the Philomel story is
      the pattern that has been copied.
40   **that mean ... thee** the means to sew (i.e., hands and fingers) have been cut off
41   **craftier** because Tereus left Philomela the means to communicate by embroidery, but, knowing the
      Philomela story, Lavinia's rapist has taken away that means for communication too
44   **lily** white, like the flower
45   **Tremble ... lute** The metaphor of somebody trembling like an aspen leaf is a common poetic
      figuration that Bate (in Ard[3]) suggests is derived from Golding ('stoode trembling like an aspen leafe'
      [3.46]; 'I trembling like an aspen leaf stood' [14.245]). This seems likely, as Golding's examples are the
      earliest ones that turn up in a collocation search in EEBO. In other early modern instances, the image
      is often a way of expressing fear, but here it describes the quick delicacy of Lavinia's musical touch.
      Using the image of shaking leaves to represent the movement of fingers on a lute is another strained
      poetic conceit in a speech that is full of them.

38 why] *Q1–2; not in Q3, F*   41 cousin, hast thou met] *Q1–2;* hast thou met *Q3;* hast thou met withall *F*

And make the silken strings delight to kiss them,
He would not then have touched them for his life.
Or had he heard the heavenly harmony
Which that sweet tongue hath made,
He would have dropped his knife and fell asleep,   50
As Cerberus at the Thracian poet's feet.
Come, let us go and make thy father blind,
For such a sight will blind a father's eye.
One hour's storm will drown the fragrant meads:
What will whole months of tears thy father's eyes?   55
Do not draw back, for we will mourn with thee.
O, could our mourning ease thy misery.   *Exeunt.*

49   **Which ... made** an unusually short iambic trimeter line
50–1   **fell asleep ... feet** The Thracian poet Orpheus is imagined soothing Cerberus, the three-headed dog
        who guards the entrance to the classical underworld, to sleep with music on his way to attempt the
        rescue of his deceased wife Eurydice – a well-known episode recounted in book 4 of Virgil's *Georgics*
        and elsewhere. Marcus' conceit is that Lavinia's song would have charmed the bestial rapist to sleep
        too had he but heard it.
54   **meads** meadows
55   **tears thy father's** tears do to thy father's

[3.1] *Enter the [Tribunes as] Judges and [the] Senators, with* TITUS' *two sons* [QUINTUS *and* MARTIUS] *bound, passing on the stage to the place of execution, and* TITUS *going before pleading.*

TITUS

Hear me, grave fathers, noble tribunes: stay
For pity of mine age, whose youth was spent
In dangerous wars whilst you securely slept.
For all my blood in Rome's great quarrel shed,
For all the frosty nights that I have watched,   5
And for these bitter tears which now you see
Filling the aged wrinkles in my cheeks,
Be pitiful to my condemned sons,
Whose souls is not corrupted as 'tis thought.
For two-and-twenty sons I never wept   10
Because they died in honour's lofty bed.

Andronicus lieth down, and the Judges pass by him.

0.1 *[Tribunes as] Judges* Most editors since Capell have added Tribunes to the ranks named in this stage direction because Titus specifically addresses them in the speech that follows. Sisson likewise argues that Tribunes other than Marcus must be included among the Senators (2:139). Since Titus speaks to the tribunes as judges, we concur with Ard³ that their entry is implied by the stage direction as it stands in Qq and F.

0.2 *on* It may well be that this unusual formulation was the Q1 compositor's misreading of an abbreviated version of *over* ('ou") in manuscript, as postulated in Oxf¹. We print the word as it appears in all the early texts and note that the meaning would not be changed by emendation.

5 **watched** remained vigilant
7 **aged** agèd
8 **condemned** condemnèd
9 **souls is** grammatically acceptable in idiomatic Early Modern English (see 2.1.26n.)
10 **two-and-twenty** At the beginning of the play, Titus indicates that he had 25 sons and that 21 died in the war (1.1.82). He may now be including Mutius among the honourably killed, or this number may be an authorial mistake.

3.1] *Actus Tertius. F; not in Qq*   0.1 *the Tribunes ... Senators] Ard³; The Judges and Senatours Qq, F; Senators, Tribunes, &c. and Officers of Justice / Capell*   0.2 QUINTUS *and* MARTIUS] *Capell subst.*   *on] Qq, F; over Oxf¹*   9 *is] Qq, F; are F2*

For these, tribunes, in the dust I write
My heart's deep languor and my soul's sad tears.
Let my tears staunch the earth's dry appetite;
My sons' sweet blood will make it shame and blush.   15

                                         Exeunt [all but Titus].

O earth, I will befriend thee more with rain
That shall distil from these two ancient ruins
Than youthful April shall with all his showers.
In summer's drought I'll drop upon thee still;
In winter with warm tears I'll melt the snow,   20
And keep eternal springtime on thy face,
So thou refuse to drink my dear sons' blood.

12   **For ... write** Editors have often emended this line by adding another one-syllable word before 'tribunes' for metrical reasons. We retain the reading from Qq, F rather than introducing a word as a placeholder.

13   **languor** sorrow, distress

14   **staunch** satisfy (*OED v.* 3.b). Since Titus goes on to suggest that staunching the earth's appetite with tears will prevent bloodshed, the word may also carry a secondary, metaphorical association with the stopping of blood flow (as in *OED* 2.a).

15   **shame and blush** Consuming the sons' blood would give earth the red appearance of a blush.

15 SD   *The SD, which is omitted in Qq, appears at 16 in F. It was probably placed there because there wasn't enough room for it in F's column of text at 15, where there is a natural break in the speech. When and how the dignitaries pass across the stage is a performance choice. By including many actors as Judges and Senators, a performance can highlight the overwhelming power of the Roman state, and such a procession could itself take place over the course of several lines. The SD after 11 indicating that the Judges and Senators 'pass by' Titus may also imply that the procession crosses the stage quickly and exits, and so Cam[1] adds 'Exeunt' there. In Lucy Bailey's 2014 Shakespeare's Globe production, Titus (played by William Houston) and the tribunes entered through the audience, and the tribunes, along with an executioner carrying a large axe, exited by 11. Having the officials leave while Titus is speaking, as in F, emphasizes his utter disenfranchisement.

17   **distil** fall in droplets
       these two ancient ruins his eyes

22   **So** as long as; Titus' image of the earth drinking blood resonates with the image of the 'blood-drinking pit' at 2.2.224.

12 these] Qq, F; these, these F2; these, good *Boswell;* these, O *Hudson²;* these two *Oxf¹ (conj. Jackson, Z.)*   15 SD *Exeunt] RSC; at line 16 in F; not in Qq*   *all but Titus] Capell subst.*   17 ruins] Qq, F; urns *Hanmer*   21 on thy] Q2–3, F; outhy Q1

Enter LUCIUS *with his weapon drawn.*

O reverend tribunes, O gentle aged men,
Unbind my sons, reverse the doom of death,
And let me say, that never wept before,   25
My tears are now prevailing orators.

LUCIUS

O noble father, you lament in vain.
The tribunes hear you not. No man is by,
And you recount your sorrows to a stone.

TITUS

Ah Lucius, for thy brothers let me plead.   30
Grave tribunes, once more I entreat of you.

LUCIUS

My gracious Lord, no tribune hears you speak.

TITUS

Why, 'tis no matter, man. [*Rises.*] If they did hear,

---

23   **aged** agèd.
24   **doom** judgement, sentence
26   **prevailing orators** i.e., persuasive speakers; the movement in this scene from Titus' final attempt at
        public oratory to the jarring indecorum of his laughter at 265 epitomizes the collapse of decorous
        oratory as an instrument of civic order within the play's imagined Roman milieu. Mansky argues that
        the first half of the play stages 'the history of rhetorical decline under monarchy' (89).
28   **hear you not** F's alterative reading – 'hear not' – makes sense, but ruins the metre and so is likely
        an error.
33 SD   *Capell adds a stage direction indicating that Titus rises in the middle of this line; other editors indicate
        that Titus rises at 40, 47 or 52. Just as the amount of time it takes the Judges and Senators to cross
        the stage is a performance decision, so too is the amount of time Titus spends kneeling. The prompt
        book for Peter Brook's 1955 RSC production indicates that Titus (played by Laurence Olivier) should
        rise at 52.

23 reverend] F3; reuerent *Qq, F*   28 hear you not] *Qq*; hear not F   33 SD] *Capell;* at 40 *Collier;* at 47 *Dyce;*
at 52 *Oxf²*

They would not mark me; if they did mark,
They would not pity me: yet plead I must, 35
And bootless unto them.
Therefore, I tell my sorrows to the stones,
Who though they cannot answer my distress,
Yet in some sort they are better than the tribunes
For that they will not intercept my tale. 40
When I do weep, they humbly at my feet
Receive my tears and seem to weep with me,
And were they but attired in grave weeds
Rome could afford no tribunes like to these.

34–7 **They would ... stones** The compositor of Q3 mangles these lines by dropping 35 altogether, altering
36 and rendering 37 hypermetrical and redundant: 'They would not marke me; or if they did marke, /
All bootlesse unto them. / Therefore I tell my sorrowes bootles to the stones'. F is mostly set from Q3,
but in this case the compositor seems to have consulted some other source in order to make sense of
what he found in Q3. F reads: 'They would not marke me; oh if they did heare / They would not pity
me. / Therefore I tell my sorrows bootless to the stones'. How editors treat this tangle depends upon
what source they imagine the compositor of F might have turned to: Ard² posited that F's compositor
consulted a prompt copy, which if true might lend authorial weight to that text's omission of 36. But if
that were the case we might also expect Q3's hypermetrical version of 37 to be improved upon in F, and
it is not. It is also possible that F's compositor simply consulted an earlier quarto copy (or a corrected
copy of Q3) here but omitted 36 because of the use of the word 'bootless' in Q3's version of the next
line. We use the Q1 version of these lines because we think the variants in F seem primarily like a failed
effort to fix the confusion of the Q3 compositor (see also pp. 40–1). Q2 follows Q1 but adds a syllable
to correct the metre in line 34 ('or if they did marke'). The half-line at 36 is omitted in Oxf¹, but there are
other half-lines in the play (such as 2.1.9), and the raggedness of Titus' rhetorical flow suits the situation
(as suggested in Ard³, 100–1).
36 **bootless** uselessly
39 **they are** pronounced as a contraction ('they're'); some later editors have emended the line to fix
the metre
40 **intercept** interrupt (*OED* 1.c, now obsolete)
42 **seem ... with me** The stones seem to be crying too because they are wet with Titus' tears.
43 **attired ... weeds** attirèd; the primary meaning of 'grave weeds' is dignified clothing: Titus, imagining
the stones as tribunes, says they might acquire grave weeds in order to play that role. There is also a
punning reference to the weeds that might grow around stones or even gravestones.
44 **afford** provide

34 if they did mark] *Q1*; or if they did marke *Q2–3*; oh, if they did hear *F* 35 They ... must] *Q1–2*; *not in Q3*;
They would not pitty me. *F* 36 And ... them] *Q1–2*; all ... them *Q3*; *not in F*; *om. in Oxf¹* 37 sorrows to] *Q1–2*;
sorrows bootles to *Q3, F* 39 they are] *Qq, F*; they're *Pope*; are *Hanmer* 44 tribunes] *Q1*; Tribune *Q2–3, F*.

A stone is as soft wax; tribunes more hard than stones.   45
A stone is silent, and offendeth not,
And tribunes with their tongues doom men to death.
But wherefore stand'st thou with thy weapon drawn?

LUCIUS

To rescue my two brothers from their death,
For which attempt the judges have pronounced   50
My everlasting doom of banishment.

TITUS

O happy man, they have befriended thee.
Why, foolish Lucius, dost thou not perceive
That Rome is but a wilderness of tigers?
Tigers must prey, and Rome affords no prey   55
But me and mine. How happy art thou then
From these devourers to be banished.
But who comes with our brother Marcus here?

Enter MARCUS *and* LAVINIA.

MARCUS

Titus, prepare thy aged eyes to weep,
Or if not so, thy noble heart to break.   60
I bring consuming sorrow to thine age.

---

45   **A ... stones** a hexameter line
        stone ... wax Wax is proverbially soft and malleable (Dent, W135.1), and so antithetical to the
        proverbial hardness of stones (S878). In Titus' compressed and paradoxical expression, even hard
        stones seem soft and yielding as wax when compared to the hardness of the Tribunes.
54   **wilderness ... tigers** Titus signals the utter collapse of the distinction between Roman/civilized and
        barbaric/wild that has often been evoked during the play's first two acts.
57   **banished** banishèd
59   **aged** agèd
61   **consuming** could have a range of associated meanings, such as dispersing (*OED* consume *v.*[1] 1) or
        destroying (*v.*[1] 2), but in a play that culminates with cannibalism the connotation of devouring (*v.*[1] 6a)
        is both resonant and proleptic

45] Q1; F *lines* waxe, / stones: / stone is as soft] F; stone is soft as *Qq*   56 me and] *Qq*; me and and F   58.1 *and*]
F; *with* Q1   59 aged] Q1; noble Q3, F

TITUS

Will it consume me? Let me see it then.

MARCUS

This was thy daughter.

TITUS

Why, Marcus, so she is.

LUCIUS [*Falls to his knees.*]

Ay me, this object kills me.   65

TITUS

Faint-hearted boy, arise and look upon her.   [*Lucius rises.*]
Speak Lavinia, what accursed hand
Hath made thee handless in thy father's sight?
What fool hath added water to the sea,
Or brought a faggot to bright-burning Troy?   70
My grief was at the height before thou cam'st,
And now like Nilus it disdaineth bounds.
Give me a sword; I'll chop off my hands too,
For they have fought for Rome, and all in vain,
And they have nursed this woe in feeding life.   75

63–5   **This ... is** Some editors treat 63 and 64 as a single line. But it would have been quite easy to create one perfect metrical line (by dropping the 'why', for instance) had that been intended. The slowing down caused by interruption of the metrical flow is fully appropriate to the subject-matter.

65   **object** spectacle; 'something placed before or presented to the eyes' (*OED* 1.a)

67–8   **accursed ... handless** The first of several instances in Act 3 where the hand as a conventional metaphor for agency is juxtaposed with the literalizing spectacle of a severed hand.
accursed accursèd

69   **added ... sea** The image of casting water into the sea is a proverbial (Dent, W106). Titus' language is more figurative and inventive and involves more shifting between different kinds of speech after he has been subject to trauma and cut off from his social position in Rome. Here, he juxtaposes a highly colloquial phrase with a more literary equivalent touching on the story of the destruction of Troy that means roughly the same thing (in the next line) as if he is code switching.

70   **faggot ... Troy** A faggot is a bundle of sticks used as fuel for fire. The image of adding fuel to the already-raging fire of Troy is another way of indicating foolish redundancy.

72   **Nilus** in mythology, the god of the Nile river; here synonymous with the Nile itself, which was known for overflowing its banks

73   **I'll chop off my hands too** Titus' line ironically anticipates events later in the scene.

---

65 SD] *Oxf¹ subst.*   66 SD] *Oxf¹*   75] *Q1; F lines* woe, / life: /

In bootless prayer have they been held up,
And they have served me to effectless use.
Now all the service I require of them
Is that the one will help to cut the other.
'Tis well Lavinia that thou hast no hands,   80
For hands to do Rome service is but vain.

LUCIUS

Speak, gentle sister: who hath martyred thee?

MARCUS

O, that delightful engine of her thoughts,
That blabbed them with such pleasing eloquence,
Is torn from forth that pretty hollow cage   85
Where, like a sweet melodious bird, it sung
Sweet varied notes, enchanting every ear.

LUCIUS

O, say thou for her; who hath done this deed?

---

76   **prayer** disyllabic here
77   **effectless** fruitless; a newfangled word in English at the time; the use in *Tit* is the earliest usage we find in the EEBO-TCP corpus.
81   **hands ... is** as in 9 above, the agreement of a plural noun with a singular, third-person, present-tense verb. It may be understood here that having hands is what is in vain, or that all service to Rome is done in vain.
82   **martyred** here and at 108 understood in its purely secular sense: to disfigure, mutilate or torture. But the word's association with sectarian violence may be worth remembering, too, since there are other anachronistically Christian terms in this scene (for instance, 'limbo' at 150).
83   **engine** Lavinia's tongue, in the sense of 'tool' or 'implement' (*OED* II.5)
84   **blabbed** spoke freely (*OED v.*[1] 1); the word can imply indiscretion (*OED v.*[1] 2), but Marcus presumably does not mean to imply any such criticism of Lavinia here.
86   **bird** Lavinia's tongue is imagined as a pet bird living in the cage of her mouth. Lavinia is likened to several kinds of animals in this scene, especially birds and deer; see 90 and 92, as well as 211 and 251, where there are puns on heart and hart (male deer). In Michael Sexton's 2011 production at the Public Lab, Lavinia was figured with a bird's head.

88] *Q1; F lines* her, / deed? /

MARCUS

O, thus I found her, straying in the park,
Seeking to hide herself, as doth the deer   90
That hath received some unrecuring wound.

TITUS

It was my deer, and he that wounded her
Hath hurt me more than had he killed me dead.
For now I stand as one upon a rock,
Environed with a wilderness of sea,   95
Who marks the waxing tide grow, wave by wave,
Expecting ever when some envious surge
Will in his brinish bowels swallow him.
This way to death my wretched sons are gone.
Here stands my other son, a banished man,   100
And here my brother, weeping at my woes.
But that which gives my soul the greatest spurn
Is dear Lavinia, dearer than my soul.
Had I but seen thy picture in this plight
It would have madded me; what shall I do   105

---

89   **park** An area reserved by royal grant for hunting; the term is dictated by the extended, courtly conceit
      that Lavinia is a wounded deer, and so is not necessarily meant to be literally descriptive of the actual
      place where she was discovered.
90–1 **Seeking … wound** i.e., 'trying to hide herself as does a wounded deer that has received an incurable
      wound'; the idea that a wounded deer withdraws itself to die is an Elizabethan commonplace.
      Compare, for instance, *AYL* 2.1.33–40. According to the *OED* and the EEBO-TCP database, Shakespeare
      is the only person to use 'unrecuring', although cognates like 'recuring', 'unrecured' and 'unrecurable'
      do appear several times in print earlier in the sixteenth century.
92   **deer** spelled 'deare' in Qq and F, both here at 90; the punning conflation of 'deer' and 'dear' is common
      in early modern literature, often facilitated as here by fluid spelling conventions. Depending upon
      which of the two meanings one prioritizes, Titus may be asserting his affection for his 'dear' Lavinia, or
      he may be asserting possession over her as his 'deer'.
96   **marks** watches
      waxing rising
97   **Expecting ever when** always expectantly awaiting
      envious spiteful
102   **spurn** an insulting kick; used metaphorically
105   **madded me** driven me mad

92] *Q1; F lines* Deare, / her, /   96] *Q1; F lines* tide, / waue, /   96 marks] *Qq, F; makes* F2–4

Now I behold thy lively body so?
Thou hast no hands to wipe away thy tears,
Nor tongue to tell me who hath martyred thee.
Thy husband he is dead, and for his death
Thy brothers are condemned, and dead by this.   110
Look, Marcus, ah, son Lucius, look on her:
When I did name her brothers, then fresh tears
Stood on her cheeks, as doth the honeydew
Upon a gathered lily almost withered.

MARCUS

Perchance she weeps because they killed her husband;   115
Perchance because she knows them innocent.

TITUS

If they did kill thy husband then be joyful,
Because the law hath ta'en revenge on them.
No, no, they would not do so foul a deed;
Witness the sorrow that their sister makes.   120

---

106   **lively body** living body; references to the lively body of Christ or to Christians as lively members of
       Christ's body are commonplace and idiomatic in early modern devotional literature, so referring to
       Lavinia's 'lively body' may suggest the language of Christian martyrdom hinted at in 82 and 108.
110   **by this** by now
111   **look on her** Titus' lines may have originally indicated some specific demonstration of emotion on
       Lavinia's part. Performances differ dramatically with regard to Lavinia's actions in the scene. For
       example, in Peter Brook's 1955 RSC production, Vivien Leigh's Lavinia was haunted but demur, while
       in Lucy Bailey's 2006 Shakespeare's Globe production, Laura Rees was traumatized into a stupor. In
       Matthew R. Wilson's 2014 Faction of Fools production, on the other hand, Lavinia was portrayed by
       the deaf actress Miranda Medungo, who was demonstratively annoyed that her father was attempting
       to interpret her non-signed emotions.
113   **honeydew** 'a sugar-rich sticky liquid ... sometimes found on the leaves and stems of trees and plants,
       and formerly thought to originate from the sky in a manner similar to dew' (*OED*)
114   **a gathered ... withered** Lilies were often associated with a woman's white beauty and/or chaste purity,
       as in *Cym*, where Iachimo sneaks into Innogen's bedroom and voyeuristically surveys her sleeping
       body: 'Fresh lily, / And whiter than the sheets' (2.2.15–16). Titus' image of Lavinia as a gathered lily
       about to wither is one of sexual violence, or of deflowering, even though he does not fully understand
       the extent of her sexual violation until later.
115–16 **Perchance ... Perchance** Perhaps ... or perhaps
120   **makes** expresses; presumably the actor playing Lavinia has responded gesturally to Titus. Ravenscroft,
       who added several SDs to supply Lavinia's gestural reactions, added a stage direction here: 'Lav. *makes
       signs of sorrow lifting up her eyes & then hanging down her head & moving her stumps*' (p. 30).

116 them] Q1; him Q3, F

Gentle Lavinia, let me kiss thy lips
Or make some signs how I may do thee ease.
Shall thy good uncle and thy brother Lucius
And thou and I sit round about some fountain,
Looking all downwards to behold our cheeks,   125
How they are stained, like meadows yet not dry,
With miry slime left on them by a flood?
And in the fountain shall we gaze so long
Till the fresh taste be taken from that clearness
And made a brine pit with our bitter tears?   130
Or shall we cut away our hands like thine?
Or shall we bite our tongues and in dumb shows
Pass the remainder of our hateful days?
What shall we do? Let us that have our tongues
Plot some device of further miseries   135
To make us wondered at in time to come.

LUCIUS

Sweet father, cease your tears, for at your grief
See how my wretched sister sobs and weeps.

---

127   **miry** swampy, as from a mire
129   **clearness** purity, as of fresh water
132–3   **shall we … days** A dumb show is a portion of an early modern play performed in mime and without
        speech, so Titus is suggesting that perhaps they should fall silent. Because Hieronimo, the revenger in
        Thomas Kyd's *Spanish Tragedy*, bites out his tongue, and because that play contains dumb shows, there
        is a possible metatheatrical allusion here, as if Titus, as he casts about for a suitable reaction to the
        violence Lavinia has suffered, is somehow thinking of Kyd's revenge play. On the importance of Kyd's
        play for *Tit*, see pp. 64–7.
138   **See how** Lucius calls attention to Lavinia's non-verbal communication. Once again the directorial/
        performance options vary wildly with regard to Lavinia's actions. She may signal that Lucius'
        interpretation of her sobs is correct (as in Deborah Warner's 1987 RSC production), she may remain
        unresponsive (Lise Bruneau's 2013 Riot Grrrls production) or she may physically signal dissent
        (Matthew R. Wilson's 2014 Faction of Fools production). This continues to be the case for 144ff.
        Ravenscroft adds a SD just before Lucius' speech: 'Lav. *turns up her eyes & then hangs down her head as
        weeping*' (p. 31).

---

122 signs] F; signe Qq   126 like] Q1; in Q2–3, F   135 miseries] F; miserie Qq

MARCUS

  Patience, dear niece. Good Titus, dry thine eyes.

  [*Offers handkerchief to Titus.*]

TITUS

  Ah Marcus, Marcus, brother, well I wot   140

  Thy napkin cannot drink a tear of mine,

  For thou, poor man, hast drowned it with thine own.

LUCIUS

  Ah, my Lavinia, I will wipe thy cheeks.

TITUS

  Mark, Marcus, mark. I understand her signs.

  Had she a tongue to speak, now would she say   145

  That, to her brother, which I said to thee:

  His napkin with his true tears all bewet

  Can do no service on her sorrowful cheeks.

  O, what a sympathy of woe is this,

  As far from help as limbo is from bliss.   150

                    Enter AARON *the Moor alone.*

140   **wot** know
141   **napkin** handkerchief
143   **I will … cheeks** In Ravenscroft, Marcus' offer to wipe Lavinia's tears is answered by the following
       SD: 'Lav. *Shakes her head & points at* Mar. handkercher *as refusing to have her eyes wip'd*' (p. 31).
144   **Mark, Marcus, mark** The unexpected sonic playfulness of this half-line may be meant to seem
       indecorous, and perhaps correlates to Titus' growing sense in this scene that his words are politically
       useless. Wright discusses this half-line as a play upon the poetic convention of beginning a line with a
       spondee created by repeating a monosyllabic word (Wright, *Metrical*, 303–4 n.3).
147   *with his** 'with her' in all the early versions until F4; an error likely stemming from the Q1 compositor's
       misreading of 'his' as 'hir'
149   **sympathy** agreement, accord
150   **limbo** technically, a region on the borders of Hell supposed to be inhabited by virtuous pagans and
       unbaptized infants, but sometimes used as a synonym for Hell (*OED* 1.c); despite the pagan setting of
       Tit, the term is Catholic.

139 SD] *Cam*[3] *subst.*   147 with his] *F4*; with her *Qq, F–F3*

AARON

    Titus Andronicus, my lord the Emperor

    Sends thee this word: that if thou love thy sons,

    Let Marcus, Lucius, or thyself old Titus,

    Or any one of you, chop off your hand

    And send it to the king. He, for the same,   155

    Will send thee hither both thy sons alive,

    And that shall be the ransom for their fault.

TITUS

    O gracious emperor, O gentle Aaron.

    Did ever raven sing so like a lark

    That gives sweet tidings of the sun's uprise?   160

    With all my heart I'll send the Emperor my hand.

    Good Aaron, wilt thou help to chop it off?

LUCIUS

    Stay father, for that noble hand of thine

    That hath thrown down so many enemies

    Shall not be sent. My hand will serve the turn.   165

    My youth can better spare my blood than you,

    And therefore mine shall save my brothers' lives.

MARCUS

    Which of your hands hath not defended Rome

    And reared aloft the bloody battleaxe,

---

151 SP In Qq and F, the SP for Aaron is 'Moore' until 200 when it switches to 'Aron'. Unlike Othello, Aaron is much more frequently referred to by his first name (24 times) than he is called Moor (12 times) by the other characters in the play. Despite the fact that Othello is a general and Aaron is initially enslaved by the Romans, Aaron is more consistently individuated by the other characters in the play.

159   **raven** Aaron is frequently linked to black birds/animals (as at 2.3.83, where he is described as Tamora's 'raven-coloured love'); these are metatheatrical references of a kind that often work in tandem with the use of racial prosthetics (make-up, vizards, wigs, stockings, etc.) to indicate blackness in Renaissance plays (see Vaughan, and Smith, 'White Skin'; see also 206 below).

161   **With ... hand** Some editors have emended this line because it is hypermetrical. Capell replaces 'emperor' with 'king' for instance. Bate, in Ard³, defends the line as 'a purposeful hexameter'.

151 SP *Moore*] *Qq, F*   161 Emperor] *Qq, F*; king *Capell*

Writing destruction on the enemy's castle?   170
O, none of both but are of high desert.
My hand hath been but idle; let it serve
To ransom my two nephews from their death;
Then have I kept it to a worthy end.

AARON

Nay, come, agree whose hand shall go along,   175
For fear they die before their pardon come.

MARCUS

My hand shall go.

LUCIUS   By heaven it shall not go.

TITUS

Sirs, strive no more. Such withered herbs as these
Are meet for plucking up, and therefore mine.

LUCIUS

Sweet father, if I shall be thought thy son,   180
Let me redeem my brothers both from death.

MARCUS

And for our father's sake, and mother's care,
Now let me show a brother's love to thee.

---

170   **castle** Theobald speculated that 'castle' might have been a compositor's misreading of 'casque', a synonym for helmet, arguing that it is more feasible to split a helmet with a battle axe than to cut down a castle with one. Ard³ follows Theobald, adducing a similar image from *R2*: 'let thy blows, doubly redoubled, / Fall like amazing thunder on the casque / Of thy adverse pernicious enemy' (1.3.80–2), though Bate notes too that 'castle' could also mean 'helmet' (*OED* II.10). We retain Q1's reading because the line does not require speculative emendation. Any metrical objection is answered if 'enemy's' scans as two syllables ('en'mies'), and the line's military image may be more generalized than Theobald allowed, reflecting a battle against enemies with a castle rather than against a single helmed foe. In which case, as Hughes puts it in Cam³, 'castle' is just 'a medieval anachronism'.

171   **none ... desert** both are very deserving

178   **withered herbs** His hands are like withered herbs (more impermanent than other kinds of plants: *OED* 1) in that, as an old man, they are almost past their period of usefulness.

179   **meet** suitable, proper

182   **for ... mother's care** one of the only times in this play where a mother's care is imagined as a normal, healthy part of Roman life; the mother of Titus' children is absent, as are the mothers of other Andronici like Publius and Young Lucius, so Tamora represents the play's predominant image of the maternal.

---

170 castle] *Qq, F*; Casque *Theobald*; cask *Hanmer*

TITUS

    Agree between you. I will spare my hand.

LUCIUS

    Then I'll go fetch an axe.   185

MARCUS

    But I will use the axe.   *Exeunt [Lucius and Marcus].*

TITUS

    Come hither, Aaron. I'll deceive them both.

    Lend me thy hand and I will give thee mine.

AARON [*aside.*]

    If that be called deceit, I will be honest

    And never whilst I live deceive men so.   190

    But I'll deceive you in another sort,

    And that you'll say ere half an hour pass.

        He cuts off Titus' [left] hand.

           Enter LUCIUS *and* MARCUS *again.*

---

184   **spare** This is doublespeak on Titus' part, since 'spare' can either mean 'save' or 'do without' (as noted in McDonald).

186 SD *While Lucius and Marcus clearly exit before Aaron cuts off Titus' hand, it is a directorial/performance decision if/how long Lavinia stays on stage. Many directors opt to have Lavinia exit with Lucius and Marcus, but some also opt to have her remain on stage to witness her father's mutilation.

188   **Lend ... give** A parody of the language of good fellowship. Titus giving Aaron his severed hand literalizes – and in doing so spoofs – both the idea of lending a hand and the practice of clasping hands to signify agreement (see Kendall; Rowe, K., 65–9).

191   **in another sort** in another way

192 SD1 **cuts ... hand** On stage, the act of chopping off a hand would have involved a dummy hand of some kind as a prop (see Karim-Cooper, *Hand*, 200–21).
       left because at 3.2.7 Titus asserts that he still has his right hand

---

186 SD *Lucius and Marcus*] Theobald; not in Qq, F   189 SD] Rowe   192 SD *left*] Oxf²

TITUS

Now stay your strife. What shall be is dispatched.

Good Aaron, give his majesty my hand.

Tell him it was a hand that warded him   195

From thousand dangers. Bid him bury it:

More hath it merited; that let it have.

As for my sons, say I account of them

As jewels purchased at an easy price,

And yet dear too, because I bought mine own.   200

AARON

I go, Andronicus, and for thy hand

Look by and by to have thy sons with thee.

[aside] Their heads I mean! O, how this villainy

Doth fat me with the very thoughts of it!

Let fools do good and fair men call for grace,   205

Aaron will have his soul black like his face.   *Exit.*

---

193   **stay** cease

        What ... dispatched 'shall' carried a secondary sense of necessity, as what was fated or appointed to
        take place (*OED* II.i.4). Here the phrase means, 'what had to be done has been done'.

195   **warded** guarded, protected

197   **that** i.e., burial

199   **easy** inexpensive

200   **dear** costly

202   **Look** expect

203   **Their heads I mean** Aaron's cruel joke is reminiscent of the sadistically comic tone of Ovid's Procne,
        who reassures Tereus that his son is within ('*intus habes, quem poscis*') just before revealing that he has
        inadvertently eaten him (*Met.* 6.653–5), and also of Seneca's Atreus, who promises to return Thyestes'
        sons to him (*Thy.* 998) just before displaying their severed heads and revealing that their flesh and
        blood has been their father's banquet (1004–34).

204   **fat** feed

205–6   **fair ... face** Aaron's blackness is consistently noted and mentioned by characters in the text. Here,
        though, Aaron himself appropriates the racist assumption that a black skin signifies an evil soul.

193 your] *Q1*; you *F*   194 my] *Q1*; me *F*   198 As for] *Qq*; As for for *F*   203 SD] *Rowe; not in Qq, F*   204
thoughts] *Qq, F*; thought *F2–4*

TITUS [*Kneels.*]

O, here I lift this one hand up to heaven
And bow this feeble ruin to the earth.
If any power pities wretched tears,
To that I call. [*To Lavinia, who kneels.*]
               What, wilt thou kneel with me?   210
Do then, dear heart, for heaven shall hear our prayers,
Or with our sighs we'll breathe the welkin dim
And stain the sun with fog, as sometime clouds
When they do hug him in their melting bosoms.

MARCUS

O brother, speak with possibility,   215
And do not break into these deep extremes.

TITUS

Is not my sorrows deep, having no bottom?
Then be my passions bottomless with them.

---

208   **ruin** i.e., his old body. Compare 17 above.

209–10 **If … call** This plea revises Titus' first speech in the scene, where instead he hoped his tears would be 'prevailing orators' (26) to Rome's tribunes.

210 SD *We follow modern editorial convention in supplying stage directions to indicate that Lavinia kneels with Titus, as Titus' remark would seem to imply. This is one of several moments in the text where our only clues to Lavinia's actions come from her male relatives as they speak for her emotions and desires. It is important always to remember that in performance Lavinia may be resistant or indifferent to her father, uncle and brother.

211   **heaven** pronounced as one syllable ('heav'n')

212   **sighs … dim** darken the sky ('welkin') with mist or fog from our exhalations

213   **sometime** sometimes

214   **him** i.e., the sun
        melting liquefying, as in rain

215   **with possibility** realistically

216   **break into** give utterance to

217   ***sorrows** The early texts read 'sorrow', but this is usually emended to 'sorrows' to agree with 'them' in the next line. The resulting combination of plural noun with singular verb is grammatical in Elizabethan English (see 2.1.26n.).

218   **passions** outbursts of strong emotion

---

207 SD] *Bevington subst.*   210 SD] *Bevington subst.* wilt] *F;* wouldst *Q1;* would *Q2–3* 215 possibility] *Q1;* possibilities *Q3, F* 217 sorrows] *Dyce²;* sorrow *Qq, F*

MARCUS

But yet let reason govern thy lament.

TITUS

If there were reason for these miseries,   220
Then into limits could I bind my woes.
When heaven doth weep, doth not the earth o'erflow?
If the winds rage, doth not the sea wax mad,
Threatening the welkin with his big-swollen face?
And wilt thou have a reason for this coil?   225
I am the sea. Hark how her sighs doth flow;
She is the weeping welkin, I the earth.
Then must my sea be moved with her sighs;
Then must my earth with her continual tears
Become a deluge, overflowed and drowned,   230
For why my bowels cannot hide her woes,
But like a drunkard must I vomit them.

---

221   **into … bind** I could contain within limits
222–30 **When heaven … drowned,** The oceanic and atmospheric language of overwhelming and overflowing grief may owe something to Hieronimo's passionate sorrow in Act 3 of Kyd's *Spanish Tragedy* (see Ard³, Appendix 1, 285–6).
223   **wax** grow
224   **Threatening … face** The blank-verse metre requires elided pronunciation of 'threat'ning' and 'swoll'n', and the spellings of these words in the early texts reflect this ('threatning'; Qq have 'bigswolne' and F has 'big-swolne').
225   **coil** agitation, disturbance; i.e., Titus' expressive outburst
226   **flow** Many editors print 'blow' here, on the authority of F2, because Lavinia's sighs are airy exhalations. She is also described as a 'weeping welkin' in 227, however. A search of EEBO-TCP reveals several contemporary instances in which sighs are said to 'blow', but also several in which sighs and tears together are said to 'flow'. Since either reading is plausible, we choose not to correct the early texts.
228   **moved** movèd
231   **For why** because
       bowels the interior of the body, here imagined as the seat of compassion
       her The referent is Lavinia. Editors since Theobald have wondered if 'her' might here be an archaic form of the word 'their', but see Hope 1.3.2f.

---

226 doth] Q1; do Q2-3, F   flow] Qq, F; blow F2   231 her] Qq, F; their *Theobald*

Then give me leave, for losers will have leave
To ease their stomachs with their bitter tongues.

Enter a Messenger *with two heads and a hand.*
[*Titus and Lavinia rise.*]

MESSENGER

Worthy Andronicus, ill art thou repaid   235
For that good hand thou sent'st the Emperor.

233–4   **losers ... tongues** an elaboration upon the proverbial notion that it is wise to let those who have lost
      vent their feelings in words (Dent, L458)
      stomachs Stomach is here 'used ... to designate the inward seat of passion' (*OED n.* 6.a). By extension,
      giving expression to extreme passion is imagined as vomiting.

234.1–2   Because this is the Messenger's only appearance in the play, he seems inorganic to the action. In Julie
      Taymor's 1999 film version of *Tit*, the messenger's brief, onstage appearance is replaced by a
      'Felliniesque' interpolated scene (Cartelli, 169) in which a clown and his assistant set up for what
      looks to be an impromptu show and then set up a 'still life' tableau including the heads in what
      are meant to be 'specimen jars' and Titus' hand on a 'mound of black velvet' before delivering a
      shortened, affectless version of the Messenger's speech through a megaphone (Taymor, *Screenplay*,
      107). The use of a generic, unnamed messenger is presumably meant to seem reminiscent of classical
      and neoclassical drama, where tragic violence is usually reported by messenger rather than shown.

234.1   **heads ... hand** Katherine Rowe reads the return of Titus' severed hand to the stage as a parodic
      literalization of the way handclasps represent social bonds in heroic literature (*Dead Hands*, 65–9). The
      spectacle of heads and hand together may also evoke *Thy.*, 764, where Atreus is said to set aside heads
      and hands while slaughtering his nephews ('*tantum ora servat et datas fidei manus*'; 'just the faces
      he keeps and the hands given in trust'). As Tarrant notes, Atreus wants the heads for identification,
      but the hands are 'grotesque souvenirs of ... pretended reconciliation' (200). Since 3.1 begins with
      Titus' efforts at public oratory and then devolves into the grotesque, the spectacle of dismembered
      heads and a severed hand may also evoke the fate of great orator Cicero, whose head and hands were
      cut off on Mark Antony's orders and placed over the rostra where orations were delivered in Rome.
      Shakespeare would have known the latter story from Plutarch, *Lives* (p. 937).

234.2   ***Titus ... rise** Titus indicates that he is kneeling at 207 and that Lavinia knelt at 210. There is no clear
      indication in the text concerning when they rise again, but the arrival of the Messenger perhaps
      indicates the start of a new action and so Titus and Lavinia may rise to meet the newcomer here.

235–6   **Worthy ... Emperor** Because the Messenger is abruptly inserted into the action, and not otherwise
      connected to any of the play's characters or their factions, it is jarring that he has such intimate
      knowledge of Aaron's prank. He is apparently being used by Aaron despite his expressions of sympathy
      for Titus.

234.2] *Ard³ subst.; at 276 in Oxf²*

Here are the heads of thy two noble sons,
And here's thy hand in scorn to thee sent back.
Thy grief, their sports. Thy resolution mocked,
That woe is me to think upon thy woes   240
More than remembrance of my father's death.   *Exit.*

MARCUS

Now let hot Etna cool in Sicily,
And be my heart an ever-burning hell!
These miseries are more than may be borne.
To weep with them that weep doth ease some deal,   245
But sorrow flouted at is double death.

LUCIUS

Ah that this sight should make so deep a wound
And yet detested life not shrink thereat.
That ever death should let life bear his name

---

239   **Thy ... sports** 'your sorrow is their entertainment'
240–1   **That ... remembrance of** i.e., so that it grieves me more to think upon your woes than to remember
242   **Etna** A volcano in Sicily, often used in classical Roman literature as a metaphor for the experience of turbulent passions such as love (e.g., *Met.* 13.868; *Phae.* 102–3) or anger (e.g., *HF* 106; *Med.* 409; *Thy.* 583). Violence and passion in this play are frequently depicted via self-consciously classicizing language and allusion.
245   **To weep ... weep** an echo of Romans 12:15: 'Rejoice with them that rejoice, and weep with them that weep'; the juxtaposition of a self-consciously classical mode of expressing emotional extremity ('Etna') with this anachronistic scriptural language perhaps registers the degree to which Marcus has now become untethered from his characteristically Roman sense of decorum.
        some deal somewhat
246   **flouted at** mocked
248   **shrink** wither or shrivel away
249   **let ... name** allow life to be called life

239 grief ... sports] Q1; griefes ... sports Q3, F   241 SD] F; *not in* Qq

Where life hath no more interest but to breathe.   250
    [*Lavinia kisses the severed heads of her brothers.*]

MARCUS

Alas, poor heart, that kiss is comfortless
As frozen water to a starved snake.

TITUS

When will this fearful slumber have an end?

MARCUS

Now farewell flattery: die, Andronicus.
Thou dost not slumber. See thy two sons' heads,   255
Thy warlike hand, thy mangled daughter here,
Thy other banished son with this dear sight
Struck pale and bloodless, and thy brother, I,
Even like a stony image, cold and numb.
Ah, now no more will I control thy griefs.   260

---

250   **interest** a right or title to share in something; Lucius is using legal language to complain that life's only share of living now is to breathe.

250 SD   *Marcus' remark at 251 is a reaction to a kiss, but there is no internal, textual basis upon which to determine who has kissed whom. A wide range of performance interpretations are possible. A note on performance provided in the RSC edition indicates that Lavinia here kissed Titus in Michael Fentiman's 2013 RSC production, but that she instead kissed the severed heads in Blanche McIntyre's 2017 RSC production. We follow the only extant textual evidence for an early performance choice in the German play *Tito Andronico*, which may contain traces of the performance of some earlier dramatic version of the Titus Andronicus story. In an equivalent episode in that play, the Lavinia character kisses the heads of her brothers (*Tito*, SD at 4.3.80). For the same reason, Ard³ opted to have Lavinia kiss the heads. Other editors, however, have imagined that Lavinia here kisses Lucius or Titus. In Ravenscroft's reconfigured adaptation of the play, Marcus' line about a comfortless kiss is instead a reaction to Lucius, who has kissed 'one head' (p. 36).

252   **starved** starvèd; almost dead from cold (*OED* v. 4), hence the comfortlessness of frozen water in particular

254   **flattery** pronounced as two syllables ('flatt'ry'); in the figurative sense of pleasing self-delusion (*OED* 2)

257   **dear** grievous (*OED adj.*² 2)

260   **control** restrain

---

250 SD] Ard³ subst.; *Lavinia kisses him / Johnson; Lavinia kisses Titus / Cam¹*   256 hand] *Qq*; hands F   257 son] *Qq*; sonnes F   260 thy] *Q1*; my *Q2–3*, F

Rend off thy silver hair, thy other hand
Gnawing with thy teeth, and be this dismal sight
The closing up of our most wretched eyes.
Now is a time to storm. Why art thou still?

TITUS

Ha, ha, ha.   265

MARCUS

Why dost thou laugh? It fits not with this hour.

TITUS

Why, I have not another tear to shed;
Besides, this sorrow is an enemy
And would usurp upon my watery eyes
And make them blind with tributary tears.   270
Then which way shall I find Revenge's cave?
For these two heads do seem to speak to me
And threat me I shall never come to bliss

---

265   **Ha, ha, ha** 'The play's pivotal indecorum' (Ard³); the indecorum of laughter in this context evokes a
       similar moment in Kyd's *Spanish Tragedy*, a play that helped set the generic conventions for Elizabethan
       revenge tragedy. There, too, the aggrieved revenger's laughter is indicative of his complete breakdown
       (see p. 65).

267   **Why** in the sense of introducing a reason why and so answering the question; compare *Lear*: 'Why I do
       trifle thus with his despair is done to cure it' (4.6.33)

269   **usurp upon** take control of
       watery pronounced with two syllables ('wat'ry')

270   **tributary tears** As at 1.1.162, the sense is that the tears are given as tribute, but with a secondary
       evocation of tributary rivers flowing into a larger body of water.

271   **Revenge's cave** Given the echo of Virgil at 2.3.236, and the play's propensity for webs of intertextual
       allusion, the image likely owes something to the dreadful cave ('*specus horrendum*' [7.568]) to which
       the vengeful fury Allecto flies in *Aen*.7. Later in *Tit*, Publius humours Titus by imagining Pluto sending
       Revenge to earth (4.3.37–41). The same notion underpins the disguise that Tamora eventually adopts
       in 5.2. If Titus is here thinking of an underworld cave, then the compensatory quality of his fantasy
       also recalls Hieronimo's madness in Act 3 of *The Spanish Tragedy*: 'Though on this earth justice will not
       be found, / I'll down to hell, and in this passion / Knock at the dismal gates of Pluto's court' (*Spanish
       Tragedy*, 3.13.108–10).

273   **threat** threaten

---

261 Rend] *Qq, F* (Rent)   267 Why, I] *Theobald*; Why I *Qq, F*; Why? I *Ard³*

Till all these mischiefs be returned again
Even in their throats that hath committed them.   275
Come, let me see what task I have to do.
You heavy people circle me about
That I may turn me to each one of you
And swear unto my soul to right your wrongs.
          [*They gather around Titus to make a vow.*]

The vow is made. Come, brother, take a head,   280
And in this hand the other will I bear;
And, Lavinia, thou shalt be employed in these things.
Bear thou my hand, sweet wench, between thy teeth.
As for thee, boy, go get thee from my sight;
Thou art an exile and thou must not stay.   285
Hie to the Goths and raise an army there,

274–5   **returned ... in their throats** idiomatic; a combatant might respond to an affront or slander by offering
         to return the lie to its speaker's throat (as at 2.1.55); used figuratively here, as an image of revenge: to
         return an evil to its perpetrators' throats is to make them eat it.

277   **heavy** sorrowful

282   **And ... things** an editorial crux, partly because the line is metrically irregular; the line in Qq reads 'And
         Lavinia thou shalt be imployde in these Armes'. The sense of the Qq line has also proven confusing,
         though this concern is solved by the F reading, which we adopt. The editors of Cam[1] speculated that
         282–3 in a lost authorial MS might have read 'And, Lavinia, thou shalt be imployd / Beare thou my
         hand sweet wench betweene thy teeth' (6.534), and that somebody unwilling to imagine Lavinia with
         a severed hand in her mouth corrected the MS by writing 'arms' above 'teeth', thereby misleading
         Q1's compositor. Ard[3] adopts the reconstructed line from Cam[1] quoted above. The editors of Oxf[3]
         emend the line to read 'And [in these things] Lavinia thou shalt be employed'. F2 improves the metre,
         but does not fix it entirely, by cutting the 'And' at the start of the line. In performance, as elsewhere,
         Lavinia's willingness to serve as a handmaiden to Titus' revenge is a directorial/performance decision.
         She can be portrayed as being eager and willing to participate in the revenge (as in Trevor Nunn's
         1972 RSC production, with Janet Suzman as Lavinia), or she may be highly resistant, even attempting
         to flee, from taking the hand (Matthew R. Wilson's 2014 Faction of Fools production). Most opt for
         something in between, with Lavinia so traumatized that she is pliant (Julie Taymor's 1994 Theatre for
         a New Audience production with Miriam Healy-Louie as Lavinia; Michael Sexton's 2011 Public Lab
         production with Jennifer Ikeda as Lavinia; and Yukio Ninagawa's 2006 production with Hitomi Manaka
         as Lavinia).

---

275 hath] *Q1*; haue *Q2–3, F*   279 SD] *This edn; They form a circle about Titus and he pledges each. Bevington;
They make a vow. Ard[3]*   282 And ... these things] *F*; And *om. F2*; And ... these Armes *Qq*; And ... these aims
Hudson; And, Lavinia, thou shalt be employed *Ard3*; And [in these things], *Lauinia*, thou shalt be imployde *Oxf[3]*

And if ye love me as I think you do,
Let's kiss and part for we have much to do.　　　*Exeunt. Manet Lucius.*

LUCIUS

Farewell, Andronicus, my noble father,
The woeful'st man that ever lived in Rome.　　　290
Farewell, proud Rome, till Lucius come again;
He loves his pledges dearer than his life.
Farewell, Lavinia, my noble sister,
O, would thou wert as thou tofore hast been.
But now nor Lucius nor Lavinia lives　　　295
But in oblivion and hateful griefs.
If Lucius live, he will requite your wrongs
And make proud Saturnine and his empress
Beg at the gates like Tarquin and his queen.
Now will I to the Goths and raise a power　　　300
To be revenged on Rome and Saturnine.　　　*Exit Lucius.*

288 *Manet* (Latin) remains
292 **his pledges** those he is now pledged to protect and revenge (i.e., his family)
294 **tofore** previously
296 **in oblivion** in complete, abject obscurity
297 **requite** avenge
299 **Tarquin** Lucius Tarquinius Superbus, the last king of Rome, who was deposed and – with his wife Tullia – exiled after his son Sextus Tarquinius raped Lucrece (see 2.1.108n). In Livy, Tarquinius Superbus is away at war when the Roman people rebel, and he returns to find the gates of the city closed against him (1.60).

287 ye] Q1; you Q2–3, F　288 SD *Manet Lucius*] F; *not in* Qq　299 like] Qq; likes F

[3.2] *A banquet [set out]. Enter* [TITUS] Andronicus, MARCUS, LAVINIA,
and the boy [YOUNG LUCIUS].

TITUS

So, so, now sit, and look you eat no more
Than will preserve just so much strength in us
As will revenge these bitter woes of ours.
Marcus, unknit that sorrow-wreathen knot:
Thy niece and I, poor creatures, want our hands   5
And cannot passionate our tenfold grief
With folded arms. This poor right hand of mine
Is left to tyrannize upon my breast,
Who, when my heart, all mad with misery,
Beats in this hollow prison of my flesh,   10
Then thus I thump it down.
[*to Lavinia*] Thou map of woe, that thus dost talk in signs,
When thy poor heart beats with outrageous beating,
Thou canst not strike it thus to make it still.
Wound it with sighing, girl, kill it with groans,   15

<hr>

3.2   This entire scene was first printed in F, and probably first performed in a Jacobean revival of this
        enduringly popular play. On authorship and dating, see pp. 28–30.
0.1   *set out* On stage, the scene must begin with a table, chairs and dishes representing a meal being set
        out for the Andronici.
1   look you see to it that you
4   sorrow-wreathen knot i.e., his arms, folded in a manner that Titus takes to indicate unhappiness
6   passionate express or perform passion
        tenfold greatly magnified
7–8   right ... is left Titus' language is playful and inventive, though in a manner that is meant to seem
        unsuitable for his tragic experiences and situation. Here, he is punning on right and left while
        complaining about the loss of his left hand.
8   to tyrannize to domineer or act like a tyrant; Titus says that his right hand attempts to control his
        beating heart by thumping his chest.
12   map epitome (*OED* II.5.a), but also, here, an image that requires interpretation
13   outrageous excessive
14   canst ... it because Lavinia is lacking both hands

<hr>

3.2] *entire scene first printed in F; not in Qq; numbered by Capell*   0.1 banquet] F (*Bnaket*); Banquet F2   set out]
Bevington   TITUS] *Rowe*   0.2 YOUNG LUCIUS *Rowe subst.*   12 SD] *Johnson*   13 with outrageous] F2; without
ragious F

Or get some little knife between thy teeth
And just against thy heart make thou a hole,
That all the tears that thy poor eyes let fall
May run into that sink and, soaking in,
Drown the lamenting fool in sea-salt tears.   20

MARCUS

Fie, brother, fie: teach her not thus to lay
Such violent hands upon her tender life.

TITUS

How now? Has sorrow made thee dote already?
Why, Marcus, no man should be mad but I:
What violent hands can she lay on her life?   25
Ah, wherefore dost thou urge the name of hands
To bid Aeneas tell the tale twice o'er
How Troy was burnt, and he made miserable?
O handle not the theme to talk of hands,
Lest we remember still that we have none.   30

16–17 **little knife ... hole** It was proverbial that nightingales kept themselves awake by pressing their breasts against thorns (Dent, N183) and the heroine of Shakespeare's *Luc* draws on this image when comparing herself to Philomela, who – after being metamorphosed into a nightingale – is said to have pressed her breast against a thorn 'To keep [her] sharp woes waking' (*Luc* 1136). On the basis of this chain of associations Bate (Ard³) argues that Titus' suggestion that Lavinia might stab a hole over her heart 'sustains the image of Lavinia as Philomel'.

19 **sink** generally, a receptacle for waste water, but here the hole near Lavinia's heart that Titus imagines as a receptacle for her tears

20 **fool** a term of pitying endearment as for a naive innocent; here, still referring to Lavinia's heart

23 **dote** act irrationally

27–8 **Aeneas ... miserable** referring to the beginning of *Aen.* 2, where Aeneas speaks of how painful it is to recount for Dido the story of the fall of Troy

29 **handle ... hands** After criticizing Marcus for using the word 'hand' unthinkingly, Titus' playfully awkward repetition of the word is symptomatic of his madness: he becomes caught up in his own obsessive wordplay. The same pun occurs in *T&C* 1.1.49–53 ('Thou answer'st 'she is fair', / Pour'st in the open ulcer of my heart / Her eyes, her hair, her cheek, her gait, her voice; / Handlest in thy discourse, O, that her hand / In whose comparison all whites are ink ... '), but here it has a special, grotesque indecorum, simultaneously reminding audiences of how pervasive hands are in figurative language and ensuring that the characters' literal dismemberments remain fresh in mind. There is also an echo of Psalm 115 here, as rendered in the Sternhold and Hopkins psalter, an extremely well-known English-language metrical translation of the Psalms: 'And handes they have, and handle not' (Sternhold and Hopkins, 292). See also 37n. below. Titus' language insistently evokes Christian registers of prayer (as at 41–2) and sacred sacrifice ('martyred', l. 36), as if this banquet scene were partly conceived of as a parodic pastiche of communion and the last supper.

Fie, fie, how franticly I square my talk
As if we should forget we had no hands
If Marcus did not name the word of hands.
Come, let's fall to, and, gentle girl, eat this.
Here is no drink? Hark, Marcus, what she says;   35
I can interpret all her martyred signs.
She says she drinks no other drink but tears,
Brewed with her sorrow, mashed upon her cheeks.
Speechless complainant, I will learn thy thought;
In thy dumb action will I be as perfect   40
As begging hermits in their holy prayers.
Thou shalt not sigh nor hold thy stumps to heaven,
Nor wink, nor nod, nor kneel, nor make a sign,
But I of these will wrest an alphabet,
And by still practice learn to know thy meaning.   45

---

31   **square** put in order, organize
34   **fall to** begin eating
35   **Here is no drink?** Titus is making a show of serving Lavinia and he notices that she does not have
     a drink. The question mark is from F, but is sometimes rendered as an exclamation point. Since the
     question is performative and rhetorical, the difference in punctuation makes little difference to the feel
     of the exchange. Her reaction to him is unspecified within the text and therefore open to interpretation
     in performance.
37   **she drinks ... tears** Another echo of the Psalms, this time from Psalm 80: 'Thou dost them fede with
     sorrowes depe their breade with teares they eate: / And drinke the teares that they do wepe in measure
     full and greate' (Sternhold and Hopkins, 199).
38   **mashed** part of the process of brewing beer or ale (OED mash v.[1] II.5.a)
39   *__complainant__ a plaintiff or one who lodges a formal complaint (OED); F's 'complaynet' is often
     emended to Capell's 'complainer', which is also plausible. 'Complainant' – an emendation first inserted
     by Collier in his copy of F2 – was a less common word, which may account for the compositor's
     confusion. To call Lavinia a speechless complainant is to see her as impotent and in need of advocacy
     and legal redress. She has become, for Titus, an emblem of the failure of both language and justice in
     Rome (Neill, 191).
40   **dumb action** hand gestures unaccompanied by speech
     perfect thoroughly expert
42–5 **Thou shalt ... meaning** Though the play has featured moments earlier in which characters try to make
     sense of Lavinia's mute gestures, this dynamic is foregrounded by Titus in a manner that asserts control
     by exaggerating her unintelligibility.
45   **still** continual

---

35 drink?] F; drink. Cam[1]; drink! Oxf[1]   38 mashed] F (mesh'd)   39 complainant] Riv (conj. Collier MS);
complaynet F; complaint F2; complainer Capell

YOUNG LUCIUS

    Good grandsire leave these bitter deep laments;

    Make my aunt merry with some pleasing tale.

MARCUS

    Alas, the tender boy, in passion moved,

    Doth weep to see his grandsire's heaviness.

TITUS

    Peace, tender sapling, thou art made of tears,   50

    And tears will quickly melt thy life away.

      Marcus strikes the dish with a knife.

    What doest thou strike at, Marcus, with thy knife?

MARCUS

    At that that I have killed, my lord: a fly.

TITUS

    Out on thee, murderer! Thou kill'st my heart!

    Mine eyes are cloyed with view of tyranny.   55

    A deed of death done on the innocent

    Becomes not Titus' brother. Get thee gone;

    I see thou art not for my company.

MARCUS

    Alas, my lord, I have but killed a fly.

---

50   **sapling** a young tree and so, metaphorically, a youth

55   **cloyed** overloaded

59   **killed a fly** This episode (in a scene that is, after all, a late addition to the play) may have been suggested by Aaron's later remark (5.1.142) that he has done dreadful things 'as willingly as one would kill a fly'.

52 thy] F2; *not in* F   53 fly] F2; Flys F   54 thee] F3; the F, F2   55 are] F2; *not in* F

TITUS

'But'? How if that fly had a father and mother?   60
How would he hang his slender gilded wings
And buzz lamenting doings in the air.
Poor harmless fly,
That with his pretty buzzing melody
Came here to make us merry, and thou hast killed him.   65

MARCUS

Pardon me, sir, it was a black ill-favoured fly,
Like to the Empress' Moor. Therefore, I killed him.

---

60   **'But'? ... mother?** Some editors have emended and/or relineated this hypermetrical line, though we
      here print the line as it appears in F. The lineation in the Folio text is often erratic, and this whole
      speech is exceptionally irregular from a metrical standpoint, which may indicate some kind of anomaly
      in the process of its transmission to print. Hudson attributed to Ritson the suggestion that the line be
      emended to 'But how if that fly had a father, brother?' and he first adopted this emendation himself in
      Hudson². It has the advantage of clarifying the referent of 'he' in 61, but it also changes the meaning
      of the F text significantly. The prompt book for Deborah Warner's 1987 RSC production indicates that
      she changed the line to 'and brother'. The Titus of Act 1 never mentions his wife or the mother of his
      children, so if 'mother' is not an error then the author of this scene apparently imagines Titus' views of
      family as having changed.

61   **he** The referent is unclear: the fly? The fly's father? The latter seems to make more sense given the
      content of 61–2, but only if the fly's mother isn't also mentioned in the previous line.

62   **buzz ... air** Because it is unclear what exactly it means to 'buzz ... doings', this line has sometimes been
      emended to say that the fly buzzed 'dolings' (as in laments) or that he buzzed 'dronings' (a suggestion
      that Hudson adapted from Theobald, *Restored*, 184). Such emendations seem too speculative to adopt,
      however, and wind up being confusing in their own right. The general sense is that the fly is buzzing
      around and doing whatever a fly does, but lamentingly.

63   **Poor ... fly** another unmetrical line in a speech that presents numerous unresolvable editorial
      problems

65   **Came ... him** In F, which is the only authoritative text for this scene, this iambic line is divided in two.
      The folio text for the rest of the play often breaks metrically regular lines from Qq into shorter lines –
      there are approximately 50 instances of this noted in the t.n. – so even though F is the only copy text
      for this scene it still makes sense to relineate for metre where a line of blank verse is split in two.

66   **black ill-favoured** 'favour' means face; the black fly has a bad face. Marcus and Titus link blackness
      with evilness, ugliness and undesirableness throughout this scene, and they also link those images with
      Aaron the Moor, clearly signalling an explicitly racialized epistemology.

---

60 'But'? ... mother?] F; *Ard³ lines* 'But'? / mother? /   60 a father and mother] F; a father and a mother *Craig*;
a father, brother *Hudson² (conj. Ritson)*   62 buzz lamenting doings] F; buzz lamenting dolings *Theobald*; buzz
laments and dolings *Hanmer*; buzz lamenting dronings *Hudson²*   65 Came ... him] *Capell*; F *lines* merry,
/ him. /   66 Pardon ... fly, *Pope*; F *lines* sir, / fly, /

TITUS

Oh, oh, oh!
Then pardon me for reprehending thee,
For thou hast done a charitable deed.   70
Give me thy knife, I will insult on him,
Flattering myself as if it were the Moor
Come hither purposely to poison me.
    [*Takes knife from Marcus and strikes.*]
There's for thyself, and that's for Tamora!
Ah, sirrah!   75
Yet, I think, we are not brought so low
But that between us we can kill a fly
That comes in likeness of a coal-black Moor.

MARCUS

Alas, poor man; grief has so wrought on him,
He takes false shadows for true substances.   80

TITUS

Come, take away. Lavinia, go with me;
I'll to thy closet and go read with thee
Sad stories chanced in the times of old.
Come boy, and go with me: thy sight is young,   84
And thou shalt read when mine begin to dazzle.   *Exeunt*

71   **insult on** triumph contemptuously over
73   **to poison me** because the episode takes place over a meal
75   **sirrah** a contemptuous or condescending mode of address to an inferior, here addressed to the fly
81   **take away** clear the table
82   **closet** private chamber
83   **chanced** that occurred
85   **mine** my eyes
      dazzle lose the capacity for steady vision (*OED* 1)

72 myself] *F2*; my selfes *F*   73 SD] *Bevington subst.*   74–5 There's … sirrah!] *Capell; one line in F*

[4.1]   *Enter* YOUNG LUCIUS, *and* LAVINIA *running after him, and the boy*
[YOUNG LUCIUS] *flies from her with his books under his arm. Enter* TITUS *and*
MARCUS. [YOUNG LUCIUS *drops his books and runs to them.*]

YOUNG LUCIUS

    Help, grandsire, help! My aunt Lavinia
    Follows me everywhere, I know not why.
    Good uncle Marcus, see how swift she comes!
    Alas, sweet aunt, I know not what you mean.

MARCUS

    Stand by me, Lucius; do not fear thy aunt.   5

TITUS

    She loves thee, boy, too well to do thee harm.

YOUNG LUCIUS

    Aye, when my father was in Rome she did.

MARCUS

    What means my niece Lavinia by these signs?

TITUS

    Fear not, Lucius, somewhat doth she mean.

4.1   On the scholarly controversy concerning the authorship of this scene, see the Introduction, pp. 24–5.

0.3   *YOUNG LUCIUS ... them* In Oxf² a SD indicating that Young Lucius drops his books is added after 4. But, as Bate argues in Ard³, Young Lucius' remark at 25 ('which made me down to throw my books and fly') makes it sound as though he dropped the books before fleeing. Our version of the SD spells out the action as proposed in Ard³: Young Lucius enters via one door pursued by Lavinia, sees Marcus and Titus entering at the other door and then drops his books and runs to them for protection.

1–4   **grandsire ... sweet aunt** If, as we believe, 3.2 is a Jacobean-era addition to the play, then this may originally have been Young Lucius' first entrance. The reiteration of his relations to other family members may initially have served to orient the audience as to the identity of this newly introduced character (see Kramer).

7   **Aye ... did** A surprising and vivid indicator of how vulnerable Young Lucius feels in this play's Rome without his father.

9   **somewhat** something

4.1] *Rowe; Actus Quartus* F; *not in* Qq   0.1 *Enter* YOUNG LUCIUS] F; *Enter Lucius sonne* Qq   0.2   YOUNG LUCIUS] *this edn*   0.3 YOUNG LUCIUS ... them] *this edn*; *He drops the books* Ard³; *he drops his books* Oxf² *after line 4*   5 thy] F; *thine* Qq   9 Fear not] F; *Fear her not* Qq

MARCUS

See, Lucius, see how much she makes of thee.   10
Somewhither would she have thee go with her.
Ah, boy, Cornelia never with more care
Read to her sons than she hath read to thee
Sweet poetry and Tully's *Orator*.
Canst thou not guess wherefore she plies thee thus?   15

YOUNG LUCIUS

My lord, I know not, I, nor can I guess,
Unless some fit or frenzy do possess her,
For I have heard my grandsire say full oft
Extremity of griefs would make men mad;
And I have read that Hecuba of Troy   20
Ran mad for sorrow: that made me to fear
Although, my lord, I know my noble aunt
Loves me as dear as e'er my mother did,

10 SP   *Lines 9–15 are given to Titus in all the early texts, but Young Lucius' response speaks of Titus in the
third person and seems to be directed as if in answer to Marcus. Capell dealt with this problem by
assigning only 15 to Marcus. But the repetition of Lucius' name in 9 and 10 would make for a very
clumsy speech, and the direct address to Lucius by name in 10 makes this seem like the start of a new
speech. In a scene with several characters on stage together, naming the addressee towards the start
of a new speech helps audience and actors keep the action straight. So, like most modern editors, we
accept Hudson's emendation and give lines 10–15 to Marcus.

11   **Somewhither** somewhere

12   **Cornelia** A virtuous Roman widow and mother who took a famously active role in the education of
her children (Tiberius and Gaius Gracchus, notable public Roman figures of the second century BCE).
In early modern English books she is often associated with eloquence and matronly virtue.

14   **Tully's *Orator*** Tully is another name for the hugely influential philosopher and statesman Marcus
Tullius Cicero. The book alluded to is either his *De Oratore* ('On the Orator', 55 BCE) or his *Orator*
(46 BCE).

15   **plies** assails vigorously or persistently (*OED v.*² I.4.a)

20–1   **Hecuba ... sorrow** Hecuba, the last queen of Troy, was associated with extreme motherly grief, which
is prominently depicted in well-known works by Euripides, Virgil, Ovid and Seneca, among others.
Depictions of Hecuba as having been driven frighteningly mad are less common, but Peele describes
her as 'worne with sorrow, wexen fell and mad' (Peele, *Farewell*, 20). It is also possible, as Nørgaard first
suggested, that Young Lucius is imagined as drawing upon student reference works like Cooper, which
contains a biographical dictionary whose entry for Hecuba suggests that 'shee finally waxed madde,
and did bite and strike all men that she mette, wherefore she was called dogge'.

10 SP MARCUS] *Hudson²; not in Qq, F, which continue to Titus*   12 Ah] *Q1 (A); Ah Q3, F*   21 for] *Q1–2;*
through Q3, F

And would not but in fury fright my youth,
Which made me down to throw my books and fly,   25
Causeless perhaps. But pardon me, sweet aunt,
And, madam, if my uncle Marcus go,
I will most willingly attend your ladyship.

MARCUS
Lucius, I will.
    [*Lavinia turns over the books which Lucius has let fall.*]

TITUS
How now, Lavinia? Marcus, what means this?   30
Some book there is that she desires to see.
Which is it, girl, of these? Open them, boy.
[*to Lavinia*] But thou art deeper read and better skilled:
Come and take choice of all my library,
And so beguile thy sorrow, till the heavens   35
Reveal the damned contriver of this deed.
What book? Why lifts she up her arms in sequence thus?

MARCUS
I think she means that there were more than one
Confederate in the fact. Aye, more there was,
Or else to heaven she heaves them to revenge.   40

---

24   **fury** 'fierce passion, disorder or tumult of mind approaching madness' (*OED* 1.a)
27   **go** i.e., go with us, as for protection
33   **thou** Lavinia
35   **heavens** one syllable here ('heav'ns')
37   **What book? ... thus?** The question 'what book' is not in Qq, and is set as a freestanding line in F. The question in F is sometimes taken to be a compositor's error, accidentally transposed and copied in from the middle of Titus' question at 41, but we agree with the editors of Oxf³ that this seems like an implausible explanation: it makes more sense to think of this as an intentional addition. F's lineation is often determined by the narrowness of its columns, and (as Oxf³ also notes), there are other hexameter lines in this scene that are very similar to this one (e.g., 46 and 54 below).
39   **Confederate in the fact** allied in the deed
40   **them** her arms

---

29 SD] *Malone*   33 SD] *Oxf³*   37 What book?] *F, not in Qq* What book? ... thus?] *Oxf³*; *F lines* book? / thus? /
38 were] *Q1–2*; was *Q3, F*   40 to] *F*; for *Qq*

TITUS

Lucius, what book is that she tosseth so?

YOUNG LUCIUS.

Grandsire, 'tis Ovid's *Metamorphoses*.

My mother gave it me.

MARCUS   For love of her that's gone,

Perhaps she culled it from among the rest?

TITUS

Soft, so busily she turns the leaves;   45

Help her – what would she find? Lavinia, shall I read?

This is the tragic tale of Philomel,

And treats of Tereus' treason and his rape;

And rape, I fear, was root of thy annoy.

MARCUS

See, brother, see: note how she quotes the leaves.   50

TITUS

Lavinia, wert thou thus surprised, sweet girl?

Ravished and wronged as Philomela was?

41   **tosseth** searches through, flips through the pages of
42   **Ovid's *Metamorphoses*** a key imaginative source for Shakespeare and other Renaissance writers; as
        becomes clear at 47, it contains the story of Philomela, which underpins so much of the action of this
        play. See p. 62.
45–6   **Soft ... read** 45–6 are printed as they appear in Qq, F, though both lines are irregular. 45 is a syllable
        short and 46 is a hexameter line. Some editors since Dyce have wondered if 'help her' might be an
        'instance of a stage-direction having crept into the text' (Dyce², 370n). The editorial problem is in
        some ways analogous to that posed by the phrase 'stand up' at 1.1.487 (and see note). However, as
        noted at 37, this is one of several hexameter lines in this scene. Perhaps Titus' excitement about what
        Lavinia is doing here is reflected both in the breakdown of the poetic line as well as in the way Titus
        first urges Marcus to assist Lavinia and then goes to help her himself.
46   **what ... find?** what does she want to find?
48   **treats of** depicts
49   **annoy** trauma; 'A mental state akin to pain arising from the involuntary reception of impressions'
        (*OED n.* 1.a)
50   **quotes the leaves** scrutinizes the pages
51–3   **Lavinia, wert ... woods?** Titus spells out explicitly an allusive analogy that has already been self-
        evident to the characters in the play since Act 2: see, for instance, 2.3.43, 2.4.38. The unusually explicit
        citational gesture – bringing Ovid on stage and having the characters process their own allusive
        relation to *Metamorphoses* – ensures that audiences understand the relation between the action and
        its citational models as part of the play's explicit thematic content.

42 *Metamorphoses*] Qq, F (Metamorphosis)   46 Help her] Qq, F; as SD Dyce² ('Helping her')   49 thy] Q1; thine
Q2–3, F   50 quotes] Q1 (coats); *quotes* Q2–3, F

Forced in the ruthless, vast, and gloomy woods?
    [*Lavinia nods her head.*]
See, see! Aye, such a place there is where we did hunt –
O, had we never, never hunted there! –   55
Patterned by that the poet here describes,
By nature made for murders and for rapes.

MARCUS

O why should nature build so foul a den,
Unless the gods delight in tragedies?

TITUS

Give signs, sweet girl, for here are none but friends,   60
What Roman lord it was durst do the deed.
Or slunk not Saturnine, as Tarquin erst,
That left the camp to sin in Lucrece' bed?

MARCUS

Sit down, sweet niece; brother, sit down by me.
Apollo, Pallas, Jove or Mercury,   65
Inspire me that I may this treason find.
My lord, look here; look here, Lavinia:
This sandy plot is plain; guide, if thou canst,

53.1   ***Lavinia nods her head** The German *Tito* play omits the business with Ovid, but in the equivalent scene, when the Lavinia-like character's father asks questions about what was done to her, she nods (*Tito*, SDs after 5.1.30 and 32).

55   **See, see! ... hunt** – Another hexameter line; compare the notes at 37 and 45–6 above

56   **Patterned ... describes** 'similar to what the poet here describes'. It is also literally true that the woods in Act 2 are 'patterned' on those in Ovid. See 2.3.12–15n.

59   **tragedies** in the general sense of bad events that cause suffering and death; but with self-referential implications, too, in the context of this tragic drama

62–3   **Tarquin erst ... bed** Titus, drawing on the story of what Tarquin erst (long ago) did, i.e., rape Lucrece, imagines that Saturninus might have been the culprit. The story of the rape of Lucrece is another of the play's recurring allusive models. See, for instance, 2.1.108, 3.1.299, and notes. See also pp. 62–4.

---

52 Philomela] *Q1 (Phlomela);* Philomela *Q2–3, F*   53 Forced] *Q1 (frocd);* forc'd *Q2–3, F*   54 SD] *Ard³ subst.*
62 erst] *Qq;* ersts *F*

This after me.

He writes his name with his staff and guides it with feet and mouth.

      I have writ my name

Without the help of any hand at all.   70

Cursed be that heart that forced us to that shift.

Write thou, good niece, and here display, at last,

What god will have discovered for revenge.

Heaven guide thy pen to print thy sorrows plain,

That we may know the traitors and the truth.   75

She takes the staff in her mouth and guides it with her stumps and writes.

O do ye read, my lord, what she hath writ?

TITUS

'Stuprum – Chiron, Demetrius'.

---

69 SD   *In Qq and F, the stage direction indicating Marcus' sand writing occurs after 68, though in Q1–2 68 ends with a comma as if the articulated thought were ongoing and not interrupted by stage business. Line 69, meanwhile, is choppy and a syllable short, and has attracted speculative emendation for metrical reasons. Moving the SD to the middle of the line, following Collier, makes sense dramatically and also means that the line's metrical irregularity would likely go unnoticed.

71   **shift** 'an ingenious means of achieving an end' (*OED* III.3.b)

73   **What god ... revenge** 'What god wants to have revealed for revenge'; Marcus imagines that god will reveal Lavinia's assailants in order to facilitate vengeance.

75.1 SD   The explicit SD has not always been accepted by directors. The prompt book for Deborah Warner's 1987 RSC production indicates that Lavinia (played by Sonia Ritter) 'takes the staff between her stumps & writes (rejects mouth)', and in Michael Sexton's 2011 Public Lab production Lavinia (played by Jennifer Ikeda) painted on plywood boards without the use of her mouth.

77 SP   *In Q1, Marcus' speech runs all the way from 64–77, but it is followed immediately at 78 by a SP indicating that Marcus speaks again, so there is an obvious compositional error here. The compositor of Q3, recognizing the error, gave 76–7 to Titus. But though Titus does sarcastically refer to Bassianus as 'my lord' at 1.1.277, that is not generally how Titus would address Marcus. Rather, as Maxwell pointed out (Ard²), it is characteristic of the way Marcus refers to Titus (first at 1.1.357, for instance). We therefore follow Ard² in assigning only 77 to Titus.

77   **Stuprum** (Latin) rape

---

69 SD] *Collier; after line 68 in Qq, F*   I have] *Qq, F;* I here have *Oxf¹*   71 that shift] *F;* this shift *Qq*   76 writ] *Qq;* writs *F*   77 SP] *Ard²; not in Q1–2, which continues to Marcus; at line 77 in Q3, F*   Demetrius] *Q1 (Dmetrius);* Demetrius *Q2–3, F*

MARCUS

What? What? The lustful sons of Tamora
Performers of this heinous, bloody deed?

TITUS

Magni dominator poli,   80
Tam lentus audis scelera, tam lentus vides?

MARCUS

O calm thee, gentle lord – although I know
There is enough written upon this earth
To stir a mutiny in the mildest thoughts
And arm the minds of infants to exclaims.   85
My lord, kneel down with me; Lavinia, kneel;
And kneel, sweet boy, the Roman Hector's hope;   [*All kneel.*]

80–1   *Magni dominator … vides?* (Latin) 'Ruler of the great heavens, do you listen to crimes so calmly, see
       them so calmly?' These lines are adapted from a key moment in Seneca's *Phaedra*, where Hippolytus
       learns that his stepmother Phaedra is in love with him and reacts with shocked horror and a call for
       divine vengeance ('*Magne regnator deum, / tam lentus audis scelera? Tam lentus vides?*' 'Great monarch
       of the gods, do you listen to crimes so calmly, see them so calmly?' [*Phae.* 671–2]). But the phrase in
       80 – '*Magni dominator poli*' – differs from Seneca's play and is likely alluding to the first line of a poem
       or prayer translated and attributed to the Greek stoic philosopher Cleanthes in Seneca's *Moral Epistle*
       107: a call for obedience to god and nature that begins '*Duc, o parens celsique dominator poli*' ('lead
       me, o my father, master of the lofty heavens' [Seneca, *Epistles*, 107.11]). This short stoic prayer was
       quite well-known among early modern scholars and St Augustine used it to illustrate ironies of stoic
       appeals to fate (Augustine, 5.8). Titus' intertextually allusive Latin outburst thus seems to combine a
       call for divine retribution with a stoic prayer for patience. See the Introduction, pp. 65–7.

85   **exclaims** outcries

87   **Roman Hector's hope** Addressed to Young Lucius. Hector was the great military champion of Troy, and
       Lucius is said to be the current Roman equivalent. Though this reference is in keeping with the Virgilian
       tenor of the Andronicus family's brand of Roman-ness, the comparison might also strike a pessimistic
       note since Hector was defeated and his son, Astyanax, was eventually sacrificed by the victorious
       Greeks. In Peele's *Troublesome Reign of John, King of England* (1591), however, there is a reference to an
       alternative history in which the son of Hector went on to found France (Peele, *Troublesome* pt. 2, 7.12),
       so if Peele wrote this scene he may have had that more optimistic story in mind (Hulse, 874).

87 SD In the seventeenth-century German play, an elaborate ritual oath-taking is staged by the Andronici
       after the names of Titus' daughter's assailants are revealed: '*Tito Andronico kneels and begins to sing a
       dirge; the others sit down by the heads. He takes up his hand, raises it, and looks to heaven, sighs, utters
       an oath, strikes his breast, and puts down the hand after having sworn. He then takes up the heads and
       swears by each of them in turn. Finally, he approaches Andronica* [Titus' daughter in that play] *and
       swears by her as before with the others. This done, they all rise*' (*Tito*, 5.1.61.1–8).

---

87 hope] Q1 (hop *or* lop – *set to the right and with* h *damaged*); hope Q2–3, F   87 SD] Bevington (*conj.*
Collier MS)

And swear with me – as, with the woeful fere
And father of that chaste dishonoured dame,
Lord Junius Brutus sware for Lucrece' rape –   90
That we will prosecute, by good advice,
Mortal revenge upon these traitorous Goths,
And see their blood or die with this reproach.   [*They rise.*]

TITUS

'Tis sure enough, an you knew how.
But if you hunt these bear-whelps then beware: 95
The dam will wake, and if she wind ye once
She's with the lion deeply still in league,
And lulls him whilst she playeth on her back;
And when he sleeps will she do what she list.
You are a young huntsman, Marcus: let alone.   100
And come, I will go get a leaf of brass
And with a gad of steel will write these words

88–90   **as … Lucrece' rape** Lucius Junius Brutus led the uprising that resulted in the expulsion of the Tarquins
and the founding of the Roman republic in retribution for the rape of Lucrece. Marcus anticipates the
way the Romans scapegoat outsiders at the end of the play, implying that they will clean up Rome by
taking care of the Goth interlopers. Titus, who has imagined Saturninus as Tarquin at 63–4, is more
attuned than his brother to the way that Rome itself has enabled the evils that have befallen them,
and he makes this explicit in his reply.
         fere husband
91   **prosecute, by good advice** pursue prudently
93   **reproach** shame
94   **an you knew how** if you knew how to achieve it
95   **bear-whelps** Whelps are the young of wild animals. Chiron and Demetrius are being compared to
young bears that the Andronici must hunt down and kill in revenge.
96   **dam** the mother bear, Tamora
         wind get the wind of, catch the scent of
97   **the lion** Saturninus, here likened to the lion because he's the ruler (the idea that the lion was king of
the animals predates the early modern period). Titus is expanding on his admonitory animal allegory,
warning his kinsmen that hunting Tamora and her sons will be dangerous because she has Saturninus
in thrall and so they have the power of Rome at their disposal.
100   **young** inexperienced
         let alone leave it alone
101–3   **I will … by** Titus, in his sorrowful madness, imagines memorializing the crime of Chiron and Demetrius
by engraving the words written in the sand upon a sheet ('leaf') of brass with a steel stylus ('gad'), as an
alternative to avenging it. This remark literalizes the proverbial idea that 'injuries are written in brass',
which as a proverb refers to the fact that people remember injuries done to them more than they
remember benefits (Dent, I71).

---

90 sware] *Qq, F* (sweare)   93 SD] *Bevington*   96 ye] *Q1;* you *Q2–3, F*   100 let] *Q1–2;* let it *Q3, F*

And lay it by. The angry northern wind
Will blow these sands like Sibyl's leaves abroad,
And where's our lesson then? Boy, what say you?   105

YOUNG LUCIUS
I say, my lord, that if I were a man,
Their mother's bedchamber should not be safe
For these base bondmen to the yoke of Rome.

MARCUS
Aye, that's my boy. Thy father hath full oft
For his ungrateful country done the like.   110

YOUNG LUCIUS
And, uncle, so will I, and if I live.

TITUS
Come, go with me into mine armory;
Lucius, I'll fit thee, and withal my boy
Shall carry from me to the Empress' sons
Presents that I intend to send them both.   115
Come, come – thou'lt do my message, wilt thou not?

YOUNG LUCIUS
Aye, with my dagger in their bosoms, grandsire.

TITUS
No, boy, not so. I'll teach thee another course.
Lavinia, come. Marcus, look to my house.

103–5   **The angry … then** In Book 3 of Virgil's *Aen.,* Aeneas learns that he will have to visit the Cumaean Sibyl,
a prophetess who writes on oak leaves which are scattered by the wind when anyone enters her cave
(441–52). Titus compares the sand in which Lavinia has written to the ephemerality of the Sibyl's
leaves.

108   **bondmen to … Rome** 'slaves to the conquest of Rome'; recalling that Chiron and Demetrius were
initially brought to Rome in bondage

110   **done the like** only in the most general terms: Lucius has fought manfully against Goths on behalf
of Rome

113   **fit thee** furnish you with weapons

119   **look to** look after

105 our] Q1; you Q2; your Q3, F   108 base] Q1; bad Q2–3, F   116 my] Q1; thy Q2–3, F

Lucius and I'll go brave it at the court.   120
Aye, marry, will we, sir, and we'll be waited on.

                          Exeunt [all but Marcus].

MARCUS
O heavens, can you hear a good man groan
And not relent or not compassion him?
Marcus, attend him in his ecstasy
That hath more scars of sorrow in his heart   125
Than foemen's marks upon his battered shield.
But yet so just that he will not revenge:
Revenge the heavens for old Andronicus.   *Exit.*

[4.2]   *Enter* AARON, CHIRON, *and* DEMETRIUS *at one door, and at another door* YOUNG LUCIUS *and another [an Attendant], with a bundle of weapons and verses writ upon them.*

CHIRON
Demetrius, here's the son of Lucius;
He hath some message to deliver us.
AARON
Aye, some mad message from his mad grandfather.
YOUNG LUCIUS
My lords, with all the humbleness I may,
I greet your honours from Andronicus –   5
[aside] And pray the Roman gods confound you both.

120   **brave it** swagger and self-present in a showy manner
123   **compassion** have compassion for
124   **ecstasy** madness
127–8 **But yet ... Andronicus** Marcus mistakes Titus' antic disposition for a staunch adherence to a stoic
       idea of justice, which would preclude personal vengeance. Confusion about Titus' motives relates to
       the ambiguity of the Senecan Latin quoted above at 81–2, which seems to combine a call for swift
       vengeance with a prayer for calm resignation.

121 SD] *all but Marcus*] *Capell subst.*   122 good man] Q2–3, F; goodman Q1   4.2] *Pope; not in Qq, F*   0.1
another] Q2–3, F; the other Q1   0.2 *an Attendant*] *this edn*   6 SD] *Capell*

DEMETRIUS

Gramercy, lovely Lucius; what's the news?

YOUNG LUCIUS   [aside]

That you are both deciphered, that's the news,

For villains marked with rape. [to them] May it please you,

My grandsire, well advised, hath sent by me   10

The goodliest weapons of his armoury

To gratify your honourable youth,

The hope of Rome, for so he bid me say,

And so I do, and with his gifts present

Your lordships, that whenever you have need,   15

You may be armed and appointed well.

    [Attendant delivers weapons.]

And so I leave you both [aside] like bloody villains.

                        Exit [Young Lucius with Attendant].

DEMETRIUS

What's here? A scroll and written round about.

Let's see [reads]:

Integer vitae, scelerisque purus,   20

Non eget Mauri iaculis, nec arcu.

---

7   **Gramercy** thank you

8   **deciphered** detected, but secondary meanings associated with textual interpretation and decoding
     are also germane to Titus' approach to revenge at this point in the play, since he is sending his enemies
     oblique literary clues

15   ***lordships, that whenever** Pope's emendation – adding 'that' – has been widely accepted by modern
     editors as it both improves the metre and clarifies the sense.

16   **armed** armèd

16.1 *Attendant* This SD, which was initially added by Bevington, makes sense because the entry SD at the
     start of the scene indicates that Young Lucius enters with 'another'.

20-1 *Integer ... arcu* (Latin) 'he who lives a sound life and is free of crime needs no Moorish javelins or
     bow'. The lines are quoted from Horace, *Odes*, 1.22.1–2. Modern editions of Horace have 'Mauris',
     but 'Mauri' is the way the word was rendered in the Latin grammar Shakespeare would have used
     as a student, which is also alluded to anachronistically by Chiron in the next speech (see Binns, 123).
     The quotation (as only Aaron realizes) is obviously meant to hint at the criminality of Chiron and
     Demetrius as Aaron's associates.

---

7 what's] *Q1, Q3, F;* what *Q2*   8 SP] *Qq (Puer); not in F*   SD] *Capell*   8 That ... news,] *Qq; not in F*   9 villains]
Qq; villanie's *F*   SD] *Ard³*   13 bid] *Q1-2;* bad *Q3, F*   15 that] *Pope; not in Qq, F*   16 SD] *Bevington*   17
SD1] *Capell*   SD2] *Capell subst.; Exit Qq, F*   20–21 *Integer ... arcu] as Theobald; One line in Qq; F*

CHIRON

O 'tis a verse in Horace; I know it well.

I read it in the grammar long ago.

AARON

Aye, just; a verse in Horace; right you have it.

[aside] Now, what a thing it is to be an ass.   25

Here's no sound jest! The old man hath found their guilt,

And sends them weapons wrapped about with lines

That wound, beyond their feeling, to the quick.

But were our witty empress well afoot

She would applaud Andronicus' conceit;   30

But let her rest in her unrest awhile.

[to them.] And now, young lords, was't not a happy star

Led us to Rome, strangers – and more than so,

Captives – to be advanced to this height?

It did me good, before the palace gate,   35

To brave the tribune in his brother's hearing.

DEMETRIUS

But me more good to see so great a lord

---

23   **the grammar** i.e. William Lily's *A Shorte Introduction of Grammar*, a standard Elizabethan schoolboy
        textbook, where Shakespeare too may have first encountered these lines from Horace (Lily, pt. 1, sig.
        C8^r; pt. 2, sig. G7^r)
24   **just** correct
        right ... it right you are
26   **Here's no sound jest!** This exclamation registers Aaron's recognition that the jest is not 'sound', in the
        sense of honest or straightforward (*OED* 10.a), because of the hidden accusation it carries.
28   **to the quick** to the core; in a painful way
29   **well afoot** up and about, as opposed to being away preparing to give birth
31   **rest in her unrest** remain in her discomfort; here and elsewhere in the scene Aaron alludes to the fact
        that Tamora is lying in and preparing to give birth.
33   **strangers** foreigners
34   **advanced** advancèd
35–6   **It did ... hearing** 'it did me good, before the palace gate, to defy ('brave') Marcus while his brother
        could hear'; this, while fitting with regard to Aaron's character, does not refer to a specific event that
        has taken place in the play. Gesturing to a social reality beyond what has been staged is one way a play
        can create the illusion of a realistic milieu for its action.

21 *eget Mauri*] *Qq*; *egit maury F   arcu*] *Q1*; *arcus Q2–3, F   25 SD*] *Johnson   27 them*] *Q1–2*; *the Q3, F   32*
SD] *Oxf^1 subst. (conj. Collier MS)   was't not*] *Q1–3*; *wa's tnot F*

226

Basely insinuate and send us gifts.

AARON

Had he not reason, Lord Demetrius?

Did you not use his daughter very friendly?   40

DEMETRIUS

I would we had a thousand Roman dames

At such a bay, by turn to serve our lust.

CHIRON

A charitable wish, and full of love.

AARON

Here lacks but your mother for to say 'amen'.

CHIRON

And that would she, for twenty thousand more.   45

DEMETRIUS

Come, let us go and pray to all the gods

For our beloved mother in her pains.

AARON

Pray to the devils. The gods have given us over.   *Flourish.*

DEMETRIUS

Why do the Emperor's trumpets flourish thus?

38   **insinuate** try to ingratiate himself with us; this is how Demetrius has understood the weapons given
      to them by Young Lucius at the start of the scene
42   **At such a bay** a metaphor from hunting, comparing victims to animals who are cornered by baying
      (barking) hounds
43   **A charitable … love** continuing the sarcastic tone set by Aaron
44   **Here lacks but** 'we're only missing'
45   **twenty thousand more** i.e., more Roman dames to assault
47   **beloved** belovèd
      pains in childbirth

44 your] Qq; you F   48 SD] F; *Trumpets sound. Qq*

CHIRON

    Belike for joy the Emperor hath a son.   50

DEMETRIUS

    Soft, who comes here?

              Enter NURSE *with a blackamoor child.*

NURSE

    God morrow, lords.

    O tell me, did you see Aaron the Moor?

AARON

    Well, more or less, or ne'er a whit at all.

    Here Aaron is, and what with Aaron now?   55

NURSE

    O, gentle Aaron, we are all undone.

    Now help, or woe betide thee evermore.

AARON

    Why, what a caterwauling dost thou keep –

    What dost thou wrap and fumble in thy arms?

NURSE

    O, that which I would hide from heaven's eye,   60

    Our empress' shame and stately Rome's disgrace:

    She is delivered, lords, she is delivered.

---

50   **Belike** in all likelihood

      the Emperor hath a son If this implies that Saturninus expects Tamora's son to be his biological offspring, as opposed to a son he can adopt, then it would seem that Tamora was not visibly pregnant when he met her in 1.1. Events in the play up to 3.1 take place in just a few days, and though it is not explicitly clear how much time has elapsed between the end of 3.1 and the beginning of Act 4, it is hard to imagine that months have passed. This would seem to be what in film terms is called a continuity error; early modern English plays are very often sloppy in this way.

51–65   This portion of the play, in all the early texts, is metrically irregular to an unusual degree; all editors therefore have a series of decisions to make about relineation and about how – and whether – to create metrical lines out of what is preserved. We have tried to reconstruct metrical lines where it seemed possible to arrive at plausible approximations without indulging in too much speculative emendation of the language. See t.n.

52   **God morrow** Q1's 'God morrow' and Q3's 'Good morrow' are both once-common shortened versions of the expression 'God give you good morrow'. On the latter, see the OED entry for 'Good morrow'. Both occur multiple times in Shakespeare; we retain the reading from Q1.

54   **Well ... at all** Aaron responds playfully to the Nurse's question with a pun on 'Moor' and 'more': one may have seen Aaron more, or less, or not at all ('ne'er a whit'). There may also be a pun on 'whit' and 'white', especially given the focus on skin colour in the exchange that follows.

55   **what with** what do you want with

56   **gentle** 'used in addressing or referring to someone in a courteous or respectful manner' (*OED* 3.c)

58   **caterwauling** whining like an agitated cat

---

52 God] *Q1–2; Good Q3, F*   52–53 God ... Moor?] *F lines; one line in Qq*   59 thy] *Q1; thine Q2–3, F*

AARON

    To whom?

NURSE   I mean she is brought abed.

AARON

    Well, God give her good rest; what hath he sent her?

NURSE

    A devil.   65

AARON

    Why then, she is the devil's dam; a joyful issue.

NURSE

    A joyless, dismal, black, and sorrowful issue!
    Here is the babe, as loathsome as a toad
    Amongst the fair-faced breeders of our clime:
    The Empress sends it thee – thy stamp, thy seal –   70
    And bids thee christen it with thy dagger's point.

AARON

    Out, you whore, is black so base a hue?
    Sweet blowze, you are a beauteous blossom, sure.

63   **To whom?** Aaron intentionally mistakes the Nurse's meaning, replying as if she had meant that Tamora had been handed over ('delivered') to somebody.

66   **Why ... issue** a hexameter line
    devil's dam Aaron, still playful, uses a proverbial expression about 'the devil and his dam' (Dent, D225) to deflect the Nurse's sense of urgency.
    issue Aaron is again punning: the word means both offspring and event.

69   **fair-faced** pretty because white, or light complexioned.
    breeders women who produce children (*OED* 2.b.i)
    clime climate, environment

70   **thy stamp, thy seal** Although paternity is often treated as uncertain in early modern texts, Aaron's paternity is marked on the child's dark skin as if it were by a stamp, an emblem of ownership, that seals the wax of a letter.

72   **Out** The Qq reading – which contains the exclamation 'Zounds', which is short for 'God's wounds' – takes God's name in vain. In 1606, Parliament passed the Act to Restrain Abuses of Players, which sought to crack down on this sort of routine blasphemy. So the reading in F (which we adopt) may have been swapped in to keep the play on the safe side of the law. If so, it also presumably reflects the way the line was performed after 1606.

73   **blowze** a coarse, ruddy-complexioned woman (see *OED* blowze 2, which cites the first part of Thomas Heywood's *King Edward the Fourth* [1599]: 'My Besse is faire, And Shoares wife but a blouze, comparde to her'); Aaron responds sarcastically to the nurse's remarks about the ugliness of the baby's skin colour by pointing out that she is not so 'fair-faced' herself.

63 To ... abed] *Cam¹*; *Qq*, *F lines* whome. / a bed. /   64 Well ... her?] *Qq*; *F lines* rest, / her? /; *Capell lines* god / her? / 65–6 A ... issue.] *Qq*, *F*; *Hanmer lines* devil. / dam; / issue. /   69 fair-faced] *Q1–2* (fairefast); fairest *Q3, F*   72 Out, you] *F*; Zounds, ye] *Qq*

DEMETRIUS

Villain, what hast thou done?

AARON

That which thou canst not undo. 75

CHIRON

Thou hast undone our mother.

AARON

Villain, I have done thy mother.

DEMETRIUS

And therein, hellish dog, thou hast undone her.

Woe to her chance and damned her loathed choice:

Accursed the offspring of so foul a fiend. 80

CHIRON

It shall not live.

AARON

It shall not die.

NURSE

Aaron, it must; the mother wills it so.

AARON

What, must it, Nurse? Then let no man but I

Do execution on my flesh and blood. 85

DEMETRIUS

I'll broach the tadpole on my rapier's point.

Nurse, give it me. My sword shall soon dispatch it.

---

76   **undone** ruined reputationally
77   **done** had sex with (*OED* do *v.* I.18., citing this instance as its earliest example); the explicit sexual boast
      allows Aaron to get the upper hand in an exchange hinging on shifting meanings of the word 'done'.
79   **chance** luck, fate
      damned damned be
      loathed loathèd
80   **fiend** devil; devils were often presented as black-skinned in medieval drama, and the phrase 'black
      fiend' was idiomatic (as at *FQ* 2.7.41, l. 9); Demetrius' choice of invective to use against his erstwhile
      associate is thus a response to Aaron's blackness.
86   **broach** impale

---

77 villain ... mother.] *Qq; not in F*   78 her] *Q1–2; not in Q3, F*

AARON

Sooner this sword shall plow thy bowels up.

[*Takes child from Nurse.*]

Stay, murderous villains, will you kill your brother?

Now, by the burning tapers of the sky   90

That shone so brightly when this boy was got,

He dies upon my scimitar's sharp point

That touches this, my first-born son and heir.

I tell you, younglings, not Enceladus,

With all his threatening band of Typhon's brood,   95

Nor great Alcides, nor the god of war,

Shall seize this prey out of his father's hands.

What, what, ye sanguine, shallow-hearted boys,

Ye white-limed walls, ye alehouse painted signs?

---

88 SD   *Editors since Capell have supplied substantially the same SD, which represents the simplest and most
direct way for Aaron to take control of his child. In the German adaptation of the Titus story, however,
the empress' son takes the child from the nurse and is ready to kill it before Aaron seizes it from him
(*Tito*, SD after 6.1.47).

91   **got** begotten; conceived

92   **scimitar's sharp point** sharp point of a scimitar, which is 'a short single-edged sword with a curved
blade that typically broadens before the point, used chiefly in Turkey and the Middle East' (*OED*);
mentioning this weapon highlights Aaron's potential Muslim origins in a manner that contrasts with
his comfortable mastery of Greco-Roman mythology in the remainder of the speech.

94   **Enceladus** one of the primordial giants said in classical mythology to have fought against the gods

95   **Typhon's brood** Typhon was another ancient giant who fought the Olympian gods. Aaron's sense is
'Enceladus together with all of the other giants'.

96   **Alcides** Hercules
         the god of war Mars

97   **prey** pursued creature

98   **sanguine** red-faced; this initiates a series of remarks about how black skin is superior to white skin.
Aaron starts by noting that whites blush and thus reveal their inner thoughts; black skin makes no
such revelation. Aaron returns to this idea at 117 below.
         shallow-hearted weak-willed

99   **white-limed** painted, as a wall, with a white paint made of lime and water; Aaron, played by a
white English actor in racial prosthetics, treats the (Gothic) whiteness of Chiron and Demetrius as
something painted on. Waith (in Oxf²) notes that a white-limed or whitewashed wall is sometimes
also emblematic of hypocrisy in earlier English texts.
         alehouse painted signs crudely painted signs meant to convey the names of alehouses

---

88 SD] *Capell subst.*   96 Alcides] *Q2; Alciades Q1*   99 white-limed] *Q1 (whitelimde); white-limbde Q2–3;*
white-limb'd *F*

Coal-black is better than another hue,   100
In that it scorns to bear another hue:
For all the water in the ocean
Can never turn the swan's black legs to white,
Although she lave them hourly in the flood.
Tell the Empress, from me, I am of age   105
To keep mine own, excuse it how she can.

DEMETRIUS
Wilt thou betray thy noble mistress thus?

AARON
My mistress is my mistress, this myself:
The vigour and the picture of my youth.
This before all the world do I prefer;   110
This maugre all the world will I keep safe,
Or some of you shall smoke for it in Rome.

DEMETRIUS
By this our mother is forever shamed.

CHIRON
Rome will despise her for this foul escape.

NURSE
The Emperor in his rage will doom her death.   115

100–1 **Coal-black ... hue** Aaron takes up the proverbial notion that 'black will take no other hue' (Dent, B436) and renders it as a correlative for his own prideful autonomy ('scorns to bear'). The word 'bear' also hints at the way blackness provides proof of his paternity of the biracial child to whom Tamora has given birth.

102–4 **all the water ... flood** Aaron draws again on proverbial language – in this case, the idea that it is futile to attempt to wash ('lave') black skin white (as in Dent, E186) – but in an unconventional way, celebrating the constancy of the swan's black legs. This statement also echoes the celebration of essentialism in *R2* 3.2.54–5, when the king declares 'Not all the water in the rough rude sea / Can wash the balm from an anointed king'.

102   **ocean** pronounced with three syllables

104   **lave** wash

106–7 **I am ... mine own** 'I'm old enough to hold onto what is mine'; depending on how old Aaron is taken to be this might be sarcastic or not.

108   **this** the child

111   **maugre** in defiance of

112   **smoke for it** suffer mortal wounds; the image behind this idiom is associated with steam rising from open, bloody wounds, as in *Mac* 1.2.17–18: 'his brandished steel ... smoked with bloody execution'.

114   **escape** transgression

CHIRON

I blush to think upon this ignominy.

AARON

Why, there's the privilege your beauty bears;
Fie, treacherous hue, that will betray with blushing
The close enacts and counsels of thy heart.
Here's a young lad framed of another leer: 120
Look how the black slave smiles upon the father,
As who should say, 'Old lad, I am thine own'.
He is your brother, lords, sensibly fed
Of that self blood that first gave life to you,
And from that womb, where you imprisoned were,   125
He is enfranchised and come to light.
Nay, he is your brother by the surer side,
Although my seal be stamped in his face.

NURSE

Aaron, what shall I say unto the Empress?

DEMETRIUS

Advise thee, Aaron, what is to be done,   130

116   **ignominy** public shame
117   **privilege** advantage; Aaron is being sarcastic
118   **treacherous hue** The white skin that, Aaron implies, constitutes the ideal form of 'beauty' for the
       Goths is also treacherous in that it betrays their secrets via blushing.
119   **close enacts** secret actions or purposes
120   **leer** complexion, appearance, hue (*OED n.*¹ 2)
122   **As who should say** as one who might say
       Old lad an affectionate and familiar form of address
123   **sensibly** evidently
124   **self** self-same
125   **that** Editors have generally accepted the Q3, F reading ('that') over Q1–2's 'your' because it makes
       more sense and because it would be very easy for a compositor to misread the former (often
       abbreviated as 'yᵗ') for the latter (often abbreviated as 'yʳ').
126   **enfranchised** enfranchisèd; set free
127   **the surer side** i.e., through the mother; compare the proverbial saying that 'the mother's side is the
       surer side' (Dent, M1205).
128   **stamped** stampèd
130   **Advise thee** give thought to

116 ignominy] F; ignomy *Qq*   119 thy] *Q1–2*; the *Q3, F*   125 that] *Q3, F;* your *Q1–2*

And we will all subscribe to thy advice:
Save thou the child, so we may all be safe.

AARON

Then sit we down and let us all consult.
My son and I will have the wind of you.
Keep there. Now, talk at pleasure of your safety.   [*They sit.*]   135

DEMETRIUS [*to the Nurse*]

How many women saw this child of his?

AARON

Why, so, brave lords. When we join in league
I am a lamb, but if you brave the Moor,
The chafed boar, the mountain lioness,
The ocean, swells not so as Aaron storms.   140
But say again: how many saw the child?

NURSE

Cornelia the midwife, and myself,
And none else but the delivered Empress.

AARON

The Empress, the midwife and yourself?

---

132   **so** so long as
134   **have ... you** keep downwind from you. As hunters or predatory animals keep downwind to be able to
       observe their prey without being noticed, so Aaron keeps his own wary distance.
135   **talk at pleasure of** discuss as freely as you wish
135 SD *Ravenscroft supplies a detailed SD here: '*All sit down on the ground, and the Moor at a distance with
       his Sword between*' (p. 40). Because Aaron, at 133, says 'then sit we down and let us all consult', editors
       since Rowe have usually supplied a SD indicating that the characters all sit down here. The ensuing
       stage business may be a bit awkward, however, with people sitting on the stage and getting up quickly,
       and it may be possible that Aaron means the phrase more abstractly, in the sense of 'we should calmly
       deliberate together'.
137   **so** just so; 'this is good'
138   **brave** defy
139   **chafed boar** chafèd; angry wild boar: a ferocious beast, as opposed to the proverbially mild lamb
140   **swells** intensifies, grows in force (*OED* 4.a)
141   **But say again** Demetrius has tried to take the lead by addressing the nurse at 135, and Aaron reasserts
       his command of the situation by re-posing the question.
142   **Cornelia** the name was chosen, perhaps, for its maternal associations (on which, see 4.1.12n.)
143–4 **Empress** pronounced with three syllables in each instance

---

135 SD *Rowe subst.*   136 SD] Oxf²   140 as] *Qq*; at *F*   143 none] *F*; no one *Qq*

Two may keep counsel when the third's away.   145
Go to the Empress. Tell her this I said –   *He kills her.*
'Wheak, wheak' – so cries a pig prepared to the spit!   [*All stand up.*]

DEMETRIUS
What mean'st thou, Aaron? Wherfore didst thou this?

AARON
O Lord, sir, 'tis a deed of policy.
Shall she live to betray this guilt of ours?   150
A long-tongued, babbling gossip? No, lords, no.
And now be it known to you my full intent:
Not far, one Mulitius my countryman –
His wife but yesternight was brought to bed.
His child is like to her, fair as you are: 155

---

145   **Two ... away** Aaron again has recourse to a proverbial phrase (Dent, T642.1: 'Two may keep counsel if the third be away [but the third never]'), though he is speaking more to provide cover for his actions than to persuade.

147   **Wheak, wheak** a squealing pig noise
        prepared preparèd; if the pig noise is included in the verse, as is the case in Qq, F, then this scans as a hexameter line

147 SD   *If everyone has been sitting, they must jump to attention at this point. Ravenscroft also has a SD to this effect when the Nurse is killed: '*Aron stabs the Woman. She dyes, all stands up*' (40).

149   **policy** strategic expediency

151   **long-tongued** overly talkative

153   *Mulitius** In Q1, this line reads 'Not farr, one *Muliteus* my Countriman', and the other early texts are substantively similar. Steevens[2] speculated that the name 'Muliteus', which renders the line metrically irregular, was the result of a compositor's erroneous misreading of the phrase 'Muly lives', a suggestion which is adopted in Ard[3]. Muly is the name of the flamboyantly villainous Moor in Peele's *Battle of Alcazar* (1588–9), but the justification for such drastic emendation of the name is highly speculative and the name as it appears in the early texts might in fact represent an attempt at Latinization of the name Muly, as if it were borrowed from Peele's drama and then back-projected into the play's Roman milieu. We retain the reading from the early texts but alter the spelling slightly to make it more clearly a Roman-style name. The line has no end punctuation in the early texts, which also renders it grammatically difficult to parse (unless, as the editors of Oxf[3] suggest, the 'his wife' in 154 is the obsolete form of the possessive, which seems unlikely too given the absence of this idiom in the rest of the play). This might also suggest compositorial error. We have added a dash at the end of the line to help with the sense.

155   **like to ... are** In other words, this other biracial child of a Moor and a Roman woman resembles its mother and is as fair as Chiron and Demetrius.

---

145 the] *Qq*; the the *F*   147 SD] *Ard*[3]   148] *Q1; F lines* Aaron? / this? /   153 Mulitius] *this edn; Muliteus Qq, F; Muliteus lives Rowe; Muly lives Ard*[3] *(conj. Steevens*[2]*)*   countryman—] *this edn; punctuation not in Qq, F*

Go pack with him, and give the mother gold,
And tell them both the circumstance of all,
And how by this their child shall be advanced
And be received for the Emperor's heir
And substituted in the place of mine   160
To calm this tempest whirling in the court;
And let the Emperor dandle him for his own.
Hark ye, lords, you see I have given her physic,
  [*Gestures towards body of the Nurse.*]
And you must needs bestow her funeral:
The fields are near, and you are gallant grooms.   165
This done, see that you take no longer days,
But send the midwife presently to me.
The midwife and the nurse well made away,
Then let the ladies tattle what they please.

CHIRON

Aaron, I see thou wilt not trust the air   170
With secrets.

---

156   **pack** conspire
158   **by this** i.e., by Aaron's scheme to swap the babies, so that Mulitius' son is accepted as the child of
       Saturninus and Tamora
159   **received** receivèd
162   **dandle** play with a baby by moving it in one's arms or on one's knee (*OED* 1.a), or, more generally,
       'make much of' (*OED* 2)
163   **physic** medicine, ironically; Aaron has taken care of her as a problem.
164   **bestow her funeral** 'find a place for her body to be laid'; 'bestow' here has the sense of 'provide with
       a resting place' (*OED* 3.b)
165   **grooms** men (*OED* 2), but perhaps also with the denigrating meaning that they are acting as his
       manservants (*OED* 3.a)
166   **take no longer days** do not delay
167   **presently** at once
168   **made away** killed
170   **trust the air** a proverbial description of suspiciousness (Dent, A94.2: 'to trust the air'), but perhaps
       also with a pun on air/heir

163 you] *Q1–2*; ye *Q3, F*   163 SD] *Johnson subst.*   170–71 Aaron ... secrets.] *Theobald; one line in Qq, F*

DEMETRIUS   For this care of Tamora,
Herself and hers are highly bound to thee.

Exeunt [Chiron and Demetrius,
with the Nurse's body].

AARON

Now to the Goths, as swift as swallow flies,
There to dispose this treasure in mine arms
And secretly to greet the Empress' friends.   175
Come on, you thick-lipped slave, I'll bear you hence,
For it is you that puts us to our shifts.
I'll make you feed on berries and on roots,
And fat on curds and whey, and suck the goat,
And cabin in a cave, and bring you up   180
To be a warrior and command a camp.   *Exit.*

---

175   **secretly … friends** It is not clear who Aaron plans to meet with, but here at the end of a scene of
      conspiracy there is a hint in soliloquy at further schemes that are as yet undisclosed.
176   **thick-lipped slave** a term of endearment here, with perhaps the secondary implication that the
      baby is weak and dependent; 'slave' could mean something like 'rascal' (*OED* I.3.b), but since
      Aaron (and Chiron and Demetrius) were all enslaved by the Romans in 1.1 the epithet is a charged
      one. On the physical description, compare *Oth* 1.1.65–6: 'What a full fortune does the thicklips
      owe / If he can carry't thus!' As in the rest of this scene, Aaron appropriates and repurposes racist
      terminology.
177   **puts … shifts** forces us to resort to clever schemes
179   **fat** Qq, F all have 'feed', which is awkwardly redundant given that the same word is used in the
      previous line. Hanmer proposed emending the word to 'feast', and Oxf¹ suggested 'fat'. We adopt the
      Oxf¹ reading because it is a striking term that Aaron has already used at 3.1.204.
      curds and whey the solid and liquid components of curdled milk
      suck suckle
178–81 **I'll make … camp** As Bate points out in Ard³, Aaron imagines giving his son 'the diet of Tacitus'
      idealized Germans'. In Tacitus' *Germania* it is also implied that there is a link between the austerity
      of this diet and German warlike valour; Aaron is planning to raise his son in a manner conducive of
      Tacitus' idealized Germanic manliness.
180   **cabin** take shelter

---

172 SD *Chiron … body]* Capell *subst.*   179 fat] Oxf¹ *(conj. Cartwright);* feed Qq, F; feast Hanmer

[4.3]   *Enter* TITUS, *old* MARCUS, YOUNG LUCIUS, *and other Gentlemen* [,
kinsmen of the Andronici, including PUBLIUS,] *with bows; and*
TITUS *bears the arrows with letters on the ends of them.*

TITUS

Come, Marcus, come; kinsmen, this is the way.

Sir boy, let me see your archery.

Look ye draw home enough, and 'tis there straight.

Terras Astrea reliquit – be you remembered, Marcus:

She's gone, she's fled. Sirs, take you to your tools.   5

You, cousins, shall go sound the ocean,

And cast your nets: haply you may catch her in the sea,

Yet there's as little justice as at land.

0.1–2   Both Titus and Marcus refer to the assembled characters as kinsmen, and indeed the logic of the
play's political story implies the Andronici are now isolated in Rome. Publius has lines later in this
scene and is identified in dialogue as Titus' nephew; other named characters – Sempronius (10) and
Caius (55) – are non-speaking: mentioning these names indicates that the play wants a gathering of
kinsmen larger than in other episodes, and the names help to create the effect of a complex social
world extending beyond the play's immediate action. But the names are decorative in the sense that
they are not necessarily connected to specific actors.

2   **Sir boy** Young Lucius; 'Sir' is ordinarily an honorific title given to a knight, but when paired here with   ·
'boy' it becomes a mock title (as in *OED* I.3.a).

3   **draw home** pull the bowstring back to its proper extent

4–7   ***Terras ... sea*** All the early texts have the same lineation here, but the metre is irregular and editors
have often relineated this portion of the text to render a greater proportion of the passage as blank
verse. Since each of the proposed emendations introduces new metrical irregularities, we have left the
lines as they are in Qq, F.

4   ***Terras Astrea reliquit*** (Latin) 'Astraea has abandoned the earth'; this line is quoted from Ovid
(*Met.* 1.150), where the departure of Astraea, goddess of justice, attends the moral degradation
associated with the age of Iron (after ages of Gold, Silver and Bronze [1.89–150]). In the remainder
of this speech, and later in this scene, Titus imagines deputizing his remaining kinsmen to search for
the missing Astraea, which is a literalized way of expressing his sense that there is no more justice to
be had in Rome. Hieronimo, the revenger in *The Spanish Tragedy*, likewise signals his despair about
worldly justice by imagining himself going to the underworld in search of Astraea (3.13.107–13,
138–40).

6   **sound** investigate the depths of
ocean pronounced with three syllables

7   **haply** perhaps

8   **there's** i.e., in the sea

4.3] *Capell; not in Qq, F*   0.2 *kinsmen ... Andronici*] Ard³ *subst.*   *including* PUBLIUS] *Bevington subst.*   0.3 *ends*]
Qq; end F   4–7] *Qq, F; Capell lines* reliquit: / fled. – / shall / nets; / sea. /; Ard² *lines* Marcus, / tools. / ocean /
nets: / sea; /   7 *haply*] F; *happily Qq*   *catch*] Q1–2; *finde Q3, F*

No, Publius and Sempronius, you must do it:
'Tis you must dig with mattock and with spade,   10
And pierce the inmost centre of the earth.
Then, when you come to Pluto's region,
I pray you deliver him this petition:
Tell him it is for justice and for aid,
And that it comes from old Andronicus,   15
Shaken with sorrows in ungrateful Rome.
Ah, Rome. Well, well, I made thee miserable,
What time I threw the people's suffrages
On him that thus doth tyrannize o'er me.
Go, get you gone, and pray be careful, all,   20
And leave you not a man-of-war unsearched.
This wicked emperor may have shipped her hence,
And, kinsmen, then we may go pipe for justice.

MARCUS

O Publius, is not this a heavy case,
To see thy noble uncle thus distract?   25

PUBLIUS

Therefore, my lords, it highly us concerns
By day and night t'attend him carefully
And feed his humour kindly as we may,
Till time beget some careful remedy.

10   **mattock** a tool for breaking up hard ground
12   **Pluto's region** the classical underworld, presided over by the god Pluto; 'region' is pronounced here as
        a three-syllable word
18   **What time** when
        suffrages votes
21   **man-of-war** battle ship
22   **her** i.e., Astraea, and thus also justice
23   **pipe for** seek in vain
24   **heavy case** sad circumstance
25   **distract** mad, in the sense of mentally pulled apart (from Latin *distrahere*, to tear apart)
28   **feed his humour** play along with his madness, as the other characters do; the word 'humour' here has
        the sense of an irrational fantasy (*OED* 6.a).
29   **careful** full of care, attentive

25 thus] Q1, Q3, F; this Q2

MARCUS

    Kinsmen, his sorrows are past remedy.   30

    Join with the Goths and with revengeful war

    Take wreak on Rome for this ingratitude,

    And vengeance on the traitor Saturnine.

TITUS

    Publius, how now? How now, my masters?

    What, have you met with her?   35

PUBLIUS

    No, my good lord, but Pluto sends you word

    If you will have Revenge from hell, you shall.

    Marry, for Justice, she is so employed –

    He thinks with Jove in heaven, or somewhere else –

    So that perforce you must needs stay a time.   40

TITUS

    He doth me wrong to feed me with delays.

    I'll dive into the burning lake below

    And pull her out of Acheron by the heels.

30–1   **remedy. / Join** In Q1, 30 is the last line on a page (sig. G4ᵛ) and is followed by a catchword indicating that the first line on the next page should begin with the word 'But'. 31 is the first line on the next page, so either the catchword is wrong for some reason, or some portion of text beginning with the word 'But' has accidentally been omitted. Some editors use ellipses to indicate a gap in the text, and Bate supplies a plausible but speculative line linking 30 to 31: 'But [let us live in hope that Lucius will]' (Ard³). Since none of the other early texts notes the error or supplements Q1, since there is another catchword error in Q1 (see the note at 2.4.14), and since the speech makes sense without the line that is apparently missing, we print it without ellipses or emendation, as it appears in all the early texts.

32   **wreak** revenge

33   **traitor** To call an emperor with seemingly unlimited political authority a 'traitor' suggests that he has violated something more fundamental to Roman society than just a political constitution.

35   **her** Astraea (justice), again

37   **Revenge** Publius' improvised conceit – which is also reminiscent of *The Spanish Tragedy* – uncannily anticipates Tamora's later efforts to manipulate Titus by dressing as Revenge and playing to his madness; the similarity, which is otherwise unexplained, gives the sense that all the characters are using the same shared cultural code.

40   **stay** wait, i.e., for Justice to be done with whatever other tasks she is occupied with at present

43   **Acheron** a river in the classical underworld; in Elizabethan texts it is sometimes (as here) referred to as a lake of fire, probably because of the influence of Christian imagery on the Renaissance reimagining of the classical underworld.

30–1 Kinsmen ... war] *Qq, F; Q1 catchword* 'but' *missing*   43 Acheron] *Qq, F1* (Acaron); *Acheron F2*

Marcus, we are but shrubs, no cedars we,

No big-boned men framed of the Cyclops' size,   45

But metal, Marcus, steel to the very back,

Yet wrung with wrongs more than our backs can bear.

And sith there's no justice in earth nor hell,

We will solicit heaven and move the gods

To send down Justice for to wreak our wrongs.   50

Come, to this gear. You are a good archer, Marcus.

He gives them the arrows.

'Ad Jovem', that's for you; here 'ad Apollinem';

'Ad Martem', that's for myself.

Here, boy, 'to Pallas'; here 'to Mercury'.

'To Saturn', Caius, not to Saturnine –   55

You were as good to shoot against the wind.

To it, boy. Marcus, loose when I bid.

44   **shrubs, no cedars** an idiomatic way of saying 'we are low, not high'; since it was proverbial wisdom that 'high cedars fall when low shrubs remain' (Dent, C208), Titus may also be imagining taking revenge on those in power.

45   **Cyclops'** a mythical race of one-eyed giants

46   **metal ... back** The expression 'steel to the back' was a proverbial way of praising warlike toughness (Dent, S842).

47   **wrung** subjected to anguish and distress

48–9   **And ... gods** As Douce first noted (2:116), Titus inverts a well-known line from Virgil: '*flectere si nequeo superos, Acheronta movebo*' ('If I cannot prevail upon the gods, I will stir up the underworld', *Aen.* 7.312).

48   **sith** since

51   **gear** business, matter at hand

52–5   **Ad Jovem ... Saturn** These are the arrows with letters attached mentioned in the entry SD at the beginning of the scene. Titus indicates which arrows are meant for which gods. The first set of letters ('*Ad Jovem*' ... '*ad Apollinem*' ... '*ad Martem*') are in Latin indicating that one arrow is directed to Jove, another to Apollo and a third to Mars. The addressees of the others are apparently translated by Titus as he hands the arrows out: they are to Pallas (Minerva), Mercury and Saturn.

55   *****To ... Saturnine** The line, as it appears in all of the early texts, makes no sense: 'To *Saturnine*, to *Caius*, not to *Saturnine*'. Presumably this is a printing-house error. The line as first emended by Capell is printed here: it suits the situation because the pursuit of justice from Saturn is necessitated by Saturninus' unjust tyranny.

56   **You ... wind.** To shoot against the wind was a proverbial expression for futility (Dent, W435.2).

57   **loose** shoot (your arrow)

47 backs] Qq; backe F   50 wrongs] Q1–3; wongs F   52 Apollinem] Rowe³; Apollonem Qq, F   55 To Saturn, Caius] Capell subst.; To Saturnine, to Caius Qq, F

Of my word, I have written to effect:
There's not a god left unsolicited.

MARCUS

Kinsmen, shoot all your shafts into the court: 60
We will afflict the Emperor in his pride.

TITUS

Now, masters, draw. [*They shoot.*] O, well said, Lucius:
Good, boy, in Virgo's lap. Give it Pallas.

MARCUS

My lord, I aim a mile beyond the moon;
Your letter is with Jupiter by this.   65

TITUS

Ha, ha, Publius! Publius, what hast thou done?
See, see, thou hast shot off one of Taurus' horns.

---

58   **Of my word** upon my word
62   **They shoot** Shooting even blunted arrows in a crowded theatre could have been dangerous, and this
        may possibly be the only staged archery in early modern English commercial drama (Cohen, 206). If
        real arrows of some kind were shot from the stage – as is suggested by their mention in the SDs at
        the start of the scene and at 52.1 – the effect might also have made audiences uneasy. In Lucy Bailey's
        2014 Shakespeare's Globe production, the actors aimed the arrows into the audience, but through a
        sleight of hand did not let them loose. Titus' one-handed shot was staged for laughs as he used his feet
        and one hand to aim and his arrow went directly up and down on the stage.
        well said The phrase 'well said' can sometimes have the general meaning 'well done', but here it also
        continues the conceit that the letters attached to the arrows are a mode of address to the gods.
63   **Virgo's lap ... Pallas** Virgo is a zodiacal constellation mythographically associated with the virgin
        goddess Astraea; Pallas (Minerva) was also emblematic of virginity. Titus' image – of shooting into the
        lap of virginal goddesses – is one of sexual aggression.
64   **I aim ... moon** Marcus alludes to the proverbial idea that one who 'casts beyond the moon' indulges
        in wild conjecture (Tilley, M1114): he is simultaneously playing along with Titus and acknowledging
        that the entire conceit is madness. Most modern editors render 'aim' in the past tense, which would
        indeed be required if Marcus were speaking only literally about his just-completed shot. The present
        tense, used in all the early texts, makes sense if Marcus is expressing his feelings about participating in
        an ongoing charade.
65   **by this** by now
67   **Taurus' horns** Taurus is an astrological constellation in the shape of a bull; Aries at 70 is another
        constellation in the shape of a ram. This exchange, with its zodiac imagery, continues the idea that
        arrows have been shot to the stars and moon.

---

62 SD] *Rowe*   64 aim] *Qq, F;* aimed *Hudson²*

MARCUS

This was the sport, my lord, when Publius shot:
The bull, being galled, gave Aries such a knock
That down fell both the Ram's horns in the court, 70
And who should find them but the Empress' villain!
She laughed and told the Moor he should not choose
But give them to his master for a present.

TITUS

Why, there it goes. God give his lordship joy.

Enter the CLOWN *with a basket and two pigeons in it.*

News! News from heaven – Marcus, the post is come. 75
Sirrah, what tidings? Have you any letters?
Shall I have justice? What says Jupiter?

CLOWN   Ho, the gibbet-maker? He says that he hath taken

71-3   **who should ... present** playing on the familiar association between horns and cuckoldry: Aaron has made Saturninus a cuckold and thus has (figuratively) given him horns

71   **villain** Originally the word designated somebody of low social class, and it became a pejorative from there, suggesting somebody of low morals. Both senses are implied: Aaron is described as Tamora's social inferior or underling and also as a bad person.

74   **There it goes** glossed in Cam² as 'the hunter's cry of encouragement' because it is used in that context by Ariel at *Tem* 4.1.226 ('There it goes, Silver'); but the phrase also appears in other early modern plays as an exclamation meaning something like 'that's the real truth'. An example of this occurs in the Q1 version of Hamlet's 'To be or not to be' speech: 'to sleep, to dream – ay, marry, there it goes' (*Ham* Q17.117). Here, Titus is responding affirmatively to the idea that Saturninus has been cuckolded by Aaron.

74.1   **CLOWN** a low, rustic person, but also sometimes the actor who played such characters for laughs (as noted in Oxf²)

75   **News ... come** This line is printed as two short lines in all the early texts, though editors since Rowe have joined them into one hexameter line. In Q1, also, the short lines are assigned to the Clown. This reads like an error a compositor might make, if he assumed that the person entering the scene would bring news. Instead, Titus, improvising a role in his fantasy, imagines that the Clown brings answers from the petitioned gods. The error is corrected in Q2 where the lines are assigned to Titus.

78   **gibbet-maker** The Clown mistakes Titus' reference to Jupiter (which is spelled 'Jubiter' throughout in Q1) as having something to do with gibbets; perhaps he thinks 'gibbeter' is somebody who makes gibbets? A gibbet is either a gallows – a mode of administering capital punishment – or a structure on which an executed body could be publicly displayed after hanging. Since Titus' question seems to be about gibbets and justice, the Clown is responding as best he can.

---

74 his] *Q1–2; your Q3, F*   75 News ... come.] *Rowe³; Qq, F lines* heauen, / come. /   SP] *Q2–3, F repeat SP Titus.; Clowne. Q1*   76] *Q1 has SP Titus.*

them down again, for the man must not be hanged till the
next week.   80

TITUS

But what says Jupiter, I ask thee?

CLOWN   Alas, sir, I know not Jupiter: I never drank with him in all
my life.

TITUS

Why, villain, art not thou the carrier?

CLOWN

Aye, of my pigeons, sir; nothing else.   85

TITUS

Why, didst thou not come from heaven?

CLOWN   From heaven? Alas, sir, I never came there. God

78–80   **taken them ... week** i.e., the gibbets have been taken down because somebody who was going to be
hanged has had his execution postponed

82   **Jupiter** In Q1, the god's name is spelled 'Jubiter' at 65, 77, 81 and 82. In Q2–3 and F the name is spelled
'Jupiter' all four times. Because of the way the Clown mishears the name at 78, some editors since
Dover Wilson (Cam²) have used the Q1 spelling (with a b) here and Jupiter in each other instance.
Since there is nothing in the early texts to indicate a difference in spelling and nothing in the comic
business that requires a different spelling, we have used the modernized spelling throughout. The
Clown's mistake at 78 may after all imply that the word was pronounced 'Jupiter' in 77 as well.

82–3   **Alas, sir ... life** The Clown's speeches are usually prose, and are usually set as prose in the early
texts. These lines are set in all the early texts as verse, possibly because a compositor saw that the
second of the two resulting lines scans as blank verse: 'Alas sir, I know not *Iubiter* / I neuer dranke
with him in all my life' (Q1). The first of the lines is not metrical, however, so the compositor who
first set the lines as verse probably erred. Capell first set these lines as prose, and most editors have
followed suit.

84   **carrier** messenger, i.e., carrier of a response from the gods

87–9   **God forbid ... days** Given the Christian anachronism about saying grace later in this exchange, the
Clown seems to be stating that he is too young to die. The speech could also make sense as a kind
of naive, unambitious modesty on the Clown's part if (as seems possible) he misunderstands Titus'
question.

82–83] *prose Capell; Q1 lines Iubiter, / life. /*

forbid I should be so bold to press to heaven in my
young days. Why, I am going with my pigeons to the
tribunal plebs to take up a matter of brawl betwixt   90
my uncle and one of the Emperal's men.

MARCUS [*to Titus*]   Why, sir, that is as fit as can be to serve for
your oration, and let him deliver the pigeons to the Emperor
from you.

TITUS   Tell me, can you deliver an oration to the Emperor   95
with a grace?

CLOWN   Nay, truly, sir; I could never say grace in all my life.

89–91   **I am ... men** The Clown's errand is thematically appropriate to the scene: he too seeks justice, though
he has 'a less elevated sense than Titus of what justice entails' (Barker, 166).
    Why, This part of the Clown's speech is set on a new line and left-justified as if it were the start of a
new speech in Qq. Since we believe that the printed version of this episode preserves two different
versions of the same exchange between the Clown and Titus, one of which was meant to supersede
the other, it is possible that this unusual and an unnecessary typesetting effect may be evidence of a
late textual insertion in whatever manuscript the Q1 compositor was working with. On the idea that
there are two versions of the same exchange preserved in the text of Qq, F in this scene, see p. 36 and
also 92–7n. and 103–4n. below.

90   **tribunal plebs** This is the Clown's malapropism for the Latin title *Tribuni Plebis*, 'the Tribunes of the
people'. The Latin title is common in early modern writing about Rome, and Shakespeare might have
encountered it, for instance, in Plutarch's 'Life of Coriolanus', where (in North's translation) the Senate
inaugurates the office of '*Tribuni Plebis*, whose office should be to defend the poore people from
violence and oppression' (Plutarch, *Lives*, 240).
    take up settle

91   **Emperal's** a malapropism for 'Emperor's'

92–7   **Why, sir ... life.** In Qq, F, Titus repeats the question he asks at 95–6 almost verbatim a few lines later.
This has led to speculation (since Cam²) that some part or other of this exchange may be an early
draft of a dramatic idea that was then superseded or rewritten but that somehow made it into the
printed text anyway (compare 1.1.35–6n.). Dover Wilson (in Cam²) speculated that 92–7 were meant
to be superseded, and these lines are presented within wavy brackets in Ard³, to indicate that they
represent a false start. This is also the only spot in the text where Marcus speaks in prose, which has
made it seem anomalous and which might be taken as evidence that this part of the exchange was
a late addition to the text. We believe there are compelling arguments for leaving this portion of
the exchange intact and addressing the redundancy via a later cut: see the Introduction, p. 36, and
103–4n. below.

93   **oration** prepared speech

96   **with a grace** in a graceful manner

97   **I could ... grace** a jokey misunderstanding – taking 'grace' to refer to a short Christian prayer
before eating – that locates the Clown in the audience's Christian moment rather than in the play's
Roman one

---

89 Why ...] *Set as the start of a new paragraph in Qq*   91 Emperal's] Q1; Emperialls Q2–3, F   92 SD] *Oxf*

TITUS

Sirrah, come hither. Make no more ado,
But give your pigeons to the Emperor: 100
By me thou shalt have justice at his hands.
Hold, hold. Meanwhile, here's money for thy charges.
[*Gives money.*]
Give me pen and ink.   [*Writes.*]
Sirrah, hast thou a knife? Come, let me see it.
Here, Marcus, fold it in the oration.   105
   [*Takes a knife from the Clown and gives it with the letter to Marcus.
   Marcus folds knife into letter and hands both to the Clown.*]

---

102   **charges** inconvenience (*OED* charge *n.* I.1.b)
103–4   *In between these lines, the early texts all include a bit of banter that repeats Titus' question at
         95–6 and which seems therefore to represent a different version of the same exchange. See 92–7n.
         and t.n. We follow Oxf² in addressing this redundancy, and find Waith's discussion there clarifying
         (211–12): since in the omitted lines Titus indicates that he will be at hand when the Clown delivers
         his message but at 108 he implies that he will be at home, the lines we have omitted seem to be
         based on a different overall conception of the scene's action. We omit these lines because we think it
         is most likely that this passage was meant to be superseded by 92–7; that both scenes were printed
         accidentally when the Q1 compositor misunderstood the cut; and that the omitted passage was not
         actually spoken in early performances.
103   **Give ... ink** This scene begins with the Andronici shooting off arrows with handwritten notes on
         them, so it is not unreasonable to assume that somebody might have a pen and ink. Titus presumably
         makes his request at large to all the other family members who are still on stage, and any one of them
         could then give Titus the writing implements he asks for.
105.1–2 *Titus gives the 'oration' to Marcus because having two hands makes it easier to fold up a letter. The
         enigma of the next line (see note) has rendered the action in this exchange unclear, but it would seem
         that Titus gives the letter to Marcus, who then gives it to the Clown, to whom Titus then addresses
         his next remarks.

---

102 SD] *Bevington subst.*   103 SD] *Oxf²*   103–04 ink ... Sirrah] *Oxf²*; inke. / Sirra, can you with grace
deliuer vp a Supplication? / *Clowne.* I sir. / *Titus.* Then here is a Supplication for you; and when you / come
to him, at the first approach you must kneele, then / kisse his foote, then deliuer vp your pidgeons, and
then / looke for your reward. Ile bee at hand, sir; see you doe it / brauelie. / *Clowne.* I warrant you sir, let
me alone. / *Titus.* Sirra *Qq, F*   105 SD] *this edn*

[*to Clown*] For thou hast made it like an humble suppliant,
And when thou hast given it to the Emperor,
Knock at my door and tell me what he says.   108
CLOWN   God be with you sir, I will.   *Exit.*
TITUS
Come, Marcus let us go. Publius, follow me.   *Exeunt.*

[4.4]   *Enter Emperor* [SATURNINUS] *and Empress* [TAMORA,] *and her two sons*[, CHIRON *and* DEMETRIUS, *with Attendants.*] *The Emperor* [SATURNINUS] *brings the arrows in his hand that Titus shot at him.*

SATURNINUS
Why, lords, what wrongs are these! Was ever seen
An emperor in Rome thus overborne,
Troubled, confronted thus, and for the extent
Of egall justice used in such contempt?
My lords, you know, as know the mightful gods,   5

---

106   **thou hast made** As Ard³ points out, Titus always refers to Marcus as 'you' in this scene, and so the use of 'thou' instead of 'you' implies that he is speaking to the Clown, and telling him how to present the oration. Titus refers to the Clown as both 'you' (at 95) and 'thou' (104) in this scene. The line is confusing and is often emended for sense because the Clown has not in any sense 'made' the oration. It is possible, however, to see Titus as instructing the Clown on how to present himself: as one who has made this folded-up document 'like an humble suppliant'.

110   **Exeunt.** Titus addresses only Marcus and Publius here, but the other non-speaking kinsmen who were present for the arrow-shooting episode at the start of the scene are still presumably on stage and they must all leave.

0.2   ***with Attendants** Any scenario in which a petitioner could approach the emperor would presumably require attendants, and the Clown is seized and taken away by Saturninus' guards after 48.

2   **overborne** oppressed

3   **the extent** the exercising of; pronounced 'th'extent'

4   **egall** equal, impartial

5   ***you know, as know** This line as it appears in the early texts ('My lords you know the mightfull Gods',) is metrically short and hard to understand. The addition of 'as know' – generally accepted in modern editions – was first suggested in Cam¹ on the theory that the repetition of the word 'know' may have caused the typesetter to lose his place and skip ahead.

---

106 SD] Ard³ subst.   106 thou hast made] Qq, F; thou must hold Ard³ (conj. T.W. Craik); thou must take RSC; then hast made Riv   107 to] Q1–2; not in Q3, F   4.4] Capell; not in Qq, F   0.1 SATURNINUS] Cam¹ subst.   TAMORA] Cam¹ subst.   0.2 CHIRON AND DEMETRIUS] Cam¹ subst.   with Attendants] Malone subst.   SATURNINUS] Cam¹ subst.   1] Q1 lines Lords, / seene /   5 you know, as know] Cam¹; you know Qq, F

However these disturbers of our peace
Buzz in the people's ears, there nought hath passed
But even with law against the wilful sons
Of old Andronicus. And what and if
His sorrows have so overwhelmed his wits?   10
Shall we be thus afflicted in his wreaks,
His fits, his frenzy and his bitterness?
And now he writes to heaven for his redress.
See, here's to Jove, and this to Mercury;
This to Apollo, this to the god of war –   15
Sweet scrolls to fly about the streets of Rome!
What's this but libelling against the senate
And blazoning our injustice everywhere?
A goodly humour, is it not, my lords?
As who would say in Rome no justice were.   20
But, if I live, his fained ecstasies
Shall be no shelter to these outrages,
But he and his shall know that Justice lives

---

7   **Buzz** spread rumours; the earliest use of this meaning for 'buzz' attested to in the OED is from 1616,
      but its adjectival form (OED buzzing 2: 'full of busy talk') predates the play and clearly informs the
      meaning of the word here.
8   **even with law** in accordance with the law
      wilful governed by will rather than reason, and thus morally perverse
9   **what and if** what if
11   **wreaks** harms done from vindictive motives (OED 1.a)
13   **heaven** pronounced with one syllable
17   **libelling** spreading defamatory ideas; this terminology might have evoked a comparison, for early
      modern London audiences, between Titus' letters and the often-scurrilous verse libels about
      public figures and events that were sometimes posted anonymously (on Titus' arrows as libels, see
      Mansky, 104–10).
18   **blazoning** proclaiming; itemizing
20   **As who would say** as if he should say
21   **fained** fainèd, i.e., faked
      ecstasies throes of madness

18 injustice] Qq (uniustice); iniustice F

In Saturninus' health, whom, if she sleep,
He'll so awake as she in fury shall 25
Cut off the proud'st conspirator that lives.

TAMORA

My gracious lord, my lovely Saturnine,
Lord of my life, commander of my thoughts,
Calm thee and bear the faults of Titus' age,
Th'effects of sorrow for his valiant sons 30
Whose loss hath pierced him deep and scarred his heart,
And rather comfort his distressed plight
Than prosecute the meanest or the best
For these contempts. (*Aside.*) Why, thus it shall become
High-witted Tamora to gloze withal. 35
But, Titus, I have touched thee to the quick.
Thy life-blood out, if Aaron now be wise,
Then is all safe, the anchor in the port.

Enter CLOWN.

How now, good fellow, wouldst thou speak with us?

CLOWN

Yea, forsooth, and your mistress-ship be emperial. 40

24–5 *she ... she** Rowe's emendation of the pronouns for justice from 'he ... he' to 'she ... she' makes sense as Saturninus is railing at Titus' missives, which may have contained reference to the idea (so prominent in 4.3, where the arrows are fired) of Astraea as a female personification of Justice. Justice is often personified as female, including at 4.3.38. Oxf² retains the reading from the early texts on the theory that Saturninus is referring to himself here; as the editors of Oxf³ note, this may in any event be what the compositor who originally set the lines thought was meant.

32 **distressed** distressèd
33 **the meanest ... best** the lowest or the most elevated in rank and social standing
35 **gloze** speak smoothly and deceptively
36 **to the quick** i.e., somewhere that really hurts
37 **Thy life-blood out** i.e., when you have been killed

24–5 she ... she] *Rowe;* he ... he *Qq, F* 34 SD] *F (after 35); not in Qq* 35 withal] *Pope;* with all *Qq, F* 38 anchor] *Q1–2;* Anchor's *Q3, F*

TAMORA

Empress I am, but yonder sits the Emperor.

CLOWN   'Tis he. God and Saint Stephen give you good e'en,
I have brought you a letter and a couple of pigeons here.

[*Saturninus*] *reads the letter* [*and discovers the knife*].

SATURNINUS

Go, take him away and hang him presently!

CLOWN

How much money must I have?   45

TAMORA

Come, sirrah, you must be hanged.

CLOWN   Hanged? By'r Lady, then I have brought up a neck
to a fair end.   *Exit* [*guarded*].

SATURNINUS

Despiteful and intolerable wrongs!

Shall I endure this monstrous villainy?   50

I know from whence this same device proceeds.

---

42   **God ... good e'en** The Clown, once again, speaks like an early modern stage clown, couching his
politeness in a Christian epithet instead of anything associated with pagan Rome. The evocation in
passing of Saint Stephen – an early Christian martyr – may register as ironic in relation to the Clown's
own subsequent slaughter and the sacrificial violence in the play as a whole (see, e.g., Moschovakis,
'Irreligious', 471–2).

43 *SD A knife was folded into the letter in 4.3, and is part of what provokes Saturninus' reaction.

46   **Come ... hanged** The tetrameter rhythm of Tamora's response echoes the Clown's question, perhaps
mockingly.

47   **By'r Lady** a contraction of 'by our Lady'; another exclamation couched in a Christian register

47–8   **I have ... end** The Clown is remarking ironically on how hanging is a fine end for his neck, and has
one small comic flourish on his way out: 'neck' could also mean impudence (*OED n.*[1] P1b), and
there is a pun on 'end' as in death and 'end' as in 'hanging from the end of a rope'. The unnecessary
violence of the Clown's death, which may be obscured by his joking, is often underscored in
production. In Lucy Bailey's 2014 Shakespeare's Globe production, the Clown's neck was broken
onstage immediately after he says the word end, and then his body was dragged offstage. In Michael
Fentiman's 2013 RSC production, the Clown was hanged on stage during the interval between
4.4 and 5.1.

51   **device** scheme, contrivance

---

42 good e'en] Q1–2 (godden); good den Q3, F   43 SD *Saturninus*] *Johnson subst.; He Qq, F   *and discovers ...
the knife*] *this edn*   47 By'r Lady] F (ber.Lady); be Lady Qq   48 SD] *guarded*] *Capell*

May this be borne? As if his traitorous sons,
That died by law for murder of our brother,
Have by my means been butchered wrongfully!
Go, drag the villain hither by the hair: 55
Nor age nor honour shall shape privilege.
For this proud mock I'll be thy slaughterman,
Sly frantic wretch, that holp'st to make me great
In hope thyself should govern Rome and me.

                    Enter nuntius EMILLIUS.

SATURNINUS

What news with thee, Emillius?   60

EMILLIUS

Arm, my lords. Rome never had more cause:
The Goths have gathered head and with a power
Of high-resolved men, bent to the spoil,
They hither march amain, under conduct
Of Lucius, son to old Andronicus,   65
Who threats, in course of this revenge, to do
As much as ever Coriolanus did.

---

56   **shape privilege** make immunity [for him]
57   **slaughterman** killer, butcher; compare *3H6* 1.4.169–70: 'Had he been slaughter-man to all my kin, /
      I should not for my life but weep with him'.
58   **holp'st** helped
59   **In hope ... me** This accusation is unwarranted, but is consistent with Saturninus' paranoid perception
      of Titus' motives. Compare 1.1.307–9.
59.1 **nuntius** (Latin) messenger; though it would technically be possible to have Emillius played by the
      same actor who plays the unnamed Messenger in 3.1, Emillius seems to be a much more socially
      elevated figure, both here and in 5.3: he is an active participant in the most important formal affairs
      of state.
62   **gathered head ... power** 'gained strength and with an army'
63   **high-resolved** high-resolvèd
      bent to the spoil intent on plundering
64   **amain** forcefully
      conduct leadership; the word is stressed on the second syllable
67   **Coriolanus** A Roman general in the early republic who, having engendered political conflict in Rome,
      was banished and then returned to attack Rome with an army of his erstwhile foes. The story is the
      subject of one of Shakespeare's late tragedies.

---

52 borne? As if] F; borne as if Q1; borne, as if Q2–3   59 SD nuntius] Q1 (nutius); nuntius Q2–3, F

SATURNINUS

   Is warlike Lucius general of the Goths?

   These tidings nip me, and I hang the head

   As flowers with frost, or grass beat down with storms.   70

   Aye, now begins our sorrows to approach.

   'Tis he the common people love so much:

   Myself hath often heard them say,

   When I have walked like a private man,

   That Lucius' banishment was wrongfully,   75

   And they have wished that Lucius were their emperor.

TAMORA

   Why should you fear? Is not our city strong?

SATURNINUS

   Aye, but the citizens favour Lucius

   And will revolt from me to succour him.

TAMORA

   King, be thy thoughts imperious like thy name: 80

   Is the sun dimmed that gnats do fly in it?

   The eagle suffers little birds to sing

   And is not careful what they mean thereby,

   Knowing that with the shadow of his wings

   He can at pleasure stint their melody: 85

---

69   **nip** rebuke

      I hang the head i.e., 'I hang my head' (as in despair)

72   **he ... people love** Saturninus' jealous calculations resemble the king's concerns in *R2*, where Richard notes that he has 'observed' a rival's 'courtship to the common people – / How he did seem to dive into their hearts' (1.4.24–5).

74   **When I ... man** actions we have not seen staged; there are depictions of rulers walking incognito amongst their subjects to eavesdrop in *H5* and *MM*.

      walked walkèd

75   **wrongfully** i.e., wrongfully done

79   **succour** assist; support

80   **like thy name** i.e., like the god Saturn, who ruled in the golden age

82   **suffers** allows

83   **careful** concerned with

85   **stint** put an end to

77 our] *F*; your *Qq*

Even so mayst thou the giddy men of Rome.
Then cheer thy spirit, for know thou, Emperor,
I will enchant the old Andronicus
With words more sweet and yet more dangerous
Then baits to fish or honey-stalks to sheep,   90
When as the one is wounded with the bait,
The other rotted with delicious feed.

SATURNINUS

But he will not entreat his son for us.

TAMORA

If Tamora entreat him, then he will.
For I can smooth and fill his aged ears   95
With golden promises, that were his heart
Almost impregnable, his old ears deaf,
Yet should both ear and heart obey my tongue.
[to Emillius] Go thou before to our ambassador;
Say that the Emperor requests a parlay   100
Of warlike Lucius, and appoint the meeting
Even at his father's house, the old Andronicus.

---

86 **giddy** inconstant
87 **spirit** pronounced with one syllable; spirit and sprite were often used interchangeably in early modern texts, and the metre suggests pronunciation that favours the latter.
90 **honey-stalks** sweet stalks or flowers of plants, especially clover, which were thought to induce animals to eat themselves to death; this is the earliest instance cited in the OED.
91 **When as** as in instances when
95 **smooth** flatter
    aged agèd
96 **that** such that
99 **Go thou ... ambassador** In Qq, this line reads 'Go thou before to be our ambassador', which implies that Emillius himself is being sent as ambassador. The F version of the line (which we print here) suggests instead that Emillius is being sent to speak to some other personage. The F version of the line offers a vaguer sense of the communications going on around the play's action, and cleans up the metre by getting rid of the extra syllable in the Qq version of the line.
100 **parlay** conference with an enemy to discuss the terms of a truce

---

92 feed] Q2–3; seede Q1; foode F   97 ears] F; yeares Qq   99 SD] Rowe   to] F; to be Qq   102 Even ... Andronicus.] Q1-2; not in Q3, F

SATURNINUS

Emillius, do this message honourably,
And if he stand in hostage for his safety,
Bid him demand what pledge will please him best.   105

EMILLIUS

Your bidding shall I do effectually.   *Exit.*

TAMORA

Now will I to that old Andronicus
And temper him, with all the art I have,
To pluck proud Lucius from the warlike Goths.
And now, sweet emperor, be blithe again,   110
And bury all thy fear in my devices.

SATURNINUS

Then go successantly and plead to him.   *Exeunt.*

---

103   **do** deliver
104   **stand in hostage** insist upon hostages
106   **effectually** thoroughly
108   **temper** mollify, bring into a well-managed frame of mind
110   **blithe** cheerful
111   **bury … devices** forget (*OED* bury *v.* 2.b) your fears in (trusting) my plans
112   **successantly** This is the only appearance of this word in the entire corpus of EEBO-TCP; the *OED* offers
        an entry for the word, with this as the only example, and the speculative definition 'in succession'.
        Some editors have suggested replacements (such as 'successfully' or 'incessantly'), but since the word
        appears in all the early texts of *Tit* it did not seem conspicuously nonsensical to compositors. The
        meaning, from context, would seem to be something like 'immediately' (as in, 'next in succession after
        what we are now doing').

---

112 successantly] *Qq, F*; successfully *Rowe*; incessantly *Capell*;   to] *Qq*; for *F*

[5.1]   *Flourish. Enter* LUCIUS *with an army of Goths [including* 1 Goth]
with Drums and Soldiers.

LUCIUS

Approved warriors, and my faithful friends,
I have received letters from great Rome,
Which signifies what hate they bear their emperor,
And how desirous of our sight they are.
Therefore, great lords, be as your titles witness,   5
Imperious, and impatient of your wrongs,
And wherein Rome hath done you any scathe,
Let him make treble satisfaction.

1 GOTH

Brave slip sprung from the great Andronicus,
Whose name was once our terror, now our comfort,   10

---

1   **Approved** approvèd; proven, battle-tested
        faithful friends evocative of Bassianus' appeal to his followers at the start of the play (1.1.9), and so also
        indicative of a possible return to a style of republican manliness that was banished when Saturninus
        became emperor; ironic in that Lucius also in this speech asks his Goth allies to be 'imperious' and to
        act on the basis of old hostility towards Rome
2   **received** receivèd
3   **signifies** On the agreement of the plural noun with singular verb form, see 2.1.26n.
5–6   **be ... wrongs** i.e., 'be what your military titles suggest, imperious, and so be unwilling to let wrongs go
        unavenged'
7   **scathe** harm
8   **Let him ... satisfaction** Lucius shifts pronouns ('you ... him') in mid-thought, but the idea is that
        anyone who has suffered harm from Rome should seek triple vengeance in the battle to come. The
        metre suggests that 'satisfaction' would have been pronounced with five syllables.
9 *SP   **1 GOTH** There are clearly different Goths speaking in this scene, but they all receive the same
        undifferentiated SP ('*Goth*') in the early texts. Editors since Capell have used numbers to distinguish
        the speakers, and we follow suit.
9   **slip** a cutting taken from a plant for replanting or grafting and so, figuratively, offspring; the metaphor
        imagines reproduction as taking place without a mother, and so it fits rhetorically with the lack of
        mention of Lucius' mother (Titus' wife) throughout the entire play. It also fits with Lucius' attempt
        to remove Tamora and restore the older, masculine idea of Roman virtue associated with Titus
        Andronicus in the first section of Act 1.

5.1] Rowe; *Actus Quintus F*   0.1 *Flourish*] F   *including* 1 Goth] *this edn*   0.2 *Drums*] Q1 (*Drum s*); *Drums*
Q2; *Drum Q3, F*   7 scathe] Q1 (*skath*); scathe Q3, F   9 SP] Capell *subst.; Goth Qq*, F

Whose high exploits and honourable deeds
Ingrateful Rome requites with foul contempt,
Be bold in us. We'll follow where thou lead'st,
Like stinging bees in hottest summer's day
Led by their master to the flowered fields   15
And be avenged on cursed Tamora.

ALL GOTHS

And as he saith, so say we all with him.

LUCIUS

I humbly thank him, and I thank you all.
But who comes here, led by a lusty Goth?

Enter a Goth [2 Goth] leading of AARON *with his child in his arms.*

2 GOTH

Renowned Lucius, from our troops I strayed   20
To gaze upon a ruinous monastery,
And as I earnestly did fix mine eye
Upon the wasted building, suddenly

---

11   **exploits** stress is on the second syllable
12   **requites** repays
13   **bold** confident
15   **their master** It was generally assumed through the early seventeenth century that the orderly society
      of bees was ruled by a king. The analogy between bees and well-governed human societies was
      commonplace even in classical times, as in the following, from Plutarch, *Morals*: 'a wise man and a
      politician is by nature alwaies the governour and chiefe magistrate of a citie, like as the king among the
      Bees' (p. 366).
16   **cursed** cursèd; the specific cause of the Goth's hostility towards their former queen is unspecified
17 *SP The line itself clearly implies that it is spoken in response, and on behalf of all the Goths ('we all'), but
      the implied SP was first supplied in F2.
19   **lusty** vigorous
20   **Renowned** Renownèd
21   **ruinous monastery** This is anachronistic, but also evocative of a suggestive association between
      Romans and Roman Catholicism. The idea that the play's landscape includes old monasteries now
      fallen to ruin and disuse may also create an imaginary link between the play's Rome and post-
      Reformation England.

---

13 Be bold] *Qq*; behold *F*   17 SP] *F2 (Omn.); not in Qq, F*   19.1 2 Goth] *this edn*   20 SP] *Capell subst;*
Goth *Qq, F*

I heard a child cry underneath a wall.
I made unto the noise, when soon I heard   25
The crying babe controlled with this discourse:
'Peace, tawny slave, half me and half thy dam,
Did not thy hue bewray whose brat thou art,
Had nature lent thee but thy mother's look,
Villain, thou mightst have been an emperor.   30
But where the bull and cow are both milk-white
They never do beget a coal-black calf.
Peace, villain, peace' – even thus he rates the babe –
'For I must bear thee to a trusty Goth
Who, when he knows thou art the Empress' babe,   35
Will hold thee dearly for thy mother's sake'.
With this, my weapon drawn, I rushed upon him,
Surprised him suddenly, and brought him hither
To use as you think needful of the man.

26   **controlled** in the sense of having its emotions subdued; calmed
27   **tawny** brown-skinned; compare with *AC* 1.1.2–6, 'Those goodly eyes, / That o'er the files and musters
      of the war / Have glowed like plated Mars, now bend, now turn / The office and devotion of their view
      / Upon a tawny front'; *MoV* SD 2.1, 'Enter Morocco, a tawny Moor all in white'; and *MND* 3.2.263, 'Out,
      tawny Tartar, out!'
      dam mother; Q1 has 'dame', and Q2–3 and F all have 'dam'. We take dame in Q1 to be an alternative
      spelling of dam and so adopt the more familiar version from Q2.
28   **bewray** reveal
      brat child; 'in 16th and 17th centuries sometimes used without contempt' (*OED n.*² a)
30   **Villain** sometimes used playfully and without sinister connotation, as in *T&C* 3.2.31: 'It is the prettiest
      villain!'
33   **rates** berates, scolds
34   **a trusty Goth** Here, Aaron's friend is said to be a Goth, but when Aaron first explains his plans (4.2.153–
      62) he says that he is going to visit a 'countryman' of his whose 'fair' wife has just given birth to a
      white-presenting baby. This is either another of the play's potential continuity errors or a revelation
      that Aaron was lying to Chiron and Demetrius about the existence of 'Mulitius' and his family.
37   **With this** at this point
39   **To use ... man** 'to use the man as you think necessary'

27 dam] Q1 (Dame); dam Q2–3; F

LUCIUS

O, worthy Goth, this is the incarnate devil   40
That robbed Andronicus of his good hand.
This is the pearl that pleased your empress' eye,
And here's the base fruit of her burning lust.
Say, wall-eyed slave, whither wouldst thou convey
This growing image of thy fiendlike face?   45
Why dost not speak? What, deaf? Not a word?
A halter, soldiers, hang him on this tree
And by his side his fruit of bastardy.

AARON

Touch not the boy; he is of royal blood.

LUCIUS

Too like the sire for ever being good.   50
First hang the child that he may see it sprawl,
A sight to vex the father's soul withal.

---

40   **incarnate devil** Devils in medieval drama were often depicted as black-skinned, so this is a racializing
     epithet when used of Aaron.
42   **the pearl ... eye** Lucius refers to the proverbial idea that 'a black man is a pearl in a fair woman's eye'
     (Dent, M79). The expression hinges on the visual contrast between a white pearl and black skin and
     thus can imply, as Lucius does here, that women's sexual taste is inherently perverse. Compare *TGV*
     5.2, where Thurio and Proteus first agree that the former's face is 'black' (10), and not 'fair' (9) as Silvia
     has allegedly stated, and then note that 'pearls are fair; and the old saying is, / "Black men are pearls in
     beauteous ladies' eyes"' (11–12).
43   **base fruit ... lust** i.e., the despicable child
44   **wall-eyed** having glaring, angry eyes (*OED* 2); since the primary meaning of the term pertains to having
     eyes of 'an excessively light colour' (*OED* 1), Lucius also seems to be commenting in a racializing manner
     on the way Aaron's eyes stand out against black skin.
45   **growing ... fiendlike face** i.e., the growing child who bears his face; on 'fiendlike', see the remarks on the
     phrase 'incarnate devil' at 40n.
46   **Why ... word?** The line is a syllable short, and seems to need a one-syllable word (like 'what' again)
     before 'Not a word'.
47   **halter** a rope with a noose
50   **sire** father
51   **sprawl** convulse
52   **vex** afflict

---

43 here's] Q1 (her's); here's Q2; heeres Q3, F   her] Q1–2; his Q3, F   44 whither] Q1–2; wether Q3, F

AARON

    Get me a ladder. Lucius, save the child,

    And bear it from me to the Empress.

    If thou do this, I'll show thee wondrous things   55

    That highly may advantage thee to hear.

    If thou wilt not, befall what may befall,

    I'll speak no more, but 'vengeance rot you all'.

        [*Goths bring a ladder; Aaron climbs it, guarded.*]

LUCIUS

    Say on, and if it please me which thou speak'st,

    Thy child shall live and I will see it nourished.   60

AARON

    And if it please thee? Why, assure thee, Lucius,

    'Twill vex thy soul to hear what I shall speak,

    For I must talk of murders, rapes, and massacres,

    Acts of black night, abominable deeds,

    Complots of mischief, treason, villanies,   65

    Ruthful to hear yet piteously performed,

---

53   **Get me a ladder** Pope[2] (acting on a suggestion from Theobald, *Restored*, 155) first assigned this half-line to Lucius, and subsequent editors have followed suit. After all, Lucius is the one commanding that Aaron and his child be hanged. The early texts, however, all assign the whole line to Aaron, which might imply that he is attempting to forestall Lucius' murder of the child by taking command of the situation and offering to hang himself. While the power relations in this scene certainly make it more realistic to reassign the command to Lucius, the line as it stands in the early texts is true to the way Aaron is characterized and depicted throughout, showing him seizing control of the action and upstaging his captors; we have left it as it is in Qq, F.

54   **Empress** pronounced with three syllables

58 SD   ***Goths ... guarded*** There is no SD concerning the ladder in the early texts, and modern editions often provide SDs specifying that Aaron is forced to ascend. If Aaron is assertively offering his own life and testimony in exchange for his son's life then he does not need to be rendered abject here.

65   **Complots** conspiracies, as at 2.3.265

66   **Ruthful ... performed** lamentable to hear of, and performed in such a way as to arouse pity in others; Aaron, who is trying to persuade his listeners that they need to hear what he has to say, emphasizes the emotional impact his tale will have.

---

53 SP] Qq, F; *After* 'Get me a ladder.' *in* Pope[2] *(conj. Theobald)*   58 SD] *This edn*   64 night] Q1–2, F; nights Q3

And this shall all be buried in my death
Unless thou swear to me my child shall live.

LUCIUS

Tell on thy mind; I say thy child shall live.

AARON

Swear that he shall, and then I will begin.   70

LUCIUS

Who should I swear by? Thou believest no god.
That granted, how canst thou believe an oath?

AARON

What if I do not, as indeed I do not?
Yet for I know thou art religious
And hast a thing within thee called conscience,   75
With twenty popish tricks and ceremonies
Which I have seen thee careful to observe,
Therefore I urge thy oath; for that I know
An idiot holds his bauble for a god
And keeps the oath which by that god he swears,   80
To that I'll urge him. Therefore thou shalt vow,
By that same god, what god soe'er it be

---

74   **for** because
      religious pronounced with four syllables
75   **called** callèd
76   **popish ... ceremonies** The term 'popish' is obviously anachronistic to the play's classical Roman
      setting, and Aaron (though self-identified as an atheist at 73) echoes Protestant anti-Catholic
      rhetoric denigrating Catholicism as empty ceremony. This strengthens the association between
      the Romans and the Roman Catholics established in the Goth soldier's narrative at 21 above.
79   **bauble** a trinket or toy, but also a stick topped with a carved ass' head used by a court jester
      as mock staff of office (*OED* III.7.a., which cites this instance); Dent compares Aaron's remark to
      an idiomatic or proverbial put-down, saying that somebody dotes more on something 'than a
      fool on his bauble' (F509). Aaron is likening religious devotion to the folly of worshipping such
      an item.

---

67 in] Q1–2; by Q3, F   69] Q1; F lines minde, / liue. /   71] Q1; F lines by, / God, /

That thou adorest and hast in reverence,
To save my boy, to nourish and bring him up,
Or else I will discover nought to thee.   85

LUCIUS

Even by my god I swear to thee I will.

AARON

First know thou I begot him on the Empress.

LUCIUS

O, most insatiate and luxurious woman!

AARON

Tut, Lucius, this was but a deed of charity
To that which thou shalt hear of me anon.   90
'Twas her two sons that murdered Bassianus;
They cut thy sister's tongue and ravished her,
And cut her hands off and trimmed her as thou sawest.

LUCIUS

O detestable villain, call'st thou that trimming?

---

83   **adorest** pronounced 'ador'st'
      hast in reverence hold in high esteem
84   **nourish** Editors sometimes change this to 'nurse' because a one-syllable word is required; in fact, the
      two words may be regarded as alternative versions of each other from the same etymological roots. We
      follow Qq and F, but here and at 60 the word was probably pronounced with a single syllable ('nour'sh')
      in a manner rendering it close to nurse.
85   **discover** reveal
86   **Even** pronounced 'ev'n'
88   **luxurious** lecherous
90   **To** compared to
93   **trimmed** A particularly nasty remark, as Lucius' response makes clear. Aaron is referring to Lavinia's
      visible condition ('as thou sawest') with her hands and tongue cut off, and though 'trimmed' as a
      verb could just mean something general like 'outfitted', Aaron means something like 'having had
      irregularities cut off' (*OED* II.11.a), as happens to meat in the process of being prepared for cooking
      (see 95n. below). The word could also mean 'prepared for some purpose or use' (*OED* II.2), and it could
      be sexual slang, including for sexual predation (Williams, *Dictionary*, 1423, provides several examples).

---

84 nourish] *Qq, F;* nurse *Ard*³   86 to] *Qq;* to to *F*   87] *Q1; F lines* thou, / Empresse. /   88 and] *Q1–2; not*
in Q3, F   93 hands off] *F;* hands *Qq*   94] *Q1; F lines* villaine! / Trimming? /

AARON

Why, she was washed and cut and trimmed,   95
And 'twas trim sport for them which had the doing of it.

LUCIUS

O barbarous, beastly villains, like thyself.

AARON

Indeed, I was their tutor to instruct them.
That codding spirit had they from their mother,
As sure a card as ever won the set;   100
That bloody mind I think they learned of me,
As true a dog as ever fought at head.
Well, let my deeds be witness of my worth:
I trained thy brethren to that guileful hole
Where the dead corpse of Bassianus lay;   105
I wrote the letter that thy father found,
And hid the gold within that letter mentioned,

95-6 **Why, she … it** Editors have sometimes created two pentameter lines by moving the phrase 'and 'twas' up to the end of 95. But, as Waith argues in Oxf², this puts 'false metrical emphasis' on the word 'twas' and so robs the speech of its natural rhythm.

95   **washed … and trimmed** 'like dead meat' (Ard³); see also the note on 'trimmed' as sexual slang in 93n. above. The objectifying, sexual meaning of the word is also insinuated by Aaron's remark about 'trim sport' at 96.

96   **trim** fine

99   **codding** lustful; this is a plausible gloss offered by the OED that is based on context and on 'cod' as early modern slang for the scrotum or testicles. The word in this sense does not appear anywhere else in the EEBO-TCP corpus, however.

100   **As sure … set** Aaron is either describing Tamora as a kind of trump card whose effectiveness reinforces the evil of her children, or he is noting that her nature determined theirs as surely as certain cards determine the outcome of a game. The language is proverbial (Dent, C74) and downplays the seriousness of the violence described.

102   **fought at head** attacked head on

104   **trained** lured

106   **thy father found** See 2.3.293–5n.

95-6 Why … it] Qq, F; Capell lines 'twas / it. /   96] which Q1; that Q2–3, F

Confederate with the queen and her two sons.
And what not done, that thou hast cause to rue,
Wherein I had no stroke of mischief in it? 110
I played the cheater for thy father's hand,
And when I had it, drew myself apart
And almost broke my heart with extreme laughter.
I pried me through the crevice of a wall
When for his hand he had his two sons' heads, 115
Beheld his tears, and laughed so heartily
That both mine eyes were rainy like to his.
And when I told the Empress of this sport
She sounded almost at my pleasing tale,
And for my tidings gave me twenty kisses. 120

1 GOTH

What, canst thou say all this and never blush?

AARON

Aye, like a black dog, as the saying is.

LUCIUS

Art thou not sorry for these heinous deeds?

---

108 **Confederate with** in league with
109 **what not done** what was not done
111 **cheater** the word's modern meaning applies, but Aaron also means that he has played the escheator (i.e., posed as an officer appointed to look after property seized by the crown): Aaron pretended to be taking Titus' hand on behalf of Saturninus.
112 **drew myself apart** 'went off by myself'
113 **extreme** the metre requires emphasis on the first syllable
114 **pried me** spied
119 **sounded** swooned, fainted
122 **like ... saying is** 'To blush like a black dog' was proverbial, a way of describing impudence (Dent, D507), and is also related to the proverbial idea that 'blushing is virtue's color' (B480). This line echoes Aaron's earlier remarks about how black skin does not show blushing (4.2.117–20), and also reveals Aaron's keen awareness of Roman anti-black stereotypes.

---

107 that] Q1; the Q2–3, F   121 SP] Capell subst.; goth Qq, F

AARON

Aye, that I had not done a thousand more.
Even now I curse the day – and yet I think   125
Few come within the compass of my curse –
Wherein I did not some notorious ill,
As kill a man, or else devise his death,
Ravish a maid, or plot the way to do it,
Accuse some innocent and forswear myself,   130
Set deadly enmity between two friends,
Make poor men's cattle break their necks,
Set fire on barns and haystacks in the night
And bid the owners quench them with their tears.
Oft have I digged up dead men from their graves   135
And set them upright at their dear friend's door,
Even when their sorrows almost was forgot,
And on their skins, as on the bark of trees,
Have with my knife carved in Roman letters,
'Let not your sorrow die though I am dead'.   140
But I have done a thousand dreadful things
As willingly as one would kill a fly,

125-7   **Even now … ill** Maxwell (Ard², xxi) noted a strong parallel between Aaron's lines here and these lines,
         spoken by King John in Peele's dramatization of that king's demise: 'How, what, when and where have
         I bestowed a day / That tended not to some notorious ill' (Peele, *Troublesome*, pt. 2, 8.81–2). The
         parallel is suggestive because that play is now generally ascribed to Peele, but this scene is considered
         to be Shakespeare's. If Peele did not have a hand in Aaron's speech here then perhaps Shakespeare
         was writing with imitation of Peele in mind?
132-40   **Make poor … dead** Aaron presents himself as demonic, in that his villainies are unmotivated; the
         catalogue of evil deeds echoes those in Marlowe, *JoM* 2.3.176–214. See pp. 67–8 and Ard³ 330–1.
137   **Even** pronounced 'ev'n'
139   **carved** carvèd
141   **But** Q2 changed this to 'Tut' and the change is carried through to Q3 and thence to F. As noted in
         Oxf³, however, this 'But' is also a catchphrase used in Q1 to guide the printer in compiling the book,
         and so it cannot there have been a compositor error and must have been included in whatever
         manuscript was the basis for the text in Q1.
142   **fly** see 3.2.59n

---

126 the] *Qq*; few F   133 haystacks] *Q1* (haystalks); haystakes Q2; Haystackes Q3, F   134 their] *Qq*; the F
141 But] *Q1*; Tut Q2–3, F

And nothing grieves me heartily indeed
But that I cannot do ten thousand more.

LUCIUS

Bring down the devil, for he must not die   145
So sweet a death as hanging presently.   [*Aaron is brought down.*]

AARON

If there be devils, would I were a devil,
To live and burn in everlasting fire,
So I might have your company in hell
But to torment you with my bitter tongue.   150

LUCIUS

Sirs, stop his mouth and let him speak no more.   [*Aaron is gagged.*]

Enter [3 Goth *with*] EMILLIUS.

3 GOTH

My lord, there is a messenger from Rome
Desires to be admitted to your presence.

LUCIUS

Let him come near.
Welcome, Emillius, what's the news from Rome?   155

EMILLIUS

Lord Lucius and you princes of the Goths,
The Roman emperor greets you all by me,

---

146   **presently** at once
149   **So** So that
151.1   ***3 Goth *with*** It would be possible to stage this by having Emillius enter and confer silently with one
          of the Goths who is already on stage, but the simplest and most likely scenario is that a different
          Goth enters with Emillius and introduces him.
155   **Welcome, Emillius** The fact that Lucius already knows Emillius' name suggests that he has a prior
          history among the elites of Rome.
157   **emperor** pronounced with two syllables

---

146 SD] *Bevington*   151 SD] *Bevington*   151.1 3 Goth *with*] *Malone subst.*   152 SP] *Capell subst.; goth Qq, F;*
a goth Oxf   155 what's] *Qq;* what *F*

And for he understands you are in arms
He craves a parlay at your father's house,
Willing you to demand your hostages   160
And they shall be immediately delivered.

1 GOTH

What says our general?

LUCIUS

Emillius, let the Emperor give his pledges
Unto my father and my uncle Marcus,   164
And we will come. March away!   *Flourish. Exeunt.*

---

158   **And for** Because
160   **Willing you ... hostages** i.e., Saturninus invites Lucius to demand hostages as collateral to ensure the
       safety of the parlay
162 *SP The early texts do not distinguish between the different Goths who speak in this scene, but since
       the first Goth to speak in this scene took a leadership role, we follow Capell in assigning this line
       to him.
163   **pledges** i.e., the hostages offered at 160
165   **March away** It is certainly possible, as Steevens suggested, that 'march away' was meant to be a SD
       in Q1, for there is no other exit SD there. Q3 and F remedy this by retaining the phrase and adding
       'Exeunt'. F also adds a 'flourish' at 164, which, like other SDs added in the Folio text, may possibly
       reflect performance; if so, this flourish is also a suitable accompaniment to Lucius giving formal
       marching orders to the assembled soldiers. Also, the inclusion of the Goth's inquiry at 162 sets up
       Lucius to speak first to Emillius and then to the army. The line as written is metrically short.
165 SD *Flourish* In F this SD is placed at the end of 164, but that would seem to be a space-saving decision
       due to the narrowness of columns which would not allow both 'Flourish' and Exeunt' to fit at the end
       of 165.

---

162 SP] *Capell subst.; Goth Qq, F*   165 March away] *Qq, F; as SD Ard³ (conj. Steevens); Away. March. Exeunt.*
/ *Capell*   165 SD] *F subst.; not in Q1–2; Exeunt Q3*

[5.2]   *Enter* TAMORA *[as Revenge]*
                *and her two sons [*CHIRON *and* DEMETRIUS*] disguised.*

TAMORA

    Thus, in this strange and sad habiliment,
    I will encounter with Andronicus,
    And say I am Revenge, sent from below
    To join with him and right his heinous wrongs.
    Knock at his study, where they say he keeps   5
    To ruminate strange plots of dire revenge.
    Tell him Revenge is come to join with him
    And work confusion on his enemies.

       They knock and TITUS *opens his study door [above].*

TITUS

    Who doth molest my contemplation?
    Is it your trick to make me ope the door,   10
    That so my sad decrees may fly away

---

1   **sad habiliment** solemn outfit
3   **say I am Revenge** Tamora is attempting to manipulate Titus' madness. Her invention echoes the way
     Publius also attempts to play along with Titus, at 4.3.36–7 ('Pluto sends you word / If you will have
     Revenge from hell, you shall'). Tamora has not been privy to Titus' fantasies, though she has presumably
     seen the notes he and his kinsmen fired with their arrows in 4.3. But there is a pervasive sense in the
     play that all the characters are operating with the same cultural scripts. See also 2.3.236n. and 3.1.271n.
     In Julie Taymor's 1999 film, the uncanny collaboration of Titus and Tamora on the scenario of the play's
     denouement is registered by the fact that the costumes worn by Tamora and her sons first appear in
     what seems to be Titus' private 'nightmare' before he looks out of his window and sees them all realized
     in the flesh (see Taymor, *Screenplay*, 149–55).
5   **keeps** stays
8.1   ***above** SDs in the early texts do not spell this out, but the dialogue between Tamora and Titus (at 33
     and 43) implies that Titus enters above.
11   **sad ... away** Titus implicitly compares himself to the Cumaean Sibyl, whose prophesies are blown out
     of order if anyone enters her cave; see also 4.1.103–5n.
     sad decrees serious edicts; the juridical connotation of the word 'decrees' suggests that Titus, alone in
     his room, is fantasizing about wielding power.

5.2] *Rowe; not in Qq, F*   0.1 as Revenge] *this edn*   0.2 CHIRON and DEMETRIUS] *Rowe subst.*   8 SD above]
Capell subst.

And all my study be to no effect?
You are deceived, for what I mean to do
See here in bloody lines I have set down,
And what is written shall be executed.   15

TAMORA

Titus, I am come to talk with thee.

TITUS

No, not a word. How can I grace my talk,
Wanting a hand to give it action?
Thou hast the odds of me. Therefore, no more.

TAMORA

If thou didst know me, thou wouldst talk with me.   20

TITUS

I am not mad, I know thee well enough.
Witness this wretched stump, witness these crimson lines,
Witness these trenches made by grief and care,
Witness the tiring day and heavy night,
Witness all sorrow, that I know thee well   25

---

18   **to give it action** The reading in Qq ('Wanting a hand to give that accord') is plausible – if Titus is
      saying 'I can't speak because I can't shake hands on any agreement reached' – but the version in F,
      which we use here, makes more sense in relation to the idea of gracing one's talk: Titus is saying that he
      cannot perform his role correctly without a hand to make the appropriate hand gestures. Discussions
      of delivery (*actio*) in classical rhetorical handbooks treat hand gestures as part of the appropriate
      performance of a speech. Maxwell (in Ard²) argued in favour of F's reading and suggested that 'accord'
      might have been the result of a compositor's misreading of something like 'acc(i)one' in the original
      manuscript, where the 'i' might be replaced in an abbreviated version and the 'e' might be mistaken
      for 'd'. Titus uses the word 'action' similarly when he speaks of Lavinia's 'dumb action' at 3.2.40, and the
      same sense occurs in 2H6: 'This hand was made to handle nought but gold. / I cannot give due action
      to my words, / Except a sword or sceptre balance it' (5.1.7–9).
19   **Thou hast ... me** you have the advantage of me
22   **Witness ... lines** a hexameter line
      these crimson lines possibly the 'bloody lines' referred to at 14
23   **trenches** deep wrinkles

---

18 it action] *F*; that accord *Qq*   20] *Q1*; *F lines* me, / me. /   22] *Q1*; *F lines* stump, / lines, /

For our proud empress, mighty Tamora.
Is not thy coming for my other hand?

TAMORA

Know thou, sad man, I am not Tamora;
She is thy enemy and I thy friend.
I am Revenge, sent from th'infernal kingdom   30
To ease the gnawing vulture of thy mind
By working wreakful vengeance on thy foes.
Come down and welcome me to this world's light,
Confer with me of murder and of death.
There's not a hollow cave or lurking place,   35
No vast obscurity or misty vale,
Where bloody murder or detested rape
Can couch for fear, but I will find them out
And in their ear tell them my dreadful name,
Revenge, which makes the foul offender quake.   40

TITUS

Art thou Revenge? And art thou sent to me
To be a torment to mine enemies?

31-2 **To ease … foes** F changes 'thy' in 31 to 'the' and 'thy' in 32 to 'my', so that these lines in F read 'To ease the gnawing Vulture of the mind, / By working wreakfull vengeance on my foes'. While these changes are possible, we retain the Qq reading and treat the F reading as compositor error: the changes introduced by F here are consistent with other obviously erroneous small changes that F's compositor makes elsewhere, such as swapping in 'the' for 'their' at 5.1.134 and errors concerning possessive adjectives at 1.1.259–60, 1.1.270, 3.1.193–4 and 4.2.44. And the F version, which has Tamora focusing less on Titus in a scene where she is playing a role tailored to his mania, seems like a departure from the intended purpose of the action.
     gnawing vulture of thy mind A vivid figure for mental unrest drawing on the myth of Prometheus (see 2.1.17n.). Though in that myth the bird gnawing at Prometheus' liver is an eagle, it is often conflated with a vulture in early modern allusion. For instance, the Elizabethan satirist William Rankins describes Prometheus as having 'a Vulture continually gnawing his lyver' (Rankins, 12).

32 **wreakful** vengeful

36 **misty vale** Shakespeare may be thinking again of the mistiness of the Vale of Amsanctus, as described by Virgil: see 2.3.236n.

38 **couch** hide

31 thy] Qq; the F   32 thy] Qq; my F   38 them out] Q1 (the mout); them out Q2–3, F   40 offender] Q1–2; offenders Q3, F

TAMORA

    I am, therefore come down and welcome me.

TITUS

    Do me some service ere I come to thee:
    Lo, by thy side where Rape and Murder stands,   45
    Now give some surance that thou art Revenge:
    Stab them, or tear them on thy chariot wheels,
    And then I'll come and be thy waggoner,
    And whirl along with thee about the globes,
    Provide thee two proper palfreys, black as jet,   50
    To hale thy vengeful wagon swift away
    And find out murderers in their guilty caves.
    And when thy car is loaden with their heads,
    I will dismount and, by thy wagon wheel,

45   **Rape and Murder** Chiron and Demetrius enter 'disguised' at the start of this scene, but it is Titus who
      first offers up the allegorical names for them.
46   **surance** assurance
49   **whirl … globes** 'globes' is usually emended to 'globe', since Titus is imagining worldly revenge, but
      the version in the early texts, which we retain, suggests that Titus is indulging in a flight of fancy
      and imagining Revenge as traversing all the spheres and planets. Titus' language evokes the whirling
      sometimes associated with planetary motion, as in Jasper Heywood's translation of the second choral
      ode from Seneca's *Troades*: 'with what whirle, the twyse six signes do flie, / With course as swift as
      rector of the Spheares, / Doth guide those glistering Globes eternally' (*Tenne*, 2: 26).
50   **proper palfreys** suitable riding horses
51   **hale** an alternative form of the word 'haul'
52   ***And … caves** In all the early texts, the line is 'And find out murder in their guilty cares'. Capell's
      emendation of 'murder' to 'murderers' makes good sense, especially if the word is then pronounced
      with two syllables ('murd'rers'). F2 corrects 'cares' to 'caves', which calls back the imagery of l. 35. Though
      'cares' makes some sense, it isn't as true to the literalized fantasy of revenge rehearsed throughout this
      exchange.

49 globes] *Qq, F*; globe *Dyce (conj. Capell)*   50 black] *Q1–2*; as blacke *Q3, F*
52 murderers] *Capell*; murder *Qq, F*   caves] *F2*; cares *Qq, F*   54 thy] *Q1*; the *Q2–3, F*

Trot like a servile footman all day long,   55
Even from Hyperion's rising in the East
Until his very downfall in the sea.
And day by day I'll do this heavy task,
So thou destroy Rapine and Murder there.

TAMORA
These are my ministers and come with me.   60

TITUS
Are they thy ministers? What are they called?

TAMORA
Rape and Murder, therefore called so
'Cause they take vengeance of such kind of men.

TITUS
Good Lord, how like the Empress' sons they are,
And you the Empress! But we worldly men   65
Have miserable, mad, mistaking eyes.
O sweet Revenge, now do I come to thee,
And if one arm's embracement will content thee,
I will embrace thee in it by and by.   *[Exit above.]*

56–7 **Hyperion's … downfall** Hyperion's, in F2, makes sense of Q1's 'Epeons', which may have resulted from misunderstanding a manuscript where the 'per' in 'Epereon' was abbreviated (McManaway, 144). Hyperion is a sun god, so literally Titus is saying that he'd attend upon Revenge from sunrise to sunset. Bate suggests in Ard³ that the whole image, of chariots and of the downfall of Hyperion, evokes the story of Phaëton trying and failing to drive the chariot of the sun (as told in *Met.* 1.944–2.420).

58 **heavy** burdensome

59 **Rapine** a word generally used for robbery or plunder, but here as a synonym for rape (which was sometimes understood as a property crime against men, as at 1.1.406)

60 **ministers** attendants

63 **of … men** i.e., 'upon men who commit rapes and murders'; Tamora may have wanted her sons to be disguised only as the ministers of Revenge. Titus gave them the names 'Rape and Murder' at 45, and Tamora accepts these names to play along with him but reframes them to fit her prior conception of the masquerade.

65 **worldly** mortal

---

56 Hyperion's] *F2; Epeons Qq; Eptons F*   61 they thy] *F2; them thy Qq, F*   65 worldly] *Q2–3, F; wordie Q1*
69 SD] *Rowe subst.*

TAMORA

This closing with him fits his lunacy.   70
Whate'er I forge to feed his brainsick humours
Do you uphold and maintain in your speeches,
For now he firmly takes me for Revenge,
And being credulous in this mad thought,
I'll make him send for Lucius his son,   75
And whilst I at a banquet hold him sure,
I'll find some cunning practice out of hand
To scatter and disperse the giddy Goths,
Or at the least make them his enemies.
See, here he comes, and I must play my theme.   80

[*Re-enter* TITUS *below.*]

TITUS

Long have I been forlorn, and all for thee:
Welcome, dread Fury, to my woeful house;
Rapine and Murder, you are welcome too.
How like the Empress and her sons you are!
Well are you fitted, had you but a Moor: 85

70   **closing** coming to agreement (*OED* close *v.* 14), but also with the more predatory sense of closing in on,
        as in a battle of wits (*OED* close *v.* 13)
71   **forge** contrive
72   **maintain** pronounced with the emphasis on the first syllable
77   **out of hand** extemporaneously, without premeditation
78   **giddy** inconstant, presumably because now they have sided with her enemy; she also says this of the
        Romans at 4.4.86
80   **play my theme** enact my plan; the *OED* cites this line to illustrate the word 'theme' as meaning 'a
        subject that is treated by action (instead of by discourse)' (1.b), but the literary connotations of the
        word ('a subject of a … composition' [1.a]) matter here too since Tamora and Titus are each attempting
        to outdo each other in a game of wits that is heavily mediated by a shared set of literary precedents.
82   **Fury** The furies were underworld figures associated with the impulse to vengeance in classical myth
        and literature.
85   **fitted** outfitted or shaped: made to look like the empress and her sons

71 humours] *Q1;* fits *Q2–3, F*   80 play] *F;* ply *Qq*   80 SD] *Rowe subst.*

Could not all hell afford you such a devil?
For well I wot the Empress never wags
But in her company there is a Moor,
And would you represent our queen aright
It were convenient you had such a devil.   90
But welcome, as you are. What shall we do?

TAMORA
What wouldst thou have us do, Andronicus?

DEMETRIUS
Show me a murderer; I'll deal with him.

CHIRON
Show me a villain that hath done a rape,
And I am sent to be revenged on him.   95

TAMORA
Show me a thousand that hath done thee wrong,
And I'll be revenged on them all.

TITUS [to Demetrius]
Look round about the wicked streets of Rome,
And when thou find'st a man that's like thyself,
Good Murder, stab him: he's a murderer.   100
[to Chiron]
Go thou with him, and when it is thy hap
To find another that is like to thee,

---

86   **devil** On the racial meaning of this epithet, here and at 90, see 5.1.40n.
87–8 **I wot … Moor** I know the empress never goes anywhere without the Moor.
93–5 **Show me … him** Tamora's sons – who were named Murder and Rape by Titus at 45 – attempt to play along.
97   **revenged** revengèd
101   **hap** chance or fortune

---

96 hath] Q1; haue Q2–3, F   97] I'll F; I will Qq   98 SD] Oxf²   101 SD] Oxf²

Good Rapine, stab him: he is a ravisher.

[*to Tamora*]

Go thou with them, and in the Emperor's court,

There is a queen, attended by a Moor;   105

Well shalt thou know her by thine own proportion,

For up and down she doth resemble thee.

I pray thee, do on them some violent death:

They have been violent to me and mine.

TAMORA

Well hast thou lessoned us; this shall we do.   110

But would it please thee, good Andronicus,

To send for Lucius, thy thrice-valiant son,

Who leads towards Rome a band of warlike Goths,

And bid him come and banquet at thy house?

When he is here, even at thy solemn feast,   115

I will bring in the Empress and her sons,

The Emperor himself and all thy foes,

And at thy mercy shall they stoop and kneel,

And on them shalt thou ease thy angry heart.

What says Andronicus to this device?   120

TITUS

Marcus, my brother, 'tis sad Titus calls.

Enter MARCUS.

---

107   **up and down** from head to toe
110   **lessoned** taught
120   **device** purpose, plan (*OED* 2); Tamora's use of the word is playfully ironic, since the word could also
       mean 'an ingenious or clever expedient; often one of an underhand or evil character; a plot, stratagem,
       trick' (*OED* 6; see also 4.4.51n.) and Tamora feels she is playing a trick on mad Titus. Titus brings her
       promise to fruition with a device of his own. The dramatic irony is worth noting because so much of
       the play's denouement unfolds as a battle of wits between Titus and Tamora.
*121.1 Marcus' entry is indicated a line earlier in the early texts, at the end of Tamora's speech. But the first line
       of Titus' speech self-evidently calls him in.

---

104 SD] *Bevington*   106 shalt] *Q1; maist Q2–3, F*   thine] *Q1–2; thy Q3, F*   121 SD] *placed here by Theobald;
after l. 120 in Qq, F*

Go, gentle Marcus, to thy nephew Lucius:
Thou shalt enquire him out among the Goths.
Bid him repair to me and bring with him
Some of the chiefest princes of the Goths.   125
Bid him encamp his soldiers where they are.
Tell him the Emperor, and the Empress too,
Feasts at my house, and he shall feast with them.
This do thou for my love, and so let him
As he regards his aged father's life.   130

MARCUS
   This will I do, and soon return again.   [*Exit.*]

TAMORA
   Now will I hence about thy business,
   And take my ministers along with me.

TITUS
   Nay, nay, let Rape and Murder stay with me,
   Or else I'll call my brother back again,   135
   And cleave to no revenge but Lucius.

TAMORA [*aside to her sons*]
   What say you, boys? Will you abide with him
   Whiles I go tell my lord the Emperor
   How I have governed our determined jest?
   Yield to his humour, smooth and speak him fair,   140
   And tarry with him till I turn again.

124   **repair** return
128   **Feasts** The Qq reading ('Feast') now seems more grammatical, but compare 2.1.26 and note.
130   **aged** agèd
136   **cleave to** cling or hold fast to
140   **smooth** flatter
141   **turn** return

128 Feasts] *F;* Feast *Qq*   131 SD] *F2*   137 SD] *Hanmer*   abide] *Q1;* bide *Q2–3, F*   140 Yield] *Q1* (yee'd – *I may be broken*); yeede *Q2;* yeelde *Q3;* yeeld *F*

TITUS [*aside*]

   I knew them all, though they supposed me mad,
   And will o'erreach them in their own devices;
   A pair of cursed hellhounds and their dam.

DEMETRIUS

   Madam, depart at pleasure. Leave us here.   145

TAMORA

   Farewell, Andronicus. Revenge now goes
   To lay a complot to betray thy foes.

TITUS

   I know thou dost; and, sweet Revenge, farewell.   [*Exit Tamora.*]

CHIRON

   Tell us, old man, how shall we be employed?

TITUS

   Tut, I have work enough for you to do.   150
   [*Calling*] Publius, come hither; Caius, and Valentine.

        [*Enter* PUBLIUS, Caius, *and* Valentine.]

PUBLIUS

   What is your will?

TITUS

   Know you these two?

PUBLIUS

   The Empress' sons, I take them: Chiron, Demetrius.

144   **cursed** cursèd
147   **lay a complot** set up a scheme
*151.1 An entry is clearly called for here, and Titus calls out for Publius, Caius and Valentine by name (even
       though neither is a speaking role).

142 SD] *Rowe*   knew] *Q1*; know *Q2–3, F*   supposed] *Q1*; suppose *Q2–3, F*   144] dam *Q1–2* (Dame);
Dam *Q3, F*   148 SD] *Capell*   150 Tut] *Q1–2, F*; But *Q3*   151 SD1] *This edn*   151 SD2] *Bevington*; Enter
Publius and Servants / *Rowe*   154] *Q1*; *F* lines Sonnes, / Demetrius. /

TITUS

    Fie, Publius, fie; thou art too much deceived: 155
    The one is Murder, and Rape is the other's name,
    And therefore bind them, gentle Publius.
    Caius and Valentine, lay hands on them.
    Oft have you heard me wish for such an hour,
    And now I find it. Therefore, bind them sure.   [*Exit.*]

CHIRON

    Villains, forbear! We are the Empress' sons.   161

PUBLIUS

    And therefore do we what we are commanded.
    Stop close their mouths; let them not speak a word.
      [*They bind and gag Chiron and Demetrius.*]
    Is he sure bound? Look that you bind them fast.

     Enter TITUS *Andronicus, with a knife, and* LAVINIA, *with a basin.*

TITUS

    Come, come, Lavinia. Look, thy foes are bound.   165
    Sirs, stop their mouths. Let them not speak to me,
    But let them hear what fearful words I utter.
    O villains, Chiron and Demetrius,
    Here stands the spring whom you have stained with mud,

---

160   **bind them sure.** In all the Qq texts, Titus' speech has one additional line after this one: 'And stop their mouths if they begin to cry'. We follow F because otherwise it is harder to understand what Titus means when he again says to stop the mouths of Chiron and Demetrius at 166.

163   **Stop close** gag tightly

164   **Look ... fast** F has an '*Exeunt*' SD at the end of 164, but it is not clear who could possibly leave at this point, since Titus addresses his attendants at 166.

169   **Here ... mud** In *Luc*, when Lucrece is attempting to persuade Tarquin not to violate the rules of sociability and friendship, she says: 'Mud not the fountain that gave drink to thee' (577). Other Elizabethan and Jacobean uses of this idiomatic expression (discovered via proximity searches in EEBO-TCP) refer to blasphemers who muddy the pure fountain or spring of religion. Titus' larger implication is not just that Lavinia herself has been soiled, but also that her rape is a violation of principles whose maintenance underpins society's well-being.

---

156 Murder, and Rape] *Q1*; Murder, Rape *Q2–3, F*   160 sure.] *F*; sure, / And stop their mouthes if they begin to cri. *Q1*   SD] *Rowe subst.*   163 SD] *Oxf*, *after 162*   164 fast.] *Qq*; fast. *Exeunt. F*

This goodly summer with your winter mixed.   170
You killed her husband, and for that vile fault
Two of her brothers were condemned to death,
My hand cut off and made a merry jest,
Both her sweet hands, her tongue, and that more dear
Than hands or tongue, her spotless chastity,   175
Inhuman traitors, you constrained and forced.
What would you say, if I should let you speak?
Villains, for shame you could not beg for grace.
Hark, wretches, how I mean to martyr you:
This one hand yet is left to cut your throats,   180
Whiles that Lavinia, 'tween her stumps, doth hold
The basin that receives your guilty blood.
You know your mother means to feast with me,
And calls herself Revenge and thinks me mad.
Hark, villains, I will grind your bones to dust,   185
And with your blood and it I'll make a paste,
And of the paste a coffin I will rear,
And make two pasties of your shameful heads,
And bid that strumpet, your unhallowed dam,
Like to the earth, swallow her increase.   190

170   **This ... mixed** Again, Titus treats the violence done to Lavinia as larger than a personal violation: it is a
      disruption of the natural order. Compare Titania's account of seasonal disorder resulting from conflict
      in *MND*: 'the spring, the summer, / The childing autumn, angry winter, change / Their wonted liveries;
      and the mazed world, / By their increase, now knows not which is which' (2.1.111–14).
176   **constrained** compelled, with the sense that is against nature
179   **martyr** As at 3.1.82, the word is here used in its secular sense: Titus is planning to inflict a cruel death
      on Chiron and Demetrius.
181   **Whiles that** while
187   **coffin** a pie crust or a mould for a pie made out of a paste (*OED* 4.a); the macabre double meaning is
      clearly intended, however.
188   **pasties** meat pies
189–90 **bid that ... increase** compare 2.3.239n.
190   **increase** offspring

181 Whiles] Q1; whilst Q2–3, F

This is the feast that I have bid her to,
And this the banquet she shall surfeit on:
For worse than Philomel you used my daughter,
And worse than Procne I will be revenged.
And now, prepare your throats. Lavinia, come   195
Receive the blood, and when that they are dead,
Let me go grind their bones to powder small,
And with this hateful liquor temper it,
And in that paste let their vile heads be baked.
Come, come! Be everyone officious   200
To make this banquet, which I wish might prove
More stern and bloody than the Centaurs' feast.
   He cuts their throats.
So now bring them in, for I'll play the cook,
And see them ready gainst their mother comes.

                                  Exeunt [with the bodies].

192   **surfeit on** gorge herself upon
193–4 **worse than Philomel ... revenged** The Ovidian story of Philomela's rape is a touchstone throughout
       the play (see, for instance, 2.3.43 and 2.4.26) and is literally gestured to on stage in 4.1. In the Ovidian
       story, Procne discovers that her sister, Philomela, has been raped by her husband, Tereus; she takes her
       revenge with Philomela's help by killing and cooking the child she has had with Tereus as a banquet
       for him. Titus' idea is that just as Chiron and Demetrius have outdone Tereus' crime, so he will outdo
       Procne's revenge by preparing a larger cannibal banquet for more guests.
195   **prepare** There is nothing Chiron and Demetrius can do to prepare except brace themselves for what is
       about to happen to them. Perhaps Titus takes sadistic pleasure in the culinary meaning of the word (as
       in 'to prepare a dish'; *OED* 2)?
198   **temper** mix together and moisten
200   **officious** attentive to their duties
202   **the Centaurs' feast** a wedding celebration that degenerated into a prolonged and violent battle
       between the Lapithae and centaurs, as described by Ovid in *Met.* 12.210–535
203   **So ... cook** A metrically awkward line, but the inelegance may be appropriate to the weird indecorum
       Titus announces: that of a once-elevated tragic protagonist assuming the role of a cook.
204   **ready** i.e., readied, made ready
       gainst against; in preparation for when

191 her] F; her owne Qq   199 vile] Q1–2; vilde Q3; vil'd F   201 might] F; may Qq   204 gainst] F; against Qq
204 SD *with the bodies*] Capell subst.

TITUS ANDRONICUS

[5.3]   *Enter* LUCIUS, MARCUS,
[YOUNG LUCIUS,] *and the Goths[, including* 1 Goth,
with AARON *as a prisoner and his child held by an Attendant].*

LUCIUS

Uncle Marcus, since 'tis my father's mind
That I repair to Rome, I am content.

1 GOTH

And ours with thine, befall what fortune will.

LUCIUS

Good uncle, take you in this barbarous Moor,
This ravenous tiger, this accursed devil.   5
Let him receive no sustenance. Fetter him
Till he be brought unto the Empress' face

0.1–2   **Enter ... Goths** When Titus sent instructions to Lucius in 5.2, he asked Lucius to 'encamp his soldiers where they are' (126). Lucius has apparently not followed this instruction, presumably because he fears an attack (as he explains at 9–10).

0.2   **YOUNG LUCIUS** Lucius' son speaks at 171 but his entry is not specified in the early texts. Editors since Malone have had him enter later, along with Titus and Lavinia, but there is no indication that he has been recruited into their macabre plan, as he is not among those present when Chiron and Demetrius are killed in 5.2. It makes more sense, therefore, to have him enter the scene accompanying Marcus.

2   **That ... Rome** As Waith notes (in Oxf²), this makes it sound as though 'they were on their way to Rome from their meeting place outside the city'. The next part of the scene sounds as though they had arrived at the house but not taken stock of the situation fully, and Aaron is brought 'in' after 15. The banquet itself might be imagined as taking place in a courtyard of some kind, since attendants are sent into the house to bring Aaron out at 141. The effective and efficient fluidity of the way this scene conceptualizes space is enabled by the relatively bare early modern stage.

3 SP   *As in 5.1, the early texts have the undifferentiated SP 'Goth' here; presumably the same actor who was the leading Goth soldier in 5.1 is speaking here.

3   **ours** i.e., our minds; the Goth soldier confirms that the minds of the soldiers agree with Lucius.

5   **ravenous** predatory, ferocious; perhaps also a pun on raven, the black bird Aaron is associated with earlier in the play: see 2.3.83, 2.3.149 and 3.1.159
    accursed accursèd

6–8   **Fetter ... testimony** Lucius apparently expects there to be some kind of juridical proceeding whereby Tamora would be forced to face or confess her crimes.

6   **sustenance** the spelling in Q1–2 may reflect pronunciation: 'sustnance'
    Fetter him bind him with chains

5.3] *Capell; not in* Qq, F   0.1 YOUNG LUCIUS] *this edn   including* 1 Goth] *this edn   0.2 with ... prisoner]* Rowe subst. *and ... Attendant]* Kittredge subst.   3 SP] *Capell subst.;* Goth Qq, F   7 Till] Q1, Q3, F; Tell Q2 Empress'] Q1–2; Emperours Q3; Emperous F

For testimony of her foul proceedings;
And see the ambush of our friends be strong.
I fear the Emperor means no good to us.   10

AARON

Some devil whisper curses in my ear,
And prompt me, that my tongue may utter forth
The venemous malice of my swelling heart.

LUCIUS

Away, inhuman dog, unhallowed slave.
Sirs, help our uncle to convey him in.   15

                    [*Exit Aaron under guard.*] *Flourish.*
The trumpets show the Emperor is at hand.

Sound Trumpets. Enter Emperor [SATURNINUS] *and* Empress [TAMORA]
    with Tribunes and Others [*including* EMILLIUS *and* ROMAN LORD].

SATURNINUS

What, hath the firmament more suns than one?

---

9   **ambush** i.e., 'a body of soldiers … concealed in order to surprise an enemy' (*OED* 2)
12   **prompt** inspire
14   **unhallowed** unholy, wicked
15 SD   *Flourish* F has both this trumpet flourish announcing the imminent arrival of the emperor and 'Sound
        Trumpets' in the SD after 16 when Saturninus and Tamora enter. Qq have only the latter, and editors
        sometimes consider the duplication in F to be an error. It is clear from 16 that trumpets have just
        sounded, though, and trumpets accompany the stately entry of the emperor elsewhere in the play
        (1.1.400.1), so it seems possible that the SDs in F may actually reflect the way trumpets are used to
        emphasize both the impending and then the actual arrival of the emperor for what is meant to be an
        important and stately event.
16.2   **with Tribunes and Others** This is a well-attended state event even if Titus himself does not treat it
        as one.
        [**including** EMILLIUS … **Lord**] Ard³ notes that Emillius has to enter here, and so does the unnamed
        Roman Lord who speaks at 71.
17   **What … one?** The phrase 'two suns cannot shine in one sphere' was a proverbial way of speaking about
        conflict over political authority (Dent, S992). Saturninus is complaining that his singular authority as
        emperor is being challenged by Lucius and his army.

---

10 I fear] *Qq*; If ere *F*   11 my] *Q1, F*; mine *Q2–3*   15 SD *Exit Aaron under guard.*] Ard³   *Flourish*] *F*;
not in *Qq*   16.1 SATURNINUS] *this edn*   Tamora] *this edn*   16.2 *including* EMILLIUS] *Dyce subst.*   and
ROMAN LORD] *this edn*   17 more] *F*; mo *Qq*

LUCIUS

What boots it thee to call thyself a sun?

MARCUS

Rome's emperor, and nephew, break the parle:

These quarrels must be quietly debated.   20

The feast is ready, which the careful Titus

Hath ordained to an honourable end,

For peace, for love, for league and good to Rome.

Please you, therefore, draw nigh and take your places.

SATURNINUS

Marcus, we will.   25

Hautboys. A table brought in.

Enter TITUS *like a cook, placing the meat on the table, and* LAVINIA

with a veil over her face.

18   **What boots it thee** what use is it to you
19   **break the parle** begin the formal discussion
21–3 **The feast ... Rome** These stately and formal lines are heavily ironic, given what the audience has learned
      about Titus' plans at the end of 5.2. Marcus exited to communicate with Lucius before Titus revealed
      his plans in in 5.2, though, and he returns with Lucius at the start of this scene, so he may not know all
      the macabre details of his brother's plan.
22   **ordained** arranged
25.1–3 This edition generally adopts SDs from F, and F has the music of hautboys (early modern precursors
      of the oboe) playing while Titus and his attendants lay out the banquet. Qq have 'Sound Trumpets'.
      Since the different locations in which the action of this scene takes place are not sharply demarcated,
      the difference in instruments might help indicate a subtle shift of venue: hautboys for banqueting
      instead of the trumpets that typically announce high-political events or the arrival of the emperor.
      Hautboys accompany the laying out of 'a great banquet' near the beginning of *Tim* (1.2.0.1–2), and
      Mac 1.7 begins with the SD '*Hautboys. Torches. Enter a Sewer and divers Servants with dishes and
      service over the stage*' (1.7.0.1–2). In the German Titus play, the stage direction at the beginning of
      the equivalent scene (*Tito*, 8.2) begins '*Music. Enter servants who dress a table and bring out the pies.*'

25.1–3 SD] F; *Trumpets sounding, Enter Titus like a Cooke, placing the dishes, and Lavinia with a vaile over her
face.* Q1

TITUS

    Welcome, my gracious lord; welcome, dread queen;
    Welcome, ye warlike Goths; welcome, Lucius;
    And welcome, all. Although the cheer be poor,
    'Twill fill your stomachs. Please you, eat of it.

SATURNINUS

    Why art thou thus attired, Andronicus?   30

TITUS

    Because I would be sure to have all well
    To entertain your highness and your empress.

TAMORA

    We are beholden to you, good Andronicus.

TITUS

    And if your highness knew my heart, you were.
    My lord the Emperor, resolve me this: 35

26   *gracious The addition of this word in Q2–3 and F fixes the metre in a line that has only four feet in Q1. As the editors of Oxf³ note, this is the last line on a page (sig. K2ʳ) in Q1, and it would not have been possible to include another word, so something may well have been left out in Q1 by a compositor trying to fit the dialogue into the available space. 'Gracious' may or may not have been what was omitted in Q1, but it creates a nice rhetorical balance that is appropriate to Titus' elaborately put-on show of fawning hospitality.

        dread revered

30   thus attired i.e., like a cook, as in his entry SD; Titus' putative madness allows him to dress in a manner that would otherwise be indecorous for a man of his stature. In the German version of the play, Tito enters the final banquet *'wearing the blood-stained apron, with a knife in his hand'* (*Tito*, Entry SD at 8.2.0.3–4).

34   And if if

26] *Q1; F lines* Lord, / Queene, /   my gracious lord] *Q2–3, F;* my Lord *Q1*

Was it well done of rash Virginius
To slay his daughter with his own right hand
Because she was enforced, stained, and deflowered?

SATURNINUS

It was, Andronicus.

TITUS   Your reason, mighty lord?

SATURNINUS

Because the girl should not survive her shame,   40
And, by her presence, still renew his sorrows.

TITUS

A reason mighty, strong, and effectual;
A pattern, precedent, and lively warrant
For me, most wretched, to perform the like.
    [*Unveils Lavinia.*]

36–8   **Was it ... deflowered?** In a story from the early Roman republic that is best-known from Livy (book
        3.44–58), the upright soldier Virginius killed his daughter Virginia to prevent her from being raped by
        a powerful senator named Appius Claudius. Titus' version of the story, which more closely parallels
        his own situation with Lavinia, differs from the version in Livy in that the daughter is killed after being
        raped. Nørgaard, who first suggested that Shakespeare might have had a source for his alternative
        version of the story, called particular attention to Lodowick Lloyd's *The Pilgrimage of Princes* (1573),
        a relatively popular Elizabethan book, in which Appius is said to have 'willyngly and wilfully ravished
        Virginia, the daughter of *Virginius*, which after that hir owne father slue hir in the open sight of Rome'
        (Lloyd, sig. M3ᵛ).
43–4   **A pattern, ... like** By using the exemplary story of Appius and Virginia as a precedent to warrant his
        own shocking murder, Titus implies that the violence he enacts is in keeping with Roman values.
43   **lively** convincing
44 SD   ***Unveils Lavinia*** Lavinia enters veiled, and this seems to be the obvious moment for a revelation of
        her identity, especially since Titus says her name in 45. The episode is carefully scripted by Titus, and it
        would make sense to assume that he wants it to be understood by his guests. In Ravenscroft, however,
        a SD is added indicating that Titus unveils Lavinia immediately after he has killed her (p. 53).

---

44 SD] *Ard³*

Die, die Lavinia, and thy shame with thee,   45

And with thy shame thy father's sorrow die.   *He kills her.*

SATURNINUS

What hast thou done? Unnatural and unkind!

TITUS

Killed her for whom my tears have made me blind.

I am as woeful as Virginius was,

And have a thousand times more cause than he.   50

SATURNINUS

What, was she ravished? Tell who did the deed.

TITUS

Will't please you eat? Will't please your highness feed?

TAMORA

Why hast thou slain thine only daughter thus?

---

46 SD   *He kills her* There is no indication of Lavinia's onstage reaction and a wide range of theatrical interpretations seem possible. In Michael Fentiman's 2013 RSC production, Titus (played by Stephen Boxer) had to grapple and subdue Lavinia (played by Rose Reynolds), who seemed unaware of his plan. Yet in Julie Taymor's 1994 TFANA production, Lavinia (played by Miriam Healy-Louie) impaled herself on one of her prosthetic talons/hands.

48   **Killed ... blind** Titus pointedly rhymes with Saturninus' last line, creating a jarring and dissonant effect that takes over the play from 52–65. First Titus keeps rhyming with what the others say, and then Lucius does. It is as if the making of rhyme becomes a proxy for the question of who will have the last word in the battle of wits between Titus and Tamora. The fact that the play shifts into rhyming couplets as its cannibalistic horrors are revealed, and as so many of the central characters kill each other in quick succession, contributes to the tonal complexity of this final scene, rendering the action an unstable mixture of horror and farce. See also pp. 1–3.

50   **than he** In the Qq texts, Titus' speech continues for one additional line, which is cut in F: 'to doe this outrage, and it now is done'. This could be an accidental omission, but cutting the line does not impact the sense and may represent a Jacobean change.

52   **Will't please you eat?** Titus obliquely answers Saturninus' question. 'Who raped Lavinia? The contents of these pasties did.' Tamora, at least, must have eaten some of the meat earlier in this scene, as Titus states at 59, and perhaps she has been eating while Saturninus and Titus have been speaking. As the meal begins, an audience will pay close attention to whomever unwittingly consumes the cannibal banquet (e.g., does Lucius partake too?). Tamora's first bite is an essential dramatic moment, since it completes Titus' revenge, but its precise timing is not indicated in the text.

---

46 SD] Q3, F; *not in* Q1–2   47 thou] *Qq; not in* F   50 he.] F; he, / To doe this outrage, and it now is done. Q1–2; he, / To doe this outrage, and it is now done. Q3   52] Q1; F *lines* eat, / feed? /   53 thus] Q1–2; *not in* Q3, F

TITUS

Not I, 'twas Chiron, and Demetrius –
They ravished her and cut away her tongue,   55
And they, 'twas they, that did her all this wrong.

SATURNINUS

Go fetch them hither to us presently.

TITUS

Why, there they are, both baked in this pie
Whereof their mother daintily hath fed,
Eating the flesh that she herself hath bred.   60
'Tis true, 'tis true; witness my knife's sharp point.   *He stabs the Empress.*

SATURNINUS

Die, frantic wretch, for this accursed deed.   [*He stabs Titus.*]

LUCIUS

Can the son's eye behold his father bleed?
There's meed for meed, death for a deadly deed.
            [*He stabs Saturninus. Company in confusion. A great tumult.*
            Lucius, Marcus, and others go up to the balcony.]

---

58   **baked** bakèd
59   **daintily** with delicate attention to the palate (*OED* 2)
62   **accursed** accursèd
64   **meed for meed** Tilley cites this as a variation on the proverbial phrase 'measure for measure' (M880).
      The literal sense is something like 'here's payment in exchange for payment'. The repeated internal
      rhyme may evoke the way rhymed couplets are sometimes used in early modern tragedy to sum up
      or bring an episode or scene to an end (as at 145–6 below). But it may also signify an escalation of
      the scene's indecorous, unexpected rhyming and so may underscore the farcical quality of this odd,
      murderous sequence.
64.1–2 *Lucius ... balcony* Most editors since Cam¹ have the surviving Andronici going aloft to restore order,
      and the rhetoric at 127–32 does suggest that they are aloft (though Ard² disputes this and finds it
      unusual that there is no dialogue to cover the time it takes for the characters to get to the balcony).
      Having the Andronici go aloft here, in a manner reminiscent of the split-level staging of 1.1, reinforces
      the fact that the surviving Andronici are attempting to restore Rome to the way it was at the opening
      of the play.

---

58 this] *Q1;* that *Q2–3, F*   61 knife's] *Qq, F* (kniues); knife's *Rowe*   62 SD] *Rowe*   64 SD *He stabs Saturninus]*
Rowe subst.   Company ... tumult] Capell   Lucius ... balcony] Cam¹

MARCUS [*aloft*]

You sad-faced men, people and sons of Rome,   65
By uproars severed, as a flight of fowl
Scattered by winds and high tempestuous gusts,
O let me teach you how to knit again
This scattered corn into one mutual sheaf,
These broken limbs again into one body.   70

ROMAN LORD

Let Rome herself be bane unto herself,
And she, whom mighty kingdoms curtsy to,
Like a forlorn and desperate castaway,
Do shameful execution on herself.

---

69   **corn** wheat
      mutual bundled together

70   **broken limbs ... body** A metaphor that may register as ironic, or hard to accept, after all the actual
      dismemberment staged in this play. Maxwell (Ard²) suggests as a parallel *Thy.* 432–3, where Thyestes
      is told that a reunion with his brother will rejoin the limbs of his dismembered family ('*lacerae
      domus / componit artus*'). This vain hope, in *Thy.*, makes possible the cannibal banquet that is the
      play's denouement. Another ironizing Senecan parallel might be the grotesque moment at the end
      of *Phaedra* where Theseus tries, and fails, to reassemble the dismembered limbs of his son (*Phae.*,
      1256–68).

71 SP   The quarto texts assign 71–93 to an unnamed Roman Lord; F assigns them to a Goth. F cannot
      be correct, and the error (as first suggested in Oxf¹) likely has to do with a hasty misreading of
      the first line, in which the speaker wishes a bane upon Rome. The Quarto speech prefix makes
      more sense thematically, since the play's final segment is all about Rome reconstituting itself and
      scapegoating outsiders. Capell (followed by some modern editions) saw the whole speech up to 93
      as a continuation of Marcus' short speech at 65–70: the speaker is apparently aged like Marcus (as
      indicated at 76) and it may seem odd to give such a prolonged speech to an unnamed character.
      But it is hard to image why Q1 would erroneously add a confusing SP here if it were not intended,
      and thematically it makes some sense to have a generic and representative figure of Roman
      respectability (some of whom entered the scene along with Saturninus and Tamora) respond to
      Marcus' plea.

71–4   **Let Rome ... herself** Let Rome just kill herself (to be bane to something is to be the cause of its
      death or destruction). A pessimistic thing to say in response to Marcus' optimistic rhetoric, but
      then the character has just witnessed cannibalism and mass murder. As Bate suggests in Ard³, the
      pessimism about Rome in these lines may have prompted F to assign the speech to a Goth.

---

65 SD] Ard³   66 as] Q1–2; like Q3, F   71 SP] Qq; Goth F; *continues with Marcus / Capell*

But if my frosty signs and chaps of age,   75
Grave witnesses of true experience,
Cannot induce you to attend my words,
Speak, Rome's dear friend, as erst our ancestor,
When with his solemn tongue he did discourse
To lovesick Dido's sad-attending ear   80
The story of that baleful burning night
When subtle Greeks surprised King Priam's Troy.
Tell us what Sinon hath bewitched our ears,
Or who hath brought the fatal engine in
That gives our Troy, our Rome, the civil wound.   85

MARCUS [*aloft*]

My heart is not compact of flint nor steel,

---

75   **frosty signs ... age** white hair and an old man's wrinkles
77   **to attend my words** to act on what I have said (i.e., that Rome should end)
78–82   **Speak, Rome's ... Troy** Editions that give these lines to Marcus often follow Rowe in indicating that he
        is here addressing Lucius. But if the speaker is an older Roman Lord, then he might be more likely to
        address Marcus – a contemporary and colleague – as 'Rome's dear friend'. The ancestor mentioned is
        Aeneas, who, in Book 2 of *Aen.*, recounts for Dido the story of the fall of Troy and the final defeat of King
        Priam. The Roman Lord is using the example of Aeneas having to recount the fall of Troy as an emblem
        of having to relive a bad memory: an early modern commonplace. Compare 3.2.27–8n.
83–5   **what Sinon ... wound** The Roman Lord elaborates on his invocation of the fall of Troy, and tries to
        draw a parallel between that story and what has unfolded in this scene. As Aeneas tells Dido in Virgil's
        Aen. (2.57–198), Sinon posed as a captive deserter in order to trick the Trojans into bringing the Trojan
        horse (the 'fatal engine', or fateful contrivance) into their city. The parallel is clumsy and inexact, but it
        reveals the scapegoat logic by which Rome will try to reconstitute itself: the Lord uses his recollected
        Virgil to pivot from despairing about Rome to reimagining its 'civil wound' as the result of the incursion
        of outsiders.
86 SP   In Qq (and Oxf³) the entire speech (lines 71–94) is given to Roman Lord. As noted in the discussion of
        the SP at 71 above, some editors since Capell have also felt that the entire speech belongs to Marcus.
        We think the emotional tenor of 86–93, in particular, would seem to imply that the speaker has been
        directly and personally shattered by the preceding tragic action; it is unclear why an unnamed Lord
        should feel compelled to account for what has happened or to 'force ... commiseration' from his
        audience, as in 91–2. The solution suggested in Ard³, which we adopt, makes best dramatic sense, even
        though it does require positing that the compositor of the Q1 text accidentally dropped an SP: there
        are several other instances in Q1 where this occurs (see the notes at 1.1.476, 4.1.10 and 4.1.77). If Q1's
        Roman Lord is accepted as Marcus' interlocutor, then other aspects of the exchange fall nicely into
        place. In 86–93, Marcus responds to the Roman Lord's request at 78 ('speak ... ') but professes to be
        unable to do so without weeping. So he calls upon Lucius to speak for him, and Lucius does (94–116).
        Then, after Lucius' long speech, Marcus indicates that he is now composed enough to speak formally
        ('Now is my turn' [117]).

86 SP] *Ard³; not in Qq, F*   86 SD] *Ard³*

Nor can I utter all our bitter grief,
But floods of tears will drown my oratory
And break my utterance, even in the time
When it should move ye to attend me most,   90
And force you to commiseration.
Here's Rome's young captain. Let him tell the tale,
While I stand by and weep to hear him speak.

LUCIUS [*aloft*]

Then, gracious auditory, be it known to you
That Chiron and the damned Demetrius   95
Were they that murdered our emperor's brother,
And they it were that ravished our sister.
For their fell faults our brothers were beheaded,
Our father's tears despised, and basely cozened
Of that true hand that fought Rome's quarrel out   100
And sent her enemies unto the grave;
Lastly myself, unkindly banished,

---

90   ye you; plural pronoun because Marcus is speaking to the assembled Romans here
91   **commiseration** pronounced with six syllables
92   **Rome's young captain** Since the assignment of these lines differs in different editions, it is worth noting
      (with Ard³) that a Roman Lord might be less likely to refer to Lucius in these terms than would Marcus,
      who is actively attempting to broker reconciliation between his family and the Roman elite. Lucius has
      in fact been leading an army of Goths threatening Rome.
94   **Then ... you** a hexameter line
      auditory a gathering of listeners
96   **murdered** murderèd
      emperor's pronounced 'emp'ror's'
97   **ravished** ravishèd
98   **fell** villainous
99   **and basely cozened** basely cheated: the subject (i.e., 'our father was') is implied by the previous clause
100   **fought ... out** fought Rome's war to its conclusion
102   **unkindly** unjustly or in violation of kind; see also 1.1.61n. and 1.1.86n.
      banished banishèd

---

89 my] Q1–2; my very Q3, F   90 ye] Q1; you Q2–3, F   91 And ... to] Q1; Lending your kind Q2–3; Lending
your kind hand F   92 Here's Rome's young] Q1; Heere is a Q2–3, F   93 While I stand by] Q1; Your harts will
throb Q2–3, F   94 SD] Ard³   Then] Qq; This F   gracious] Q1; noble Q2–3, F   95 Chiron and the damned]
Q1; Cursed *Chiron* and Q2–3, F

The gates shut on me, and turned weeping out
To beg relief among Rome's enemies,
Who drowned their enmity in my true tears,   105
And op'd their arms to embrace me as a friend.
I am the turned-forth, be it known to you,
That have preserved her welfare in my blood
And from her bosom took the enemy's point,
Sheathing the steel in my adventurous body.   110
Alas, you know I am no vaunter, I;
My scars can witness, dumb although they are,
That my report is just and full of truth.
But soft, methinks I do digress too much,
Citing my worthless praise. O pardon me,   115
For when no friends are by, men praise themselves.
MARCUS [aloft]
    Now is my turn to speak.   [Points to Aaron's baby]
                    Behold the child.

---

106   **to embrace** pronounced 't'embrace'
107   **turned-forth** exiled one
108   **her** i.e., Rome's; Lucius frames his defection as an act of public defence.
110   **adventurous** risk-taking; pronounced with three syllables
111   **vaunter** braggart
116   **when no ... themselves** Dent cites this as a variation on the proverbial saying that 'he dwells far from neighbors that is fain to praise himself' (N117), which is sometimes used as a way to call attention to the antisocial nature of self-praise.
117 SD   ***Points to Aaron's baby** Since the baby is on stage now, it has presumably been on stage in the arms of an onlooker since the beginning of this scene. To avoid the potential for distraction that an actual baby would entail, the child was probably represented by a swaddled doll. In addition to explaining the events of the play to bystanders, Marcus draws the audience's attention to the fate of the child, and thus to the question of whether or not Lucius will keep his word. Julie Taymor's 1994 TFANA production, perhaps influenced by a similar choice in the 1985 BBC film (Howell, BBC), made it clear that the baby had not survived: a tiny black coffin was presented at this moment. In Yukio Ninagawa's 2006 production, Kentaro Nishimoto's Young Lucius wailed tragically as he cradled a newborn baby in his arms.

---

107 I am the] Q1–2; and I am the Q3; And I am F   117 SD1] Ard³   SD2 Points ... baby] Oxf²   the] Q1–2; this Q3, F

Of this was Tamora delivered,
The issue of an irreligious Moor,
Chief architect and plotter of these woes.   120
The villain is alive in Titus' house,
And, as he is to witness, this is true.
Now judge what cause had Titus to revenge
These wrongs, unspeakeable, past patience,
Or more than any living man could bear.   125
Now have you heard the truth; what say you, Romans?
Have we done aught amiss, show us wherein,
And, from the place where you behold us pleading,
The poor remainder of Andronici
Will hand in hand all headlong hurl ourselves,   130
And on the ragged stones beat forth our souls
And make a mutual closure of our house.
Speak, Romans, speak; and if you say we shall,
Lo, hand in hand, Lucius and I will fall.

EMILLIUS
　　Come, come, thou reverend man of Rome,   135

118　　**delivered** deliverèd
120　　**architect** contriver
122　　**he is to witness** he is to confirm
124　　**patience** pronounced with three syllables
127　　**Have we done** if we have done
129–32　**The poor ... house** Marcus draws an implicit analogy between the balcony from which the Andronici
　　　　might hurl themselves on the Tarpeian rock, a steep cliff used as a site of execution for serious crimes
　　　　such as treason in republican-era and early imperial Rome. It is rhetorically astute of Marcus to
　　　　demonstrate his ancient Roman *bona fides* while offering to undergo judgement for being treasonous
　　　　to Rome.
131　　**ragged** sharp and uneven; pronounced with two syllables
132　　**make ... house** 'put an agreed-upon end to our family'
134　　**Lucius and I** If Marcus is offering the 'closure' of the house of the Andronici, then Young Lucius must
　　　　also be up on the balcony ready to jump as well.
135　　**Come ... Rome** a tetrameter line
　　　　reverend esteemed

122 true.] F; true, *Qq*　123 cause] *F4*; course *Qq*, F　126 have you] *Q1*; you haue *Q2–3*, F　128 pleading] *Q1*;
now *Q2–3*, F　130 hurl ourselves] *Q1*; cast vs downe *Q2–3*, F　131 souls] *Q1*; braines *Q2–3*, F

And bring our emperor gently in thy hand:
Lucius, our emperor, for well I know
The common voice do cry 'it shall be so'.

MARCUS [aloft]

Lucius, all hail, Rome's royal emperor!
Go, go into old Titus' sorrowful house,   140
And hither hale that misbelieving Moor
To be adjudged some direful slaughtering death
As punishment for his most wicked life.   [Attendants exit.]

ALL ROMANS

Lucius, all hail, Rome's gracious governor!

LUCIUS

Thanks, gentle Romans. May I govern so,   145
To heal Rome's harms and wipe away her woe.
            [A long flourish till Lucius and Marcus come down.]

139 SP The early texts give 139–44 to Marcus, and most editors since Capell have emended the text by giving 139 and 144 to the assembled Romans. It is true that Emillius has just spoken of the 'common voice', and it might seem risky for Marcus to proclaim his own nephew emperor before common acclaim has fully been signalled. But Marcus is speaking on behalf of the common voice in his role as Tribune, as he also does at 1.1.231–4 (as noted in Ard³).

143 SD *Attendants The early texts have no SD indicating who fetches Aaron here in response to Marcus' request. Aaron is taken into the house under guard by members of Lucius' Goth army near the start of the scene, but by this point the action is concerned with reconsolidating Roman authority; the Goths are something of an afterthought. The attendants should therefore likely be Roman.

144 *SP This line, like 139, is given to Marcus in Qq, F. While it is tempting to think of this political ritual as being so insular as not even to allow for other voices, Lucius' reply at 145 does address and thank the assembled Romans, so a moment of collective assent is needed. If the assembled Romans proclaim Lucius here and not at 139, then they are echoing Marcus and following his lead.

146 *SD Though there are no SDs in Qq or F, it is clear that Marcus and Lucius must come down to the main stage here to interact with Titus' body. Most editors have the descent a few lines earlier, either just before or just after the expression of popular acclaim at 144. But Lucius' couplet at 145–6 concludes the episode of his coronation (Ravenscroft too has the Andronici come down after Lucius has thanked the assembled Romans [p. 56]). This SD, which we adopt from Ard³ but shift to a few lines later, is modelled on the one provided in F for Saturninus' coronation (after 1.1.234).

139 SP] Qq, F; Rom. Capell   SD] Ard³   142 adjudged] Q3, F; adiudge Q1–2   143 SD] Cam¹ subst.   144 SP] Capell subst.; continues to Marcus in Qq, F   hail] Q1; haile to Q2–3, F   146 SD long ... down] Ard³ subst., after 144; Lucius, and the rest, come down; with them, young Lucius / Capell, after 144

But, gentle people, give me aim awhile,
For nature puts me to a heavy task.
Stand all aloof, but uncle draw you near
To shed obsequious tears upon this trunk.   [*Kisses Titus.*]   150
O, take this warm kiss on thy pale, cold lips,
These sorrowful drops upon thy bloodstained face,
The last true duties of thy noble son.

MARCUS

Tear for tear and loving kiss for kiss,
Thy brother Marcus tenders on thy lips.   [*Kisses Titus.*]   155
O, were the sum of these that I should pay
Countless and infinite, yet would I pay them.

LUCIUS

Come hither, boy; come, come, and learn of us
To melt in showers. Thy grandsire loved thee well;
Many a time he danced thee on his knee,   160
Sung thee asleep, his loving breast thy pillow;
Many a story hath he told to thee,
And bid thee bear his pretty tales in mind
And talk of them when he was dead and gone.

---

147   **give me aim** A term from archery meaning 'give assistance with my aim'; Lucius is asking for the
      assembled Romans to stand by him as he faces the difficult task of dealing with his father's death.
150   **obsequious** funereal; suitable for obsequies
      trunk lifeless body (*OED* 3)
163–9 **And ... him** Lines 163–7 occur at the bottom of sig. K4ʳ in Q1. They were apparently damaged beyond
      legibility in the copy of Q1 that was used in the making of Q2, because Q2 has five lines added to fill
      out the play and replace them. Whoever wrote these lines was also missing the SP at 165 and so was
      unaware that Marcus speaks here. The replacement lines simply provide a bridge from 163 to the lines
      (168–9) that occur on the next printed page in Q1, and the whole speech is assigned to Lucius. So, in
      Q2 (and thus, with minor variations in punctuation, in Q3 and F as well) Lucius' speech is extended.
      See t.n.

---

150 SD] *Johnson, after 152*   152 bloodstained] *F3;* blood slaine *Q1–2;* bloud-slaine *Q3, F*   155 SD]
Bevington   161 Sung] *Q2–3, F;* Song *Q1*   162 story] *Q1;* matter *Q2–3, F*   163-67 And ... kiss,] *Q1;* Meete
and agreeing with thine infancie, / In that respect then, like a louing child. / Shed yet some small drops from
thy tender spring, / Because kind nature doth require it so, / Friends should associate friends in griefe and
woe. *Q2–3, F subst.*

MARCUS

How many thousand times hath these poor lips,   165
When they were living, warmed themselves on thine.
O now, sweet boy, give them their latest kiss;
Bid him farewell, commit him to the grave.
Do him that kindness and take leave of him.

YOUNG LUCIUS

O grandsire, grandsire, even with all my heart   170
Would I were dead, so you did live again.   [*Kisses Titus.*]
O lord, I cannot speak to him for weeping;
My tears will choke me if I ope my mouth.

[*Enter Attendants with* AARON.]

ROMAN LORD

You sad Andronici, have done with woes.
Give sentence on this execrable wretch,   175
That hath been breeder of these dire events.

LUCIUS

Set him breast-deep in earth and famish him.
There let him stand and rave and cry for food.
If anyone relieves or pities him,
For the offence he dies. This is our doom.   180

---

167   **latest** last
171   **Would ... again** 'I would give up my life if that meant you could live again'
173   **ope** open
174   *SP Qq give these lines to an unnamed Roman, and F gives the speech to 'Romans'. Since a spoken line must be assigned to an actor, we assign it to the same Roman Lord who has spoken on behalf of the assembled Romans earlier in the scene. Ravenscroft attributes this speech to Emillius (p. 56), as editors have done since Dyce: this is harder to square with Qq, F though it otherwise makes sense.
175   **execrable** detestable, accursed
176   **breeder** origin, cause; the word is strongly associated with giving birth, as when the Nurse remarks on the 'fair-faced breeders of our clime' at 4.2.69. The language in which the Roman speaker is blaming Aaron thus links his malevolent agency to his miscegenetic union with Tamora.
180   **our doom** our judgement (against Aaron, but rhetorically ambiguous since it can sound like dooming the Andronici)

---

169 him ... him] *F*; them ... them *Qq* 170 even] *Q1–2* (eu'n); euen *Q3, F*   171 SD] *Bevington*   173
SD] *Capell*   174 SP] *this edn*; *Romane Qq*; *Romans F*; *Aemil. Dyce²*

Some stay to see him fastened in the earth.

AARON

O, why should wrath be mute and fury dumb?
I am no baby, I, that with base prayers
I should repent the evils I have done.
Ten thousand worse than ever yet I did   185
Would I perform if I might have my will.
If one good deed in all my life I did
I do repent it from my very soul.

LUCIUS

Some loving friends convey the Emperor hence,
And give him burial in his fathers' grave.   190
My father and Lavinia shall forthwith
Be closed in our household's monument.
As for that ravenous tiger, Tamora,
No funeral rite, nor man in mourning weed,
No mournful bell shall ring her burial,   195

---

181   **Some stay** If Lucius is ordering his attendants to stay behind and punish Aaron, then it is likely that
        the gruesome punishment described is meant to occur after the play's conclusion though (as Sale
        discusses) it would be possible to show Aaron set 'breast-deep in earth' using the stage's trapdoor, as
        they do in Blanche McIntyre's 2017 RSC production.
189   **Emperor** i.e., Saturninus, whose memory is actively being recuperated
190   **fathers'** 'fathers' in Qq, F could refer either to the grave of his father – the emperor prior to the start
        of the play – or in a family tomb, the grave of his fathers; given the emphasis on the family tomb of the
        Andronici in Act 1, the latter is perhaps more likely.
192   **closed** closèd
193   **ravenous** predatory, voracious; it echoes the phrase Lucius uses for Aaron at the beginning of the scene
        (5.3.5)

---

182 O] *F*; Ah *Qq*   190 fathers'] *Riv (conj. in Cam¹)*; fathers *Qq, F*; father's *Rowe*

But throw her forth to beasts and birds of prey.
Her life was beast-like and devoid of pity,
And, being dead, let birds on her take pity. *Exeunt [with the bodies].*

Finis the Tragedy of Titus Andronicus.

197-8   **pity ... pity** As mentioned in 163–9n. above, the Q1 copy from which Q2 was made seems to have
sustained damage, making the bottom of the last pages (sigs K4^{r-v}) difficult to read. Probably because
the last line was damaged and because it was not clear how much text was missing, Q2 rewrites the
play's last line and goes on to provide an additional four lines not found in Q1. See the t.n. The fact that
the concluding couplet in Q1 repeats the word 'pity' rather than offering a true rhyme makes these last
lines come across as heavy-handed and perhaps unimaginative on Lucius' part. At key moments earlier
in the play, Lavinia (2.3.147) and Titus (3.1.2) are refused pity. The concluding couplet emphasizes just
how absolutely lacking in pity Rome remains. Compare also the note at 2.3.151–2.

198 SD   ***with the bodies** The bodies of the Roman dead are to be buried in their respective family tombs.
Tamora's body is to be thrown forth to beasts and birds of prey, so it too should be carried off. In more
stylized productions, like Tang Shu-wing's 2009 No Man's Land production (Hong Kong), the staging
options are more varied. Tang had his actors sit in silence and twirl in circles for long stretches of time
to invoke the need for meditative reflection at the end of the play.

193 ravenous] Q1; hainous Q2–3, F   194 mourning] Q1–2; mournefull Q3, F   weed] Q1; weeds Q2–3, F   196
of] F; to Qq   197 beast-like] F; beastlie Qq   198 And ... pity] Q1; And being so, shall haue like want of
pitty. / See iustice done on *Aron* that damn'd Moore, / By whom our heauie haps had their beginning: / Than
afterwards to order well the state, / That like euents may nere it ruinate. Q2–3; And being so, shall haue like
want of pitty. / See Iustice done on *Aaron* that damn'd Moore, / From whom, our heauy happes had their
beginning: / Then Afterwards, to Order well the State, / That like euents, may ne're it Ruinate. F   198.1 SD *with
the bodies]* Bevington subst.

ABBREVIATIONS AND REFERENCES

Quotations and references to works by Shakespeare other than *Titus Andronicus* are from The Arden Shakespeare, Third Series unless otherwise stated. In all references, the place of publication is London unless otherwise indicated. All Bible references are to the Geneva (1560) edition. Even in otherwise unmodernized quotations from early modern texts, we have silently modernized i/j and u/v.

ABBREVIATIONS

ABBREVIATIONS USED IN THE NOTES

*	precedes commentary notes involving readings altered from Qq or F
conj.	conjectured by
edn	edition
Ff	all folio editions
LCL	Loeb Classical Library
n.	note
NQ	*Notes & Queries*
om.	omitted in
Qq	all quarto texts
RD	*Renaissance Drama*
RES	*The Review of English Studies*
rev edn	revised edition
RSC	Royal Shakespeare Company
SB	*Shakespeare Bulletin*
SD	stage direction
sig. / sigs.	signature / signatures
SP	speech prefix
SQ	*Shakespeare Quarterly*
SS	*Shakespeare Survey*
subst.	substantially
t.n.	textual notes

WORKS BY AND PARTLY BY SHAKESPEARE

A&C	*Antony and Cleopatra*
Ado	*Much Ado About Nothing*

AWW	All's Well That Ends Well
AYL	As You Like It
Cor	Coriolanus
Cym	Cymbeline
Err	The Comedy of Errors
Ham	Hamlet
1H4	Henry IV, Part 1
2H4	Henry IV, Part 2
H5	Henry V
1H6	Henry VI, Part 1
2H6	Henry VI, Part 2
3H6	Henry VI, Part 3
H8	Henry VIII
JC	Julius Caesar
John	King John
LC	A Lover's Complaint
Lear	King Lear
LLL	Love's Labour's Lost
Luc	The Rape of Lucrece
Mac	Macbeth
MM	Measure for Measure
MND	A Midsummer Night's Dream
MV	The Merchant of Venice
MWW	The Merry Wives of Windsor
Oth	Othello
Per	Pericles
PP	The Passionate Pilgrim
Phx	The Phoenix and Turtle
R&J	Romeo and Juliet
R2	Richard II
R3	Richard III
Son	Sonnets
T&C	Troilus and Cressida
Tem	The Tempest
TGV	Two Gentlemen of Verona
Tim	Timon of Athens
Tit	Titus Andronicus
TN	Twelfth Night
TNK	Two Noble Kinsmen
Shr	The Taming of the Shrew
V&A	Venus and Adonis
WT	The Winter's Tale

REFERENCES

EDITIONS OF SHAKESPEARE COLLATED

Adams	*Shakespeare's Titus Andronicus: The first quarto, 1594, reproduced in facsimile from the unique copy in the Folger Shakespeare library, with an introduction by Joseph Quincy Adams* (New York, 1936)
Aldus	*The Tragedy of Titus Andronicus*, ed. Jennie Ellis Burdick et al., The Aldus Shakespeare (New York, 1909)
Ard¹	*The Lamentable Tragedy of Titus Andronicus*, ed. H. Bellyse Baildon, The Arden Shakespeare (1904)
Ard²	*Titus Andronicus*, ed. J. C. Maxwell, The Arden Shakespeare (1953; 2nd edn, 1961)
Ard³	*Titus Andronicus*, ed. Jonathan Bate, The Arden Shakespeare (third series) (1995; rev edn, 2018)
Bevington	*Complete Works*, ed. David Bevington (1951; 3rd edn, Glenview IL, 1980)
Blayney, *Folio*	Peter W. M. Blayney, *The First Folio of Shakespeare* (Washington, DC, 1991)
Boswell	*Plays and Poems*, ed. James Boswell (1821)
Cam¹	*Works*, ed. William George Clark and William Aldis Wright, 9 vols (Cambridge, 1863–6)
Cam²	*Titus Andronicus*, ed. John Dover Wilson (Cambridge, 1948)
Cam³	*Titus Andronicus*, ed. Alan Hughes, The New Cambridge Shakespeare (1994; rev edn, Cambridge, 2006)
Capell	*Comedies, Histories, and Tragedies*, ed. Edward Capell, 10 vols (1767–8)
Collier	*Works*, ed. John Payne Collier, 8 vols (1842–4)
Collier MS	The Perkins Folio; copy of F2 with handwritten annotations likely forged by John Payne Collier: Huntington Library RB 36516
Craig	*Complete Works*, ed. W. J. Craig, The Oxford Shakespeare (Oxford, 1891)
Dyce	*Works*, ed. Alexander Dyce, 6 vols (1857)
Dyce²	*Works*, ed. Alexander Dyce, 9 vols (1864–7)
F	*Mr. William Shakespeare's Comedies, Histories, and Tragedies* (1623) (first folio)
F2	*Mr. William Shakespeare's Comedies, Histories, and Tragedies* (1632) (second folio)
F3	*Mr. William Shakespeare's Comedies, Histories, and Tragedies* (1663) (third folio)
F4	*Mr. William Shakespeare's Comedies, Histories, and Tragedies* (1685) (fourth folio)
Folg	*Titus Andronicus*, ed. Barbara A. Mowat and Paul Werstine, Folger Shakespeare Library (New York, 2005)
Herford	*Works*, ed. C. H. Herford, 10 vols (1899)
Hudson	*Works*, ed. Henry N. Hudson, 11 vols (Boston, 1851–6)
Hudson²	*Complete Works*, ed. Henry N. Hudson, 20 vols (Boston, 1880–1)
Jansen	Matthew Trey Jansen, 'A New Critical Edition of Shakespeare's *Titus Andronicus*', PhD dissertation (University of Nevada, Reno, 2013)
Johnson	*Plays*, ed. Samuel Johnson, 8 vols (1765)
Keightley	*Plays*, ed. William Keightley, 6 vols (1864)
Kittredge	*Complete Works*, ed. George Lyman Kittredge (Boston, 1936)
Malone	*Plays and Poems*, ed. Edmond Malone, 10 vols (1790)
McDonald	*Titus Andronicus*, ed. Russ McDonald, The Pelican Shakespeare (New York, 2000)
Oxf¹	*Complete Works*, ed. Stanley Wells, Gary Taylor, John Jowett and William Montgomery (Oxford, 1986)
Oxf²	*Titus Andronicus*, ed. Eugene M. Waith (Oxford, 1984)

Oxf³	*Complete Works, Critical Reference Edition*, ed. Gary Taylor, John Jowett, Terri Bourus, Gabriel Egan et al., 2 vols, The New Oxford Shakespeare (Oxford, 2017)
Pope	*Works*, ed. Alexander Pope, 6 vols (1723–5)
Pope²	*Works*, ed. Alexander Pope and George Sewell, 10 vols (1728)
Q1	*The Most Lamentable Roman Tragedy of Titus Andronicus* (1594)
Q2	*The Most Lamentable Roman Tragedy of Titus Andronicus* (1600)
Q3	*The Most Lamentable Tragedy of Titus Andronicus* (1611)
Ravenscroft	Edward Ravenscroft, *Titus Andronicus, or the Rape of Lavinia* (1687)
Riv	*The Riverside Shakespeare*, ed. G. Blakemore Evans (Boston, 1974)
Rowe	*Works*, ed. Nicholas Rowe, 6 vols (1709)
Rowe²	*Works*, ed. Nicholas Rowe, 2nd edn, 6 vols (1709)
Rowe³	*Works*, ed. Nicholas Rowe, 8 vols (1714)
RSC	*Complete Works*, ed. Jonathan Bate, Eric Rasmussen, et al. (2007; 2nd edn, New York, 2022)
Steevens	*Plays*, ed. George Steevens and Samuel Johnson (1773)
Steevens²	*Plays*, ed. George Steevens, Samuel Johnson and Isaac Reed, 4th edn, 15 vols (1793)
Theobald	*Works*, ed. Lewis Theobald, 7 vols (1733)
Yale	*The Tragedy of Titus Andronicus*, ed. A. M. Witherspoon (New Haven, 1926)

OTHER WORKS CITED

Aen.	Virgil, *Aeneid*, from *Virgil*, 2 vols, LCL (Cambridge, MA, 1916–18)
Aga.	*Agamemnon*, in Seneca, *Tragedies*
Aldridge review	'A Review of Ira Aldridge's *Titus* at the Britannia, Huxton', *The Era* (26 April 1857), reprinted in Kolin, 377–9
Augustine	Augustine, *The City of God Against the Pagans*, ed. and trans. R. W. Dyson (Cambridge, 1998)
Barbour	Reid Barbour, 'Peele, George (bap. 1556, d. 1596), Poet and Playwright', in *ODNB*
Barker	Francis Barker, *The Culture of Violence: Essays on Tragedy and History* (Chicago, 1993)
Barnes	Barnabe Barnes, *Parthenophil and Parthenophe. Sonnets, Madrigals, Elegies and Odes* (1593)
Barthelemy	Anthony Gerard Barthelemy, *Black Face, Maligned Race: The Representation of Blacks in English Drama from Shakespeare to Southerne* (Baton Rouge, LA, 1987)
Beauman	Sally Beauman, *The Royal Shakespeare Company: A History of Ten Decades* (Oxford, 1982)
Bennett	Paul E. Bennett, 'An Apparent Allusion to *Titus Andronicus*', *NQ* 200 (1955), 422–24
Billington, 'Brutal'	Michael Billington, '"A brutal sort of interrogation": Michael Billington Hails Antony Sher in a Politically Focused *Titus Andronicus*, Over Here from the Market Theatre, Johannesburg', *The Guardian* (14 July 1995)
Billington, 'Horror'	Michael Billington, 'Horror and Humanity', *The Guardian* (14 May 1987), reprinted in Kolin, 473–5
Billington, Review	Michael Billington, 'Titus Andronicus', *The Guardian* (22 June 2006)
Binns	J. W. Binns, 'Shakespeare's Latin Citations: The Editorial Problem', *SS* 35 (1982), 119–28
Bishai	Nadia Bishai, '"At the Signe of the Gunne": *Titus Andronicus*, the London Book Trade, and the Literature of Crime, 1590–1615', in Liberty Stanavage and Paxton Hehmeyer, eds, *Titus out of Joint: Reading the Fragmented Titus Andronicus* (Newcastle upon Tyne, 2012), 7–48
Blayney, *Bookshops*	Peter W. M. Blayney, *The Bookshops in St. Paul's Cross Churchyard*, Occasional Papers of the Bibliographical Society 5 (1990)

Bolton, 'Authentic'	Joseph S. G. Bolton, 'The Authentic Text of *Titus Andronicus*', PMLA 44 (1929), 765–88
Bolton, 'Notes'	Joseph S. G. Bolton, 'Two Notes on *Titus Andronicus*', *Modern Language Notes* 45 (1930), 139–41
Bowers	Fredson Bowers, *Bibliography and Textual Criticism* (Oxford, 1964)
Boyd	Brian Boyd, 'An Obstacle Removed in *Titus Andronicus*', RES 55 (2004), 196–209
Brook	Peter Brook, 'Search for Hunger', *Encore* 8.4 (1961), 8–21
Bruster and Smith	Douglas Bruster and Geneviève Smith, 'A New Chronology for Shakespeare's Plays', *Digital Scholarship in the Humanities* 31 (2016), 301–20
Buckley	Thea Buckley, '*The Hungry* by Microwave (review)', SB 37 (2019), 288–92
Bullough	Geoffrey Bullough, ed., *Narrative and Dramatic Sources of Shakespeare*, 8 vols (1957–75)
Callaghan	Dympna Callaghan, *Shakespeare Without Women: Representing Gender and Race on the Renaissance Stage* (2000)
Cantrell and Williams	Paul L. Cantrell and George Walton Williams, 'Roberts' Compositors in *Titus Andronicus* Q2', *Studies in Bibliography* 8 (1956), 27–38
'Carados'	Carados (R. Chance Newton), 'Titus at the Old Vic, 1923', *The Referee* (14 October 1923), reprinted in Kolin, 381–3
Cartelli	Thomas Cartelli, 'Taymor's *Titus* in Time and Space: Surrogation and Interpolation', RD 34 (2005), 163–84
Cartwright	Robert Cartwright, *New Readings in Shakespeare* (1866)
Catalogue	*A Catalogue of Maps, Prints [etc.] Printed and Sold by William and Cluer Dicey, at their Warehouse, Opposite the South Door of Bow-Church, in Bow-Church-Yard, London* (1754)
Chambers, *Stage*	E. K. Chambers, *The Elizabethan, Stage*, 4 vols (Oxford, 1923)
Chambers, 'First'	E. K. Chambers, 'The First Illustration to "Shakespeare"', *The Library* s4–5 (1925), 326–30
Chaudhuri	Pramit Chaudhuri, 'Classical Quotation in *Titus Andronicus*', ELH 81 (2014), 787–810
Choy	Howard Y. F. Choy, 'Toward a Poetic Minimalism of Violence: On Tang Shu-wing's *Titus Andronicus* 2.0', *Asian Theatre Journal* 28 (2011), 44–66
Cicero, *DND*	Cicero, *De Natura Deorum; Academica*, LCL (Cambridge, MA, 1933)
Cicero, *Letters*	Cicero, *Letters to Friends*, ed. D. R. Shackleton Bailey, 3 vols, LCL (Cambridge, MA, 2001)
Clines	Robert Clines, 'Men Think About Rome Almost Every Day. That's a Problem. But It Doesn't Have to Be', *The Sundial* (September 2023): https://medium.com/the-sundial-acmrs/men-think-about-rome-almost-every-day-thats-a-problem-but-it-doesn-t-have-to-be-6b5a2393dcbe
Clubb	Louise George Clubb, 'Looking Back on Shakespeare and Italian Theater', RD 36/37 (2010), 3–19
Cohen	Ralph Alan Cohen, '"Did you see that?!": *Titus Andronicus* and Theatrical Transgression', in Karim-Cooper, SoP, 203–19
Cook	Judith Cook, *Shakespeare's Players* (1983)
Cooper	Thomas Cooper, *Thesaurus Linguae Romanae & Britannicae* (1565)
Cosin	Richard Cosin, *Conspiracy for Pretended Reformation, Viz. Presbyterial Discipline. A Treatise Discovering the Late Designments and Courses Held for Advancement Thereof, by William Hacket Yeoman, Edmund Coppinger, and Henry Arthington Gent.* (1592)

Crawford	Kevin Crawford, 'A "black, black, black man": Aaron's Represented Blackness on Stage and Screen', *Journal X* 7.2 (2003), 101–28
Crosbie	Christopher Crosbie, 'The Longleat Manuscript Reconsidered: Shakespeare and the Sword of Lath', *English Literary Renaissance* 44 (2014), 221–40
Dawson	Giles E. Dawson, 'An Early List of Elizabethan Plays', *The Library* s4: 15 (1935), 445–56
Dent	R. W. Dent, *Shakespeare's Proverbial Language: An Index* (Berkeley, 1981)
Dessen	Alan C. Dessen, 'Exploring the Script: Shakespearean Pay-offs in 1987', *SQ* 39 (1988), 217–26
Dessen and Thomson	Alan C. Dessen and Leslie Thomson, *A Dictionary of Stage Directions in English Drama, 1580–1642* (Cambridge, 1999)
Discursive	John Harvey, *A Discursive Problem Concerning Prophesies, how Far they are to be Valued, Or Credited, According to the Surest Rules, and Directions in Divinity, Philosophie, Astrology, and Other Learning* (1588)
Douce	Francis Douce, *Illustrations of Shakespeare and of Ancient Manners*, 2 vols (1807)
Drew-Bear	Annette Drew-Bear, *Painted Faces on the Renaissance Stage: The Moral Significance of Face-Painting Conventions* (Lewisburg, PA, 1994)
Ebanks	Jared Ebanks, 'Deaf Lead Paves Way for Inclusivity in *Titus Andronicus* Performance', *The Daily Illini* (11 November 2019)
Ebbs	John Dale Ebbs, 'A Note on Nashe and Shakespeare', *Modern Language Notes* 66 (1951), 480–1
Edmondson and Wells	Paul Edmondson and Stanley Wells, eds, *The Shakespeare Circle: An Alternative Biography* (Cambridge, 2015)
EEBO	*Early English Books Online*. https://proquest.libguides.com/eebopqp/home
EEBO-TCP	*Early English Books Online, Text Creation Partnership*. https://quod.lib.umich.edu/e/eebogroup/index.html
Eliot	T. S. Eliot, *Selected Essays, 1917–1932* (New York, 1932)
Erne	Lukas Erne, *Shakespeare and the Book Trade* (Cambridge, 2013)
Estill et al.	Laura Estill, Dominic Klyve and Kate Bridal, '"Spare your arithmetic, never count the turns": A Statistical Analysis of Writing About Shakespeare, 1960–2010', *SQ* 66 (2015), 1–28
Evans	Lewis Evans, *The Hateful Hypocrisy and Rebellion of the Romish Prelacy* (1570)
Fables	*Babrius and Phaedrus: Fables*, trans. Ben Edwin Perry, LCL (Cambridge, MA, 1965)
Fenne	Thomas Fenne, *Fenne's Fruits* (1590)
Fletcher	John Fletcher, *The Faithfull Shepherdess* (1610)
FQ	Edmund Spenser, *The Faerie Queene*, ed. A. C. Hamilton (2001; rev edn, 2007)
Friedman	Michael Friedman, *Shakespeare in Performance: Titus Andronicus* (Manchester, 2013)
Gainsborough	Thomas Gainsborough, portrait of James Quin (1693–1766), oil on canvas, 1760–3, Royal Collection Trust. https://www.rct.uk/collection/search#/14/collection/405949/james-quin-1693-1766
Gardiner	Samuel Gardiner, *The Portraiture of the Prodigal Son, Lively Set Forth in a Three-Fold Discourse* (1599)
Goffe	Thomas Goffe, *The Careless Shepherdess a Tragi-Comedy Acted before the King & Queen, and at Salisbury [...] with an Alphabetical Catalogue of all such Plays that Ever were Printed* (1656)
Golding	Arthur Golding, trans, John Frederic Nims, ed., *Ovid's Metamorphoses* (Philadelphia, 2000)

Goy-Blanquet	Dominique Goy-Blanquet, 'Titus Resartus: Warner, Stein and Mesguich have a cut at *Titus Andronicus*', in Dennis Kennedy, ed., *Foreign Shakespeare: Contemporary Performance* (Cambridge, 1993), 36–55
Greg, *Folio*	W. W. Greg, *The Shakespeare First Folio: Its Bibliographical and Textual History* (Oxford, 1955)
Groves	Beatrice Groves, *The Destruction of Jerusalem in Early Modern English Literature* (Cambridge, 2015)
Hadfield	Andrew Hadfield, ' "Suum Cuique": Natural Law in *Titus Andronicus*, I.i.284', *NQ* ns 52 (2005), 195–6
Helms	Lorraine Helms, ' "The High Roman Fashion": Sacrifice, Suicide, and the Shakespearean Stage', *PMLA* 107 (1992), 554–65
Henslowe	R. A. Foakes, ed., *Henslowe's Diary* (1961; 2nd edn, Cambridge, 2002)
Herodian	Herodian, *History of the Empire*, trans. C. R. Whittaker, 2 vols, LCL (Cambridge, MA, 1969–70)
Heywood, *Troia*	Thomas Heywood, *Troia Britanica: Or, Great Britain's Troy* (1609)
HF	*Hercules Furens*, in Seneca, *Tragedies*
Higgins	Ben Higgins, *Shakespeare's Syndicate: The First Folio, Its Publishers, and the Early Modern Book Trade* (Oxford, 2022)
Hinds	Stephen Hinds, 'Landscape with Figures: Aesthetics of Place in the *Metamorphoses* and its Tradition', in Philip Hardie, ed., *The Cambridge Companion to Ovid* (Cambridge, 2002), 122–49
Hinman	Charlton Hinman, *The Printing and Proof-Reading of the First Folio of Shakespeare*, 2 vols (Oxford, 1963)
Hope	Jonathan Hope, *Shakespeare's Grammar* (2003)
Horace, *Satires*	*Horace: Satires, Epistles, and Art of Poetry*, trans. H. Rushton Fairclough, LCL (1926; Cambridge, MA, 1929)
Horace, *Odes*	*Horace: Odes and Epodes*, trans. C. E. Bennett, LCL (1914; Cambridge, MA, 1995)
Hornback	Robert Hornback, *Racism and Early Blackface Comic Traditions: From the Old World to the New* (Cham, Switzerland, 2018)
Howard-Hill	T. H. Howard-Hill, 'New Light on Compositor E of the Shakespeare First Folio', *The Library* s6-2 (1980), 156–78
Howell, BBC	*Titus Andronicus*, DVD, Directed by Jane Howell, BBC production (New York, 1985)
Hulse	Mark C. Hulse, 'The Case for Peele's Authorship of *Titus Andronicus* 4.1: Cross-Examining Attribution Methods in a Disputed Scene', *RES* 72 (2021), 860–81
Hunter	G. K. Hunter, 'Sources and Meanings in *Titus Andronicus*', in J. C. Gray, ed., *Mirror up to Shakespeare: Essays in Honour of G.R. Hibbard* (Toronto, 1984), 171–88
Imbracsio	Nicola M. Imbracsio, 'Stage Hands: Shakespeare's *Titus Andronicus* and the Agency of the Disabled Body in Text and Performance', *Journal of Literary & Cultural Disability Studies* 6.3 (2012), 291–306
Jackson, *Abraham*	Ken Jackson, *Shakespeare & Abraham* (Notre Dame, IN, 2015)
Jackson, *Attribution*	MacDonald P. Jackson, *Studies in Attribution: Middleton and Shakespeare* (Salzburg, 1979)
Jackson, 'Determining'	MacDonald P. Jackson, 'Determining Authorship: A New Technique', *Research Opportunities in Renaissance Drama* 41 (2002), 1–14
Jackson, 'Editions'	MacDonald P. Jackson, 'Editions and Textual Studies', *SS* 38 (1986), 238–54
Jackson, 'Play'	MacDonald P. Jackson, '*Titus Andronicus*: Play, Ballad, and Prose History', *NQ* ns 36 (1989), 315–17

Jackson, 'Stage Directions' MacDonald P. Jackson, 'Stage Directions and Speech Headings in Act 1 of *Titus Andronicus* Q (1594): Shakespeare or Peel?', *Studies in Bibliography* 49 (1996), 134–48

Jackson, *Genius* Zachariah Jackson, *Shakespeare's Genius Justified* (1819)

James Heather James, 'Cultural Disintegration in *Titus Andronicus*: Mutilating Titus, Vergil and Rome', *Themes in Drama* 13 (1991), 123–40

Javanian Mohammadreza Hassanzadeh Javanian, '*Titus* and *Coriolanus* in Tehran: Shakespeare's Roman Plays and Iran's Politics', *Critical Survey* 34.4 (2022), 124–35

Jests *Merry Conceited Jests of George Peele Gentleman, Sometimes a Student in Oxford, Wherein is Shewed the Course of His Life how He Lived* (1607)

Jonson, *Bart. Fair* Ben Jonson, *Bartholomew Fair*, ed. G. R. Hibbard and Alexander Leggatt (1977; 2007)

Johnson-Haddad Miranda Johnson-Haddad, 'A Time for *Titus*: An Interview with Julie Taymor', *SB* 18.4 (2000), 34–6

Johnson, *History* Richard Johnson, *The Most Famous History of the Seven Champions of Christendom: Saint George of England, Saint Dennis of France, Saint James of Spain, Saint Anthony of Italy, Saint Andrew of Scotland, Saint Patrick of Ireland, and Saint David of Wales* (1596)

Karim-Cooper, *Cosmetics* Farah Karim-Cooper, *Cosmetics in Shakespearean and Renaissance Drama* (rev edn, Edinburgh, 2019)

Karim-Cooper, *Hand* Farah Karim-Cooper, *The Hand on the Shakespearean Stage: Gesture, Touch and the Spectacle of Dismemberment* (2016)

Karim-Cooper, *SoP* Farah Karim-Cooper, ed., *Titus Andronicus: The State of Play* (2019)

Kendall Gillian Murray Kendall, ' "Lend me thy Hand": Metaphor and Mayhem in *Titus Andronicus*', *SQ* 40 (1989), 299–316

Knack *A Most Pleasant and Merry New Comedy Entitled A Knack to Know a Knave, Newly Set Forth, as it Hath Sundry Times Been Played by Ed. Allen and His Company* (1594)

Knutson Roslyn L. Knutson, 'The Repertory', in John D. Cox and David Scott Kastan, ed., *A New History of Early English Drama* (New York, 1997), 461–80

Kolin Philip C. Kolin, ed., *Titus Andronicus: Critical Essays* (New York, 1995)

Kramer Joseph E. Kramer, '*Titus Andronicus*: The "Fly-Killing" Incident', *Shakespeare Studies* 5 (1969), 9–19

Law Robert Adger Law, 'The Roman Background of *Titus Andronicus*', *Studies in Philology* 40 (1943), 145–55

Lee Adele Lee, 'Titus in No Man's Land: The Tang Shu-wing Theatre Studio's Production', in Susan Bennett and Christie Carson, ed., *Shakespeare Beyond English: A Global Experiment* (Cambridge, 2013), 110–14

Leibler Naomi Conn Liebler, 'Getting It All Right: *Titus Andronicus* and Roman History', *SQ* 45 (1994), 263–78

Lennix and Fishburne Harry J. Lennix and Laurence Fishburne, 'Two Actors on Shakespeare, Race, and Performance: A Conversation Between Harry J. Lennix and Laurence Fishburne', *SB* 27.3 (2009), 399–414

Lesser Zachary Lesser, *Ghosts, Holes, Rips and Scrapes: Shakespeare in 1619, Bibliography in the Longue Durée* (Philadelphia, 2021)

Levin Richard Levin, 'The Longleat Manuscript and *Titus Andronicus*', *SQ* 53 (2002), 323–40

Lily	William Lily, *A Short Introduction of Grammar Generally to be Used: Compiled and Set Forth, for the Bringing Up of all those that Intend to Attain the Knowledge of the Latin Tongue* (1568)
Livy	Livy, *History of Rome*, 14 vols, LCL (Cambridge, MA, 1919–59)
Lloyd	Lodowick Lloyd, *The Pilgrimage of Princes, Penned Out of Sundry Greek and Latin Authors* (1573)
Loughnane	Rory Loughnane, 'Re-Editing Non-Shakespeare for the Modern Reader: The Murder of Mutius in *Titus Andronicus*', RES 68 (2016), 268–95
LPD	*Lost Plays Database*, ed. Roslyn L. Knutson, David McInnis, Matthew Steggle and Misha Teramura (Washington, DC). https://lostplays.folger.edu
MacDonald	Joyce Green MacDonald, 'Women and Theatrical Authority: Deborah Warner's *Titus Andronicus*', in Marianne Novy, ed., *Cross-Cultural Performances: Differences in Women's Re-Visions of Shakespeare* (Urbana, IL, 1993), 185–205.
Manley, 'From Strange's'	Lawrence Manley, 'From Strange's Men to Pembroke's Men: *2 Henry VI* and *The First Part of the Contention*', SQ 54 (2003), 253–87
Manley and MacLean	Lawrence Manley and Sally-Beth MacLean, *Lord Strange's Men and Their Plays* (New Haven, 2014)
Mansky	Joseph Mansky, *Libels and Theater in Shakespeare's England: Publics, Politics, Performance* (Cambridge, 2023)
Marlowe, *JoM*	Christopher Marlowe, *The Jew of Malta*, ed. William H. Sherman and Chloe Preedy (2021)
Marlowe, *Tamb.*	Christopher Marlowe, *Tamburlaine the Great*, ed. J. S. Cunningham (Manchester, 1981)
Marshall and Stock	Herbert Marshall and Mildred Stock, *Ira Aldridge, The Negro Tragedian* (New York, 1958)
Marston	John Marston, *The Metamorphosis of Pygmalion's Image, and Certain Satyrs* (1598)
McCandless	David McCandless, 'A Tale of Two Tituses: Julie Taymor's Vision on Stage and Screen', SQ 53 (2002), 487–511
McCarthy and Schlueter	Dennis McCarthy and June Schlueter, 'A Shakespeare/North Collaboration: *Titus Andronicus* and *Titus and Vespasian*', SS 67 (2014), 85–101
McKerrow, 'Note'	R. B. McKerrow, 'A Note on *Titus Andronicus*', *The Library* 15 (1934), 49–53
McKerrow, 'Typical'	R. B. McKerrow, 'Edward Allde as a Typical Trade Printer', *The Library* 10 (1929), 121–62
McManaway	James G. McManaway, 'Textual Studies', SS 3 (1950), 143–54
McMillin	Scott McMillin, 'Sussex's Men in 1594: The Evidence of *Titus Andronicus* and *The Jew of Malta*', *Theatre Survey* 32 (1991), 214–23
McRuer and Cassabaum	Robert McRuer and Emma Cassabaum, 'Crip Theory', in *Oxford Bibliographies in Literary and Critical Theory*, ed. Eugene O'Brien. DOI: 10.1093/OBO/9780190221911-0109
Med.	*Medea*, in Seneca, *Tragedies*
Meres	Francis Meres, *Palladis Tamia; Wit's Treasury* (1598)
Met.	Ovid, *Metamorphoses*, 2 vols, LCL (Cambridge, MA, 1916)
Metz	G. Harold Metz, '*Titus Andronicus*: Three Versions of the Story', NQ ns 35 (1988), 451–5
Mincoff	Marco Mincoff, 'The Source of *Titus Andronicus*', NQ ns 18 (1971), 131–4
Miola, *Classical*	Robert S. Miola, *Shakespeare and Classical Tragedy: The Influence of Seneca* (Oxford, 1992)

Miola, Iphigenia	Robert S. Miola, 'Early Modern Receptions of Iphigenia at Aulis', *Classical Receptions Journal* 12.3 (2020), 279–98
Moschovakis, 'Irreligious'	Nicholas R. Moschovakis, ' "Irreligious Piety" and Christian History: Persecution as Pagan Anachronism in *Titus Andronicus*', SQ 53 (2002), 460–86
Moschovakis, 'Topicality'	Nicholas R. Moschovakis, 'Topicality and Conceptual Blending: *Titus Andronicus* and the Case of William Hacket', *College Literature* 31.1 (2006), 127–50
Mueller and Scodel	Janel Mueller and Joshua Scodel, eds., *Elizabeth I: Translations, 1544–1589* (Chicago, 2009)
Mullaney	Steven Mullaney, *The Reformation of Emotions in the Age of Shakespeare* (Chicago, 2015)
Munro	Lucy Munro, 'His Collaborator John Fletcher', in Edmondson and Wells, 305–14
Murphy	Andrew Murphy, *Shakespeare in Print: A History and Chronology of Shakespeare Publishing* (Cambridge, 2003)
Nashe	Thomas Nashe, *The Unfortunate Traveller. Or, the Life of Jack Wilton* (1594)
Ndiaye, 'Aaron's Roots'	Noémie Ndiaye, 'Aaron's Roots: Spaniards, Englishmen, and Blackamoors in *Titus Andronicus*', *Early Theatre* 19.2 (2016), 59–80
Ndiaye, 'Race'	Noémie Ndiaye, 'Shakespeare, Race, and Globalization: *Titus Andronicus*', in Thompson, *Companion*, 158–74
Neill	Michael Neill, *Putting History to the Question: Power, Politics, and Society in English Renaissance Drama* (New York, 2000)
Neuburg	Victor E. Neuburg, 'The Diceys and the Chapbook Trade', *The Library* s5–24 (1969), 219–31
Nørgaard	Holger Nørgaard, 'Never Wrong But With Just Cause', *English Studies* 45.2 (1964), 137–41
ODNB	*Oxford Dictionary of National Biography* (Oxford 2004–). https://www.oxforddnb.com/
OED	*The Oxford English Dictionary.* https://www.oed.com/
Ovid, *Fasti*	Ovid, *Fasti*, trans. James G. Frazer, rev. G. P. Goold, LCL (rev edn, Cambridge, MA, 1996)
Parrott	T. M. Parrott, 'Shakespeare's Revision of *Titus Andronicus*', *Modern Language Review* 14 (1919), 16–37
Partridge	Eric Partridge, *Shakespeare's Bawdy* (1948; 3rd edn, 1968)
Peele, *Alcazar*	George Peele, *The Battle of Alcazar*, in Charles Edelman, ed., *The Stukeley Plays* (Manchester, 2005), 60–128
Peele, *Decensus*	George Peele, *Descensus Astaeae: the Device of a Pageant Borne before M. William Web, Lord Mayor of the City of London on the Day He Took His Oath, Being the 29. of October 1591* (1591)
Peele, *Edw. 1*	George Peele, *The Famous Chronicle of King Edward the First, Surnamed Edward Longshanks with His Return from the Holy Land* (1593)
Peele, *Farewell*	George Peele, *A Farewell Entitled to the Famous and Fortunate Generals of our English Forces: Sir John Norris & Sir Frauncis Drake Knights, and all Their Brave and Resolute Followers. Whereunto is Annexed: A Tale of Troy* (1589)
Peele, *Honour*	George Peele, *The Honour of the Garter Displayed in a Poeme Gratulatory: Entitled to the Worthy and Renowned Earl of Northumberland. Created Knight of that Order, and Installed at Windsor* (1593)
Peele, *Troublesome*	George Peele, *The Troublesome Reign of John, King of England*, ed. Charles R. Forker (Manchester, 2011)

Perry, 'Satire'	Curtis Perry, 'Titus's Revenge and/as Imperial Roman Satire', *Explorations in Renaissance Culture* 48 (2022), 40–60
Perry, *Senecan*	Curtis Perry, *Shakespeare and Senecan Tragedy* (Cambridge, 2021)
Petersen	Lene B. Petersen, *Shakespeare's Errant Texts: Textual Form and Linguistic Style in Shakespearean 'Bad' Quartos and Co-authored Plays* (Cambridge, 2010)
Phae.	*Phaedra*, in Seneca, *Tragedies*
Phaer	Thomas Phaer, trans., *The Whole XII Bookes of the Aeneidos of Virgil* (1573)
Pliny the Elder	*The Historie of the World. Commonly Called, the Natural History of C. Plinius Secundus. Translated into English by Philemon Holland Doctor in Physick*, 2 books (1601)
Plutarch, *Lives*	Plutarch, *The Lives of the Noble Grecians and Romanes, Compared Together by that Grave Learned Philosopher and Historiographer, Plutarch of Chaeronea: Translated Out of Greek into French by James Amyot, Abbot of Bellozane, Bishop of Auxerre, One of the Kings Privy Counsel, and Great Amner of Fraunce, and Out of French into English, by Thomas North* (1579)
Plutarch, *Morals*	Plutarch, *The Philosophie, Commonly Called, the Morals Written by the Learned Philosopher Plutarch of Chaeronea. Translated Out of Greek into English, and Conferred with the Latin Translations and the French, by Philemon Holland of Coventry, Doctor in Physick* (1603)
Pollard	Tanya Pollard, *Greek Tragic Women on Shakespearean Stages* (Oxford, 2017)
Price	H. T. Price, 'The Yew-tree In *Titus Andronicus*', *NQ* ns 10 (1963), 98–9
Pruitt	Anna Pruitt, 'Refining the LION Collocation Test: A Comparative Study of Authorship Test Results for Titus Andronicus Scene 6 (= 4.1)', in Taylor and Egan, 92–106
Rankins	William Rankins, *The English Ape, the Italian Imitation, the Footsteps of France. Wherein is Explained, the Willful Blindness of Subtle Mischief, the Striving for Stars, the Catching of Moonshine: And the Secrete Sound of Many Hollow Hearts* (1588)
Rich	Barnabe Rich, *Alarm to England, Foreshowing What Perils are Procured Where the People Live Without Regard of Martial Law* (1578)
Ritson	Joseph Ritson, *Remarks, critical and illustrative, on the text and notes of the last edition of Shakespeare* (1783)
Rowe, *Dead Hands*	Katherine Rowe, *Dead Hands: Fictions of Agency, Renaissance to Modern* (Stanford, 2000)
Royster	Francesca T. Royster, 'White-Limed Walls: Whiteness and Gothic Extremism in Shakespeare's *Titus Andronicus*', *SQ* 51 (2000), 432–55
Rutter	Carol Chillington Rutter, ed., *Documents of the Rose Playhouse* (1984; rev edn, Manchester, 1999)
Sale	Carolyn Sale, 'Black Aeneas: Race, English Literary History, and the "Barbarous" Poetics of *Titus Andronicus*', *SQ* 62 (2011), 25–52
Samuels	Alexandra Samuels, 'Father of Student Convicted of Rape: Steep Price for "20 minutes of action"', *USA Today* (6 June 2016)
Schiesaro	Alessandro Schiesaro, *The Passions in Play: Thyestes and the Dynamics of Senecan Drama* (Cambridge, 2003)
Seneca, *Epistles*	Seneca, *Epistles*, ed. Richard M. Gummere, 3 vols, LCL (Cambridge, MA, 1917–25)
Seneca, *Tragedies*	Seneca, *Tragedies*, ed. John G. Fitch, 2 vols, LCL (Cambridge, MA, 2002–4)
Sharpe	Christina Sharpe, *In the Wake: On Blackness and Being* (Durham, 2016)
Sisson	Charles Jasper Sisson, *New Readings in Shakespeare*, 2 vols (Cambridge, 1956)
Smith, 'Aldridge'	James McCune Smith, 'Ira Aldridge', *The Anglo-African Magazine* 2.1 (1860), 27–32

Smith, 'Collaborator'	Emma Smith, 'His Collaborator Thomas Middleton', in Edmondson and Wells, 297–304
Smith, 'White Skin'	Ian Smith, 'White Skin, Black Masks: Racial Cross-Dressing on the Early Modern Stage', *RD* 32 (2003), 33–67
Spencer	T. J. B. Spencer, 'Shakespeare and the Elizabethan Romans', *SS* 10 (1957), 27–38
Spanish Tragedy	Thomas Kyd, *The Spanish Tragedy*, ed. J. R. Mulryne (1970; rev edn, 1989)
SRO	Giles Bergel and Ian Gadd, *Stationers' Register Online*, CREATe, University of Glasgow. http://stationersregister.online
Staatsschauspiel	https://www.staatsschauspiel-dresden.de/spielplan/archive/t/titus-andronicus
Stern, *Documents*	Tiffany Stern, *Documents of Performance in Early Modern England* (Cambridge, 2009)
Stern, *Rehearsal*	Tiffany Stern, *Rehearsal from Shakespeare to Sheridan* (Oxford, 2008)
Sternhold and Hopkins	*The Whole Book of Psalmes Collected into English Meter by T. Sternhold, J. Hopkins, & Others* (1562)
Stoker	David Stoker, 'Another Look at the Dicey-Marshall Publications: 1736–1806', *The Library*, series 7, vol. 15 (2014), 111–57
Streete	Adrian Streete, 'Nashe, Shakespeare, and The Bishops' Bible', *NQ* ns 47 (2000), 56–8
Syme, 'Alternative'	Holger Schott Syme, 'Three's Company: Alternative Histories of London's Theatres in the 1590s', *SS* 65 (2012), 269–89
Syme, *History*	Holger Schott Syme, *Theatre History, Attribution Studies, and the Question of Evidence* (Cambridge, 2023)
T&V	'Titus and Vespasian', LPD. https://lostplays.folger.edu/Titus_and_Vespasian
Tarrant	R. J. Tarrant, ed., *Seneca's Thyestes* (1985; Atlanta, 1998)
Tavares	Elizabeth Elaine Tavares, 'The Chariots in II *Tamburlaine, The Wounds of Civil War*, and *The Reign of King Edward III*', *NQ* ns 63 (2016), 393–6
Taylor, 'Structure'	Gary Taylor, 'The Structure of Performance: Act-Intervals in the London Theatres, 1576–1642', in Gary Taylor and John Jowett, ed., *Shakespeare Reshaped, 1606–1623* (Oxford, 1993), 3–50
Taylor and Duhaime	Gary Taylor and Doug Duhaime, 'Who Wrote the Fly Scene (3.2) in *Titus Andronicus*? Automated Searches and Deep Reading', in Taylor and Egan, 67–91
Taylor and Egan	Gary Taylor and Gabriel Egan, ed., *The New Oxford Shakespeare: Authorship Companion* (Oxford, 2017)
Taylor and Loughnane	Gary Taylor and Rory Loughnane, 'The Canon and Chronology of Shakespeare's Works', in Taylor and Egan, 417–602
Taymor, *Titus*	*Titus*, DVD, Directed by Julie Taymor (New York, 1999)
Taymor, *Playing*	Julie Taymor, *Playing With Fire: Theater, Opera, Film* (1995; rev edn, New York, 1999)
Taymor, *Screenplay*	Julie Taymor, *Titus: The Illustrated Screenplay, Adapted From the Play By William Shakespeare* (New York, 2000)
Tenne	Thomas Newton et al., *Seneca His Tenne Tragedies Translated into English*, 2 vols (1927; Bloomington, IN, 1966)
Teramura, 'Black'	Misha Teramura, 'Black Comedy: Shakespeare, Terence, and *Titus Andronicus*', *ELH* 85 (2018), 877–908
Teramura, 'Titus &'	Misha Teramura, 'Titus & Andronicus: One or Two?' Paper presented at the 8th International Marlowe Society of America Conference, Wittenberg, Germany, July 2018
Theater Iran	https://theater.ir/en/120520
Theobald, *Restored*	Lewis Theobald, *Shakespeare Restored: Or, A Specimen Of The Many Errors, As Well Committed As Unamended By Mr. Pope In His Late Edition Of This Poet* (1776)

Thompson, *Companion*	Ayanna Thompson, ed., *The Cambridge Companion to Shakespeare and Race* (Cambridge, 2021)
Thompson, *Documentary*	George A. Thompson, Jr., *A Documentary History of the African Theatre* (Evanston, IL, 1998)
Thy.	*Thyestes*, in Seneca, *Tragedies*
Tilley	Morris Palmer Tilley, *A Dictionary of the Proverbs in England in the Sixteenth and Seventeenth Centuries* (Ann Arbor, MI, 1950)
Tito	*Tito Andronico*, in *Early Modern German Shakespeare: Titus Andronicus and The Taming of the Shrew*, ed. Lukas Erne, Florence Hazrat and Maria Shmygol (2022)
Ungerer	Gustav Ungerer, 'An Unrecorded Elizabethan Performance of *Titus Andronicus*', SS 14 (1961), 102–9
Vaughan	Virginia Mason Vaughan, *Performing Blackness on English Stages, 1500–1800* (Cambridge, 2005)
Vickers	Brian Vickers, *Shakespeare, Co-Author: A Historical Study of Five Collaborative Plays* (Oxford, 2002)
Weber	William W. Weber, 'Shakespeare After All?: The Authorship of *Titus Andronicus* 4.1 Reconsidered', SS 67 (2014), 69–84
Wells, *Re-editing*	Stanley Wells, *Re-editing Shakespeare for the Modern Reader* (Oxford, 1984)
Werstine	Paul Werstine, *Early Modern Playhouse Manuscripts and the Editing of Shakespeare* (Cambridge, 2012)
Whitworth	Charles Whitworth, 'George Peele', in Bruce R. Smith et al., ed., *The Cambridge Guide to the Worlds of Shakespeare*, 2 vols (Cambridge, 2016), 1: 908–13.
Wiggins	Martin Wiggins and Catherine Richardson, *British Drama 1533–1642: A Catalogue* (Oxford, 2012–)
Williams, *Dictionary*	Gordon Williams, *A Dictionary of Sexual Language and Imagery in Shakespearean and Stuart Literature* (2001)
Williams, *Glossary*	Gordon Williams, *Shakespeare's Sexual Language: A Glossary* (2006)
Wilson, *Three*	Robert Wilson, *The Pleasant and Stately Moral, of the Three Lords and Three Ladies of London with the Great Joy and Pomp Solemnized at their Marriages* (1590)
Witherspoon	A. M. Witherspoon, 'Staging of *Titus Andronicus* Gives Alpha Delta Phi Place in Shakespearean History', *The Yale Daily News* (16 April 1924), reprinted in Kolin, 385–7
Wright, *Metrical*	George T. Wright, *Shakespeare's Metrical Art* (Berkeley, 1988)
WSB	World Shakespeare Bibliography Online. https://www.worldshakesbib.org/
Zolidis	Don Zolidis, *My Little Titus Andronicus* (New York, 2020)
Zornosa	Laura Zornosa, 'An Imaginary Play, Dreamed Into Existence', *The New York Times* (21 August 2021)

LIST OF MODERN PRODUCTIONS CITED

In chronological order; for those RSC productions marked with a **, we have also referenced original prompt books held in the Royal Shakespeare Company Archives.

1923	Old Vic dir. Robert Atkins
1924	Yale University dir. Montillion 'Monty' Woolley
1955	RSC dir. Peter Brook**
1956	New York Shakespeare Festival dir. Joseph Papp
1963	Birmingham Repertory Company dir. Ronald Eyre

1967	New York Shakespeare Festival dir. Gerald Freedman
1972	RSC dir. Trevor Nunn**
1978	New Vic Bristol dir. Adrian Noble
1978	Stratford, Ontario Festival dir. Brian Bedford
1981	American Players Theatre dir. Anne Occhiogrosso & Mik Derks
1987	RSC dir. Deborah Warner**
1989	Shakespeare Festival (Stratford, Ontario) dir. Jeanette Lambermont
1990	St. Louis Shakespeare Festival dir. Donna Northcott
1991	Theater Links der Isar (Munich) dir. Erica Prahl
1993	Octagon Theatre (Bolton) dir. Carole Tweedy & Lawrence Till
1993	Hampshire Shakespeare Company dir. Sarah Wilson
1994	Theatro (Graz) dir. Dorothee Steinbauer
1994	Theatre for a New Audience dir. Julie Taymor
1995	Market Theatre dir. Gregory Doran
1998	Landestheater Schwaben (Memmingen) dir. Eva Maria Niedermeiser
1999	Courtyard Theatre (London) dir. Annecy Lax
2006	Shakespeare's Globe dir. Lucy Bailey
2006	RSC dir. Yukio Ninagawa
2007	Academy Shakespeare Company dir. Takayuki Ayanogki
2009	No Man's Land dir. Tang Shu-wing
2010	Yamanote Jijo Sha dir. Yasuhiro Yosuda
2010	Star Dust 21 dir. Eiji Nishizawa
2011	Shakespeare Festival dir. Hideki Yashiro
2011	Kusunoki Mitsuka Lonely Shakespeare dir. Mitsuka Kusunoki
2011	Public Lab dir. Michael Sexton
2012	Staatsschauspiel Dresden dir. Jan Klata
2013	RSC dir. Michael Fentiman
2013	Riot Grrrls dir. Lise Bruneau
2014	Shakespeare's Globe dir. Lucy Bailey
2014	Faction of Fools dir. Matthew R. Wilson
2017	RSC dir. Blanche McIntyre
2019	IranShahr Theater dir. Masoud Tayebi

INDEX